An Author's Guide to Social Work Journals

NASW PRESS   FOURTH EDITION

NASW PRESS

National Association of Social Workers
Washington, DC

Jay J. Cayner, ACSW, LISW, President
Josephine Nieves, MSW, PhD, Executive Director

Linda Beebe, Executive Editor
Nancy A. Winchester, Editorial Services Director
Sarah Lowman, Production Editor
Fran Pflieger, Maben Publications, Inc., Copy Editor
Beth Gyorgy, Shenandoah Publications, Inc., Proofreader

Library of Congress Cataloging-in-Publication Data

NASW Press.
    An author's guide to social work journals / NASW Press.
    4th ed.
       p.   cm
    Includes bibliographical references.
    ISBN 0-87101-271-5
    1. Social service—United States—Periodicals—Directories.
    2. Social service literature—Publishing—United States. I. Title.
HV85.A93 1997
016.3613'05—dc21   96-49622
                               CIP

Printed in the United States of America

Contents

Contents

Foreword

The success of the previous three editions of *An Author's Guide to Social Work Journals,* as well as changes in the social work profession, human services, and other related fields, made a fourth edition inevitable. This book has become an important resource in the advancement of social work scholarship. The fourth edition has been expanded to cover nearly 200 journals. Users will find greater coverage of publications on children and families, sex therapy, violence, aging, and occupational therapy. Some of the new journals featured in this edition are *Violence Against Women, Social Work and Christianity, Computers in the Schools,* and the *Journal of Interpersonal Violence.*

An Author's Guide to Social Work Journals is an essential reference tool for potential authors, researchers, social work faculty, librarians, and students. As with the previous editions, the fourth edition provides standard information such as editorial focus, special issues, where indexed and abstracted, circulation, and acceptance rates. New foreign titles, e-mail addresses, and home page URLs are new features that give the users even more access to journal publishing.

A special thanks goes to Henry Mendelsohn—editor of the first three editions—whose dedication and insight made this book possible. He has given the profession an important tool for advancing its knowledge base. Thanks also to Linda Beebe, executive editor, for overseeing the development and design of this latest edition.

Jeanne C. Marsh
Dean
School of Social Service Administration
University of Chicago

Categories of
Information
for Each Journal

Title	Name of journal.
Previous Title	Previous name of journal, if applicable.
Editorial Focus	The types of articles (research, review, theoretical, and so forth) that the editor or editorial board seek, in addition to such features as letters, notices, research in brief, book reviews, and so forth.
Audience	Discipline and types of subscribers, such as practitioners, faculty, libraries, and so forth.
Special Themes	Content or subject areas of particular interest to the journal.
Where Indexed/ Abstracted	Sources where the journal is indexed or abstracted.
Year Established	Year of first volume; if there have been interruptions or if the journal has been retitled at any point, please note.
Circulation	Size of subscriber list.
Frequency	How often the journal is published each year.
Months Issued	The months or seasons the journal is published.
No. of Articles	Number of articles per issue.

SUBMISSIONS

Address	Full address for submission of manuscripts.
Number of Copies	Number of copies the author should submit.
Disk Submission	Are disks required for submission? Are they required for accepted manuscripts? What word processing formats are accepted?

FORMAT OF MANUSCRIPT

Cover Sheet	Information to be included on a cover sheet, if required.
Abstract	Number of words needed, if an abstract is required.
Key Words	Are key words required? How many?
Length	Desired or maximum number of pages.
Margins	Correct margin settings.
Spacing	Spacing—single, double, or triple—required.

STYLE

Name of Guide	Suggested style guide or statement of availability of style sheets from editor or publisher.

Subheadings	How to include, if required.
References	Proper style.
Footnotes	How to include, if required or accepted.
Tables or Figures	Format. Is camera-ready copy required for all art? Or does the journal provide graphic services for a fee?

REVIEW PROCESS

Type	Information on review process, whether it is anonymous or not.
Queries	Does the editor welcome or accept query letters?
Acknowledgment	Method by which manuscripts are acknowledged; also, instructions for including a self-addressed, stamped envelope or postcard, if required.
Review Time	Estimated length of time from receipt of manuscript to the time the author is notified of a decision.
Revisions	How revisions are handled; requirements for resubmission.
Acceptance Rate	Estimate of the approximate percentage of manuscripts accepted.
Return of Manuscript	Are manuscripts returned? Should authors include a self-addressed, stamped envelope for return of manuscript?
Lag Time to Print	Estimate of the usual length of time between acceptance and publication.

CHARGES TO AUTHOR

Author Alterations	Does the journal charge authors for alterations in proofs? If so, what are the charges?
Page Charges	Does the journal issue page charges? If so, are they for expedited publication? What are the charges?
Processing	Does the journal charge for processing manuscripts?

REPRINT, SUBSCRIPTION, AND CONTACT INFORMATION

Reprint Policy	Policy on purchase of reprints or free provision of reprints; address for reprints.
Book Reviews	Does the journal publish book reviews? Does it accept unsolicited book reviews? How should books for review or reviews be submitted? To whom and where?
Subscriptions	Address for subscription orders and cost of one-year subscription.
Affiliation	Name of professional association or institution, if any, with which journal is affiliated.
E-Mail Address	Editor's or publisher's address, if any; purposes for use.
Home Page URL	Home page of publisher or journal.

Journals Arranged by Subject Categories

ADMINISTRATION

Administration in Social Work
The Clinical Supervisor
Computers in Human Services
Evaluation and Program Planning: An International Journal
The Journal of Applied Social Sciences
Journal of Health and Social Policy
Journal of Long-Term Care Administration
Journal of Nonprofit & Public Sector Marketing
Journal of Policy Analysis and Management
Journal of Social Service Research
Journal of Volunteer Administration
Nonprofit and Voluntary Sector Quarterly

AGING AND THE AGED

Activities, Adaptation & Aging
American Journal of Alzheimer's Disease
Clinical Gerontologist
The Gerontologist
International Journal of Aging and Human Development
Journal of Aging & Social Policy
Journal of Aging Studies
Journal of Elder Abuse & Neglect
Journal of Geriatric Drug Therapy
Journal of Gerontological Social Work
Journal of Nutrition for the Elderly
Omega: Journal of Death and Dying
Physical & Occupational Therapy in Geriatrics
Psychology and Aging

CHILDREN AND FAMILIES/ CHILD AND FAMILY WELFARE

American Journal of Family Therapy
Child Abuse & Neglect, The International Journal
Child & Adolescent Social Work Journal
Child & Family Behavior Therapy
Child and Youth Care Forum
Child & Youth Services
Child Maltreatment—Journal of the American Professional Society on the Abuse of Children
Child Psychiatry and Human Development
Children and Youth Services Review
Child Welfare
Families in Society: The Journal of Contemporary Human Services
Family Preservation Journal
Family Process
Family Relations: Interdisciplinary Journal of Applied Family Studies
Family Therapy
Family Violence & Sexual Assault Bulletin
Jewish Social Work Forum
Journal of Child and Adolescent Group Therapy
Journal of Child & Adolescent Substance Abuse
Journal of Child Psychology and Psychiatry & Allied Disciplines
Journal of Child Sexual Abuse
Journal of Divorce & Remarriage
Journal of Family Issues
Journal of Family Ministry
Journal of Family Psychology
Journal of Family Psychotherapy
Journal of Family Social Work
Journal of Feminist Family Therapy
Journal of Marriage & the Family
Journal of Pediatric Psychology
Journal of Sex and Marital Therapy
Journal of Sex Education and Therapy
Journal of Sexual Aggression
Journal of Youth and Adolescence
Marriage & Family Review
Merrill-Palmer Quarterly: Journal of Developmental Psychology
Physical & Occupational Therapy in Pediatrics

Residential Treatment for Children and Youth
Student Assistance Journal

EDUCATION/SCHOOLS

Arete
The British Journal of Social Work
Computers in the Schools
Early Childhood Education Journal
Journal of Baccalaureate Social Work
Journal of Continuing Social Work Education
Journal of Lesbian Studies
Journal of Sex Education and Therapy
Journal of Social Work Education
Journal of Teaching in Social Work
The New Social Worker: The Magazine for
    Social Work Students and Recent Graduates
Social Work Education
Social Work in Education
Special Services in the Schools

GENERAL SOCIAL WORK

American Sociological Review
Arete
Australian Social Work
Behavioral & Social Sciences Librarian
British Journal of Psychotherapy
The British Journal of Social Work
Groupwork
The Indian Journal of Social Work
Research in Pharmaceutical Economics
Research on Social Work Practice
Scandinavian Journal of Social Welfare
Smith College Studies in Social Work
Social Work
Social Work and Social Sciences Review
Social Work Research
Society

HEALTH AND HEALTH CARE

Alcohol Health & Research World
Alternative Therapies in Clinical Practice
The American Journal of Hospice & Palliative
    Care
Death Studies
Healing Ministry
Health Affairs

Health & Social Work
Health Care Financing Review
Health Psychology
Home Health Care Services Quarterly
The Hospice Journal
Journal of Health and Social Policy
Journal of Long-Term Care Administration
Journal of Neuro-AIDS
Journal of Neurovascular Disease
Journal of Psychosocial Oncology
Occupational Therapy in Health Care
Omega: Journal of Death and Dying
Physical & Occupational Therapy in Geriatrics
Physical & Occupational Therapy in Pediatrics
Research in Pharmaceutical Economics
SCI (Spinal Cord Injury) Psychosocial Process
Social Work in Health Care
Women and Health

MENTAL HEALTH/MENTAL ILLNESS

American Journal of Orthopsychiatry
American Psychologist
British Journal of Psychotherapy
Bulletin of the Menninger Clinic
The Canadian Journal of Human Sexuality
Clinical Gerontologist
Clinical Social Work Journal
The Clinical Supervisor
Death Studies
Developmental Psychology
Groupwork
Healing Ministry
Health Affairs
Health & Social Work
Health Psychology
The Indian Journal of Social Work
International Journal of Mental Health
The International Journal of Psychiatry in
    Medicine
Journal of Abnormal Psychology
Journal of Analytic Social Work
Journal of Applied Research in Intellectual
    Disabilities
Journal of Autism and Developmental Disorders
Journal of Child Psychology and Psychiatry &
    Allied Disciplines

Journal of Child Sexual Abuse
Journal of College Student Psychotherapy
Journal of Consulting and Clinical Psychology
Journal of Counseling Psychology
Journal of Emotional Abuse
Journal of Gay & Lesbian Psychotherapy
The Journal of General Psychology
Journal of Genetic Psychology
Journal of Homosexuality
Journal of Interpersonal Violence
The Journal of Mind and Behavior
Journal of Offender Rehabilitation
Journal of Pediatric Psychology
Journal of Personality and Social Psychology
Journal of Poetry Therapy
The Journal of Police Negotiations, Crisis
    Management, and Suicidology
Journal of Psychology & Human Sexuality
Journal of Psychopathology and Behavioral
    Assessment
Journal of Sex and Marital Therapy
Journal of Sex Education and Therapy
Journal of Sexual Aggression
The Journal of Social Psychology
Journal of Traumatic Stress
Merrill-Palmer Quarterly: Journal of Develop-
    mental Psychology
Occupational Therapy in Mental Health
Psychiatric Rehabilitation Journal
Psychiatric Services
Psychological Assessment
Psychology and Aging
Psychotherapy
Psychotherapy in Private Practice
The Psychotherapy Patient
Small Group Research
Smith College Studies in Social Work
Social Work
Student Assistance Journal
Suicide and Life-Threatening Behavior
Women and Therapy

OCCUPATIONAL AND INDUSTRIAL SERVICES

Employee Assistance Quarterly
Occupational Therapy in Health Care
Occupational Therapy in Mental Health

SOCIAL ISSUES AND SOCIAL PROBLEMS

Affilia: Journal of Women and Social Work
American Psychologist
American Sociological Review
Federal Probation
Hastings Center Report
Information & Referral: The Journal of the
    Alliance of Information and Referral Systems
International Social Work
Journal of Community Practice
Journal of Interpersonal Violence
Journal of Offender Rehabilitation
Journal of Peace Research
The Journal of Police Negotiations, Crisis
    Management and Suicidology
Journal of Prevention & Intervention in the
    Community
Journal of Progressive Human Services
Journal of Social Issues
Journal of Social Service Research
Journal of Sociology and Social Welfare
Migration World
Public Welfare
Social Development Issues
Social Policy
Social Service Review
Social Thought (Journal of Religion in the Social
    Services)
Social Work
Social Work and Christianity: An International
    Journal
Social Work and Social Sciences Review
Society
Suicide and Life-Threatening Behavior
Violence Against Women
Women & Politics

SOCIAL POLICY/SOCIAL ACTION

Hastings Center Report
Information & Referral: The Journal of the
    Alliance of Information and Referral Systems
Journal of Health and Social Policy
Journal of Law and Social Work
Journal of Nonprofit & Public Sector Marketing
Journal of Policy Analysis and Management
Journal of Progressive Human Services

Journal of Social Service Research
Journal of Sociology and Social Welfare
Journal of Volunteer Administration
Nonprofit and Voluntary Sector Quarterly
The Public Interest
Public Welfare
Reflections: Narratives of Professional Helping
Social Policy
Social Service Review
Social Thought (Journal of Religion in the Social
    Services)
Social Work
Social Work and Social Sciences Review
Social Work with Groups

SPECIAL POPULATIONS

Affilia: Journal of Women and Social Work
Asia Pacific Journal of Social Work
Australian Social Work
Child Welfare
The Indian Journal of Social Work
Jewish Social Work Forum
Journal of Black Studies
Journal of College Student Psychotherpy

Journal of Gay & Lesbian Psychotherapy
Journal of Homosexuality
Journal of Multicultural Social Work
Journal of Offender Rehabilitation
Journal of Visual Impairment & Blindness
Journal of Volunteer Administration
Migration World
Omega: Journal of Death and Dying
Women and Health
Women & Politics
Women and Therapy

SUBSTANCE USE AND ABUSE/ALCOHOLISM

Alcohol Health & Research World
Alcoholism Treatment Quarterly
American Journal of Drug and Alcohol Abuse
Employee Assistance Quarterly
Journal of Addictive Diseases
Journal of Chemical Dependency Treatment
Journal of Child & Adolescent Substance Abuse
Journal of Drug Issues
Journal of Studies on Alcohol
Substance Abuse
Substance Use and Misuse

The Journals

Activities, Adaptation & Aging

Editorial Focus	Formal and informal research regarding the therapeutic value of activities in providing/enhancing the quality of life in a caring environment—be it institutional, residential or adult day care—for elderly persons. A multidisciplinary approach.
Audience	Activity practitioners, various therapies working with the elderly; faculty, researchers, students, others in the human services.
Special Themes	Various modalities relating to specific activity types, disease processes, adaptations, psychosocial aspects of aging.
Where Indexed/ Abstracted	Abstracts in Social Gerontology: Current Literature on Aging; Abstracts of Research in Pastoral Care & Counseling; Age Info CD-ROM AgeLine Database; Alzheimer's Disease Education & Referral Center; Brown University Geriatric Research Application Digest "Abstracts Section"; Cambridge Scientific Abstracts; Cumulative Index to Nursing and Allied Health Literature; CNPIEC Reference Guide: Chinese Directory of Foreign Periodicals; Combined Health Information Database; Communication Abstracts; Family Studies Database; Health Care Literature Information Network; Human Resources Abstracts; IBZ International Bibliography of Periodical Literature; INTERNET ACCESS & Additional Networks Bulletin Board for Libraries, JANET, etc.; Leisure, Recreation & Tourism Abstracts, c/o CAB International/CAB ACCESS; Mental Health Abstracts (online through DIALOG); National Clearinghouse for Primary Care Information; New Literature on Old Age; OT BibSys; Psychological Abstracts; Referativyni Zhurnal (Republic of Russia); Social Planning/Policy & Development Abstracts; Social Work Abstracts; Sociological Abstracts; Special Educational Needs Abstracts; Sport Database/Discus.
Year Established	1980.
Circulation	500–600.
Frequency	Quarterly.
Months Issued	Not specified.
No. of Articles	5–7 per issue.

SUBMISSIONS

Address	Phyllis Foster, ACC, Editor, *Activities, Adaptation & Aging*, 6549 South Lincoln Street, Littleton, CO 80121-2325; phone 303-794-7676.
Number of Copies	3.
Disk Submission	Authors of accepted manuscripts are asked to submit 4 hard copies and a disk, clearly identifying program used.

FORMAT OF MANUSCRIPT

Cover Sheet	Separate sheet that does not go out for review: Full title, authors' names, degrees, professional titles, designation of corresponding author with full address, phone numbers, fax number, and date of submission.

Abstract	Approximately 100 words.
Key Words	3–10 key words typed beneath the abstract.
Length	12–25 pages, including abstract and references.
Margins	1 inch on all sides.
Spacing	Double-spaced, except for title page.

STYLE

Name of Guide	Instructions for authors available from the editor. References, citations, and general style of manuscripts should follow the *Chicago Manual of Style*. References should be double-spaced and placed in alphabetic order.
Subheadings	Not specified.
Tables or Figures	Must be camera-ready, each on a separate sheet. On back of each sheet, write title of article lightly in pencil. In body of text, leave extra lines where the table or figure goes and indicate which table or figure goes there.

REVIEW PROCESS

Type	2 reviewers and the editor read the manuscript in an anonymous review.
Queries	Not specified.
Acknowledgment	Enclose a regular self-addressed, stamped envelope with submission.
Review Time	3–4 months.
Revisions	Not specified.
Acceptance Rate	Approximately 63%.
Return of Manuscript	Enclose a large, stamped, self-addressed envelope with submission.
Lag Time to Print	Approximately 6 months–1 year.

REPRINT, SUBSCRIPTION, AND CONTACT INFORMATION

Reprint Policy	Several weeks after the issue is in circulation, senior author receives 2 copies of the journal issue and 10 copies of the article. Junior author receives two copies of the journal. An order form to purchase additional copies is also sent at this time.
Book Reviews	Send books for review to: Book Review Editor, *Activities, Adaptation & Aging*, 6549 South Lincoln Street, Littleton, CO 80121-2325.
Subscriptions	The Haworth Press, Inc., 10 Alice Street, Binghamton, NY 13904-1580; phone: 800-342-9678; fax: 607-722-6362.
	One volume: $40, individual; $185, institutions; $225, libraries. Two volumes: $80, individual; $370, institutions; $450, libraries. NAAP members receive 50% discount on individual subscriptions.
Affiliation	*Activities, Adaptation & Aging* is published in cooperation with the National Association of Activity Professionals (NAAP).

Administration in Social Work

Editorial Focus	Theoretical formulations, empirical studies, case studies, critical analysis of issues. In addition to articles, issues include Notes for the Management Literature and Notes from the Field (brief articles on management practice).
Audience	Managers of social welfare agencies, academics interested in nonprofit organizations and management.
Special Themes	Performance of nonprofit social welfare agencies, organizational dynamics, management practice.
Where Indexed/ Abstracted	ABI/INFORM Research: Academic Abstracts/CD-ROM; Academic Index (online); Applied Social Sciences Index & Abstracts (Online: ASSI via Data-Star)(CD/ROM: ASSIA Plus); caredata CD; CINAHL (Cumulative Index to Nursing & Allied Health Literature); in print, also on CD-ROM from CD PLUS, EBSCO, and SilverPlatter, and online from CDP Online (Formerly BRS), Data-Star, and PaperChase; CNPIEC Reference Guide: Chinese National Directory of Foreign Periodicals; Current Contents; Expanded Academic Index; Family Studies Database (online and CD-ROM); Guide to Social Science & Religion in Periodical Literature; Health Planning and Administration (HEALTH) Database; Hospital Literature Index; Human Resources Abstracts (HRA); and others.
Year Established	1977.
Circulation	782.
Frequency	4 times per year.
Months Issued	January, April, July, October.
No. of Articles	4–5.

SUBMISSIONS

Address	Rino J. Patti, Editor, *Administration in Social Work*, University of Southern California, School of Social Work, Los Angeles, CA. 90089-0411.
Number of Copies	3.
Disk Submission	Required for accepted manuscripts.

FORMAT OF MANUSCRIPT

Cover Sheet	1 page with title and abstract only, attached to the paper; 1 page loose with title, date, author affiliation, professional title, address, phone numbers, key words, acknowledgments.
Abstract	Yes, 100 words.
Key Words	5–6.
Length	15–18 pages, including references and abstract.
Margins	1 inch on all sides.
Spacing	Double-spaced.

STYLE

Name of Guide	*Publication Manual of the American Psychological Association.*
Subheadings	Yes.
References	Author–date citation style; see style guide.
Footnotes	Discouraged.
Tables or Figures	On separate sheets of paper, camera-ready copy (not dot-matrix).

REVIEW PROCESS

Type	Anonymous.
Queries	Queries accepted.
Acknowledgment	Enclose a regular self-addressed, stamped envelope with submission.
Review Time	3–4 months.
Revisions	Author receives reviewers' critiques and a letter summarizing needed changes from the editor.
Acceptance Rate	25%.
Return of Manuscript	Manuscript returned if author encloses a self-addressed, stamped 9″ x 12″ envelope.
Lag Time to Print	1 year.

REPRINT, SUBSCRIPTION, AND CONTACT INFORMATION

Reprint Policy	The senior author receives 2 copies of the journal issue and 10 complimentary reprints. The junior author receives 2 copies of the journal issue. To order additional reprints, please contact Sample Copy Department, The Haworth Press, Inc.
Book Reviews	Book reviews published. Send books for review to Professor Madeleine Stoner, Book Review Editor, *Administration in Social Work,* University of Southern California, School of Social Work, Los Angeles, CA 90089-0411.
Subscriptions	Subscriptions are on a per-volume basis only. The following prices are for the current volume only for addresses in the United States. Subscriptions must be prepaid.
	$65—individuals (paid by personal check); $140.00—institutions (examples: corporations, departments, institutes, social and health service agencies/hospitals); $235.00—libraries and subscription agencies (whenever purchased either directly or through a subscription agency).
	All subscriptions, reprints, and advertising inquiries should be directed to The Haworth Press, Inc., 10 Alice Street, Binghamton, NY 13904-1580; phone: (607) 722-5857.
Affiliation	The National Network for Social Work Managers, Inc.
E-Mail Address	rino@sowk.usc.edu

Affilia—Journal of Women and Social Work

Editorial Focus	The journal is committed to the discussion and development of feminist values, theories, and knowledge as they relate to social work research, education, and practice.
Audience	Not specified.
Special Themes	Feminist perspectives.
Where Indexed/ Abstracted	Applied Social Sciences Index & Abstracts; caredata ABSTRACTS; caredata CD; caredata INFORMATION BULLETIN; Current Contents: Social & Behavioral Sciences; Family Resources Database; Feminist Periodicals; Health Instrument File; Human Resources Abstracts; Research Alert; Sage Family Studies Abstracts; Social Planning/Policy & Development Abstracts; Social SciSearch; Social Work Abstracts; Sociological Abstracts; Studies on Women Abstracts; Violence and Abuse Abstracts; Women Studies Abstracts.
Year Established	1985.
Circulation	2,000.
Frequency	Quarterly.
Months Issued	February, May, August, November.
No. of Articles	16.

SUBMISSIONS

Address	Dr. Emma Gross, *Affilia* Editor, Graduate School of Social Work, Social Work Building, University of Utah, Salt Lake City, UT 84112.
Number of Copies	4.
Disk Submission	A corrected copy of the manuscript saved on a disk as an ASCII text file must be returned with the final hard copy.

FORMAT OF MANUSCRIPT

Cover Sheet	Not specified.
Abstract	Under 100 words.
Key Words	None.
Length	Optimum length 14–16 pages.
Margins	Not specified.
Spacing	Double-spaced.

STYLE

Name of Guide	*Publication Manual of the American Psychological Association.*
Subheadings	Not specified.
References	Separate page.

Footnotes	Separate page.
Tables or Figures	Separate page.

REVIEW PROCESS

Type	Anonymous peer review.
Queries	Not specified.
Acknowledgment	Not specified.
Review Time	Not specified.
Revisions	Not specified.
Acceptance Rate	Not specified.
Return of Manuscript	Not specified.
Lag Time to Print	Not specified.

REPRINT, SUBSCRIPTION, AND CONTACT INFORMATION

Reprint Policy	May purchase.
Book Reviews	Miriam Dinerman, Book Review Editor, School of Social Work, Rutgers University, 536 George Street, New Brunswick, NJ 08903.
Subscriptions	Sage Publications, Inc., 2455 Teller Road, Thousand Oaks, CA 91320.
	1996–97 one-year prices: individuals, $50; institutions, $145.
Home Page URL	http://www.sagepub.com

Alcohol Health & Research World

Editorial Focus   *Alcohol Health & Research World* is a quarterly journal published by the National Institute on Alcohol Abuse and Alcoholism (NIAAA). Each issue presents an in-depth review of a topic important in alcohol research. Recent topics have included Alcohol-Related Birth Defects, The Genetics of Alcoholism, and Alcoholism and Social Policy. The editorial staff work closely with experts in the alcohol field to translate highly technical research findings into clear, understandable text that appeals to a wide range of readers. In addition to receiving careful editing, the articles are strictly reviewed to ensure that the information being presented is up-to-date and technically accurate.

Audience   The full spectrum of people involved in the alcohol field, including educators, counselors, treatment specialists, clinicians, researchers, and policymakers.

Special Themes   Each issue presents an in-depth review of a topic important in alcohol research. Topics are selected by the editorial advisory board in collaboration with NIAAA senior staff.

Where Indexed/ Abstracted   Cumulative Index of Nursing and Allied Health Literature; Current Contents/Social & Behavioral Sciences; NTIS Bibliographic Database; PsycINFO; Research Alert; Social SciSearch.

Year Established   1972.

Circulation   3,500.

Frequency   Quarterly.

Months Issued   Winter, spring, summer, fall.

No. of Articles   8–16.

SUBMISSIONS

Address   Manuscripts are solicited by the editor and managing editor. Unsolicited manuscripts are discouraged. Inquiries may be addressed to Dianne M. Welsh (editor) or Barbara B. Vann (managing editor), c/o CSR, Inc., 1400 Eye Street, NW, Suite 300, Washington, DC 20005.

Number of Copies   Not specified.

Disk Submission   Not specified.

FORMAT OF MANUSCRIPT

Not specified.

STYLE

Not specified.

REVIEW PROCESS

Type — Each article undergoes anonymous peer review by 2 experts in the field, then is reviewed and approved by NIAAA senior staff before release for publishing. Because no original research is published in the journal, these reviews focus on whether the topic has been sufficiently covered and whether the information presented is accurate and up-to-date.

Queries — Staff science writers/editors work with authors to make the necessary revisions.

Acknowledgment — Not specified.

Review Time — 2–3 weeks.

Revisions — Staff science writers/editors work with authors to make the necessary revisions.

Acceptance Rate — Because manuscripts are solicited, they rarely are rejected.

Return of Manuscript — Not specified.

Lag Time to Print — 6 months.

REPRINT, SUBSCRIPTION, AND CONTACT INFORMATION

Reprint Policy — *Alcohol Health & Research World* is a government publication. All material remains in the public domain following publication. When reprinting, proper attribution to authors and the journal is appreciated.

Book Reviews — Not specified.

Subscriptions — Superintendent of Documents, P.O. Box 371954, Pittsburgh, PA 15250-7954. Rates are $18 ($22.50 foreign).

Affiliation — National Institute on Alcohol Abuse and Alcoholism.

E-Mail Address — ARCADMAIL@AOL.COM

Home Page URL — http://www.niaaa.nih.gov

Alcoholism Treatment Quarterly

Editorial Focus To bridge the gap between research journals and information for the general public.

Audience Professional alcoholism counselors, social workers, psychologists, physicians, clergy, nurses, employee assistance professionals.

Special Themes Professional alcoholism counseling and therapy from both the counselor and therapist's view as well as that of the client.

Where Indexed/ Abstracted Abstracts in Anthropology; Abstracts of Research in Pastoral Care & Counseling; Academic Abstracts/CD-ROM; ADDICTION ABSTRACTS; ALCONLINE Database; Brown University Digest of Addiction Theory and Application; The (DATA Newsletter); Cambridge Scientific Abstracts; CNPIEC Reference Guide: Chinese National Directory of Foreign Periodicals; Criminal Justice Abstracts; Criminology, Penology and Police Science Abstracts; EAP Abstracts Plus; Excerpta Medica/Secondary Publishing Division; Family Studies Database (online and CD-ROM); Health Source Plus; Index to Periodical Articles Related to Law; INTERNET ACCESS (& additional networks) Bulletin Board for Libraries ("BUBL"), coverage of information resources on INTERNET, JANET, and other networks; Medication Use STudies (MUST) DATABASE; Mental Health Abstracts (online through DIALOG); NIAAA Alcohol and Alcohol Problems Science Database (ETOH); Psychological Abstracts (PsycINFO); Referativnyi Zhurnal (Abstracts Journal of the Institute of Scientific Information of the Republic of Russia); Social Planning/Policy & Development Abstracts (SOPODA); Social Work Abstracts; Sociological Abstracts (SA); SOMED (social medicine) Database; Studies on Women Abstracts; Violence and Abuse Abstracts: A Review of Current Literature on Interpersonal Violence (VAA).

Year Established 1994.

Circulation 417.

Frequency Quarterly.

Months Issued Not specified.

No. of Articles 6–10 per issue.

SUBMISSIONS

Address Thomas F. McGovern, PhD, Department of Psychiatry, Texas Technical University,, Health Sciences Center, P.O. Box 3864, Lubbock, TX 79430-0001.

Number of Copies 4.

Disk Submission Authors of accepted manuscripts are asked to submit a disk, preferably in Microsoft Word or WordPerfect.

FORMAT OF MANUSCRIPT

Cover Sheet	Separate sheet, which does not go out for review. Full title, author names, degrees, professional titles; designation of one author as corresponding author with full address, phone numbers, e-mail address, and fax number; date of submission.
Abstract	150–word informative abstract.
Key Words	Not specified.
Length	14–16 pages including references and tables.
Margins	1 inch on all sides.
Spacing	Double-spaced for all copy, except title page.

STYLE

Name of Guide	*Publication Manual of the American Psychological Association.*
Subheadings	Use as needed to guide reader through the article. No more than 4 levels.
References	Author–date citation style; see style guide.
Footnotes	No footnotes preferred; incorporate into text.
Tables or Figures	Type tables double-spaced. Submit camera-ready art (300 dpi printer or better) for all figures. Place each table or figure on a separate, numbered page at the end of the manuscript.

REVIEW PROCESS

Type	"Double blind" anonymous peer review. 3 reviewers plus editor-in-chief read the manuscript in an anonymous review.
Queries	Authors are encouraged to read the journal to determine if their subject matter would be appropriate.
Acknowledgment	Enclose a regular self-addressed, stamped envelope with submission.
Review Time	3–4 months.
Revisions	See journal.
Acceptance Rate	Not specified.
Return of Manuscript	Not specified.
Lag Time to Print	6 months–1 year.

REPRINT, SUBSCRIPTION, AND CONTACT INFORMATION

Reprint Policy	All authors receive 2 complimentary copies of the issue in which article appears. Authors receive reprint order forms to purchase additional reprinted copies.
Book Reviews	Send to editor.
Subscriptions	The Haworth Press, Inc., 10 Alice Street, Binghamton, NY 13904-1580. Individuals, $48; institutions, $150; libraries, $275.

Alternative Therapies in Clinical Practice

Previous Title	*Complementary Medicine International.*
Editorial Focus	To inform traditional physicians of efficacy or nonefficacy of alternative medicines.
Audience	MDs, doctors of osteopathy, and PhDs.
Special Themes	Contact publishers.
Where Indexed/ Abstracted	CINAHL; others pending.
Year Established	1994.
Circulation	Approximately 3,000.
Frequency	Bimonthly.
Months Issued	February, April, June, August, October, December.
No. of Articles	5–8.

SUBMISSIONS

Address	R. P. Gates, Managing Editor, 470 Boston Post Road, Weston, MA 02193.
Number of Copies	3
Disk Submission	Mandatory; IBM MS-DOS format disks in ASCII text, Microsoft Word 2.0 or greater, DCA, WordPerfect 5.1 or greater.

FORMAT OF MANUSCRIPT

Cover Sheet	Article title; authors' full names; highest pertinent academic degrees; affiliations; current address of each author; the author handling all correspondence; telephone number; and, if the manuscript was orally presented, the name of the organization, place, and date presented.
Abstract	100–200 words.
Key Words	Not necessary.
Length	Approximately 12–15 pages.
Margins	Wide.
Spacing	Double-spaced.

STYLE

Name of Guide	*MLA Handbook.*
Subheadings	Insert at suitable intervals.
References	Consult publisher for reference style.
Footnotes	No footnotes.
Tables or Figures	Submit 3 copies (paper) of each. Acceptable formats: TIFF, EPS, JPE6, BMP, WFM.

REVIEW PROCESS

Type	Anonymous review by 3 reviewers.
Queries	Yes, but not necessary.
Acknowledgment	By mail.
Review Time	10–15 weeks.
Revisions	Reviewer comments and suggestions are mailed to authors for approval or action. If authors choose to make or approve or suggest alternative changes, the manuscript is reviewed again for clarity and content by the previous reviewers or by another party.
Acceptance Rate	50%.
Return of Manuscript	Returned if not published.
Lag Time to Print	6–8 months.

REPRINT, SUBSCRIPTION, AND CONTACT INFORMATION

Reprint Policy	Professional reprints available at discount. Contact publisher.
Book Reviews	Query first.
Subscriptions	Publisher, 470 Boston Post Road, Weston, MA 02193.
E-Mail Address	(AOL) DeVitoR@aol.com
	(CompuServe) 76150.1602@compuserve.com
	(Internet) radjr@ix.netcom.com

American Journal of Alzheimer's Disease

Previous Title	*American Journal of Alzheimer's Disease and Related Disorders and Research.*
Editorial Focus	Research review, therapeutic interventions, editorial, book reviews, news briefs, video reviews, behavioral, environment, design for dementia.
Audience	Alzheimer's professionals and paraprofessionals, physicians, activities directors, nursing and day care administrators, home health aides, schools of nursing and gerontology, universities, libraries.
Special Themes	Anything pertaining to Alzheimer's disease.
Where Indexed/ Abstracted	Abstracts and Social Gerontology; CINAHL; SAGE.
Year Established	1984.
Circulation	3,000.
Frequency	Bimonthly.
Months Issued	February, April, June, August, October, December.
No. of Articles	5–8.

SUBMISSIONS

Address	*American Journal of Alzheimer's Disease,* Nancy Hindlian, Managing Editor, 470 Boston Post Road, Weston, MA 02193.
Number of Copies	3.
Disk Submission	Preferred.

FORMAT OF MANUSCRIPT

Cover Sheet	Author information, address, phone and fax numbers.
Abstract	Yes.
Key Words	None.
Length	8–18 pages.
Margins	1.5 inches on all sides.
Spacing	Double-spaced.

STYLE

See journal for instructions.

REVIEW PROCESS

Type	Anonymous peer review by 2 reviewers.
Queries	Letters are welcome.
Acknowledgment	By phone, card, or letter.
Review Time	6 weeks.

Revisions	Revisions are made, then seen by author.
Acceptance Rate	75%.
Return of Manuscript	Only if manuscript is rejected.
Lag Time to Print	6–12 months.

REPRINT, SUBSCRIPTION, AND CONTACT INFORMATION

Reprint Policy	Reprint orders available for a fee, upon request.
Book Reviews	Yes.
Subscriptions	*American Journal of Alzheimer's Disease,* 470 Boston Post Road, Weston, MA 02193.

	U.S.	*Canada*	*Foreign*
Individuals	$ 82	$107	$107
Institutions	$109	$142	$175
Libraries	$122	$159	$211

E-Mail Address	AOL—DevitoR@aol.com or radjr@1x.netcom.com CompuServe—76150.160Z@compuserve.com

American Journal of Drug and Alcohol Abuse

Editorial Focus	Data-based articles, articles on new scientific discoveries, articles with information that can be applied to current research and clinical practice.
Audience	Not specified.
Special Themes	None.
Where Indexed/ Abstracted	Abstracts for Social Workers; Adolescent Mental Health Abstracts; The Alcoholism Digest; Automatic Subject Citation Alert; BioSciences Information Service of Biological Abstracts (BIOSIS); British Journal of Addiction; British Medical Journal; Classified Abstracts Archive of the Alcohol Literature; Current Awareness in Biological Sciences; Current Contents: Social and Behavioral Sciences; Dokumentation Gefahrdung D. Alkohol; Excerpta Medica; Gower Academic Journals; National Clearinghouse for Alcohol Information; PASCAL/CNRS; Psychedelic Review; Psychological Abstracts; Rauchen, Drogen, Arzneimettel (Risk of Alcohol, Smoking, Drugs, and Pharmaceutics); Research Information Systems; Social Sciences Citation Index.
Year Established	Not specified.
Circulation	Unavailable.
Frequency	Quarterly.
Months Issued	Not specified.
No. of Articles	Approximately 8–11 per issue.

SUBMISSIONS

Address	Edward Kaufman, MD, 33971 Selva Road, Suite 125, Dana Point, CA 92629.
Number of Copies	1 original and 2 copies.
Disk Submission	Yes.

FORMAT OF MANUSCRIPT

Cover Sheet	Author's academic and program affiliation.
Abstract	250 words.
Key Words	None.
Length	10–25 pages.
Margins	Wide.
Spacing	Double-spaced.

STYLE

Name of Guide	Refer to "Information for Contributors."
Subheadings	Use at appropriate intervals to aid in presentation and clarify material.

References	Type double-spaced on separate page; arrange according to order in article (use numbers in parentheses).
Footnotes	See references.
Tables or Figures	Should be clear; type tables on separate sheets with data reading down rather than across. Provide original artwork for all tables and figures.

REVIEW PROCESS

Type	Anonymous review by 2 reviewers.
Queries	Not specified.
Acknowledgment	Letter sent on receipt of manuscript.
Review Time	Generally 8–12 weeks.
Revisions	Not specified.
Acceptance Rate	55%.
Return of Manuscript	Not returned, kept on file.
Lag Time to Print	8 months–1 year.

REPRINT, SUBSCRIPTION, AND CONTACT INFORMATION

Reprint Policy	20 free reprints if 100 are purchased.
Book Reviews	Yes.
Subscriptions	Marcel Dekker Publishers, P.O. Box 10018, Church Street Station, New York, NY 10249.

American Journal of Family Therapy

Previous Title	*Journal of Family Counseling.*
Editorial Focus	Articles on research, clinical practice, or that are theoretical in nature, or are literature reviews; must be concerned with some aspect of family therapy.
Audience	Mental health practitioners, graduate students, faculty.
Special Themes	Behavioral family medicine.
Where Indexed/ Abstracted	Child Development Abstracts; Current Index to Journals in Education (CIJE); International Bibliography of Sociology; Psychological Abstracts; Sage Family Studies Abstracts; Social Sciences Citation Index; Social Work Abstracts.
Year Established	1970.
Circulation	3,000.
Frequency	Quarterly.
Months Issued	January, April, July, October.
No. of Articles	7 per issue.

SUBMISSIONS

Address	Dr. S. Richard Sauber, Editor, *American Journal of Family Therapy,* 17829 Scarsdale Way, Boca Raton, FL 33496.
Number of Copies	3.
Disk Submission	Preferred.

FORMAT OF MANUSCRIPT

Cover Sheet	Separate title page should include, after the article's title, the following: an asterisked footnote to the title indicating any acknowledgments for grants or individual assistance and any previous presentations of the manuscript; author names with a double asterisk indicating job title and institutional affiliation. Type only the title on the first page of the manuscript.
Abstract	100 words.
Key Words	Yes.
Length	16–20 pages.
Margins	1 inch on all sides.
Spacing	Double-spaced.

STYLE

Name of Guide	*Publication Manual of the American Psychological Association.*
Subheadings	See style guide.
References	See style guide.

Footnotes	See style guide.
Tables or Figures	See style guide; include originals of all tables and figures.

REVIEW PROCESS

Type	Anonymous review by 2 reviewers.
Queries	Yes.
Acknowledgment	Include self-addressed, stamped envelope when submitting manuscript.
Review Time	6 weeks.
Revisions	Not specified.
Acceptance Rate	20%–25%.
Return of Manuscript	Include a 9″ x 12″ self-addressed, stamped envelope when submitting manuscript.
Lag Time to Print	6–12 months.

REPRINT, SUBSCRIPTION, AND CONTACT INFORMATION

Reprint Policy	Reprints available; contact publisher for price.
Book Reviews	Send unsolicited reviews to book review editor.
Subscriptions	Brunner/Mazel, Inc., 19 Union Square West, New York, NY 10003. Institutions, $84.

The American Journal of Hospice & Palliative Care

Editorial Focus	Research, philosophical, opinion, and anecdotal materials from the hospice field covering medical, administrative, and social aspects; for example, pain and symptom management, psychosocial care, ethics, bereavement, training, hospice team approaches, quality assurance.
Audience	Those who are actively providing care to the terminally ill, such as physicians, nurses, volunteers and volunteer coordinators, planners, administrators, pharmacists, allied health professionals, social workers, home health aides, and every member of the hospice team.
Special Themes	Contact the publisher.
Where Indexed/ Abstracted	Current Contents: Social & Behavioral Sciences; International Nursing Index/MEDLINE Medlars System; Medical Information Service of the British Library, Terminal Care Index; Sage Family Studies Abstracts; Sage Human Resources Abstracts; Social Work Abstracts.
Year Established	Not specified.
Circulation	2,300.
Frequency	Bimonthly.
Months Issued	Not specified.
No. of Articles	3–5, plus regular columns.

SUBMISSIONS

Address	R. Patrick Gates, Managing Editor, 470 Boston Post Road, Weston, MA 02193.
Number of Copies	3.
Disk Submission	Mandatory; IBM MS-DOS format, ASCII text, Microsoft Word 2.0 or greater, DCA, WordPerfect 5.1 or greater.

FORMAT OF MANUSCRIPT

Cover Sheet	Article's title; authors' full names; highest pertinent academic degrees; affiliations; current address of each author; the author handling all correspondence; telephone number; and, if the manuscript was orally presented, the name of the organization, place, and date presented.
Abstract	100–200 words.
Key Words	Not specified.
Length	12–15 pages.
Margins	Wide.
Spacing	Double-spaced.

STYLE

Name of Guide	*MLA Handbook.*
Subheadings	Insert at suitable intervals.
References	Consult publisher for reference style.
Footnotes	No footnotes.
Tables or Figures	Title charts and number them consecutively according to citation in text. If data have been published previously, include an appropriate reference. Number illustrations and legends consecutively according to appearance in the text. Provide short, descriptive legends on a separate page. Legends for figures previously published should include a complete reference to the original publication, with the copyright designation. Must provide copies of the publisher's and author's permission to use the figure. Photographs should include captions.

REVIEW PROCESS

Type	Anonymous review by 3 reviewers.
Queries	Not specified.
Acknowledgment	By mail.
Review Time	10–15 weeks.
Revisions	Reviewer comments and suggestions are mailed to authors for approval or action. If authors choose to make or approve or suggest alternative changes, the manuscript is reviewed again for clarity and content by the previous reviewers or by another party.
Acceptance Rate	60%.
Return of Manuscript	Returned if not published.
Lag Time to Print	3–8 months.

REPRINT, SUBSCRIPTION, AND CONTACT INFORMATION

Reprint Policy	Professional reprints available at discount. Contact publisher.
Book Reviews	Unsolicited book reviews rarely are used.
Subscriptions	Publisher, 470 Boston Post Road, Weston, MA 02193. Individual, $91.

American Journal of Orthopsychiatry

Editorial Focus	The journal is dedicated to informing public policy, professional practice, and knowledge production relating to mental health and human development, from an interdisciplinary prespective. Articles should have application across professional boundaries, rather than being discipline-specific. Clinical, theoretical, research, or service-system-oriented manuscripts are invited for editorial board consideration. Selection of articles for publication is based on their originality, adequacy of method, significance of findings, contribution to theory and practice, and clarity and brevity of presentation.
Audience	Social workers, psychologists, psychiatrists, psychiatric nurses, educators, and professionals in a broad range of allied disciplines.
Special Themes	Articles with a preventive orientation and those that offer reconceptualization of generally accepted tenets and practices are especially welcome.
Where Indexed/ Abstracted	Child Development Abstracts; Current Contents; Education Index; Excerpta Medica; Hospital Literature Index; Language and Language Behavior Abstracts; Mental Retardation Abstracts; Psychological Abstracts; PsycSCAN; Developmental Psychology; Social Sciences Citation Index; Social Sciences Index; Social Work Abstracts.
Year Established	1930.
Circulation	10,000.
Frequency	Quarterly.
Months Issued	January, April, July, October.
No. of Articles	Approximately15 per issue.

SUBMISSIONS

Address	Editor, *American Journal of Orthopsychiatry*, 330 Seventh Avenue, 18th Floor, New York, NY 10001.
Number of Copies	4.
Disk Submission	None for submission; disk required on acceptance.

FORMAT OF MANUSCRIPT

Cover Sheet	Separate cover sheet should include title, authors' affiliations, mailing address, daytime phone and fax numbers of corresponding author.
Abstract	50 words.
Key Words	Not required.
Length	15–20 pages.
Margins	Wide.
Spacing	Double-spaced (minimum).

STYLE

Name of Guide	Consult previous issues for general style guidance regarding text.
Subheadings	Level-one head: separate line, all capitals, flush left. Level-two head: upper/lower case, separate line, flush left. Level-three head: run in to start of paragraph; first word takes initial upper case, all else lowercase. Apply NO formatting (bold, italic, etc.) to subheads.
References	Follow style of current edition of *Publication Manual of the American Psychological Association*, except that in-text parenthetical citations should be italicized if possible (not underlined).
Footnotes	Textual footnotes are discouraged; where essential, asterisk system is used.
Tables or Figures	Tables should be prepared on a standard word processor (same as text), *not* in a special table editing, spread-sheet, or presentation program. Columns of figures must be delimited by tabs, not spaces (i.e., tab key, not spacebar). Tables should contain *no* vertical rules; horizontal rules should be done via the keyboard underline key; not a drawing tool. See prior issues for general table style and layout.

REVIEW PROCESS

Type	Double-blind review.
Queries	Letters of inquiry unaccompanied by manuscript are discouraged.
Acknowledgment	All submissions are acknowledged on receipt.
Review Time	3–5 months.
Revisions	May be requested by the editor subsequent to review; resubmissions are subject to further review.
Acceptance Rate	15%.
Return of Manuscript	Not returned.
Lag Time to Print	12–18 months.

CHARGES TO AUTHOR

Author Alterations	Only for major alterations, at prevailing rate.

REPRINT, SUBSCRIPTION, AND CONTACT INFORMATION

Reprint Policy	Authors are invited to order reprints at their own expense.
Book Reviews	None. Companion quarterly, *Readings: A Journal of Reviews and Commentary in Mental Health*, publishes book reviews, all invited by the editors.
Subscriptions	Free to members of the American Orthopsychiatric Association. Address membership inquiries to American Orthopsychiatric Association, 330 Seventh Avenue, 18th Floor, New York, NY 10001; phone: 212-564-5930; fax: 212-564-6180. Nonmember rates: $70 per volume for institutions and libraries; $45 per volume for individuals. Contact Ortho Publication Sales Office, 49 Sheridan Avenue, Albany, NY 12210.
Affiliation	American Orthopsychiatric Association.

American Psychologist

Editorial Focus	*American Psychologist* is the official journal of the American Psychological Association and, as such, contains archival documents. It also publishes articles on current issues in psychology as well as empirical, theoretical, and practical articles on broad aspects of psychology.
Audience	Researchers in the discipline, faculty, libraries.
Where Indexed/ Abstracted	Academic Index; Applied Social Sciences Index & Abstracts; Biological Abstracts; Child Development Abstracts; Communications Abstracts; Criminal Justice Abstracts; Current Advances in Ecological & Environmental Sciences; Current Contents; Current Index to Journals in Education; Index Medicus; Management Contents; PsycINFO; Research in Higher Education; Risk Abstracts; Sage Family Studies Abstracts; Science Citation Index; Social Sciences Citation Index; Social Sciences Index; Social Work Abstracts; Studies on Women Abstracts.
Year Established	1946.
Circulation	106,800.
Frequency	Monthly.
No. of Articles	13.

SUBMISSIONS

Address	Raymond D. Fowler, *American Psychologist,* 750 First Street, NE, Washington, DC 20002-4242.
Number of Copies	5.
Disk Submission	Submit manuscripts on paper; disks may be requested of accepted articles.

FORMAT OF MANUSCRIPT

Cover Sheet	Refer to Instructions to Authors in each issue.
Abstract	Manuscripts must include an abstract containing a maximum of 960 characters and spaces (approximately 120 words), typed on a separate sheet of paper.
Key Words	None.
Length	Not specified.
Margins	See style guide.
Spacing	Double-spaced.

STYLE

Name of Guide	*Publication Manual of the American Psychological Association.*
Subheadings	See style guide.
References	See style guide.

Footnotes	See style guide.
Tables or Figures	See style guide; camera-ready copy required for all art.

REVIEW PROCESS

Type	Masked review.
Queries	No query letters.
Acknowledgment	Editor acknowledges submission by mail.
Review Time	Usually 60–90 days.
Revisions	Editor will notify author if revision is desired (most manuscripts are initially rejected; most published manuscripts have gone through one or two revisions).
Acceptance Rate	13%.
Return of Manuscript	Manuscripts are not usually returned.
Lag Time to Print	8 months.

CHARGES TO AUTHOR

Author Alterations	Authors are billed for alterations in proofs.

REPRINT, SUBSCRIPTION, AND CONTACT INFORMATION

Reprint Policy	Authors may purchase reprints of their articles (order form accompanies proofs).
Book Reviews	None.
Subscriptions	Subscriptions Department, American Psychological Association, 750 First Street, NE, Washington, DC 20002-4242.
	Nonmember individual rates are $180 domestic, $220 foreign, $245 air mail; institutional rates are $313 domestic, $397 foreign, $423 airmail. Free with APA membership.
Affiliation	Published by the American Psychological Association.
Home Page URL	http://www.apa.org

American Sociological Review

Editorial Focus	The official flagship journal of the American Sociological Association, *ASR* publishes original works of interest to the discipline in general, new theoretical developments, results of research that advance our understanding of fundamental social processes, and important methodological innovations. All areas of sociology are welcomed. Emphasis is on exceptional quality and general interest.
Audience	Sociologists and other social scientists, in academic and applied settings; libraries.
Special Themes	No thematic issues are published.
Where Indexed/ Abstracted	Abstracts for Social Workers; Ayer's Guide; Current Contents; ERIC Clearinghouse; International Political Science Abstracts; Psychological Abstracts; Social Science Index/Social Science Abstracts; Sociological Abstracts; University Microfilms; others.
Year Established	1936.
Circulation	Approximately 13,500.
Frequency	Bimonthly.
Months Issued	February, April, June, August, October, December.
No. of Articles	8–15 per issue.

SUBMISSIONS

Address	Glenn Firebaugh, Editor, *American Sociological Review,* Department of Sociology, 206 Oswald Tower, Pennsylvania State University, University Park, PA 16802.
Number of Copies	5.
Disk Submission	Final versions of accepted articles are requested, not required, on disk.

FORMAT OF MANUSCRIPT

Cover Sheet	Title page should include full article title, author(s) name(s) and affiliation(s), a "running head," and approximate word count of the article.
Abstract	Separate page; limited to 150 words; omit author's name.
Key Words	Authors of accepted articles will be asked to provide key words/phrases.
Length	Generally, approximately 40 manuscript pages; comments and replies are limited to 8 pages.
Margins	1.25 inches on all sides.
Spacing	Double-spaced.

STYLE

Name of Guide	*American Sociological Association Style Guide* (1996); available from ASA office.
Subheadings	Indicate the organization of the content. Generally, 3 levels are adequate. Refer to *ASA Style Guide* for details.
References	See style guide.
Footnotes	See style guide.
Tables or Figures	See style guide.

REVIEW PROCESS

Type	Blind.
Queries	Editors' discretion.
Acknowledgment	*ASR* sends a postcard acknowledging receipt of manuscript.
Review Time	Approximately 10 weeks.
Revisions	See style guide.
Acceptance Rate	Approximately 15%–17%.
Return of Manuscript	Manuscripts are not returned.
Lag Time to Print	Approximately 8 months.

CHARGES TO AUTHOR

Author Alterations	None.
Page Charges	Voluntary contributions requested if author has research funds for that purpose.
Processing	$15; waived for student members.

REPRINT, SUBSCRIPTION, AND CONTACT INFORMATION

Reprint Policy	Authors receive 1 complimentary copy of the issue and may order reprints from journal printer.
Book Reviews	*ASR* does not review books.
Subscriptions	May be selected as free membership journal by ASA members; $60 to non-member individuals; $120 to institutions. Write: ASA Subscriptions, 1722 N Street, NW, Washington, DC 20036.
Affiliation	Published by the American Sociological Association.
E-Mail Address	publications@asanet.org (ASA Executive Office)
Home Page URL	http://www.asanet.org

Arete

Editorial Focus	Problems, issues, and new developments in social work practice, social work education, and social issues; articles of a theoretical or research nature; and manuscripts for "Education Digest."
Audience	Professionals, educators, practitioners.
Special Themes	Social work education, new teaching models, social welfare issues in the South.
Where Indexed/ Abstracted	Social Work Abstracts; Sociological Abstracts.
Year Established	1970.
Circulation	3,000.
Frequency	Semiannually.
Months Issued	May and December.
No. of Articles	5–7.

SUBMISSIONS

Address	Dr. Terry Tirrito, Editor, University of South Carolina, College of Social Work, Columbia, SC 29208.
Number of Copies	4.
Disk Submission	Yes, on acceptance.

FORMAT OF MANUSCRIPT

Cover Sheet	Title, name, address, telephone, fax, and e-mail address. Include title page that contains manuscript title, author's name and affiliation, with the first page of text repeating the title page.
Abstract	50–100 words.
Key Words	Yes.
Length	Full-length manuscripts, 16–20 pages; Education Digest, 8 pages.
Margins	Wide.
Spacing	Double-spaced.

STYLE

Name of Guide	*Publication Manual of the American Psychological Association.*
Subheadings	See style guide.
References	See style guide.
Footnotes	See style guide.
Tables or Figures	See style guide.

REVIEW PROCESS

Type	Anonymous review by 2 external reviewers and 5 internal reviewers for full-length manuscripts, and by 5 internal reviewers for Education Digest manuscripts.
Queries	Yes.
Acknowledgment	Letter is mailed to author.
Review Time	4–6 months.
Revisions	Editor specifies required revisions.
Acceptance Rate	30%.
Return of Manuscript	Not returned.
Lag Time to Print	6 months.

REPRINT, SUBSCRIPTION, AND CONTACT INFORMATION

Reprint Policy	5 complimentary copies of issue sent to each author upon publication.
Book Reviews	None.
Subscriptions	Dr. Terry Tirrito, Editor, University of South Carolina, College of Social Work, Columbia, SC 29208.
E-Mail Address	Arete@cosw.cosw.sc.edu
Home Page URL	http://www.sc.edu/index.html

Asia Pacific Journal of Social Work

Editorial Focus	Social work practice and research in Asia Pacific region.
Audience	Social workers.
Special Themes	Social work practice, research, policy, cross-cultural diversity, gender and race concerns. Fields include children, youth, elderly, family, community, health, justice, disability, and education.
Where Indexed/ Abstracted	In process.
Year Established	1991.
Circulation	250.
Frequency	Semiannually.
Months Issued	March and September.
No. of Articles	8–10 per issue.

SUBMISSIONS

Address	Managing Editor, *APJSW,* Department of Social Work & Psychology, National University of Singapore, Kent Ridge, Singapore 119260.
Number of Copies	3.
Disk Submission	Microsoft Word or WordPerfect.

FORMAT OF MANUSCRIPT

Cover Sheet	Separate sheet with author, address, and designation.
Abstract	60-word abstract.
Key Words	2–3 key words.
Length	12–16 pages (about 3,500 words).
Margins	1 inch on all sides.
Spacing	Double-spaced.

STYLE

Name of Guide	*Publication Manual of the American Psychological Association.*
Subheadings	Not specified.
References	See style guide.
Footnotes	No footnotes preferred.
Tables or Figures	Camera-ready.

REVIEW PROCESS

Type	"Double-blind" international panel of reviewers.
Queries	Address to managing editor.

Acknowledgment	By letter.
Review Time	3–6 months.
Revisions	As per reviewers' or editors' comments.
Acceptance Rate	Approximately 50%.
Return of Manuscript	Not returned.
Lag Time to Print	6 months–1 year.

REPRINT, SUBSCRIPTION, AND CONTACT INFORMATION

Reprint Policy	Authors receive 2 complimentary copies.
Book Reviews	Send books for review to managing editor.
Subscriptions	Editorial Assistant, Times Academic Press, Federal Publications (s) PTE LTD, 1 New Industrial Road, Singapore 536196.
Affiliation	APASWE, IFSW (Asia Pacific).
E-Mail Address	swktannt@nus.sg

Australian Social Work

Previous Title	*Forum, Australian Journal of Social Work.*
Editorial Focus	Original research, practice, and theoretical articles relevant to professional social workers.
Audience	Social workers and social welfare professionals—practitioners and academics, libraries.
Special Themes	Calls for papers and special theme issues are a regular feature.
Where Indexed/ Abstracted	AGIS; APAIS; DRUG; Family; MAIS; PsychLit; Social Work Abstracts; Socio File; SSI; SSCI.
Year Established	1948.
Circulation	4,700.
Frequency	Quarterly.
Months Issued	March, June, September, December.
No. of Articles	7–8.

SUBMISSIONS

Address	The Editor, 28 Ethie Road, Beacon Hill, N.S.W. 2100 Australia.
Number of Copies	3.
Disk Submission	Only required for accepted manuscripts. Text only or as an ASCII file, Macintosh format preferred.

FORMAT OF MANUSCRIPT

Cover Sheet	Name of author, address, phone and fax numbers, brief biographical details, number of words.
Abstract	Abstract required. Maximum 150 words.
Key Words	Not required, but desirable.
Length	Maximum 4,000 words.
Margins	Not specified.
Spacing	Double-spaced.

STYLE

Name of Guide	*Style Manual for Authors, Editors and Printers,* Australian Government Publishing Service.
Subheadings	Required. Type in bold.
References	Harvard (author–date) system.
Footnotes	No footnotes. Endnotes only if necessary.
Tables or Figures	Camera-ready copy preferred, but graphics services are available.

REVIEW PROCESS

Type	Anonymous review by two referees.
Queries	Manuscripts submitted for review only.
Acknowledgment	By letter. If from overseas, a self-addressed, stamped envelope required.
Review Time	3 months.
Revisions	Sent to 2 reviewers, 1 original reviewer and 1 new one.
Acceptance Rate	Approximately one-third on first attempt, sometimes with minor changes required.
Return of Manuscript	1 copy returned. Self-addressed, stamped envelope required for overseas contributors.
Lag Time to Print	9 months.

REPRINT, SUBSCRIPTION, AND CONTACT INFORMATION

Reprint Policy	2 free reprints provided. Further copies on request, also free.
Book Reviews	Book reviews are published in each issue. Sought by book review editor.
Subscriptions	AUST $90 per year to AASW LTD, P.O. Box 84, Hawker ACT 2614 Australia.
Affiliation	Australian Association of Social Workers Ltd.
E-Mail Address	aaswnat@aasw.asn.au
Home Page URL	http://www.aasw.asn.au/~aaswnat/aasw/national/journal/journal.html

Behavioral & Social Sciences Librarian

Editorial Focus	Production, collection, organization, retrieval, and use of social science information.
Audience	Scholars, researchers, publishers, database producers, librarians, and information specialists, working in public libraries, colleges and universities, government, applied research centers, data archives, foundations, professional organizations, and the commercial sector.
Special Themes	Descriptive and critical analyses of information resources with particular subdiscipline; publishing trends; use and user studies; reference service and bibliographic instruction; indexing, abstracting, thesaurus building and database construction; bibliographic and numeric databases, and social science data files and data archives.
Where Indexed/ Abstracted	Abstracts in Social Gerontology: Current Literature on Aging; Applied Social Sciences Index & Abstracts (Online: ASSI via Data–Star) (CD-ROM: ASSIA Plus); CINAHL (Cumulative Index to Nursing & Allied Health Literature); CNPIEC Reference Guide: Chinese National Directory of Foreign Periodicals; Current Awareness Bulletin; Current Contents: Clinical Medicine/Life Sciences (CC: CM/LS); Current Index to Journals in Education; Educational Administration Abstracts (EAA); Index to Periodical Articles Related to Law; Information Reports & Bibliographies; Information Science Abstracts; Informed Librarian; INSPEC Information Services; International Bulletin of Bibliography on Education; INTERNET ACCESS (& additional networks) Bulletin Board for Libraries ("BUBL"), coverage of information resources on INTERNET, JANET and other networks; Library & Information Science Abstracts (LISA); Library Literature; Newsletter of Library and Information Services; Public Affairs Information Bulletin (PAIS); Referativnyi Zhurnal (Abstracts Journal of the Institute of Scientific Information of the Republic of Russia); Sage Public Administration Abstracts (SPAA); Social Work Abstracts.
Year Established	1979.
Circulation	282.
Frequency	Semiannually.
Months Issued	Not specified.
No. of Articles	6–10 per issue.

SUBMISSIONS

Address	Editor, David Lonergan, PhD, University Libraries, Northern Illinois University, DeKalb, IL 60115.
Number of Copies	4.
Disk Submission	Authors of accepted manuscripts are asked to submit a disk, preferably in Microsoft Word or WordPerfect.

FORMAT OF MANUSCRIPT

Cover Sheet Separate sheet, which does not go out for review. Full title, author names, degrees, professional titles; designation of one author as corresponding author with full address, phone numbers, e-mail address, and fax number; date of submission.

Abstract About 100 words.

Key Words 5 or 6 words that identify article content.

Length 5–50 pages, including references and abstract. Lengthier manuscripts may be considered, but only at the discretion of the editor. Sometimes, lengthier manuscripts may be considered if they can be divided up into sections for publication in successive issues.

Margins 1 inch on all sides.

Spacing Double-spaced for all copy, except title page.

STYLE

Name of Guide *Chicago Manual of Style.*

Subheadings Use as needed to guide reader through the article. No more than 4 levels.

References Author–date citation style; see style guide.

Footnotes No footnotes preferred; incorporate into text.

Tables or Figures Type tables double-spaced. Submit camera-ready art (300 dpi printer or better) for all figures. Place each table or figure on a separate, numbered page at the end of the manuscript.

REVIEW PROCESS

Type "Double blind" anonymous peer review. 3 reviewers plus editor-in-chief read the manuscript in an anonymous review.

Queries Authors are encouraged to read the journal to determine if their subject matter would be appropriate.

Acknowledgment Enclose a regular self-addressed, stamped envelope with submission.

Review Time 3–4 months.

Revisions See journal.

Acceptance Rate Not specified.

Return of Manuscript Only if 9″ x 12″ self-addressed, stamped envelope is enclosed.

Lag Time to Print 6 months–1 year.

REPRINT, SUBSCRIPTION, AND CONTACT INFORMATION

Reprint Policy All authors receive 2 complimentary copies of the issue in which article appears. Authors receive reprint order forms to purchase additional reprinted copies.

Book Reviews Book Review Editor, Kathleen A. Walsh, 506 N. 5th Street, DeKalb, IL 60115.

Subscriptions The Haworth Press, Inc., 10 Alice Street, Binghamton, NY 13904-1580. Individuals, $42; institutions, $90; libraries, $90.

British Journal of Psychotherapy

Editorial Focus	Clinical (including comparative clinical interpretation), research, theoretical. Largely psychodynamic, with comparisons with other therapies.
Audience	Practicing psychotherapists, libraries of mental health, institutions, and teaching schools.
Special Themes	Comparison between forms of schools of psychotherapy, and between therapies.
Where Indexed/ Abstracted	Medical Abstracts; Psychological Abstracts.
Year Established	1984.
Circulation	2,500.
Frequency	Quarterly.
Months Issued	September, December, March, June.
No. of Articles	8–10.

SUBMISSIONS

Address	Dr. Jean Arundale, Editor, *British Journal of Psychotherapy*, York Clinic, Guy's Hospital, 117 Borough High Street, London SE1 1NP, England.
Number of Copies	5.
Disk Submission	Required for accepted articles. WordPerfect 5.1 or Microsoft Word for Windows 2.0.

FORMAT OF MANUSCRIPT

Cover Sheet	Submission information published in each number.
Abstract	Approximately 100 words.
Key Words	None.
Length	Approximately 5,000 words.
Margins	1 inch on all sides.
Spacing	Double-spaced.

STYLE

Name of Guide	See journal.
Subheadings	As needed.
References	Author–date citation system. See journal.
Footnotes	Incorporate into text wherever possible.
Tables or Figures	Will be typeset in journal style.

REVIEW PROCESS

Type	Peer-reviewed.
Queries	To editor.
Acknowledgment	On receipt.
Review Time	6 months.
Revisions	Submit as original.
Acceptance Rate	Approximately 40%.
Return of Manuscript	Not returned.
Lag Time to Print	6–9 months.

CHARGES TO AUTHOR

Author Alterations	For major alterations at proof.

REPRINT, SUBSCRIPTION, AND CONTACT INFORMATION

Reprint Policy	On request, at proof.
Book Reviews	Suggestions and requests to review editor.
Subscriptions	Contact Artesian Books, 18 Artesian Road, London W2 5AR, England.
Affiliation	Sponsored by Arbours Association, Association for Group and Individual Psychotherapy, Centre for Psycho-analytic Psychotherapy, Guild of Psycho-therapists, Institute for Psychotherapy and Counselling (WPF), Lincoln Clinic and Institute for Psychotherapy, London Centre for Psychotherapy, Severnside Institute for Psychotherapy.

The British Journal of Social Work

Editorial Focus	Research papers, book reviews, commentaries on research papers published in other journals.
Audience	Academics working in social work and related fields, social workers.
Special Themes	Occasional special issues on particular themes are published.
Where Indexed/ Abstracted	Abstracts in Social Work; Adolescent Mental Health Abstracts; Applied Social Sciences Index & Abstracts; Cumulative Index of Nursing and Allied Health Literature; Current Contents: Social and Behavioral Sciences; Human Resources Abstracts; International Bibliography of Sociology; Linguistics and Language Behavioral Abstracts; Middle East Abstracts Index; Psychological Abstracts; PsycINFO; PsycLIT; Research Alert; Sage Family Studies Abstracts; Sage Race Relations Abstracts; Social Planning and Policy Development Abstracts; Social Sciences Citation Index; Social Work Abstracts; Sociology Abstracts; Sociology Education Abstracts; Studies on Women Abstracts.
Year Established	1971.
Circulation	1,300.
Frequency	Bimonthly.
Months Issued	February, April, June, August, October, December.
No. of Articles	Approximately 40 per year.

SUBMISSIONS

Address	Professor Audrey Mullender, Department of Allied Social Studies, University of Warwick, Coventry CV4 7AL, England.
Number of Copies	3.
Disk Submission	Yes, preferably Microsoft Word or WordPerfect.

FORMAT OF MANUSCRIPT

Cover Sheet	See style guide.
Abstract	Yes, 150–250 words.
Key Words	None.
Length	Major research papers should not exceed 6,000 words; shorter papers are welcomed.
Margins	Wide.
Spacing	Double-spaced.

STYLE

Name of Guide	Notes for Contributors are published in journal.
Subheadings	One level is normal; two levels are optional.

References	See style guide.
Footnotes	Not normally admitted.
Tables or Figures	Camera-ready copy preferred but not essential.

REVIEW PROCESS

Type	Anonymous refereeing.
Queries	Accept and welcome.
Acknowledgment	Letter sent by editor.
Review Time	Aim for 6–8 weeks.
Revisions	Detailed letter from editor, plus comments from referees; cover letter required with resubmission.
Acceptance Rate	Approximately 20%–25%.
Return of Manuscript	Not returned.
Lag Time to Print	Currently 18 months.

CHARGES TO AUTHOR

Author Alterations	Authors may be charged for alterations where these account for more than 10% of typesetting costs.

REPRINT, SUBSCRIPTION, AND CONTACT INFORMATION

Reprint Policy	25 provided free of charge.
Book Reviews	Book reviews are published. Unsolicited reviews are not normally published. Contact: Eric Blyth, Department of Social Work, University of Huddersfield, Queensgate, Huddersfield HD1 3DH, England.
Subscriptions	Journal Subscription Department, Oxford University Press, Walton Street, Oxford OX2 6DP, England.
	Within North America: Journal Subscription Department, Oxford University Press, 2001 Evans Road, Cary, NC 27513.
	1997 Subscription Prices: Institutions: Europe £110, outside Europe $190; Individuals: Europe £45, outside Europe $84.
Affiliation	British Association of Social Workers.
Home Page URL	http://www.oup.co.uk/jnls/list/social

Bulletin of the Menninger Clinic

Editorial Focus	To provide new insights into the understanding and treatment of severe mental illness from many perspectives within a broad psychodynamic framework.
Audience	Psychiatrists, psychologists, psychoanalysts, psychiatric social workers, psychiatric nurses.
Special Themes	Current treatment approaches, specific psychiatric disorders, clinical research.
Where Indexed/ Abstracted	Abstracts on Criminology & Penology (Amsterdam); Academic Abstracts; Current Contents: Social & Behavioral Sciences; Digest of Neurology & Psychiatry; Excerpta Medica/EMBASE; Family Resources Database; Hungarian Medical Bibliography; Index Medicus/MEDLINE; Institute of Scientific Information (Moscow); International Nursing Index; National Clearinghouse for Mental Health Information/Mental Health Abstracts; Pascal Bibliographie Internationale; Psychoanalytic Abstracts; Psychological Abstracts/PsycINFO; Social Planning/Policy & Development Abstracts; Social Sciences Citation Index/Social Scisearch; Social Work Abstracts.
Year Established	1936.
Circulation	2,000.
Frequency	Quarterly.
Months Issued	January, April, July, October.
No. of Articles	8–12 per issue.

SUBMISSIONS

Address	Managing Editor, *Bulletin of the Menninger Clinic*, P.O. Box 829, Topeka, KS 66601-0829.
Number of Copies	4.
Disk Submission	Authors of accepted manuscripts are asked to submit a disk, preferably in Microsoft Word or WordPerfect.

FORMAT OF MANUSCRIPT

Cover Sheet	Separate sheet with full title of article, names, degrees, and titles of all authors, designation of one author as corresponding author with full address, phone numbers, e-mail address, fax number.
Abstract	75–100 word informative abstract.
Key Words	6 key words for indexing.
Length	20–25 pages, including references and tables; longer manuscripts may be considered at the discretion of the editor.
Margins	1 inch on all sides.
Spacing	Double-spaced for all copy, except title page.

STYLE

Name of Guide	*Publication Manual of the American Psychological Association.*
Subheadings	Use as needed to guide reader; preferably only three levels.
References	Author–date citation style; reference list includes only sources cited in text.
Footnotes	Keep footnotes to a minimum; incorporate such information into text.
Tables or Figures	Type tables double-spaced, each on a separate numbered sheet. Figures should be attached to end of manuscript and submitted as camera-ready art (600 dpi or better), but publisher reserves right to redo unsatisfactory figures and charge excessive costs to authors.

REVIEW PROCESS

Type	Anonymous peer review; editor-in chief reads all manuscripts and selects 2–3 additional reviewers.
Queries	Query letters acceptable, and authors should read journal to determine whether their manuscripts are appropriate.
Acknowledgment	Acknowledgment letter sent on receipt of manuscript.
Review Time	3–4 months.
Revisions	Submit 2 copies with cover letter describing revisions and/or explaining why revisions were not made.
Acceptance Rate	Annual rate varies from 40%–50%.
Return of Manuscript	Manuscripts are not returned.
Lag Time to Print	Approximately 6 months to 1 year.

REPRINT, SUBSCRIPTION, AND CONTACT INFORMATION

Reprint Policy	All authors receive 1 complimentary copy of issue in which article appears. Authors receive reprint order forms to purchase additional copies of article.
Book Reviews	By invitation only; send books for review to Book Review Editor, *Bulletin of the Menninger Clinic*, P.O. Box 829, Topeka, KS 66601-0829; phone: 913-350-5856; fax: 913-273-8625.
Subscriptions	*Bulletin of the Menninger Clinic,* Guilford Publications, Inc., 72 Spring Street, New York, NY 10012; phone 800-365-7006, ext. 3, or 212-431-9800; fax: 212-966-6708; e-mail: info@guilford.com or samples@guilford.com
Affiliation	The Menninger Clinic.
E-Mail Address	allenjg@menninger.edu
Home Page URL	http://www.menninger.edu

The Canadian Journal of Human Sexuality

Editorial Focus	Empirical research, critical analyses, and clinical case presentations related to human sexuality.
Audience	Researchers, educators, libraries, students, professionals whose work is related to human sexuality.
Special Themes	Not specified.
Where Indexed/ Abstracted	Applied Social Sciences Index & Abstracts; Child Development Abstracts and Bibliography; Contents Pages in Education; Excerpta Medica; Family Studies Database; International Bibliography of the Social Sciences; Psychological Abstracts; Sage Family Studies Abstracts; Social Work Abstracts; Sociological Abstracts; Sociology of Education Abstracts; Studies on Women Abstracts.
Year Established	1990.
Circulation	1,500+.
Frequency	Quarterly.
Months Issued	March, July, October, December.
No. of Articles	5–8 per issue.

SUBMISSIONS

Address	Editor, *The Canadian Journal of Human Sexuality*, SIECCAN, 850 Coxwell Avenue, East York, Ontario, M4C 5R1, Canada.
Number of Copies	3.
Disk Submission	Manuscripts should be submitted on 3-1/2″ diskettes in either WordPerfect 5.1 or WordPerfect 6.0 in IBM format.

FORMAT OF MANUSCRIPT

Cover Sheet	Separate sheet, which does not go out for review. This page should include the title of the paper, the names and affiliations of all the authors, and the complete mailing address and telephone number of the author to whom communication should be addressed.
Abstract	Approximately 200 words.
Key Words	4–5 key words or phrases (2–4 words maximum).
Length	10–30 pages.
Margins	1 inch on all sides.
Spacing	Double-spaced.

STYLE

Name of Guide	*Publication Manual of the American Psychological Association.*
Subheadings	As needed.

References	See style guide.
Footnotes	See style guide.
Tables or Figures	Tables should be numbered and referred to by number in the text. Each table should be typed on a separate sheet of paper and have an accompanying title.

REVIEW PROCESS

Type	Anonymous peer review; 2 reviewers make recommendations to editor.
Queries	Accepted.
Acknowledgment	Editor sends an acknowledgment on receipt of manuscript.
Review Time	4–8 weeks.
Revisions	Submit 3 copies with separate cover sheet describing revisions and responding to reviewers' comments.
Acceptance Rate	40%.
Return of Manuscript	Not returned.
Lag Time to Print	3 months.

REPRINT, SUBSCRIPTION, AND CONTACT INFORMATION

Reprint Policy	All authors receive 4 complimentary copies of the issue in which the paper appears. Reprints available on request.
Book Reviews	Send books for review to Editor, *The Canadian Journal of Human Sexuality*, SIECCAN, 850 Coxwell Avenue, East York, Ontario, M4C 5R1, Canada.
Subscriptions	SIECCAN, 850 Coxwell Avenue, East York, Ontario, M4C 5R1, Canada. Individuals, $40; institutions, $60.
Affiliation	*The Canadian Journal of Human Sexuality* is a publication of SIECCAN, the Sex Information and Education Council of Canada.

Child Abuse & Neglect, The International Journal

Editorial Focus Provides an international, multidisciplinary forum on all aspects of child abuse and neglect, with special emphasis on prevention and treatment. The scope extends further to all those aspects of life that either favor or hinder child development.

Audience Although contributions will primarily be from the fields of psychology, psychiatry, social work, medicine, nursing, law enforcement, legislation, education, and anthropology, the journal aims to encourage the concerned lay individual and child-oriented advocate organizations to contribute.

Where Indexed/ Abstracted Adolescent Mental Health Abstracts; Applied Social Sciences Index & Abstracts; Child Development Abstracts; Criminal Justice Abstracts; Current Contents: Social and Behavioral Sciences; Current Index of Journals in Education; ERIC/CIJE; Exceptional Child Educational Abstracts; Excerpta Medica; IBA; Index Medicus; MEDLINE; NCJRS; PASCAL-CNRS Data; Psychological Abstracts; Research Alert; Social Work Abstracts; Social Sciences Citation Index.

Year Established 1977.

Circulation 2,000 individual, 1,000 institutional.

Frequency Monthly.

No. of Articles 10–12.

SUBMISSIONS

Address *Child Abuse & Neglect,* Kempe National Center, 1205 Oneida Street, Denver, CO 80220.

Number of Copies Original plus 3 copies.

Disk Submission Disk copy requested on acceptance of manuscript; ASCII or DOS.

FORMAT OF MANUSCRIPT

Cover Sheet Title of article; authors' names and affiliations at the time the work was conducted; corresponding author's address and telephone number; a concise running title; at least 3 and no more than 5 key words for indexing purposes; and an unnumbered footnote giving address for reprint requests and any acknowledgments. A letter to the editor must be enclosed requesting review and possible publication; the letter must also state that the manuscript has not been previously published and is not under simultaneous consideration by another publication. The corresponding author's address and telephone number (as well as any forthcoming change) should be noted.

Abstract All articles except Brief Communications must have a synopsis-type abstract not to exceed 200 words in length covering the main factual points and statement of the problem, method, results, and conclusions.

Key Words At least 3 and no more than 5 key words for indexing purposes.

Length 16–20 pages.

Margins	1 inch on all sides.
Spacing	Double-spaced throughout, including references.

STYLE

Name of Guide	*Publication Manual of the American Psychological Association.*
Subheadings	See style guide.
References	See style guide.
Footnotes	None; should be incorporated into the text.
Tables or Figures	Copies of all tables and figures should be included with each copy of the manuscript. Upon acceptance of a manuscript for publication, original, camera-ready tables and/or figures must be submitted. Type figure legends on a separate sheet. Write author name, aritcle title, and figure number lightly in pencil on back of each.

REVIEW PROCESS

Type	Blind review by at least 2 editorial consultants.
Queries	Contact Mary Roth or Janina Stewart, editorial office, 303-321-3963.
Acknowledgment	Upon receipt of manuscript.
Review Time	Approximately 4–6 weeks.
Revisions	Reviews are the same as for original submissions. Authors are asked to resubmit in a timely fashion (6 weeks) or notify editorial office of expected delays.
Acceptance Rate	38%.
Return of Manuscript	Only on request, if author provides self-addressed, stamped envelope.
Lag Time to Print	6–8 months.

CHARGES TO AUTHOR

Author Alterations	Only if major alterations to page proofs.

REPRINT, SUBSCRIPTION, AND CONTACT INFORMATION

Reprint Policy	Order form for reprints included with page proofs; 25 free reprints are provided. Orders for additional reprints must be received before printing in order to qualify for lower prepublication rates.
Book Reviews	Book review editor assigns reviewers, 4–6 book reviews appear in each issue. No charge for publication of book reviews; however, not all books received are reviewed.
Subscriptions	Membership to The International Society for Prevention of Child Abuse & Neglect ($85 per year for developed countries; $45 per year for developing countries). For nonmembers, annual institutional subscription rate for North, Central, and South America is $729 per year.
Affiliation	Official journal of the International Society for Prevention of Child Abuse & Neglect.
E-Mail Address	Mary.Roth@UCHSC.edu

Child & Adolescent Social Work Journal

Editorial Focus	Clinical articles on treatment of children and adolescents and their families. Research, theoretical, policy.
Audience	Practitioners, faculty, libraries.
Special Themes	Clinical articles.
Where Indexed/ Abstracted	Abstract of Research Papers; Chicago Psychoanalytic Literature; Current Contents; Current Journal Literature; Family Abstracts; Health Instrument File; Index APA Psychological Abstracts; International Bibliography of Periodical Literature; Social Science Documentation Center; Social Work Abstracts; Sociological Abstracts; Studies on Women Abstracts.
Year Established	1994.
Circulation	Not specified.
Frequency	Bimonthly.
Months Issued	February, April, June, August, October, December.
No. of Articles	5–6.

SUBMISSIONS

Address	Dr. Thomas Kenemore, Institute for Clinical Social Work, 68 East Walker Place, Suite 1400, Chicago, IL 60601-7202.
Number of Copies	3.
Disk Submission	Yes, clearly labeled as to program, computer, disk format, and file name.

FORMAT OF MANUSCRIPT

Cover Sheet	Name and address of authors.
Abstract	1 paragraph.
Key Words	Yes.
Length	14–16 pages.
Margins	1.5 inches on all sides.
Spacing	Double-spaced, including references and quotations.

STYLE

Name of Guide	*Publication Manual of the American Psychological Association.*
Subheadings	Yes.
References	Yes, double-spaced.
Footnotes	End of article.
Tables or Figures	Camera-ready.

REVIEW PROCESS

Type	Anonymous.
Queries	Not specified.
Acknowledgment	By postcard.
Review Time	3–4 months.
Revisions	If paper is of interest, and if reviewers request changes, author is notified with suggestions. Journal is author-friendly.
Acceptance Rate	40%–50%.
Return of Manuscript	Only if accompanied by a stamped, self-addressed envelope.
Lag Time to Print	4 months.

CHARGES TO AUTHOR

Author Alterations	Some charges.

REPRINT, SUBSCRIPTION, AND CONTACT INFORMATION

Reprint Policy	Charge for reprints from publisher. Human Sciences Press, 233 Spring Street, New York, NY 10013-1578.
Book Reviews	By invitation. Send books for review to Dr. Joyce West Stevens, School of Social Work, Boston University, 264 Bay State Road, Boston, MA 02215.
Subscriptions	Human Sciences Press, 233 Spring Street, New York, NY 10013-1578. $52.

Child & Family Behavior Therapy

Editorial Focus	Not specified.
Audience	Not specified.
Where Indexed/ Abstracted	Academic Abstracts/CD-ROM; Academic Search; Behavioral Medicine Abstracts; Cambridge Scientific Abstracts; Child Development Abstracts & Bibliography; CNPIEC Reference Guide: Chinese National Directory of Foreign Periodicals; Criminal Justice Abstracts; Criminology, Penology and Police Science Abstracts; Current Contents; Developmental Medicine & Child Neurology; ERIC Clearinghouse on Counseling and Student Services (ERIC/CASS); ERIC Clearinghouse on Elementary & Early Childhood Education; Exceptional Child Education Resources (ECER), (online through DIALOG and hard copy); Family Studies Database (online and CD-ROM); Index to Periodical Articles Related to Law; International Bulletin of Bibliography on Education; INTERNET ACCESS (& additional networks) Bulletin Board for Libraries ("BUBL"), coverage of information resources on INTERNET, JANET, and other networks; MasterFILE: updated database from EBSCO Publishing; Mental Health Abstracts (online through DIALOG); PASCAL International Bibliography T205: Sciences de l'information Documentation; Psychological Abstracts (PsycINFO); Sage Family Studies Abstracts (SFSA); Social Planning/Policy & Development Abstracts (SOPODA); Social Work Abstracts; Sociological Abstracts (SA); Sociology of Education Abstracts: Special Educational Needs Abstracts; Studies on Women Abstracts; Violence and Abuse Abstracts: A Review of Current Literature on Interpersonal Violence (VAA).
Year Established	1982.
Circulation	453.
Frequency	Quarterly.
Months Issued	Not specified.
No. of Articles	6–10 per issue.

SUBMISSIONS

Address	Associate Editor, Charles Diament, PhD, *Child & Family Behavior Therapy*, Psychotherapy Associates, 41 Reckless Place, Red Bank, NY 10010.
Number of Copies	4.
Disk Submission	Authors of accepted manuscripts are asked to submit a disk, preferably in Microsoft Word or WordPerfect.

FORMAT OF MANUSCRIPT

Cover Sheet	Separate sheet, which does not go out for review. Full title, author names, degrees, professional titles; designation of one author as corresponding author with full address, phone numbers, e-mail address, and fax number; date of submission.

Abstract	About 100 words.
Key Words	5 or 6 words that identify article content.
Length	20 pages, including references and abstract. Lengthier manuscripts may be considered, but only at the discretion of the editor. Sometimes, lengthier manuscripts may be considered if they can be divided up into sections for publication in successive issues.
Margins	1 inch on all sides.
Spacing	Double-spaced for all copy, except title page.

STYLE

Name of Guide	*Publication Manual of the American Psychological Association.*
Subheadings	Use as needed to guide reader through the article. No more than four levels.
References	Author–date citation style; see style guide.
Footnotes	No footnotes preferred; incorporate into text.
Tables or Figures	Type tables double-spaced. Submit camera-ready art (300 dpi printer or better) for all figures. Place each table or figure on a separate, numbered page at the end of the manuscript.

REVIEW PROCESS

Type	"Double blind" anonymous peer review. 3 reviewers plus editor-in-chief read the manuscript in an anonymous review.
Queries	Authors are encouraged to read the journal to determine if their subject matter would be appropriate.
Acknowledgment	Enclose a regular self-addressed, stamped envelope with submission.
Review Time	3–4 months.
Revisions	See journal.
Acceptance Rate	Not specified.
Return of Manuscript	Only if 9″ x 12″ self-addressed, stamped envelope is enclosed.
Lag Time to Print	6 months–1 year.

REPRINT, SUBSCRIPTION, AND CONTACT INFORMATION

Reprint Policy	All authors receive 2 complimentary copies of the issue in which article appears. Authors receive reprint order forms to purchase additional reprinted copies.
Book Reviews	Send to associate editor.
Subscriptions	The Haworth Press, Inc., 10 Alice Street, Binghamton, NY 13904-1580. Individuals, $50; institutions, $240; libraries, $325.
E-Mail Address	VFranks@aol.com

Child and Youth Care Forum

Previous Titles	*Child Care Quarterly; Child and Youth Care Quarterly.*
Editorial Focus	An independent journal of day and residential child and youth care practice.
Audience	Administrators, supervisors, direct care practitioners, students and faculty members in the field, researchers, policymakers.
Special Themes	Direct practice, selection and training, supervision, theory and research, policy, professional issues.
Where Indexed/ Abstracted	Abstracts for Social Workers; Chicorel Abstracts to Reading and Learning Disabilities; Community Mental Health Review; Current Contents: Behavioral, Social and Educational Sciences; Education Index; Exceptional Child Education Abstracts; Health Instrument File; Psychological Abstracts; Sage Family Studies Abstracts; Social Sciences Citation Index; Sociology of Education Abstracts.
Year Established	1970.
Circulation	1,000+.
Frequency	Bimonthly.
Months Issued	February, April, June, August, October, December.
No. of Articles	Generally, 4–6.

SUBMISSIONS

Address	Professor Jerome Beker, Editor, *Child and Youth Care Forum,* Youth Studies Program, School of Social Work, University of Minnesota, 386 McNeal Hall, 1985 Buford Avenue, St. Paul, MN 55108.
Number of Copies	4.
Disk Submission	Not required.

FORMAT OF MANUSCRIPT

Cover Sheet	Yes.
Abstract	Yes.
Key Words	Not required.
Length	Most are 12–20 pages, but shorter or even considerably longer ones are considered if appropriate to the content.
Margins	1 inch on all sides.
Spacing	Double-spaced.

STYLE

Name of Guide	*Publication Manual of the American Psychological Association.*
Subheadings	See style guide.
References	See style guide.

| Footnotes | See style guide. |
| Tables or Figures | See style guide. |

REVIEW PROCESS

Type	2 reviewers per manuscript. Anonymous if the manuscript is formatted appropriately.
Queries	Welcomed by mail or e-mail.
Acknowledgment	Yes. Prefer stamped, self-addressed envelope or postcard (or e-mail address).
Review Time	Usually 4 months.
Revisions	Generally 3 copies required, with cover letter explaining revisions. Revisions are normally read by at least 1 of the original reviewers and the editor.
Acceptance Rate	Approximately 50%, often subject to revisions, for topically appropriate manuscripts.
Return of Manuscript	With return envelope and postage.
Lag Time to Print	Approximately 6 months.

CHARGES TO AUTHOR

| Author Alterations | None, except for alterations on proofs. |

REPRINT, SUBSCRIPTION, AND CONTACT INFORMATION

Reprint Policy	Order forms sent with proofs.
Book Reviews	Yes, but query first. Send books for review to the editor.
Subscriptions	Subscription Department, Human Sciences Press, 233 Spring Street, New York, NY 10013-1578; phone: 212-620-8468; fax: 212-807-1047.
	1996 prices: individuals, $52 ($61 foreign); institutions, $275 ($320 foreign).
E-Mail Address	beker001@maroon.tc.umn.edu

Child & Youth Services

Editorial Focus	Each issue focuses on a specific topic of interest, usually one that has received relatively little attention elsewhere, under the guidance of a qualified issue editor. Any topic within child and youth services is eligible for consideration. Queries and proposals from prospective issue editors are invited. (Unsolicited manuscripts not related to an announced issue should not be submitted.)
Audience	Professionals and academics interested in programs and services for children and youth.
Where Indexed/ Abstracted	Cambridge Scientific Abstracts; Child Development Abstracts and Bibliography; CNPIEC Reference Guide: Chinese National Directory of Foreign Periodicals; Criminal Justice Abstracts; Criminology, Penology and Police Science Abstracts; ERIC Clearinghouse on Counseling and Student Services; ERIC Clearinghouse on Elementary and Early Childhood Education; Exceptional Child Education Resources; Family Studies Database; IBX International Bibliography of Periodical Literature; Index to Periodical Articles Related to Law; International Bulletin of Bibliography on Education; International Access Bulletin Board for Libraries (JANET, TELNET, Gopher, www, NISSWAIS); Mental Health Abstracts; OT BibSys, American Occupational Therapy Foundation; PASCAL International Bibliography T205: Sciences de l'information Documentation; Psychological Abstracts; Referativnyi Zhurnal (Abstracts Journal of the Institute of Scientific Information of the Republic of Russia); Sage Family Studies Abstracts; Social Planning/Policy and Development Abstracts; Social Work Abstracts; Sociological Abstracts; Sociology of Education Abstracts; Studies on Women Abstracts; Violence and Abuse Abstracts: A Review of Current Literature on Interpersonal Violence.
Year Established	1976.
Circulation	Several hundred; number varies because each issue covers a different topic, and issues are sold as singles as well as by subscription.
Frequency	Semiannually.
Months Issued	Varies.
No. of Articles	6–10.

SUBMISSIONS

Address	Professor Jerome Beker, Editor, *Child and Youth Services,* Youth Studies Program, School of Social Work, University of Minnesota, 386 McNeal Hall, 1985 Buford Avenue, St. Paul, MN 55108.
Number of Copies	4 copies required, or fewer at the discretion of the issue editor.
Disk Submission	Required for final copy, after review and any revisions. Most standard programs are acceptable.

FORMAT OF MANUSCRIPT

Cover Sheet	Yes.
Abstract	Yes.

Key Words	Not required.
Length	Most are 12–20 pages total, but shorter or even considerably longer ones (including full issues) are considered if appropriate to the content.
Margins	1 inch on all sides.
Spacing	Double-spaced.

STYLE

Name of Guide	*Publication Manual of the American Psychological Association.*
Subheadings	See style guide.
References	See style guide.
Footnotes	See style guide.
Tables or Figures	See style guide.

REVIEW PROCESS

Type	The editor reviews proposals for topical special issues, usually in consultation with other members of the editorial board. Individual articles are usually invited by issue editors (often using a call for papers) and are reviewed in consultation with the editor.
Queries	Most issues develop from an initial query letter from someone interested in editing an issue on a topic of his or her choosing.
Acknowledgment	Enclose a regular self-addressed, stamped envelope with submission.
Review Time	Depends on issue editor involved; usually within 1–3 months.
Revisions	Re-reviewed by issue editor and by others at his or her discretion.
Acceptance Rate	About half of proposed issues are accepted.
Return of Manuscript	With stamped, self-addressed envelope.
Lag Time to Print	6–9 months.

CHARGES TO AUTHOR

Author Alterations	Significant author alterations in proofs are charged.

REPRINT, SUBSCRIPTION, AND CONTACT INFORMATION

Reprint Policy	Senior author receives 2 copies of the journal and 10 reprints; other authors receive 2 copies of the journal. Additional reprints can be ordered.
Book Reviews	Generally, none.
Subscriptions	The Haworth Press, Inc., 10 Alice Street, Binghamton, NY 13904-1580; phone: 800-342-9678; fax: 607-722-6362.
	Individuals, $60; institutions, $160; libraries, $200. (Canada add 30% + 7% GST; other international add 40%; all outside US sent by air mail.)
E-Mail Address	beker001@maroon.tc.umn.edu

Child Maltreatment—Journal of the American Professional Society on the Abuse of Children

Editorial Focus	Reporting current and at-issue scientific information and technical innovations in the field of child abuse and neglect.
Audience	Practitioners and researchers from mental health, child protection, law, law enforcement, medicine, nursing, and allied disciplines.
Special Themes	Treatment outcome research, the decreasing role of the federal government in child protection, medical practice standards, parent training and abuse prevention, legal options with sexual offenders.
Where Indexed/ Abstracted	Cancer Prevention and Control Database; Comprehensive School Health Database; Criminal Justice Abstracts; Health Promotion and Education Database; Linguistics and Language Behavior Abstracts; The Pilot Database: An Electronic Index to the Traumatic Stress Literature; Prenatal Smoking Cessation Database; Social Work Abstracts; Western New England College School of Law.
Year Established	1996.
Circulation	7,000.
Frequency	Quarterly.
Months Issued	February, May, August, November.
No. of Articles	10.

SUBMISSIONS

Address	Mark Chaffin, PhD, *CM* Editor, c/o APSAC, 407 S. Dearborn, Suite 1300, Chicago, IL 60605.
Number of Copies	5.
Disk Submission	After revisions have been made, an IBM-compatible disk in WordPerfect or AmiPro should accompany the final, revised manuscript.

FORMAT OF MANUSCRIPT

Cover Sheet	Author's name and affiliation should appear on separate cover page.
Abstract	150 words or less.
Key Words	None.
Length	No more than 30 pages for articles; no more than 50 pages for literature reviews.
Margins	Not specified.
Spacing	Double-spaced.

STYLE

Name of Guide	*Publication Manual of the American Psychological Association.*
Subheadings	Not specified.
References	Separate sheet.
Footnotes	Separate sheet.
Tables or Figures	Separate sheet.

REVIEW PROCESS

Not specified.

REPRINT, SUBSCRIPTION, AND CONTACT INFORMATION

Reprint Policy	May purchase.
Book Reviews	Not specified.
Subscriptions	Sage Publications, Inc., 2455 Teller Road, Thousand Oaks, CA 91320. 1996–97 one-year prices: individuals, $60; institutions, $140.
Affiliation	American Professional Society on the Abuse of Children (APSAC).
E-Mail Address	apsacpubs@aol.com
Home Page URL	http://www.sagepub.com

Child Psychiatry and Human Development

Editorial Focus	An interdisciplinary journal to promote dialogue on clinical and developmental issues regarding the mental health of children.
Audience	Mental health and child development professionals.
Special Themes	Child psychiatric diagnosis and treatment; child development; social issues affecting children; review articles; family evaluation and treatment; forensic practices; child advocacy; child abuse and neglect.
Where Indexed/ Abstracted	Abstracts Research Pastoral Care; Applied Social Sciences Index & Abstracts; Automatic Subject Citation Alert; BioSciences Information Service of Biological Abstracts; Cambridge Scientific Abstracts; Chicago Psychoanalytic Literature Index; Child Development Abstracts and Bibliography; Chioral Abstracts to Reading and Learning Disabilities; Current Contents: Behavioral; Current Contents: Clinical Practice; Educational Index; Exceptional Child Education Resources; Excerpta Medica; Family Abstracts; Health Instrument File; Index Medicus; Psychological Abstracts; Safety Science Abstracts; Sage Family Studies Abstracts; Social Sciences Citation Index; Social Work Abstracts; Sociological Abstracts; Studies on Women Abstracts. **Listed in:** Nursing Research, Psychological Readers Guide, Selected Lists of Table of Contents of Psychiatric Periodicals.
Year Established	1974.
Circulation	2,000.
Frequency	Quarterly.
Months Issued	Summer, fall, winter, spring.
No. of Articles	5–6.

SUBMISSIONS

Address	Jack C. Westman, Editor, *Child Psychiatry and Human Development;* 6001 Research Park Boulevard, Madison, WI 53719.
Number of Copies	3.
Disk Submission	Requested when article is accepted for publication.

FORMAT OF MANUSCRIPT

Cover Sheet	Full title; names of authors, including professional degrees, titles, and affiliations; designation of corresponding author with address, phone number, e-mail address, and fax number.
Abstract	6–8 lines.
Key Words	List of salient key words for indexing purposes.
Length	17 pages.
Margins	1 inch on all sides.
Spacing	Double-spaced.

STYLE

Name of Guide   *Index Medicus.*

Subheadings   No heading for introduction. Thereafter as appropriate.

References   In text cited by serially numbered superscript following punctuation. In reference section serially numbered and abbreviated in accordance with *Index Medicus.*

Footnotes   No footnotes.

Tables or Figures   Tables typed double-spaced; figures must be submitted in camera-ready format. Each table and figure must be on a separate page at end of the manuscript.

REVIEW PROCESS

Type   Peer and editorial staff review.

Queries   Detailed information about submissions is available in each issue.

Acknowledgment   Postcard sent on receipt of submission.

Review Time   1–3 months.

Revisions   Not specified.

Acceptance Rate   Approximately 40%.

Return of Manuscript   Return postage required on submission.

Lag Time to Print   6–12 months.

REPRINT, SUBSCRIPTION, AND CONTACT INFORMATION

Reprint Policy   Author may order reprints at current rates at time of proof review.

Book Reviews   To editorial office.

Subscriptions   *Child Psychiatry and Human Development,* 233 Spring Street, New York, NY 10013-1578.

Individual subscription, $52 (outside the U.S., $61).

Affiliation   American Association of Psychiatric Services for Children.

E-Mail Address   jwestman@facstaff.wisc.edu

Children and Youth Services Review

Editorial Focus	Child welfare.
Audience	Social work, social policy.
Special Themes	Foster care, adoption, child poverty, child abuse and neglect.
Where Indexed/ Abstracted	Adolescent Mental Health Abstracts; Applied Social Sciences Index & Abstracts; Automatic Subject Citation Alert; Child Development Abstracts; Current Contents: Social and Behavioral Sciences; Exceptional Child Education Abstracts; PsycINFO; Psychological Abstracts; Research Alert; Sage Family Studies Abstracts; Social Sciences Citation Index; Sociological Abstracts.
Year Established	1978.
Circulation	Approximately 2,000.
Frequency	8 issues per year.
Months Issued	January, February, April, May, July, August, October, November.
No. of Articles	7 per issue.

SUBMISSIONS

Address	Duncan Lindsey, Editor-in-Chief, School of Public Policy and Social Research, 3250 Public Policy Building, UCLA, Los Angeles, CA 90095-1652.
Number of Copies	5.
Disk Submission	No.

FORMAT OF MANUSCRIPT

Cover Sheet	See style guide.
Abstract	Yes.
Key Words	No.
Length	Open.
Margins	1 inch on all sides.
Spacing	Double-spaced.

STYLE

Name of Guide	*Publication Manual of the American Psychological Association.*
Subheadings	See style guide.
References	See style guide.
Footnotes	See style guide.
Tables or Figures	See style guide.

REVIEW PROCESS

Type	Blind review.
Queries	Reviews provided.
Acknowledgment	Yes.
Review Time	4–6 weeks.
Revisions	Often requested.
Acceptance Rate	5%.
Return of Manuscript	Not returned.
Lag Time to Print	Varies.

REPRINT, SUBSCRIPTION, AND CONTACT INFORMATION

Reprint Policy	Standard Elsevier policy.
Book Reviews	Yes. Contact Julia Henley at UCLA.
Subscriptions	Contact Elsevier.
E-Mail Address	dlindsey@ucla.edu
Home Page URL	www.childwelfare.com

Child Welfare

Editorial Focus	Material that extends knowledge in the field of child and family welfare or related service; on any aspect of administration, supervision, casework, group work, community organization, teaching, research, or interpretation; on any facet of interdisciplinary approaches to the field; or on issues of social policy that bear on the welfare of children, youths, and their families.
Audience	Social workers, administrators, child care workers and paraprofessionals, child day care staff members, board members, volunteers, faculty, students, foster and adoptive parents, librarians, juvenile court personnel, government and legislative officials, social scientists, child psychiatrists, pediatricians, and community leaders.
Special Themes	Past special issues: kinship care, research, adoption, child day care, foster care, independent living, and African American families and child welfare. Future issues: HIV/AIDS, youth development, and children of incarcerated parents.
Where Indexed/ Abstracted	Abstracts for Social Workers; Chicorel Abstracts to Reading and Learning Disabilities; Child Development Abstracts and Bibliography; Cumulative Index to Nursing and Allied Health Literature; Educational Resources Information Center/Early Childhood Education; Education Index; Exceptional Child Education Resources; National Institute for Social Work (caredata CD, caredata Abstracts, caredata Information Bulletin); Poverty and Human Resources Abstracts; PsycINFO; Psychological Abstracts; Sage Family Studies Abstracts; Selected References on the Abused and Battered Child.
Year Established	1922.
Circulation	15,000.
Frequency	Bimonthly.
Months Issued	January, March, May, July, September, November.
No. of Articles	Regular issues, 6–10; special issues, 10–12.

SUBMISSIONS

Address	Managing Editor, *Child Welfare*, c/o Child Welfare League of America, 440 First Street, NW, 3rd Floor, Washington, DC 20001-2085.
Number of Copies	4.
Disk Submission	Authors of accepted manuscripts are asked to submit their articles on disk.

FORMAT OF MANUSCRIPT

Cover Sheet	On a separate sheet, the full title of the manuscript, the full name of each author, each author's academic degree, professional title and affiliation, city, and state. Include a mailing address, phone number, fax, and e-mail address for the corresponding author.
Abstract	Approximately 75 words, on a separate sheet.
Key Words	Not necessary.
Length	Articles should be 3,500–5,000 words in length, or about 15–20 double-

spaced pages of about 250 words each, including references and tables. Text should in a 12-point serif face.

Margins	1 inch on all sides.
Spacing	Double-spaced throughout, including tables, figures, and references.

STYLE

Name of Guide	*Publication Manual of the American Psychological Association.* A copy of CWLA's *Authors' Guide* is available on request at no charge.
Subheadings	*1st level subheadings* should be in bold, upper- and lowercase type. *2nd level subheadings* should be in italic, upper- and lowercase type. *3rd level subheadings* should be set in bold, run into the text paragraph.
References	See style guide. References must be double-spaced throughout.
Footnotes	Avoid the use of footnotes.
Tables or Figures	All tables and figures should be double-spaced on a separate, numbered page at the end of the manuscript. Include reference points used in the creation of charts and graphs.

REVIEW PROCESS

Type	Peer review; 2 anonymous reviewers and the senior editor.
Queries	Not recommended. Authors should check prior issues of *Child Welfare* and CWLA's *Authors' Guide.*
Acknowledgment	By postcard, with the manuscript number assigned to their submission.
Review Time	8–12 weeks.
Revisions	Authors whose manuscripts have been accepted should return two clean copies, plus a copy on disk in WordPerfect or Microsoft Word.
Acceptance Rate	20%.
Return of Manuscript	Rejected manuscripts are returned only if a self-addressed, stamped envelope of suitable size is provided. *Child Welfare* retains copies of rejected manuscripts for 12 months from the date of rejection.
Lag Time to Print	12–18 months.

REPRINT, SUBSCRIPTION, AND CONTACT INFORMATION

Reprint Policy	Authors are expected to fulfill individual requests for reprints of their articles. Reprints may be purchased from *Child Welfare*, or authors may have their own reprints made.
Book Reviews	By invitation only. Books to be reviewed should be sent to *Child Welfare* Book Review Editor, c/o Child Welfare League of America, 440 First Street, NW, Suite 310, Washington, DC 20001-2085.
Subscriptions	*Child Welfare*, c/o Transaction, P.O. Box 10286, New Brunswick, NJ 08906-9977.
Affiliation	Child Welfare League of America, Inc.
E-Mail Address	journal@cwla.org
Home Page URL	http://www.cwla.org

Clinical Gerontologist

Editorial Focus	Practical information on assessment and management of mental health disorders in the elderly.
Audience	Mental health practitioners.
Special Themes	Dementia, depression, caregivers.
Where Indexed/ Abstracted	Most social science and medical services.
Year Established	1982.
Circulation	Not specified.
Frequency	4 times per year.
Months Issued	Not specified.
No. of Articles	Not specified.

SUBMISSIONS

Address	Dr. T. L. Brink, 1103 Church Street, Redlands, CA 92374.
Number of Copies	4.
Disk Submission	Not specified.

FORMAT OF MANUSCRIPT

Cover Sheet	Not specified.
Abstract	Yes.
Key Words	Not specified.
Length	Up to 30 pages for articles, 4 pages for case reports.
Margins	Not specified.
Spacing	Not specified.

STYLE

Name of Guide	*Publication Manual of the American Psychological Association.*
Subheadings	Not specified.
References	Not specified.
Footnotes	Not specified.
Tables or Figures	Not specified.

REVIEW PROCESS

Type	Anonymous.
Queries	Not specified.
Acknowledgment	Enclose a regular self-addressed, stamped envelope with submission.
Review Time	3–5 months.

Revisions	Not specified.
Acceptance Rate	Not specified.
Return of Manuscript	If accompanied by self-addressed, stamped envelope.
Lag Time to Print	1 year.

REPRINT, SUBSCRIPTION, AND CONTACT INFORMATION

Reprint Policy	Not specified.
Book Reviews	Yes.
Subscriptions	The Haworth Press, Inc., 10 Alice Street, Binghamton, NY 13904-1580.
E-Mail Address	tlbrink@sbccd.cc.ca.us

Clinical Social Work Journal

Editorial Focus	The interrelationship between theory and practice in clinical social work, defined as direct practice with individuals, families, and groups. Case illustrations demonstrating in detail clinical processes and the manner in which the theory or theories under discussion affect the worker–client interaction and relationship in treatment are strongly preferred. Research having a direct bearing on clinical practice is also welcomed. Scholarly papers addressing significant current controversies or issues in clinical social work may be published in a special section.
Audience	Practitioners, scholars, and students of clinical social work as well as others involved in practicing or studying psychotherapy or the human services; members of the state societies affiliated with the National Federation of Societies for Clinical Social Work, the sponsoring organization.
Special Themes	Psychodynamic, psychoanalytic, or developmental theories as these inform practice; issues in clinical education; dilemmas encountered in practice; and frameworks for considering their effects.
Where Indexed/ Abstracted	Abstracts for Social Workers; Child Development Abstracts and Bibliography; Current Contents: Social and Behavioral Sciences; Psychological Abstracts; Poverty and Human Resources Abstracts; Social Sciences Citation Index; Sociological Abstracts.
Year Established	1971.
Circulation	7,500+.
Frequency	Quarterly.
Months Issued	February, May, August, November.
No. of Articles	6–8.

SUBMISSIONS

Address	Carolyn Saari, PhD, Editor, School of Social Work, Loyola University Chicago, 820 N. Michigan Avenue, Chicago, IL 60611.
Number of Copies	3.
Disk Submission	If possible when final version has been accepted; clearly marked with type of computer and software used.

FORMAT OF MANUSCRIPT

Cover Sheet	Title and authors' names and addresses.
Abstract	Required; 50–100 words.
Key Words	Required; 3–5 key words.
Length	Maximum of 20 pages.
Margins	1 inch on all sides.
Spacing	Double-spaced for all copy including case illustrations and references.

STYLE

Name of Guide	*Publication Manual of the American Psychological Association.*
Subheadings	Use as needed to guide reader through the article; more than 3 levels discouraged.
References	In-text reference style with multiple works alphabetized; see style guide.
Footnotes	Discouraged.
Tables or Figures	Must be camera-ready. Each table must be on a separate page at the end of the manuscript. Indicate in text the approximate placement of the table.

REVIEW PROCESS

Type	Anonymous peer review by 2 consulting editors plus editor.
Queries	Discouraged.
Acknowledgment	By postcard on receipt.
Review Time	2–4 months.
Revisions	Submit 2 hard copies plus disk. Accepted papers will also require very brief biographical statement about authors.
Acceptance Rate	20%.
Return of Manuscript	Discouraged, but possible if author submits self-addressed, stamped envelope.
Lag Time to Print	Approximately 1 year.

CHARGES TO AUTHOR

Author Alterations	At discretion of the publisher.

REPRINT, SUBSCRIPTION, AND CONTACT INFORMATION

Reprint Policy	No complimentary copies.
Book Reviews	By invitation only. Send books to Terry B. Northcut, PhD, Book Review Editor, School of Social Work, Loyola University Chicago, 820 N. Michigan Avenue, Chicago, IL 60611.
Subscriptions	Subscription Department, Human Sciences Press, 233 Spring Street, New York, NY 10013-1578.
	Included in dues in most state Societies for Clinical Social Work; individual per year—$49 in U.S., $56 outside the U.S., students receive 20% discount; institutions—$245 in U.S., $285 outside the U.S.
Affiliation	Sponsored by National Federation of Societies for Clinical Social Work.
E-Mail Address	Editor: csaari@luc.edu
Home Page URL	http://www.webcom.com/nfscsw/cswj/cswj.html

The Clinical Supervisor

Editorial Focus	Supervision in psychotherapy and mental health.
Audience	Not specified.
Where Indexed/ Abstracted	Abstracts of Research in Pastoral Care & Counseling; caredata CD: the social and community care database; CINAHL (Cumulative Index to Nursing & Allied Health Literature); CNPIEC Reference Guide: Chinese National Directory of Foreign Periodicals; Family Studies Database (online and CD-ROM); INTERNET ACCESS (& additional networks) Bulletin Board for Libraries ("BUBL"), coverage of information resources on INTERNET, JANET, and other networks; Mental Health Abstracts (online through DIALOG); Psychological Abstracts (PsycINFO); Social Planning/ Policy & Development Abstracts (SOPODA); Social Work Abstracts; Sociological Abstracts (SA); Violence and Abuse Abstracts: A Review of Current Literature on Interpersonal Violence (VAA).
Year Established	1983.
Circulation	312.
Frequency	Semiannually.
Months Issued	Not specified.
No. of Articles	6–10 per issue.

SUBMISSIONS

Address	Carlton E. Munson. DSW, Editor, *The Clinical Supervisor*, Doctoral Program Director, School of Social Work, University of Maryland at Baltimore, Baltimore, MD 21201.
Number of Copies	4.
Disk Submission	Authors of accepted manuscripts are asked to submit a disk, preferably in Microsoft Word or WordPerfect.

FORMAT OF MANUSCRIPT

Cover Sheet	Separate sheet, which does not go out for review. Full title, author names, degrees, professional titles; designation of one author as corresponding author with full address, phone numbers, e-mail address, and fax number; date of submission.
Abstract	About 100 words.
Key Words	5 or 6 key words that identify article content.
Length	20 pages, including references and abstract. Lengthier manuscripts may be considered, but only at the discretion of the editor. Sometimes, lengthier manuscripts may be considered if they can be divided up into sections for publication in successive issues.
Margins	1 inch on all sides.
Spacing	Double-spaced for all copy, except title page.

STYLE

Name of Guide	*Publication Manual of the American Psychological Association.*
Subheadings	Use as needed to guide reader through the article. No more than 4 levels.
References	Author–date citation style; see style guide.
Footnotes	No footnotes preferred; incorporate into text.
Tables or Figures	Type tables double-spaced. Submit camera-ready art (300 dpi printer or better) for all figures. Place each table or figure on a separate, numbered page at the end of the manuscript.

REVIEW PROCESS

Type	"Double blind" anonymous peer review. 3 reviewers plus editor-in-chief read the manuscript in an anonymous review.
Queries	Authors are encouraged to read the journal to determine if their subject matter would be appropriate.
Acknowledgment	Enclose a regular self-addressed, stamped envelope with submission.
Review Time	3–4 months.
Revisions	See journal.
Acceptance Rate	Not specified.
Return of Manuscript	Only if 9″ x 12″ self-addressed, stamped envelope is enclosed.
Lag Time to Print	6 months–1 year.

REPRINT, SUBSCRIPTION, AND CONTACT INFORMATION

Reprint Policy	All authors receive 2 complimentary copies of the issue in which article appears. Authors receive reprint order forms to purchase additional reprinted copies.
Book Reviews	Send to journal editor.
Subscriptions	The Haworth Press, Inc., 10 Alice Street, Binghamton, NY 13904-1580. Individuals, $28; institutions, $160; libraries, $275.

Computers in Human Services

Editorial Focus	Not specified.
Audience	Human services professionals (educators, practitioners, researchers) interested in electronic information technology.
Where Indexed/ Abstracted	Abstracts of Research in Pastoral Care & Counseling; ACM Guide to Computer Literature; Applied Social Sciences Index & Abstracts (Online: ASSI via Data–Star) (CD-ROM: ASSIA Plus); Behavioral Medicine Abstracts; caredata CD: the social and community care database; CNPIEC Reference Guide: Chinese National Directory of Foreign Periodicals; Computer Abstracts; Computer Literature Index; Computing Reviews; Current Contents; Engineering Information (PAGE ONE); IBZ International Bibliography of Periodical Literature; Information Science Abstracts; INSPEC Information Services; Institute for Scientific Information; INTERNET ACCESS (& additional networks) Bulletin Board for Resources Libraries ("BUBL"), coverage of information resources on INTERNET, JANET, and other networks; Library & Information Science Abstracts (LISA); Microcomputer Abstracts; National Clearinghouse on Child Abuse & Neglect; Periodica Islamica; Psychological Abstracts (PsycINFO); Referativnyi Zhurnal (Abstracts Journal of the Institute of Scientific Information of the Republic of Russia); Sage Public Administration Abstracts; Social Planning/Policy & Development Abstracts (SOPODA); Social Work Abstracts; Sociological Abstracts (SA).
Year Established	1985.
Circulation	348.
Frequency	Quarterly.
Months Issued	Not specified.
No. of Articles	6–10 per issue.

SUBMISSIONS

Address	Editor, Dick Schoech, School of Social Work, University of Texas-Arlington, Box 19129, Arlington, TX 76019-0129.
Number of Copies	4.
Disk Submission	Authors of accepted manuscripts are asked to submit a disk, preferably in Microsoft Word or WordPerfect.

FORMAT OF MANUSCRIPT

Cover Sheet	Separate sheet, which does not go out for review. Full title, author names, degrees, professional titles; designation of one author as corresponding author with full address, phone numbers, e-mail address, and fax number; date of submission.
Abstract	About 100 words.

Key Words	5 or 6 words that identify article content.
Length	20 pages, including references and abstract. Lengthier manuscripts may be considered, but only at the discretion of the editor. Sometimes, lengthier manuscripts may be considered if they can be divided into sections for publication in successive issues.
Margins	1 inch on all sides.
Spacing	Double-spaced for all copy, except title page.

STYLE

Name of Guide	*Publication Manual of the American Psychological Association.*
Subheadings	Use as needed to guide reader through the article. No more than 4 levels.
References	Author–date citation style; see style guide.
Footnotes	No footnotes preferred; incorporate into text.
Tables or Figures	Type tables double-spaced. Submit camera-ready art (300 dpi printer or better) for all figures. Place each table or figure on a separate, numbered page at the end of the manuscript.

REVIEW PROCESS

Type	"Double blind" anonymous peer review. 3 reviewers plus editor-in-chief read the manuscript in an anonymous review.
Queries	Authors are encouraged to read the journal to determine if their subject matter would be appropriate.
Acknowledgment	Enclose a regular self-addressed, stamped envelope with submission.
Review Time	3–4 months.
Revisions	See journal.
Acceptance Rate	Not specified.
Return of Manuscript	Only if 9″ x 12″ self-addressed, stamped envelope is enclosed.
Lag Time to Print	6 months–1 year.

REPRINT, SUBSCRIPTION, AND CONTACT INFORMATION

Reprint Policy	All authors receive 2 complimentary copies of the issue in which article appears. Authors receive reprint order forms to purchase additional reprinted copies.
Book Reviews	Send to journal editor.
Subscriptions	The Haworth Press, Inc., 10 Alice Street, Binghamton, NY 13904-1580. Individuals , $45; institutions, $90; libraries, $200.

Computers in the Schools

Editorial Focus	The interdisciplinary journal of practice, theory, and applied research.
Audience	Educators, administrators, computer center directors, and special service providers in the school setting.
Special Themes	Practice, theory, and applied research.
Where Indexed/ Abstracted	Academic Abstracts/CD-ROM; ACM Guide to Computer Literature; CNPIEC Reference Guide: Chinese Directory of Foreign Periodicals; Computer Literature Index; Computing Reviews; Current Index to Journals in Education; Education Digest; Educational Administration Abstracts (EAA); Educational Technology Abstracts; Engineering Information (PAGE ONE); IBZ International Bibliography of Periodical Literature; Information Science Abstracts; INSPEC Information Services; International Bulletin of Bibliography on Education; INTERNET ACCESS (& additional networks) Bulletin Board for Libraries ("BUBL"), coverage of information resources on INTERNET, JANET, and other networks; Linguistics and Language Behavior Abstracts (LLBA); MasterFILE: updated database from EBSCO Publishing; Mathematical Didactics' (MATHDI); Microcomputer Abstracts; National Clearinghouse for Bilingual Education; Referativnyi Zhurnal (Abstracts Journal of the Institute of Scientific Information of the Republic of Russia); Social Planning/Policy & Development Abstracts (SOPODA); Social Work Abstracts; Sociological Abstracts (SA); Sociology of Education Abstracts; ZDM/International Reviews on Mathematical Education.
Year Established	1984.
Circulation	495.
Frequency	Quarterly.
Months Issued	Not specified.
No. of Articles	6–10 per issue.

SUBMISSIONS

Address	Editor, D. LaMont Johnson, *Computers in the Schools*, College of Education, University of Nevada, Reno, NV 89557-0029.
Number of Copies	4.
Disk Submission	Authors of accepted manuscripts are asked to submit a disk, preferably in Microsoft Word or WordPerfect.

FORMAT OF MANUSCRIPT

Cover Sheet	Separate sheet, which does not go out for review. Full title, author names, degrees, professional titles; designation of one author as corresponding author with full address, phone numbers, e-mail address, and fax number; date of submission.
Abstract	About 100 words.

Key Words	Not specified.
Length	10–20 pages, including references and abstract. Lengthier manuscripts may be considered, but only at the discretion of the editor. Sometimes, lengthier manuscripts may be considered if they can be divided into sections for publication in successive issues.
Margins	1 inch on all sides.
Spacing	Double-spaced for all copy, except title page.

STYLE

Name of Guide	*Publication Manual of the American Psychological Association.*
Subheadings	Use as needed to guide reader through the article. No more than 4 levels.
References	Author–date citation style; see style guide.
Footnotes	No footnotes preferred; incorporate into text.
Tables or Figures	Type tables double-spaced. Submit camera-ready art (300 dpi printer or better) for all figures. Place each table or figure on a separate, numbered page at the end of the manuscript.

REVIEW PROCESS

Type	"Double blind" anonymous peer review. 3 reviewers plus editor-in-chief read the manuscript in an anonymous review.
Queries	Authors are encouraged to read the journal to determine if their subject matter would be appropriate.
Acknowledgment	Enclose a regular self-addressed, stamped envelope with submission.
Review Time	3–4 months.
Revisions	See journal.
Acceptance Rate	Not specified.
Return of Manuscript	Only if 9″ x 12″ self-addressed, stamped envelope is enclosed.
Lag Time to Print	6 months–1 year.

REPRINT, SUBSCRIPTION, AND CONTACT INFORMATION

Reprint Policy	All authors receive 2 complimentary copies of the issue in which article appears. Authors receive reprint order forms to purchase additional reprinted copies.
Book Reviews	Send to journal editor.
Subscriptions	The Haworth Press, Inc., 10 Alice Street, Binghamton, NY 13904-1580. Individuals, $40; institutions, $85; libraries, $140.

Death Studies

Previous Title	*Death Education* (until 1985).
Editorial Focus	Areas of death education, death-related counseling, and terminal care, including hospice and bereavement counseling; research reports on all aspects of dying, death, bereavement, and suicide; manuscripts dealing with ethical, legal, and professional issues and controversies related to death; manuscripts focusing on practical issues of program implementation, such as objectives, pedagogic methods, and evaluation.
Audience	Health care and mental health professionals, social scientists, and scholars interested in death and loss issues.
Special Themes	Special issues are offered periodically on such topics as AIDS, death anxiety, and suicide, by invitation and submission. Contact editor for details.
Where Indexed/ Abstracted	Abstracts of Research in Pastoral Care and Counseling; ARECO's Quarterly Index to Periodical Literature on Aging; Contents Pages in Education; Cumulative Index to Nursing and Allied Health Literature; Hospital Literature Index; Index Medicus; Psychological Abstracts; Sage Family Studies Abstracts; Social Planning/Policy & Development Abstracts; Social Work Abstracts; Sociological Abstracts; Terminal Care Index.
Year Established	1976.
Circulation	1,000+.
Frequency	Bimonthly.
Months Issued	February, April, June, August, October, December.
No. of Articles	8.

SUBMISSIONS

Address	Robert A. Neimeyer, PhD, Death Studies, Department of Psychology, University of Memphis, Memphis, TN 38152-6400.
Number of Copies	4.
Disk Submission	Optional.

FORMAT OF MANUSCRIPT

Cover Sheet	Names and institutional affiliations of all authors and the complete mailing address of the author to whom all correspondence should be sent.
Abstract	250 words maximum; lack of an abstract may delay publication.
Key Words	4 to 5 key words encouraged.
Length	Approximately 25 pages.
Margins	1.5 inches on all sides.
Spacing	Double-spaced.

STYLE

Name of Guide	*Publication Manual of the American Psychological Association.*
Subheadings	See style guide.
References	See style guide.
Footnotes	Place at end of manuscript.
Tables or Figures	Submit camera-ready glossy prints.

REVIEW PROCESS

Type	Anonymous review by 3 reviewers.
Queries	Not specified.
Acknowledgment	Letter of notification sent on manuscript receipt.
Review Time	2–4 months.
Revisions	As stipulated in disposition letter.
Acceptance Rate	5% without revisions, 40% with revisions.
Return of Manuscript	As needed to convey revisions.
Lag Time to Print	9 months.

CHARGES TO AUTHOR

Author Alterations	Charges for alterations beyond 5%; handled by printer.

REPRINT, SUBSCRIPTION, AND CONTACT INFORMATION

Reprint Policy	Reprint order form is sent with proofs to author. The senior author of each journal will receive one complimentary copy of the journal in which the article appears.
Book Reviews	Contact: David Balk, Department of Human Development and Family Studies, Kansas State University, Manhattan, KS 66506-1403.
Subscriptions	Taylor & Francis, Inc., 1101 Vermont Avenue, NW, Suite 200, Washington DC 20002-3521.
E-Mail Address	neimeyerra@cc.memphis.edu

Developmental Psychology

Editorial Focus	*Developmental Psychology* publishes articles that advance knowledge and theory about human development across the life span. Although most papers address directly the issues of human development, studies of other species are appropriate if they have important implications for human development. The journal includes significant empirical contributions to the study of growth and development and, occasionally, scholarly reviews, theoretical articles, and social policy papers. Studies of any variables that affect human psychological development are considered. In the case of laboratory experimental studies, preference is given to reports of series of studies, and the external validity of such studies is a major consideration. Field research, cross-cultural studies, research on gender and ethnicity, and research on other socially important topics are especially welcome.
Audience	Researchers and practitioners in the discipline, faculty, libraries.
Where Indexed/ Abstracted	Addiction Abstracts; Biological Abstracts; Excerpta Medica; PsycINFO.
Year Established	1969.
Circulation	5,500.
Frequency	Bimonthly.
Months Issued	January, March, May, July, September, November.
No. of Articles	15.

SUBMISSIONS

Address	Carolyn Zahn-Waxler, 4305 Dresden Street, Kensington, MD 20895.
Number of Copies	5.
Disk Submission	Submit manuscripts on paper; disks may be requested of accepted articles.

FORMAT OF MANUSCRIPT

Cover Sheet	Refer to Instructions to Authors in each issue.
Abstract	Manuscripts must include an abstract containing a maximum of 960 characters and spaces (approximately 120 words), typed on a separate sheet of paper.
Key Words	None.
Length	Not specified.
Margins	See style guide.
Spacing	Double-spaced.

STYLE

Name of Guide	*Publication Manual of the American Psychological Association.*
Subheadings	See style guide.

References	See style guide.
Footnotes	See style guide.
Tables or Figures	See style guide; camera-ready copy required for all art.

REVIEW PROCESS

Type	Masked review.
Queries	No query letters.
Acknowledgment	Editor acknowledges submission by mail.
Review Time	Usually 60–90 days.
Revisions	Editor will notify author if revision is desired (most manuscripts are initially rejected; most published manuscripts have gone through one or two revisions).
Acceptance Rate	23%.
Return of Manuscript	Manuscripts are not usually returned.
Lag Time to Print	10 months.

CHARGES TO AUTHOR

Author Alterations	Authors are billed for alterations in proofs.

REPRINT, SUBSCRIPTION, AND CONTACT INFORMATION

Reprint Policy	Authors may purchase reprints of their articles (order form accompanies proofs).
Book Reviews	None.
Subscriptions	Subscriptions Department, American Psychological Association, 750 First Street, NE, Washington, DC 20002-4242.
	Yearly rates for nonmembers are $131 domestic, $151 foreign, $164 airmail. APA members: $65.
Affiliation	Published by the American Psychological Association.
Home Page URL	http://www.apa.org

Early Childhood Education Journal

Previous Title	*Day Care and Early Education.*
Editorial Focus	Exemplary practices in the rapidly changing field of contemporary early childhood education. *Early Childhood Education Journal* publishes feature-length articles that skillfully blend theory, research, and practice; descriptions of outstanding early childhood programs from around the world, and case studies of young children. Reviews print and nonprint media.
Audience	Child advocates, including classroom teachers (nursery through third grade), child care providers, university faculty, and administrators of early childhood programs. Experts in related fields who share a commitment to young children and their families.
Special Themes	All issues are multitopic rather than thematic.
Where Indexed/ Abstracted	Behavioral Abstracts; Book Review Index; Chicorel Abstracts to Reading and Learning Disabilities; Contents Pages in Education; Current Index to Journals in Education (ERIC); Education Digest; Education Index; Exceptional Child Education Resources; Excerpta Medica; Family Abstracts; Health Instrument File; Information Updates; Media Review Digest; Social Work Abstracts; Social Work Abstracts; Sociological Abstracts; Teachers College Record (http://www.tc.columbia.edu/~TCRECORD).
Year Established	1972.
Circulation	3,000.
Frequency	Quarterly.
Months Issued	October, January, April, July.
No. of Articles	Approximately 7 unsolicited and 7 invited per issue.

SUBMISSIONS

Address	Dr. Mary Renck Jalongo, Editor, 654 College Lodge Road, Indiana, PA 15701: phone 412-357-2417.
Number of Copies	3. Include a self-addressed 9" x 12" envelope with priority mail postage attached. (For international submissions include a postage coupon.)
Disk Submission	Yes. Final, edited copy labeled with kind of computer used, software and version number, disk format and file name of article, journal name (*ECEJ*), and author's last name.

FORMAT OF MANUSCRIPT

Cover Sheet	Separate sheet, which does not go out for review. Full title, author names, professional titles, designation of one author as corresponding author with full address, telephone numbers, e-mail address, fax number, and date of submission.
Abstract	An abstract of approximately 3–4 sentences is required.
Key Words	3 or 4 words that can be used for indexing purposes.
Length	18 double-spaced pages in 10 characters per inch type, including references and citations.

Margins	1 inch on all sides.
Spacing	Double-spaced throughout.

STYLE

Name of Guide	*Publication Manual of the American Psychological Association.* Guidelines for Contributors are published in the back of each issue.
Subheadings	Use headings and subheadings to identify major sections of the manuscript.
References	See style guide.
Footnotes	No footnotes are preferred. Incorporate information into the text.
Tables or Figures	Photographs require a model release; all tables and figures must have captions and clearly indicate placement. Camera-ready art is required.

REVIEW PROCESS

Type	Anonymous peer review. 2 members of the Editorial Board review unsolicited manuscripts.
Queries	Authors are advised to review several recent issues of the journal carefully to get a sense of style and topics that have been addressed recently.
Acknowledgment	Authors are notified after the manuscript has been reviewed.
Review Time	2–4 months.
Revisions	Submit a cover letter that describes the changes made in the manuscript in response to the recommendations for revision. Include a self-addressed 9″ x 12″ envelope with priority mail postage attached. (International submissions include a postage coupon.)
Acceptance Rate	Approximately 50%.
Return of Manuscript	Author should retain a copy. All copies of rejected manuscripts are returned if postage is provided.
Lag Time to Print	Approximately 6–18 months.

CHARGES TO AUTHOR

Author Alterations	Any substantive changes must be made prior to page proof stage.

REPRINT, SUBSCRIPTION, AND CONTACT INFORMATION

Reprint Policy	Authors may purchase reprints when article is accepted.
Book Reviews	By invitation only.
Subscriptions	Subscription Department, Human Sciences Press, 233 Spring Street, New York, NY 10013-1578; phone: 212-620-8468; fax: 212-807-1047.
	Individual rates: $29 in the U.S., $34.00 outside the U.S. Institutional rates: $125 in the U.S., $145 outside the U.S.
Affiliation	Human Sciences Press/Plenum Publishers.
E-Mail address	MJALONGO@grove.IUP.edu (Do not e-mail manuscripts.)
Home Page URL	http://www@Plenum.com

Employee Assistance Quarterly

Previous Title	*Labor–Management Alcoholism Journal.*
Editorial Focus	Research and development in the employee assistance field.
Audience	Scholars, practitioners.
Special Themes	Emerging issues in the employee assistance field, cost management, industrial social work, new modes of outpatient treatment, and employee assistance programs for the post-industrial era.
Where Indexed/ Abstracted	Brown University Digest of Addiction Theory and Application; CNPIEC Reference Guide: Chinese National Directory of Foreign Periodicals; EAP Abstracts Plus; Excerpta Medica/Secondary Publishing Division; Family Studies Database (online and CD-ROM); Human Resources Abstracts (HRA); INTERNET ACCESS (& additional networks) Bulletin Board for Libraries ("BUBL"), coverage of information resources on INTERNET, JANET, and other networks; Medical Benefits; NIAAA Alcohol and Alcohol Problems Science Database (ETOH); Personnel Management Abstracts; Psychological Abstracts (PsycINFO); Public Affairs Information Bulletin (PAIS); Social Planning/Policy & Development Abstracts (SOPODA); Social Work Abstracts; Sociological Abstracts (SA); SOMED (social medicine) Database; UP–TO–DATE Publications; Work Related Abstracts.
Year Established	1985.
Circulation	564.
Frequency	Quarterly.
Months Issued	Not specified.
No. of Articles	6–10 per issue.

SUBMISSIONS

Address	Editor, Keith McClellan, 14100 Balfour, Oak Park, MI 48237.
Number of Copies	4.
Disk Submission	Authors of accepted manuscripts are asked to submit a disk, preferably in Microsoft Word or WordPerfect.

FORMAT OF MANUSCRIPT

Cover Sheet	Separate sheet, which does not go out for review. Full title, author names, degrees, professional titles; designation of one author as corresponding author with full address, phone numbers, e-mail address, and fax number; date of submission.
Abstract	About 100 words.
Key Words	5 or 6 key words that identify article content.
Length	5–20 pages, including references and abstract. Lengthier manuscripts may be considered, but only at the discretion of the editor. Sometimes, lengthier manuscripts may be considered if they can be divided into sections for publication in successive issues.

Margins	1 inch on all sides.
Spacing	Double-spaced for all copy, except title page.

STYLE

Name of Guide	*Publication Manual of the American Psychological Association.*
Subheadings	Use as needed to guide reader through the article. No more than 4 levels.
References	Author–date citation style; see style guide.
Footnotes	No footnotes preferred; incorporate into text.
Tables or Figures	Type tables double-spaced. Submit camera-ready art (300 dpi printer or better) for all figures. Place each table or figure on a separate, numbered page at the end of the manuscript.

REVIEW PROCESS

Type	"Double blind" anonymous peer review. 3 reviewers plus editor-in-chief read the manuscript in an anonymous review.
Queries	Authors are encouraged to read the journal to determine if their subject matter would be appropriate.
Acknowledgment	Enclose a regular self-addressed, stamped envelope with submission.
Review Time	3–4 months.
Revisions	See journal.
Acceptance Rate	Not specified.
Return of Manuscript	Only if 9″ x 12″ self-addressed, stamped envelope is enclosed.
Lag Time to Print	6 months–1 year.

REPRINT, SUBSCRIPTION, AND CONTACT INFORMATION

Reprint Policy	All authors receive 2 complimentary copies of the issue in which article appears. Authors receive reprint order forms to purchase additional reprinted copies.
Book Reviews	Derek Aronoff, Associate Editor, 4800 Sherbrooke Street W, Suite 190, Montreal, QC, Canada H3Z 1H1.
Subscriptions	The Haworth Press, Inc., 10 Alice Street, Binghamton, NY 13904-1580.
	Individuals, $45; institutions, $140; libraries, $250. EASNA members: free.
Affiliation	Employee Assistance Society of North America (EASNA).

Evaluation and Program Planning: An International Journal

Editorial Focus	Interdisciplinary focus on methods in and reports of evaluation and planning efforts.
Audience	Evaluators and planners across many fields.
Special Themes	Special issues (usually half a volume to allow for individual submissions from the field) are published about 3 times per year. Suggestions for topics are most welcome.
Where Indexed/ Abstracted	Adolescent Mental Health Abstracts; Current Contents: Social and Behavioral Sciences; Current Contents: Health Services Administration; ERIC/CIJE; GEOBASE; International Development Abstracts; PsychINFO; PsycLIT; Psychological Abstracts; Social Sciences Citation Index; Sociological Abstracts.
Year Established	1975.
Circulation	Contact Geraldine Billingham at Elsevier Press: g.billingham@elsevier.co.uk
Frequency	Quarterly.
Months Issued	January–March, April–June, July–September, October–December.
No. of Articles	7–10 without special half issue, 3–5 with special half issue.

SUBMISSIONS

Address	Jonathan A. Morell, Industrial Technology Institute, P.O. Box 1485, Ann Arbor, MI 48106.
Number of Copies	4 copies of manuscript, 5 copies of abstract.
Disk Submission	Yes.

FORMAT OF MANUSCRIPT

Cover Sheet	See style guide.
Abstract	See style guide.
Key Words	See style guide.
Length	7,000 words.
Margins	See style guide.
Spacing	See style guide.

STYLE

Name of Guide	*Publication Manual of the American Psychological Association.*
Subheadings	See style guide.
References	See style guide.
Footnotes	See style guide.
Tables or Figures	See style guide.

REVIEW PROCESS

Type	Double blind.
Queries	Encouraged by editors of prospective authors or those with ideas for special issues.
Acknowledgment	Sent on receipt of manuscript.
Review Time	3–4 months.
Revisions	Often encouraged. To assist editors and reviewers, please include a detailed list of changes made.
Acceptance Rate	Acceptance with only minor revisions, 10%–15%; acceptance with more major revisions to satisfy reviewers, approximately 50%.
Return of Manuscript	Not returned.
Lag Time to Print	From acceptance of final revisions, 6–12 months.

CHARGES TO AUTHOR

Author Alterations	No charge unless large changes are requested by author after manuscript has been sent to press.

REPRINT, SUBSCRIPTION, AND CONTACT INFORMATION

Reprint Policy	25 free to senior authors; 100 additional free if author chooses to pay the page charges.
Book Reviews	1–2 per issue. Suggestions for books to be reviewed are welcome.
Subscriptions	Contact Geraldine Billingham at g.billingham@elsevier.co.uk
E-Mail Address	jam@iti.org
Home Page URL	http://www.elsevier.com/cas/estoc/contents/SAE/01497189.html

Families in Society:
The Journal of Contemporary Human Services

Previous Title	*Social Casework: The Journal of Contemporary Social Work.*
Editorial Focus	Practice-related analysis, discussions, and research; agency-based practice; public policy issues.
Audience	Social work (and allied disciplines) practitioners, educators, agencies, libraries.
Special Themes	Not specified.
Where Indexed/ Abstracted	Alcohol and Alcohol Science Problems Database (ETOH); Book Review Index; Chicago Psychoanalytic Literature Index; Current Contents; Expanded Academic Index; Hospital Literature Index; Inventory of Marriage and Family Literature; Psychological Abstracts; Psychiatric Rehabilitation; Sage Family Studies Abstracts; Social Sciences Citation Index; Social Sciences Index; Social Work Abstracts; Sociological Abstracts. In Great Britain, Applied Social Sciences Index & Abstracts; Studies on Women Abstracts.
Year Established	1920.
Circulation	3,500.
Frequency	Bimonthly.
Months Issued	January, March, May, July, September, November.
No. of Articles	10.

SUBMISSIONS

Address	Editor, *Families in Society*, 11700 W. Luke Park Drive, Milwaukee, WI 53224-3099.
Number of Copies	4.
Disk Submission	As requested after acceptance.

FORMAT OF MANUSCRIPT

Cover Sheet	Not specified.
Abstract	150 words.
Key Words	2–3 words or phrases.
Length	4,000–6,000 words, including reference list.
Margins	1 inch on all sides.
Spacing	Double-spaced, including reference list.

STYLE

Name of Guide	*Publication Manual of the American Psychological Association.*
Subheadings	3 levels, as needed for clarity.

References	See style guide.
Footnotes	Discouraged.
Tables or Figures	Tables typed double-spaced on separate pages.

REVIEW PROCESS

Type	Anonymous peer review. Manuscripts sent to 3 reviewers.
Queries	Authors should be familiar with the journal and decide on appropriateness of their manuscripts.
Acknowledgment	Send within 1 week of manuscript receipt.
Review Time	2–4 months.
Revisions	2 copies with detailed explanation of changes needed.
Acceptance Rate	37%.
Return of Manuscript	Not returned.
Lag Time to Print	9 months–1 year.

REPRINT, SUBSCRIPTION, AND CONTACT INFORMATION

Reprint Policy	Reprint order form sent to authors.
Book Reviews	Invited only. Send books for review to editorial office.
Subscriptions	Subscription Department, 11700 W. Lake Park Drive, Milwaukee, WI 53224-3099.
Affiliation	Families International, Inc., publishes in association with Family Service America, Inc.
E-Mail Address	fis@fsanet.org
Home Page URL	http://www.fsanet.org

Family Preservation Journal

Editorial Focus	Devoted to presenting theoretical and practical articles on family preservation and support: policy, practice, and evaluation.
Audience	Family preservation practitioners, policymakers, and administrators.
Special Themes	Family preservation, unities, and practice.
Where Indexed/ Abstracted	Not specified.
Year Established	1995.
Circulation	1,000.
Frequency	Semiannually.
Months Issued	Summer and winter.
No. of Articles	54 per issue.

SUBMISSIONS

Address	*Family Preservation Journal,* Department of Social Work, New Mexico State University, P.O. Box 30001, Dept. 3SW, Las Cruces, NM 88003-8001.
Number of Copies	5.
Disk Submission	Authors of accepted manuscripts are asked to include a disk using WordPerfect 5.1 or 6.l in IBM format.

FORMAT OF MANUSCRIPT

Cover Sheet	Author's name, affiliation, address, and telephone number.
Abstract	About 100 words; list title only, no authors' names.
Key Words	Not specified.
Length	Not to exceed 16 pages, excluding tables and figures.
Margins	1 inch on all sides.
Spacing	Double-spaced.

STYLE

Name of Guide	*Publication Manual of the American Psychological Association.*
Subheadings	See style guide.
References	Alphabetical list; see style guide.
Footnotes	None.
Tables or Figures	See style guide.

REVIEW PROCESS

Type	Juried.
Queries	Same as manuscript submission.

Acknowledgment	Yes.
Review Time	1–3 months.
Revisions	1 month.
Acceptance Rate	20%.
Return of Manuscript	Not returned.
Lag Time to Print	3–6 months.

REPRINT, SUBSCRIPTION, AND CONTACT INFORMATION

Reprint Policy	Request permission from publisher.
Book Reviews	By invitation.
Subscriptions	Eddie Bowers Publishing, Inc., 2600 Jackson Street, Dubuque, IA 52001.
	Individuals, $25 per year; institutions, $50 per year.
Affiliation	Family Preservation Institute, New Mexico State University.
E-Mail Address	fpi@nmsu.edu
Home Page URL	http://www.nmsu.edu/~socwork

Family Process

Audience	*Family Process* is a multidisciplinary journal that publishes clinical research, training, and theoretical contributions in the broad field of family therapy.
Special Themes	Family therapy theory and practice, multiculturalism, family therapy outcome research, systems theory.
Where Indexed/ Abstracted	Abstracts of Research in Pastoral Counseling; Abstracts for Social Workers; Care and Counseling; Family Research Database; Index Medicus; Psychological Abstracts; Sage Publications Family Studies Abstracts; Social Work Abstracts; Sociological Abstracts.
Year Established	1960.
Circulation	9,000.
Frequency	Quarterly.
Months Issued	March, June, September, December.
No. of Articles	8–10 per issue.

SUBMISSIONS

Address	Editor, *Family Process*, 149 East 78th Street, New York, NY 10021.
Number of Copies	5.
Disk Submission	Authors of accepted manuscripts are asked to submit a disk, preferably in Microsoft Word or WordPerfect.

FORMAT OF MANUSCRIPT

Cover Sheet	Separate sheet which doesn't go out for review. Should include full title, author names, degrees, professional titles, and name and location of principle institutional affiliation, corresponding author's full address, phone numbers, e-mail address, and fax number.
Abstract	Maximum 150 words covering intent, scope, general procedures, and principle findings of the article.
Key Words	None.
Length	15–25 pages.
Margins	1 inch on all sides.
Spacing	Double-spaced.

STYLE

Name of Guide	*Publication Manual of the American Psychological Association.*
Subheadings	Use as needed to guide reader through the article.
References	Author–date citation style; see style guide.
Footnotes	Footnotes should be used very sparingly, only where absolutely necessary.
Tables or Figures	Type tables double-spaced. Submit camera-ready art for all figures. Place each table or figure on a separate, numbered page at the end of the manuscript.

REVIEW PROCESS

Type	"Blind" anonymous peer review. Typically three reviewers.
Queries	Query letters are discouraged.
Acknowledgment	The editorial office sends an acknowledgement letter on receipt of the manuscript.
Review Time	3–4 months.
Revisions	Submit 5 copies with cover letter indicating changes that have been made and author's response to specific criticisms raised by reviewers.
Acceptance Rate	Approximately 25%.
Return of Manuscript	Not returned.
Lag Time to Print	Approximately 6 months–1 year.

REPRINT, SUBSCRIPTION, AND CONTACT INFORMATION

Reprint Policy	Authors receive reprint order forms to purchase reprints at time article is prepared for publication.
Book Reviews	None.
Subscriptions	Subscription Office, *Family Process*, P.O. Box 460, Vernon, NJ 07462.
	1996 one-year prices: individual U.S., $44; individual Canada and Latin America, $49; individual other, $54; institutional U.S., $80; institutional Canada and Latin America, $85; institutional other, $90.
Affiliation	*Family Process* is published by Family Process, Inc.
E-Mail Address	psteinglass@ackerman.org

Family Relations: Interdisciplinary Journal of Applied Family Studies

Previous Title	*Family Relations: Journal of Applied Family and Child Studies.*
Editorial Focus	High-quality, scholarly research with a particular emphasis on relationships across the life cycle and the implications of the research for practitioners. Content areas within the broad field of family studies are open, but all submissions should have a strong theoretical/conceptual framework.
Audience	Both scholars and practitioners.
Special Themes	Content areas within the broad field of family studies with implications for intervention, education, and public policy.
Where Indexed/ Abstracted	Adolescent Mental Health Abstracts; Book Review Index; Child Development Abstracts; Current Index to Journals in Education; International Bibliography of Sociology; Inventory of Marriage and Family Literature; Psychological Abstracts; Sage Family Studies Abstracts; Social Sciences Citation Index.
Year Established	1951.
Circulation	4,000.
Frequency	Quarterly.
Months Issued	January, April, July, October.
No. of Articles	12–15.

SUBMISSIONS

Address	Jeffrey W. Dwyer, Editor, *Family Relations,* Institute of Gerontology, 226 Knapp Bldg., 87 E. Ferry Street, Detroit, MI 48202.
Number of Copies	5.
Disk Submission	Not specified.

FORMAT OF MANUSCRIPT

Cover Sheet	Title followed by a starred footnote indicating any acknowledgment for grant or individual assistance and any previous presentations of the paper. Corresponding author with a double-starred footnote after his or her name indicating his or her contact information. Because articles are reviewed anonymously, only the title should appear on the first page of the manuscript proper. Titles should be a maximum of 15 words.
Abstract	For every article of 6 pages or longer, an abstract of no more than 75 words that introduces the topic, method of study, and implications or conclusions should precede the article. Double-space and underline.
Key Words	No more than 5 key words, underlined and in alphabetical order, to assist investigators who use computer retrieval systems to review literature.
Length	No longer than 30 pages, including references.
Margins	Lines of text should not exceed 6 inches in length, and margins should not be less than 1 inch all around. The right-hand margin should not be justified.
Spacing	Double-space the entire manuscript.

STYLE

Name of Guide	*Publication Manual of the American Psychological Association.*
Subheadings	Divide into appropriate sections with headings as follows: first-order (centered); second-order (flush left); third-order (indented 5 spaces, used as first sentence of paragraph).
References	Double-spaced. See style guide.
Footnotes	May be used with editor's permission.
Tables or Figures	Camera-ready artwork for figures required. High-quality laser acceptable.

REVIEW PROCESS

Type	Anonymous, 2–4 reviewers.
Queries	Editor welcomes query letters.
Acknowledgment	If author would like receipt of manuscript acknowledged, must include a self-addressed, stamped envelope or postcard with submission.
Review Time	Approximately 3 months.
Revisions	Must be completed within 4 months of invitation to resubmission.
Acceptance Rate	Not specified.
Return of Manuscript	Manuscripts are not returned.
Lag Time to Print	Variable.

CHARGES TO AUTHOR

Author Alterations	Minimal changes allowed at proof stage.
Processing	$15 processing fee; check payable to the National Council on Family Relations. Manuscripts submitted without fee will not be reviewed. No additional fee for manuscripts invited to be revised and resubmitted.

REPRINT, SUBSCRIPTION, AND CONTACT INFORMATION

Reprint Policy	Must order before production. Purchase reprints in multiples of 100 (minimum).
Book Reviews	By invitation. If interested in writing a book review essay or book abstract, contact Book Review Editor, Ruth E. Ray, at Family Relations, Institute of Gerontology, 226 Knapp Building, 87 E. Ferry Street, Detroit, MI 48202; or e-mail Dr. Ray, ray@iog.wayne.edu
Subscriptions	Contact National Council on Family Relations to subscribe.
	Individual, $45 in U.S., $57 outside U.S.; student: $20 in U.S., $32 outside U.S.; organization: $85 in U.S., $97 outside U.S.
Affiliation	National Council on Family Relations.
E-Mail Address	fr@iog.wayne.edu
Home Page URL	http://www.iog.wayne.edu/FR/homepage.html

Family Therapy

Previous Title	*Family Therapy: The Journal of the California Graduate School of Family Psychology.*
Editorial Focus	Articles within the broad field of family and marital therapy; clinical articles devoted to technique; content areas including therapy and counseling; marriage and family, divorce, law, alcohol and drug use, aging, children, sexuality, social psychology, domestic violence, ethnicity, codependency, sex roles, deviancy, religion and values, human development. We place special emphasis on practical, clinical manuscripts directed at therapists in the field, as opposed to researchers. Thoughtful research papers will always be well-regarded but must be written in plain English and include an explanation as to their relevance for the work-a-day practitioner.
Audience	Mental health workers, particularly those working with couples, families, and children.
Special Themes	Authors and guest editors may submit their proposals. For example, we once did an entire issue devoted to "children of the holocaust."
Where Indexed/ Abstracted	AGRICOLA; Applied Social Sciences Index & Abstracts; Behavioral Abstracts; Community Mental Health Review; Criminal Justice Abstracts; Current Contents: Social & Behavioral Sciences; Exceptional Child Education Abstracts; Institute for Psychoanalysis; MEDLINE; Psychological Abstracts; Sage Family Studies Abstracts; Social Sciences Citation Index; Social Work Abstracts; Studies on Women Abstracts; SWAB Database.
Year Established	1968.
Circulation	9,400.
Frequency	Quarterly.
Months Issued	January, April, July, September.
No. of Articles	8–10.

SUBMISSIONS

Address	*Family Therapy,* 50 Idalia Road, San Anselmo, CA 94960.
Number of Copies	1.
Disk Submission	No.

FORMAT OF MANUSCRIPT

Cover Sheet	See style guide.
Abstract	Approximately 150 words.
Key Words	None.
Length	No limit; average is 18 pages.
Margins	1 inch on all sides.
Spacing	Double-spaced.

STYLE

Name of Guide	*Publication Manual of the American Psychological Association.*
Subheadings	See style guide.
References	See style guide.
Footnotes	Keep to minimum, group at end of manuscript.
Tables or Figures	Provide clear, reproducible copies.

REVIEW PROCESS

Type of Review	Anonymous, 2 reviewers.
Queries	Yes.
Acknowledgment	Not specified.
Review Time	3 weeks.
Revisions	If major, manuscript is returned for review by author. If minor, proofs sent to author.
Acceptance Rate	40%.
Return of Manuscript	Not returned.
Lag Time to Print	3–5 months.

REPRINT, SUBSCRIPTION, AND CONTACT INFORMATION

Reprint Policy	Purchase reprints from: Libra Publishers, Inc., 3089-C Clairemont Drive, Suite 383, San Diego, CA 92117.
Book Reviews	By invitation only.
Subscriptions	Libra Publishers, Inc., 3089-C Clairemont Drive, Suite 383, San Diego, CA 92117.

	1 Year	*2 Years*	*3 Years*
In U.S.			
Individuals	$44	$86	$128
Institutions	$50	$98	$146
Outside U.S.			
Individuals	$48	$94	$140
Institutions	$54	$106	$140

Affiliation	California Graduate School of Family Psychology.

Family Violence & Sexual Assault Bulletin

Editorial Focus	Research, treatment, prevention programs, theories, legal and criminal justice, and legislation issues concerning any aspect of spouse/partner maltreatment, parent/elder maltreatment, child physical maltreatment/ neglect, child/adult sexual abuse/harassment.
Audience	Interdisciplinary professionals involved in any aspect of working with family violence or maltreatment of victims, survivors, or by offenders.
Special Themes	Varies.
Where Indexed/ Abstracted	Caredata Abstracts; caredata CD; ERIC Clearinghouse on Disabilities & Gifted Education; Mental Health Abstracts; National Clearinghouse on Child Abuse & Neglect; Sage Family Studies Abstracts; Social Work Abstracts; Sociological Abstracts.
Year Established	1984.
Circulation	2,000.
Frequency	Semiannually.
Months Issued	Generally, June and December.
No. of Articles	3.

SUBMISSIONS

Address	*Family Violence & Sexual Assault Bulletin*, c/o FVSAI, 1121 E SE Loop 323, Suite 130, Tyler, TX 75701.
Number of Copies	5 (1 original with identifying names, etc., and 4 copies without this information).
Disk Submission	Disk requested on acceptance.

FORMAT OF MANUSCRIPT

Cover Sheet	Title; authors, including degrees, positions, affiliations, address for reprint requests.
Abstract	None.
Key Words	Not required.
Length	10–20 pages, including references and tables.
Margins	1 inch on all sides.
Spacing	Double-spaced throughout.

STYLE

Name of Guide	*Publication Manual of the American Psychological Association*; instructions for authors available from Family Violence & Sexual Assault Institute.
Subheadings	See style guide.
References	See style guide.

| Footnotes | Not suggested unless absolutely needed; see style guide. |
| Tables or Figures | See style guide; all figures must be camera-ready. |

REVIEW PROCESS

Type	Anonymous review by editorial board or ad hoc reviewers.
Queries	Editor welcomes query letters or phone calls.
Acknowledgment	On receipt of manuscript, letter and copyright form sent for all authors to sign in original; must include letter-size self-addressed, stamped envelope, and an envelope for return of the manuscript with feedback.
Review Time	3–5 months.
Revisions	Feedback is given to authors for making revisions, and the number of copies to be sent back is provided. The journal encourages revisions and resubmissions, with a cover letter by the author explaining what has been done to address the concerns.
Acceptance Rate	50%.
Return of Manuscript	Manuscripts are returned with comments and a letter; self-addressed, stamped envelope needed.
Lag Time to Print	4–8 months.

REPRINT, SUBSCRIPTION, AND CONTACT INFORMATION

Reprint Policy	A sample issue is sent free.
Book Reviews	Books and book reviews accepted for publication (solicited and unsolicited).
Subscriptions	Order through Family Violence & Sexual Assault Institute, 1121 E SE Loop 323, Suite 130, Tyler, TX 75701; individuals, $30; agencies/institutions and libraries, $45. Individuals and institutions can get a discount for a 2-year subscription.
Affiliation	Family Violence & Sexual Assault Institute.
E-Mail Address	FVSAI@e-tex.com

Federal Probation

Editorial Focus	All aspects of corrections and criminal justice including community corrections, sentencing, and treatment.
Audience	Community corrections professionals at federal, state, and local levels; educators, researchers, students.
Special Themes	Management in community corrections, pretrial release and detention, sentencing guidelines.
Where Indexed/ Abstracted	Westlaw.
Year Established	1937.
Circulation	8,000.
Frequency	Quarterly.
Months Issued	March, June, September, December.
No. of Articles	Approximately 9 per issue.

SUBMISSIONS

Address	Editor, *Federal Probation,* Administrative Office of the U.S. Courts, Washington, DC 20544.
Number of Copies	2.
Disk Submission	Authors of accepted manuscripts are asked to submit a disk.

FORMAT OF MANUSCRIPT

Cover Sheet	Not specified.
Abstract	Not specified.
Key Words	Not specified.
Length	3,500–4,000 words.
Margins	1 inch on all sides.
Spacing	Double-spaced.

STYLE

Name of Guide	*Publication Manual of the American Psychological Association.*
Subheadings	Not specified.
References	See style guide.
Footnotes	See style guide.
Tables or Figures	Should be used sparingly. Author will be asked to provide camera-ready copy for figures.

REVIEW PROCESS

Type	Review by journal's editorial staff.
Queries	Prefer to review manuscripts.
Acknowledgment	Receipt of manuscript acknowledged by letter.
Review Time	3–4 months.
Revisions	Not specified.
Acceptance Rate	Approximately 40%.
Return of Manuscript	Not returned.
Lag Time to Print	Approximately 6 months.

REPRINT, SUBSCRIPTION, AND CONTACT INFORMATION

Reprint Policy	All authors receive 3 complimentary copies of the issue in which the article appears. Authors may request free reprints.
Book Reviews	Solicited by editor. Send books for review to: Editor, *Federal Probation,* Administrative Office of the U.S. Courts, Washington, DC 20544.
Subscriptions	Available from the U.S. Government Printing Office, Superintendent of Documents, P.O. Box 371954, Pittsburgh, PA 15250-7954.
	$7 per year.

The Gerontologist

Editorial Focus	This is a bimonthly, multidisciplinary journal that, through publication of research and analysis in applied gerontology, provides a multidisciplinary perspective on human aging, including social policy, program development, and service delivery. It both reflects and informs the broad community of disciplines and professions involved in understanding the aging process and serving older people. Articles should address significant policy or practice issues, report research findings, and include important implications for policy or practice that flow from the research results. Contributions from social and psychological sciences (construed broadly), health sciences, political science, economics, education, law, and the humanities are welcome. Brief descriptions of innovative practices and programs are included in the "Practice Concepts" section.
Audience	Not specified.
Special Themes	None.
Where Indexed/ Abstracted	All major behavioral and social sciences indexing and abstracting services.
Year Established	1961.
Circulation	Approximately 10,000.
Frequency	Bimonthly.
Months Issued	February, April, June, August, October, December.
No. of Articles	Approximately 15.

SUBMISSIONS

Address	Rosalie A. Kane, DSW, *The Gerontologist,* Division of Health Services Research and Policy, University of Minnesota, 420 Delaware Street SE, Box 197, Minneapolis, MN 55455.
Number of Copies	4.
Disk Submission	No.

FORMAT OF MANUSCRIPT

Cover Sheet	Title page: author names, affiliations, addresses, acknowledgments; no identifying information about the authors on any other page.
Abstract	8 lines maximum.
Key Words	3–5 key words that are not in the title.
Length	Research articles: 18–20 pages; Forum section: 18–20 pages; Symposiums: contact editor-in-chief for further guidance; Practice Concepts: 10 pages maximum; letters to the editor: 3–4 pages or less.
Margins	Wide.
Spacing	Double-spaced.

STYLE

Name of Guide	"Instructions to Authors" available from editor (style is based on *Publication Manual of the American Psychological Association*).
Subheadings	None.
References	See style guide.
Footnotes	None.
Tables or Figures	Type all tables double-spaced on separate sheets. Number consecutively, using Arabic numerals. Type table footnotes immediately below the table, using superscript letters (a,b,c) as reference marks. Use asterisks for significant probabilities on tests of significance. Do not submit original art with manuscripts for review. Send only copies or facsimiles that need not be returned. On acceptance and copyediting, submit clear glossy prints or original drawings. Drawings should be in black India ink on white paper. Type legends on a separate page, using Arabic numerals corresponding to the figures. Photographs and drawings will not be returned.

REVIEW PROCESS

Type	Anonymous review by multiple reviewers.
Queries	Yes.
Acknowledgment	None.
Review Time	8 weeks minimum.
Revisions	Not specified.
Acceptance Rate	20%.
Return of Manuscript	Not returned.
Lag Time to Print	Not specified.

CHARGES TO AUTHOR

Author Alterations	Proofs are sent to authors to check printer errors. Alterations of proofs in excess of 10% of the cost of composition are charged to the author.

REPRINT, SUBSCRIPTION, AND CONTACT INFORMATION

Reprint Policy	Reprints available. Contact publisher for price.
Book Reviews	By invitation only.
Subscriptions	The Gerontological Society of America, 1275 K Street, NW, Suite 350, Washington, DC 20005.
	$60/individuals (nonmembers)/$70 (foreign); $112/institution (nonmembers)/$112 (foreign).
Affiliation	The Gerontological Society of America.
E-Mail Address	gerontologist@maxwell.syr.edu

Groupwork

Editorial Focus	Social work with groups.
Audience	Social workers, health and education personnel, and academics with interest in group work.
Special Themes	Special issues from time to time on group work in particular settings. Previous examples include group work with offenders, group work and women, group work in education.
Where Indexed/ Abstracted	Applied Social Sciences Index & Abstracts; Bibliographie Zeitscriften-literatur aller Gebieten des Wissens; Social Care Update; Social Work Abstracts; Sociological Abstracts; Special Educational Needs Abstracts; Studies on Women Abstracts.
Year Established	1988.
Circulation	Not specified.
Frequency	3 times per year.
Months Issued	February, July, December.
No. of Articles	5-8.

SUBMISSIONS

Address	*Groupwork,* c/o Whiting and Birch Ltd, P.O. Box 872, London SE23 3HZ, England.
Number of Copies	5.
Disk Submission	Disks required for final accepted manuscripts. Any word processing format accepted, but authors using Windows should save files in DOS. Avoid Wordstar.

FORMAT OF MANUSCRIPT

Cover Sheet	Author(s) name, professional address, professional details, title of article, number of words, address/phone/fax for correspondence. Professional addresses of second and subsequent authors welcomed for future communications.
Abstract	Less than 200 words if possible.
Key Words	Maximum 8.
Length	2,500–4,000 words.
Margins	Generous.
Spacing	Double-spaced.

STYLE

Name of Guide	Notes for contributors are published in journal. Use *Publication Manual of the American Psychological Association* for points of detail.
Subheadings	Preferably no more than 3 levels. Level 1: bold, lowercase; level 2: italics, lowercase; level 3: Roman, lowercase. Never use all capitals, and do not capitalize initials except for proper names.
References	Harvard.
Footnotes	Endnotes allowed if absolutely unavoidable.
Tables or Figures	If several tables, group at end of article and indicate position in text. If only 1 or 2 simple tables, include in text. Prepare tables with single right tab between each column. Lines of hyphens should not be included between rows; we will insert rules according to house style. However, authors should add clear indications of how they wish each table to appear. For figures involving any graphics, however simple, camera-ready copy should be supplied.

REVIEW PROCESS

Type	Double anonymous.
Queries	Queries are welcomed. Editors especially keen to encourage articles from professionals in practice, and will help as possible.
Acknowledgment	Self-addressed postcard/envelope welcomed.
Review Time	3 months.
Revisions	Material may be accepted subject to minor revisions, rejected, or editors may indicate more substantial rewriting required. In latter case, resubmission required.
Acceptance Rate	40%.
Return of Manuscript	Manuscripts not returned unless specifically requested and adequate postage/international postal reply coupons supplied.
Lag Time to Print	Target is one year.

CHARGES TO AUTHOR

Author Alterations	Approximately $6 per page for significant changes. However, we do not charge for alterations that relate to genuinely unpredictable changes since submission that require acknowledgment in text.

REPRINT, SUBSCRIPTION, AND CONTACT INFORMATION

Reprint Policy	2 free copies of journal, reprints available at cost.
Book Reviews	We publish book reviews, and will accept unsolicited reviews. Submit unsolicited reviews to Book Review Editor, c/o Whiting and Birch Ltd, P.O. Box 872, London SE23 3HZ, England.
Subscriptions	Whiting and Birch Ltd, P.O. Box 872, London SE23 3HZ, England. North American rates: $85 institutions, $37.50 individuals.

Hastings Center Report

Previous Title	*Hastings Center Studies.*
Editorial Focus	Articles (general theoretical, analysis of particular topics, rarely reports of empirical research), reflective essays, and case studies (approximately 20 percent solicited, remainder unsolicited); letters to the editor, book reviews (solicited only), and "In Brief" news features.
Audience	Health care professionals, educators, academics (medicine, law, philosophy, social sciences), students (undergraduate, graduate/professional), libraries, interested lay readers.
Special Themes	Ethical issues in medicine and the life sciences; public policy relating to health care; environmental ethics (limited).
Where Indexed/ Abstracted	Current Contents; EBSCO; Information Access; Sociological Abstracts; UMI.
Year Established	1971.
Circulation	11,500.
Frequency	Bimonthly.
Months Issued	January, March, May, July, September, November.
No. of Articles	3–6 per issue, depending on length.

SUBMISSIONS

Address	Editor, The Hastings Center, 255 Elm Road, Briarcliff Manor, NY 10510.
Number of Copies	3.
Disk Submission	Unnecessary for review purposes.

FORMAT OF MANUSCRIPT

Cover Sheet	Contact name, address, phone number, fax number.
Abstract	None.
Key Words	None.
Length	20–25 pages, including references (5,000–6,000 words for main text).
Margins	1 inch on all sides.
Spacing	Double-spaced.

STYLE

Name of Guide	*Chicago Manual of Style.*
Subheadings	Not specified.
References	See style guide.
Footnotes	Not accepted.
Tables or Figures	Prefer no tables or figures.

REVIEW PROCESS

Type	Blind peer review.
Queries	Potential contributors are encouraged to submit letters of inquiry or descriptions of possible articles.
Acknowledgment	By postcard on receipt of manuscript.
Review Time	8–10 weeks.
Revisions	Not specified.
Acceptance Rate	Approximately 20%.
Return of Manuscript	Not returned.
Lag Time to Print	Varies, average 2–3 issues.

REPRINT, SUBSCRIPTION, AND CONTACT INFORMATION

Reprint Policy	Center provides 2 bound copies of journal and 5 copies of tear sheets of article. Contributors may purchase reprints; information provided along with bound copies and tear sheets after publication.
Book Reviews	Solicited only.
Subscriptions	Membership Department, The Hastings Center, 255 Elm Road, Briarcliff Manor, NY 10510; (914) 762-8500, ext. 234 or 235.
	$55 individuals; $70 institutions; $42 full-time students/seniors.
Affiliation	The Hastings Center.

Healing Ministry

Editorial Focus	Dedicated to helping those who provide spiritual care for the sick and dying.
Audience	Hospital chaplains, clergy, social workers, volunteers, hospice personnel.
Special Themes	None.
Where Indexed/ Abstracted	Pending.
Year Established	1994.
Circulation	10,000.
Frequency	Bimonthly.
Months Issued	February, April, June, August, October, December.
No. of Articles	5–8.

SUBMISSIONS

Address	R. Patrick Gates, Managing Editor, 470 Boston Post Road, Weston, MA 02193.
Number of Copies	3.
Disk Submission	Mandatory; IBM MS-DOS format disks in ASCII text, Microsoft Word 2.0 or greater, DCA, WordPerfect 5.1 or greater.

FORMAT OF MANUSCRIPT

Cover Sheet	Article's title; authors' full names; highest pertinent academic degrees; affiliations; current address of each author; the author handling all correspondence; telephone number; and, if the manuscript was orally presented, the name of the organization, place, and date presented.
Abstract	Not necessary.
Key Words	Not necessary.
Length	Approximately 12–15 pages.
Margins	Wide.
Spacing	Double-spaced.

STYLE

Name of Guide	*MLA Handbook.*
Subheadings	Insert at suitable intervals.
References	Consult publisher for reference style.
Footnotes	No footnotes.
Tables or Figures	Title charts and number them consecutively according to citation in text. If data have been published previously, include an appropriate reference. Number illustrations and legends consecutively according to appearance in the text. Provide short, descriptive legends on a separate page. Legends for

figures previously published should include a complete reference to the original publication, with copyright designation. Must provide copies of the publisher's and author's permission to use the figure. Photographs should include captions.

REVIEW PROCESS

Type	Anonymous review by 3 reviewers.
Queries	Not specified.
Acknowledgment	By mail.
Review Time	10–15 weeks.
Revisions	Reviewer comments and suggestions are mailed to authors for approval or action. If authors choose to make or approve or suggest alternative changes, the manuscript is reviewed again for clarity and content by the previous reviewers or by another party.
Acceptance Rate	60%.
Return of Manuscript	Returned if not published.
Lag Time to Print	3–8 months.

REPRINT, SUBSCRIPTION, AND CONTACT INFORMATION

Reprint Policy	Professional reprints available at discount. Contact publisher.
Book Reviews	Unsolicited book reviews rarely are used.
Subscriptions	Publisher, 470 Boston Post Road, Weston, MA 02193. Individual: $91.

Health Affairs

Editorial Focus	*Health Affairs* is a multidisciplinary, peer-reviewed journal dedicated to the serious exploration of domestic and international health policy issues.
Audience	Health services researchers, policymakers, health care development executives, students of health care administration and policy.
Special Themes	Managed care, mental health care, health spending, consumer satisfaction, Medicaid, Medicare, philanthropy.
Where Indexed/ Abstracted	Current Contents: Health Services Administration and Social and Behavioral Sciences; Excerpta Medica; Health Planning and Administration Database; Index Medicus; MEDLINE; Social Sciences Citation Index.
Year Established	1981.
Circulation	9,000+.
Frequency	Bimonthly.
Months Issued	January, March, May, July, September, November.
No. of Articles	20–25.

SUBMISSIONS

Address	John K. Iglehart, *Health Affairs*, 7500 Old Georgetown Road, Suite 600, Bethesda, MD 20814.
Number of Copies	3.
Disk Submission	Upon acceptance; most major word processing programs accepted.

FORMAT OF MANUSCRIPT

Cover Sheet	Working title, names, affiliations, complete addresses and telephone numbers of all authors; date of submission; and whether the paper has been presented at a meeting.
Abstract	100 words.
Key Words	Not required.
Length	No longer than 6,000 words (20 pages); for DataWatch section, suggested length is 3,000 words (10 pages).
Margins	Not specified.
Spacing	Double-spaced.

STYLE

Name of Guide	*Chicago Manual of Style.*
Subheadings	As needed to guide reader through the paper.
References	First and last name of author.
Footnotes	Endnotes only, numbered in the order in which they appear in the text (not alphabetically).

Tables or Figures	Should be placed at the end of the manuscript, one exhibit per page. Authors must provide numerical plotting data for all figures. Electronic media or original art for exhibits is not requested.

REVIEW PROCESS

Type	Anonymous peer review; 2–3 peer reviewers, plus *Health Affairs* editors.
Queries	Queries are discouraged.
Acknowledgment	All papers are acknowledged by letter or postcard.
Review Time	3–4 months.
Revisions	3 copies with cover sheet describing changes.
Acceptance Rate	Approximately 10%.
Return of Manuscript	One copy of manuscript is returned.
Lag Time to Print	3–12 months.

REPRINT, SUBSCRIPTION, AND CONTACT INFORMATION

Reprint Policy	All authors receive 2 complimentary copies of the issue in which their articles appear. Authors receive reprint order forms to purchase discounted reprints of the article itself.
Book Reviews	Send book reviews and books to be reviewed to: Sue Driesen, Senior Editor, *Health Affairs*, 7500 Old Georgetown Road, Suite 600, Bethesda, MD 20814.
Subscriptions	*Health Affairs*, P.O. Box 148, Congers, NY 10920; phone: 800-765-7514; fax: 914-267-3479.
	1997 one-year prices (U.S. and Canada): $79 individuals, $129 institutions.
Affiliation	*Health Affairs* is published by Project HOPE.
E-Mail Address	azuerche@projhope.org
Home Page URL	http://www.projhope.org/

Health & Social Work

Editorial Focus	Social work and service delivery in all aspects of physical and mental health. Articles on practice, social policy, planning, legislative issues, innovations in health care, and research.
Audience	Health care practitioners including social workers and other professionals, researchers, students, libraries, organizations.
Special Themes	Managed care, HIV/AIDS, substance abuse, racial and ethnic diversity.
Where Indexed/ Abstracted	Abstracts in Anthropology; Abstracts in Social Gerontology; Academic Abstracts; AgeLine; Applied Social Sciences Index & Abstracts; caredata; Cumulative Index to Nursing & Allied Health Literature (CINAHL); Current Contents: Social & Behavioral Sciences; ERIC/Cass; Exceptional Child Education Resources; Psychological Abstracts/PsycINFO/PsycLIT; Public Affairs Information Service Bulletin (PAIS); Sage Family Studies Abstracts; Social Planning/Policy & Development Abstracts (SOPODA); Social Sciences Index/Social Sciences Abstracts; Social Work Abstracts; Sociological Abstracts (SA).
Year Established	1976.
Circulation	6,500.
Frequency	Quarterly.
Months Issued	February, May, August, November.
No. of Articles	Generally 8.

SUBMISSIONS

Address	*Health & Social Work,* NASW Press, 750 First Street, NE, Suite 700, Washington, DC 20002-4241.
Number of Copies	5.
Disk Submission	Authors of accepted manuscripts are asked to submit a disk, preferably in Microsoft Word or WordPerfect.

FORMAT OF MANUSCRIPT

Cover Sheet	Separate sheet, which does not go out for review. Full title, author names, degrees, professional titles, designation of one author as corresponding author with full address, phone numbers, e-mail address, and fax number; date of submission.
Abstract	150-word informative abstract.
Key Words	Up to 5 words or key phrases (2–3 word maximum) describing the article.
Length	14–16 pages including references and tables; manuscripts exceeding 25 pages will be returned.
Margins	1 inch on all sides.
Spacing	Double-spaced for all copy, except title page.

STYLE

Name of Guide
Writing for the NASW Press: Information for Authors (free) and *Professional Writing for the Human Services* (for purchase from the NASW Press). Contact NASW Press.

Subheadings
Use as needed to guide reader through the article. No more than 3 levels.

References
Author–date citation style; see style guides.

Footnotes
No footnotes preferred; incorporate into text.

Tables or Figures
Type tables double-spaced. Submit camera-ready art (300 dpi printer or better) for all figures. Place each table or figure on a separate, numbered page at the end of the manuscript.

REVIEW PROCESS

Type
"Double blind" anonymous peer review. 3 reviewers, plus the editor-in-chief, read the manuscript in an anonymous review.

Queries
Query letters are discouraged; authors are encouraged to read the journal and *Writing for the NASW Press* to determine if their subject matter would be appropriate.

Acknowledgment
The NASW Press sends a letter on receipt of manuscript.

Review Time
3–4 months.

Revisions
Submit 5 copies with a separate cover sheet (not identifying the author) describing the changes made in the manuscript and replying to the reviewers' comments. In general, the original reviewers and the editor-in-chief read revisions.

Acceptance Rate
Approximately 25%.

Return of Manuscript
Not returned; author should retain copies.

Lag Time to Print
Approximately 6 months–1 year.

REPRINT, SUBSCRIPTION, AND CONTACT INFORMATION

Reprint Policy
All authors receive 5 complimentary copies of the issue in which the article appears. Authors receive reprint order forms to purchase additional reprinted copies.

Book Reviews
By invitation only; send books for review to: Book Review Editor, *Health & Social Work*, NASW Press, 750 First Street, NE, Suite 700, Washington, DC 20002-4241.

Subscriptions
Health & Social Work, P.O. Box 431, Annapolis JCT, MD 20701.

1996–97 one-year prices: NASW members, $45; individual nonmembers, $70; libraries/institutions, $87.

Affiliation
The NASW Press is a division of the National Association of Social Workers.

E-Mail Address
press@naswdc.org.

Home Page URL
http://www.naswpress.org

Health Care Financing Review

Editorial Focus	Original health care research; major policy issues that present information and analyses concerning health services and health financing programs (with emphasis on the Medicare and Medicaid programs; the development of particular projects or demonstrations.
Audience	Health care policymakers, planners, administrators, insurers, researchers, and providers.
Special Themes	Managed care, vulnerable populations, rural health, health care reform, quality of care.
Where Indexed/ Abstracted	Abstracts of Health Care Management Studies; Excerpta Medica; HealthSTAR; Hospital and Health Administration Index; Index to U.S. Government Periodicals; ISI Current Contents: Social and Behavioral Sciences Social SciSearch; ISI Social Sciences Citation Index Research Alert; MEDOC.
Year Established	1979.
Circulation	6,000.
Frequency	Quarterly.
Months Issued	Spring, summer, fall, winter.
No. of Articles	12–16 per issue.

SUBMISSIONS

Address	Editor-in-Chief, *Health Care Financing Review*, 7500 Security Boulevard, C3-11-07, Baltimore, MD 21244-1850; phone: 410-786-6572; fax: 410-786-5768; e-mail: LWolf@hcfa.gov
Number of Copies	4.
Disk Submission	Authors of accepted manuscripts are asked to submit a 3-1/2″ floppy disk, with manuscript in WordPerfect format and tables in either Microsoft Excel or WordPerfect format.

FORMAT OF MANUSCRIPT

Cover Sheet	Cover page should provide the following information: title of the manuscript; names, academic degrees, and affiliations of the author and all co-authors; address for reprint requests; and any grant, contract, or support information.
Abstract	100 words or fewer.
Key Words	None.
Length	Approximately 25–35 pages.
Margins	1 inch on all sides.
Spacing	Double-spaced, single-sided.

STYLE

Name of Guide	*U.S. Government Printing Office Style Manual.*
Subheadings	3 levels.
References	Author–date citation style; see "Information for Authors" section in *Health Care Financing Review* for sample citation.
Footnotes	Footnotes should be cited in text with a superior number and numbered sequentially throughout the article; notes should be listed at the bottom of the page, *not* separately at the end of the article.
Tables or Figures	Total number of tables and figures not to exceed 10; each table and figure should be on a separate sheet and be specifically cited within the text; disk copy should be provided for all tables (and figures, if possible); plotting points should be provided for each figure.

REVIEW PROCESS

Type	The executive and associate editors decide which submitted articles are relevant to the health care financing field in general and the Health Care Financing Administration in particular. Relevant articles undergo a double-blind anonymous peer review by 3 reviewers. Comments are transmitted to authors, who are expected to make revisions based on these critiques.
Queries	Queries about acceptability of manuscripts should be submitted to the submission address listed above.
Acknowledgment	An acknowledgment letter is sent on receipt of manuscript.
Review Time	3–4 months.
Revisions	Submit two copies of the manuscript along with floppy disk as described above. On a separate cover sheet, describe changes made to the manuscript and the incorporation of the peer reviewers' comments. The manuscript will undergo a final review.
Acceptance Rate	Not specified.
Return of Manuscript	Rejected manuscripts will be returned to the author; the *Review* accepts no responsibility for lost manuscripts.
Lag Time to Print	6 months–1 year.

REPRINT, SUBSCRIPTION, AND CONTACT INFORMATION

Reprint Policy	All authors receive a complimentary copy of the issue in which the article appears, as well as 50 reprints of their article.
Book Reviews	Send books for review to submission address listed above.
Subscriptions	Superintendent of Documents, U.S. Government Printing Office, P.O. Box 371954, Pittsburgh, PA 15250-7954; fax: 202-512-2250.
Affiliation	The *Health Care Financing Review* is published by the Office of Research and Demonstrations, U.S. Health Care Financing Administration.
E-Mail Address	LWolf@hcfa.gov
Home Page URL	http://www.hcfa.gov

Health Psychology

Previous Title	Previously published solely by APA's division of Health Psychology.
Editorial Focus	*Health Psychology* is a scholarly journal devoted to furthering an understanding of scientific relationships between behavioral principles on the one hand and physical health and illness on the other. The readership has a broad range of backgrounds, interests, and specializations, often interdisciplinary in nature. The major type of paper being solicited for *Health Psychology* is the report of empirical research. Such papers should have significant theoretical or practical import for an understanding of relationships between behavior and physical health. Integrative papers that address themselves to a broad constituency are particularly welcome. Suitable topics for submission include, but are not restricted to, the role of environmental, psychosocial, or sociocultural factors that may contribute to disease or its prevention; behavioral methods used in the diagnosis, treatment, or rehabilitation of individuals having physical disorders; and techniques that could reduce disease risk by modifying health beliefs, attitudes, or behaviors including decisions about using professional services. Interventions used may be at the individual, group, multicenter, or community level.
Audience	Researchers in the discipline, faculty, libraries.
Where Indexed/ Abstracted	Academic Index; Addiction Abstracts; Applied Social Sciences Index & Abstracts; Biological Abstracts; Criminal Justice Abstracts; Current Contents; Excerpta Medica; Index Medicus; Management Contents; PsycINFO; Sage Family Studies Abstracts; Social Sciences Citation Index; Social Sciences Index; Social Work Abstracts; Studies on Women Abstracts.
Year Established	Not specified.
Circulation	9,000.
Frequency	Bimonthly.
Months Issued	January, March, May, July, September, November.
No. of Articles	13.

SUBMISSIONS

Address	David S. Krantz, Department of Medical and Clinical Psychology, Uniformed Services University of Health Sciences, 4301 Jones Bridge Road, Bethesda, MD 20814-4799.
Number of Copies	5.
Disk Submission	Submit manuscripts on paper; disks may be requested of accepted articles.

FORMAT OF MANUSCRIPT

Cover Sheet	Refer to Instructions to Authors in each issue.
Abstract	Manuscripts must include an abstract containing a maximum of 960 characters and spaces (approximately 120 words), typed on a separate sheet of paper.

Key Words	4–6 key words.
Length	Not specified.
Margins	See style guide.
Spacing	Double-spaced.

STYLE

Name of Guide	*Publication Manual of the American Psychological Association.*
Subheadings	See style guide.
References	See style guide.
Footnotes	See style guide.
Tables or Figures	See style guide; camera-ready copy required for all art.

REVIEW PROCESS

Type	Masked review by request of author.
Queries	No query letters.
Acknowledgment	Editor acknowledges submission by mail.
Review Time	Usually 60–90 days.
Revisions	Editor will notify author if revision is desired (most manuscripts are initially rejected; most published manuscripts have gone through one or two revisions).
Acceptance Rate	16%.
Return of Manuscript	Manuscripts are not usually returned.
Lag Time to Print	5 months.

CHARGES TO AUTHOR

| Author Alterations | Authors are billed for alterations in proofs. |

REPRINT, SUBSCRIPTION, AND CONTACT INFORMATION

Reprint Policy	Authors may purchase reprints of their articles (order form accompanies proofs).
Book Reviews	None.
Subscriptions	Subscriptions Department, American Psychological Association, 750 First Street, NE, Washington, DC 20002-4242.
	Yearly rates for nonmembers are $67 domestic, $87 foreign, $100 air mail; institutional rates are $180 domestic, $223 foreign, $235 air mail. APA members: $34. Free with APA Division 38 membership or affiliate membership.
Affiliation	Published by the American Psychological Association.
Home Page URL	http://www.apa.org

Home Health Care Services Quarterly

Editorial Focus	Important research on the cutting edge of home care and alternatives to long-term institutional care for elderly, disabled, and other population groups that use in-home health care services. Aimed toward service providers and health care specialists involved with health care financing, evalutaion of services, organization of services, and public policy issues. New insights into delivery and management of home health and related community services.
Audience	Service providers, health care specialists, business people, professors, researchers.
Where Indexed/ Abstracted	Abstracting, Indexing & Bibliographic; Abstracts in Social Gerontology; Academic Abstracts/CD-ROM; Academic Search; Access; AgeLine Database; Alzheimer's Disease Education & Referral Center (ADEAR); Brown University Geriatric Research Application Digest "Abstracts Section"; Cabell's Directory of Publishing Opportunities in Nursing; Cambridge Scientific Abstracts; CINAHL (Cumulative Index to Nursing & Allied Health (Literature); Current Literature on Aging; Health Care Literature Information Network/HECLINET; Health Planning and Administration (HEALTH) Database; Hospital Literature Index; Human Resources Abstracts (HRA); International Pharmaceutical Abstracts; INTERNET ACCESS (& additional networks) Bulletin Board for Libraries ("BUBL"); Inventory of Marriage and Family Literature (online & hard copy); National Clearinghouse for Primary Care Information (NCPCI); Nursing Abstracts; Sage Family Studies Abstracts (SFSA); Social Planning/Policy & Development Abstracts (SOPODA); Social Work Abstracts; Sociological Abstracts.
Year Established	1981.
Circulation	Less than 1,000.
Frequency	Quarterly.
Months Issued	Spring, summer, fall, winter.
No. of Articles	Not specified.

SUBMISSIONS

Address	W. June Simmons, *Home Health Care Services Quarterly*, 520 S. La Fayette Park Place, Suite 500, Los Angeles, CA 90057.
Number of Copies	4.
Disk Submission	Authors of accepted manuscripts are asked to submit a disk, preferably in WordPerfect 5.1 or 6.0.

FORMAT OF MANUSCRIPT

Cover Sheet	On one page, indicate only the article title for anonymous refereeing. On a loose page include the title; author names; authors' academic degrees, professional titles, affiliations, mailing addresses, phone numbers; an abstract of about 100 words; and any desired acknowledgment of research support or other credit.
Abstract	100 words.

Key Words	3–10 key words.
Length	16–20 pages, including references and abstract.
Margins	At least 1 inch on all 4 sides.
Spacing	Double-spaced.

STYLE

Name of Guide	References, citations, and general style of manuscripts for this journal should follow the style of the *Publication Manual of the American Psychological Association*.
Subheadings	Use as needed to guide reader through the article.
References	References should be double-spaced and placed in alphabetical order.
Footnotes	No footnotes preferred; incorporate into text.
Tables or Figures	Must be camera-ready, cleanly typed, or artistically prepared on separate sheets of paper. On the back of these items, write article title and the journal title lightly in pencil. Indicate placement in text. Photographs are considered part of the acceptable manuscript and remain with publisher for use in additional printings.

REVIEW PROCESS

Type	"Double blind" anonymous peer review. 2 reviewers, plus the editor-in-chief, read the manuscript in an anonymous review.
Queries	A copy of the *Home Health Care Services Quarterly—Instructions for Authors* will be sent to all queries.
Acknowledgment	By letter on receipt of manuscript.
Review Time	2–3 months.
Revisions	Submit 4 copies with a separate cover sheet (not identifying the author) describing the changes made in the manuscript and replying to the reviewers' comments.
Acceptance Rate	Approximately 21%–30%.
Return of Manuscript	Manuscripts will not be returned.
Lag Time to Print	Approximately 4–6 months.

REPRINT, SUBSCRIPTION, AND CONTACT INFORMATION

Reprint Policy	The senior author will receive 2 copies of the journal issue and 10 complimentary reprints. The junior author will receive 2 copies of the journal issue. Reprints may be ordered.
Book Reviews	By invitation only; send books for review to W. June Simmons, *Home Health Care Services Quarterly*, 520 S. La Fayette Park Place, Suite 500, Los Angeles, CA 90057.
Subscriptions	*Home Health Care Services Quarterly*, The Haworth Press, Inc., 10 Alice Street, Binghamton, NY 13904-1580.
	1996–97 one-year prices: individual, $45; institution, $180; library, $265.
E-Mail Address	75151.3037@compuserve.com

The Hospice Journal

Editorial Focus	Hospice care, clinical care, and research.
Audience	Members of the National Hospice Organization (NHO).
Special Themes	Applied research or evaluation studies.
Where Indexed/ Abstracted	Abstracts in Social Gerontology: Current Literature on Aging; Abstracts of Research in Pastoral Care & Counseling; Academic Abstracts/CD-ROM; AgeLine Database; Cambridge Scientific Abstracts; CINAHL (Cumulative Index to Nursing & Allied Health Literature); CNPIEC Reference Guide: Chinese National Directory of Foreign Periodicals; Educational Administration Abstracts; Family Studies Database (online and CD)ROM); Health STAR; Health Source Plus; Health Source; Hospital and Health Administration Index; International Nursing Index; International Pharmaceutical Abstracts; Leeds Medical Information; Medication Use STudies (MUST) Database; Nursing Abstracts; Psychological Abstracts (PsycINFO); Sage Family Studies Abstracts (SFSA); Sage Urban Studies Abstracts (SUSA); Sapient Health Network; SilverPlatter Information, Inc, "CD–ROM online"; Social Planning Policy & Development Abstracts (SOPODA); Social Work Abstracts; Sociological Abstracts (SA); Violence and Abuse Abstracts: A Review of Current Literature on Interpersonal Violence (VAA).
Year Established	1985.
Circulation	514.
Frequency	Quarterly.
Months Issued	Not specified.
No. of Articles	6–10 per issue.

SUBMISSIONS

Address	Editor, Donna Lind Infeld, PhD, Professor of Health Services Management and Policy and of Health Care Sciences, 600 21st Street, NW, Washington, DC 20052.
Number of Copies	4.
Disk Submission	Authors of accepted manuscripts are asked to submit a disk, preferably in Microsoft Word or WordPerfect.

FORMAT OF MANUSCRIPT

Cover Sheet	Separate sheet, which does not go out for review. Full title, author names, degrees, professional titles; designation of one author as corresponding author with full address, phone numbers, e-mail address, and fax number; date of submission.
Abstract	About 100 words.
Key Words	5 or 6 words that identify article content.

Length	5–20 pages, including references and abstract. Lengthier manuscripts may be considered, but only at the discretion of the editor. Sometimes, lengthier manuscripts may be considered if they can be divided into sections for publication in successive issues.
Margins	1 inch on all sides.
Spacing	Double-spaced for all copy, except title page.

STYLE

Name of Guide	*American Medical Association* or *Publication Manual of the American Psychological Association.*
Subheadings	Use as needed to guide reader through the article. No more than 4 levels.
References	Author–date citation style; see style guide.
Footnotes	No footnotes preferred; incorporate into text.
Tables or Figures	Type tables double-spaced. Submit camera-ready art (300 dpi printer or better) for all figures. Place each table or figure on a separate, numbered page at the end of the manuscript.

REVIEW PROCESS

Type	"Double blind" anonymous peer review. 3 reviewers plus editor-in-chief read the manuscript in an anonymous review.
Queries	Authors are encouraged to read the journal to determine if their subject matter would be appropriate.
Acknowledgment	Enclose a regular self-addressed, stamped envelope with submission.
Review Time	3–4 months.
Revisions	See journal.
Acceptance Rate	Not specified.
Return of Manuscript	Only if 9″ x 12″ self-addressed, stamped envelope is enclosed.
Lag Time to Print	6 months–1 year.

REPRINT, SUBSCRIPTION, AND CONTACT INFORMATION

Reprint Policy	All authors receive 2 complimentary copies of the issue in which article appears. Authors receive reprint order forms to purchase additional reprinted copies.
Book Reviews	Send to journal editor.
Subscriptions	The Haworth Press, Inc., 10 Alice Street, Binghamton, NY 13904-1580. Individuals, $40; institutions, $90; libraries, $200. NHO members: free.
Affiliation	National Hospice Organization (NHO).
E-Mail Address	dlind@gw152.circ.gwu.edu

The Indian Journal of Social Work

Editorial Focus	*The Indian Journal of Social Work* is a path-breaking quarterly publication of the social work profession in India since 1940 published by Tata Institute of Social Sciences, the pioneering Institute of Social Work Education in India. It focuses on multidisciplinary knowledge development relevant to the changing perspectives of the social work profession. Preference is given to articles related to the problems of marginalized groups (among children, youth, the elderly, women, Dalits, tribals, labor, the disabled, and so on). It also includes articles which address interventions that impede as well as those that facilitate people-centeredness in social systems and processes at the local, national, and international levels. Issues related to livelihood, health, housing, education, occupation, criminality, relief and rehabilitation, disaster management, media, welfare, development, and the like are covered. The journal invites theoretical, historical, empirical, methodological, epistemological analyses; reviews of policies , programs, legislation, voluntary organizations, professional interventions; curriculum development; book reviews; discussions, and notes.
Audience	Schools of social work; research, voluntary, government, international, and other organizations; practitioners; activists; academicians.
Special Themes	Recent special themes include Volunteers: Their Role and Training; The Family; The Social Construction and Expression of Ethnicity and Identity.
Where Indexed/ Abstracted	Current Contents; Indian Psychological Abstracts and Reviews; Psychiatric Rehabilitation Journal; Social Planning/Policy and Development Abstracts; Social Sciences Citation Index; Social Work Abstracts; Sociological Abstracts.
Year Established	1940.
Circulation	669.
Frequency	Quarterly.
Months Issued	January, April, July, October.
No. of Articles	10–12.

SUBMISSIONS

Address	Associate Editor, *The Indian Journal of Social Work,* Tata Institute of Social Sciences, P.O. Box 8313, Deonar, Mumbai 400 088, India.
Number of Copies	3.
Disk Submission	Not required. If author submits a disk, should be in WordStar version 5.5.

FORMAT OF MANUSCRIPT

Cover Sheet	Title of the article, authors' names, and their institutional affiliations.
Abstract	Approximately 75 words.

Key Words	Not required.
Length	Up to 6,000 words.
Margins	1.5″ on the left side and 1″ on the other 3 sides.
Spacing	Double-spaced.

STYLE

Name of Guide	*IJSW Instructions to Authors.*
Subheadings	Not specified.
References	Author–date citation style.
Footnotes	Footnotes should be listed as notes in an appendix and not typed at the bottom of the manuscript pages on which they appear.
Tables or Figures	Type each table on a separate page. Insert a location note at the appropriate place in the text; minimize the use of the tables. Graphs, charts, and maps should each be prepared on a separate page. Retain the original drawings for submission after the paper is accepted, but send a rough copy with the manuscript. Insert a location note at the appropriate place in the text.

REVIEW PROCESS

Type	Every article is reviewed by masked peer review by 2 referees.
Queries	Not specified.
Acknowledgment	Yes.
Review Time	2 months.
Revisions	Read by the original reviewers and the associate editor.
Acceptance Rate	Approximately 20%.
Return of Manuscript	Returned only if rejected.
Lag Time to Print	1 year.

REPRINT, SUBSCRIPTION, AND CONTACT INFORMATION

Reprint Policy	All authors receive 1 copy of the issue.
Book Reviews	By invitation only.
Subscriptions	Contact Tata Institute of Social Sciences, No. 8313, Deonar, Mumbai 400 088, India; phone: 91-22-556 3289 or 91-22-556 3290; fax: 91-22-556 2912.
Affiliation	The Tata Institute of Social Sciences.
E-Mail Address	tissbom@ren.nic.in

Information & Referral: The Journal of the Alliance of Information and Referral Systems

Editorial Focus Each volume focuses on a central theme selected by the editor and the editorial board. Articles on other practical and theoretical aspects of community information and referral (including, but not limited to, such topics as information processing and management, staff training and development, the client interview and referral transaction, program development and evaluation, and interagency/intra-agency cooperation) may be appropriate to the journal's Notes from the Field section. An ongoing bibliography of print and nonprint resources also appears in the journal, as do reviews of books and other publications.

Audience Primarily individuals who work in the field of community information and referral.

Special Themes Various.

Where Indexed/ Abstracted Information Science Abstracts; INSPEC [online database]; Library & Information Science Abstracts; PAIS International in Print; Social Planning/ Policy & Development Abstracts; Sociological Abstracts.

Year Established 1979.

Circulation Approximately 1,000.

Frequency Annually.

Months Issued Varies.

No. of Articles 6–12.

SUBMISSIONS

Address Dick Manikowski, TIP Database Department, Detroit Public Library, 5201 Woodward Avenue. Detroit, MI 48202-4093; phone: 313/833-4033.

Number of Copies 1.

Disk Submission Manuscripts in Microsoft Word for Windows 6.0 preferred; second choice is unformatted ASCII text.

FORMAT OF MANUSCRIPT

Cover Sheet Title, author name, address, affiliation, daytime voice/fax phone numbers, e-mail address.

Abstract 50–200 words.

Key Words Not needed.

Length No longer than 7,500 words; most articles run 3,000–5,000 words.

Margins Author discretion.

Spacing Triple-spaced.

STYLE

Name of Guide	Author discretion. Because so many of our readers are not academics, editor strives to avoid overly formal and technical styles and approaches that might intimidate them.
Subheadings	Author discretion.
References	Author discretion.
Footnotes	Author discretion.
Tables or Figures	Author discretion.

REVIEW PROCESS

Type	Anonymous.
Queries	Editor prefers initial contact (voice, mail, e-mail) before submission.
Acknowledgment	Via e-mail.
Review Time	Varies.
Revisions	Editor works with contributor to revise first draft into something more polished before submitting to editorial review board.
Acceptance Rate	70%.
Return of Manuscript	Enclose self-addressed, stamped envelope.
Lag Time to Print	Varies.

REPRINT, SUBSCRIPTION, AND CONTACT INFORMATION

Reprint Policy	On publication, author(s) receive 2 copies of issue. On request, editor will grant permission to reprint published articles elsewhere providing that the original source of publication is cited.
Book Reviews	Unsolicited reviews accepted, but editor prefers contact before submission.
Subscriptions	Alliance of Information & Referral Systems, P.O. Box 31668, Seattle, WA 98103; phone: 206/632-2477.
	Subscription free with institutional membership; $20 for volunteer/student members; $25 for nonmember individuals; $30 for nonmember agencies.
Affiliation	Alliance of Information & Referral Systems.
E-Mail Address	rmaniko@cms.cc.wayne.edu (communications with editor) pkaairs@aol.com (subscription communications with national office)

International Journal of Aging and Human Development

Editorial Focus	Psychological, social, anthropological, and humanistic studies of aging and the aged; observations from other fields that illuminate the human side of gerontology, or use gerontological observations to illuminate problems in other fields.
Audience	Not specified.
Special Themes	Not specified.
Where Indexed/ Abstracted	Aged Care and Services Review; Applied Social Sciences Index & Abstracts; Bibliographical Index of Health Education Periodicals; Current Index to Journals in Education (CIJE); Excerpta Medica; Family Abstracts; Index to Periodical Literature to Aging; MEDLINE; Mental Health Abstracts; PREV; Social Work Abstracts; Sociological Abstracts.
Year Established	1970.
Circulation	1,700.
Frequency	8 times per year.
Months Issued	Not specified.
No. of Articles	6.

SUBMISSIONS

Address	Dr. Robert Kastenbaum, Department of Communications, Arizona State University, Box 871205, Tempe, AZ 85287-1205.
Number of Copies	3.
Disk Submission	No.

FORMAT OF MANUSCRIPT

Cover Sheet	Not required.
Abstract	100–150 words.
Key Words	Not specified.
Length	22 pages, but depends on content.
Margins	Wide.
Spacing	Double-spaced.

STYLE

Name of Guide	*Publication Manual of the American Psychological Association.*
Subheadings	Yes.
References	Should relate only to material cited in text and be listed numerically according to appearance within text. Consult editor for more details on reference style.

Footnotes	Place at the bottom of page where referenced. Number using superscript Arabic numbers without parentheses or brackets. Footnotes should be brief with an average length of 3 lines. Keep to a minimum.
Tables or Figures	*Tables:* Cite tables in text in numerical sequence. Give each a descriptive title. Superscript lowercase letters for footnotes to tables, if any. Type tables on separate pages and indicate their approximate placement in text. *Figures:* Number figure callouts in text in numerical sequence. Line art must be original drawings in black ink, proportionate to the journal's page size, and suitable for photographing. Indicate top and bottom of figure where confusion may exist. Label using 8-point type. Clearly identify all figures. Draw figures on separate pages and indicate their placement in text.

REVIEW PROCESS

Type	Anonymous review by at least 2 reviewers.
Queries	Not specified.
Acknowledgment	Within 48 hours.
Review Time	6–10 weeks.
Revisions	Authors receive detailed suggestions from reviewers. Manuscripts requiring minor revisions are reviewed again by editorial staff. Manuscripts with major revisions are re-read by reviewers.
Acceptance Rate	20% after first submission, 30%–35% after revision.
Return of Manuscript	Include a self-addressed, stamped envelope when submitting manuscript.
Lag Time to Print	Within 1 year.

REPRINT, SUBSCRIPTION, AND CONTACT INFORMATION

Reprint Policy	Authors receive 20 free reprints and information form for ordering additional copies.
Book Reviews	Contact editor. Indicate areas of expertise and interests, and include a vita.
Subscriptions	Baywood Publishing Company, Inc., 26 Austin Avenue, P.O. Box 33, Amityville, NY 11701.
	Individuals, $54; institutions, $135.

International Journal of Mental Health

Editorial Focus	Community mental health.
Audience	Mental health professionals, planners, and researchers.
Special Themes	Relapse prevention, coping with disaster, depression, among others.
Where Indexed/ Abstracted	Current Contents; Index Medicus; Psychological Abstracts.
Year Established	1970.
Circulation	1,200.
Frequency	Quarterly.
Months Issued	Not specified.
No. of Articles	10–14.

SUBMISSIONS

Address	Martin Gittelman, Editor, Department of Psychiatry, New York Medical College, Room 24A, 100 W. 94th Street, New York, NY 10025.
Number of Copies	2.
Disk Submission	3-1/2″ disk in Microsoft Word or ASCII format.

FORMAT OF MANUSCRIPT

Cover Sheet	Author names, titles, institutional affiliations, addresses, phone numbers.
Abstract	Not required.
Key Words	Not specified.
Length	Not specified.
Margins	Wide.
Spacing	Double-spaced.

STYLE

Name of Guide	Available from: B. Appelbau, Managing Editor, M. E. Sharpe, Inc., P.O. Box 1, Burlington Flats, NY 13315.
Subheadings	Not specified.
References	Not specified.
Footnotes	Not specified.
Tables or Figures	Not specified.

REVIEW PROCESS

Type	Anonymous review by 2 reviewers.
Queries	Not specified.
Acknowledgment	Include self-addressed, stamped envelope with submission.

Review Time	3–12 months.
Revisions	Not specified.
Acceptance Rate	90% are invited; of the 10% remaining, 40% are accepted.
Return of Manuscript	Manuscripts are returned.
Lag Time to Print	3–6 months.

REPRINT, SUBSCRIPTION, AND CONTACT INFORMATION

Reprint Policy	Not specified.
Book Reviews	Not specified.
Subscriptions	M. E. Sharpe, Inc., P.O. Box 1, Burlington Flats, NY 13315. Individuals, $54; institutions, $190.
Affiliation	World Association for Psychosocial Rehabilitation.

The International Journal of Psychiatry in Medicine

Editorial Focus	Topics of interest include, but are not limited to: psychosocial modifiers of illness; minor and moderate mental disorders *seen* and treated by primary care providers; physician–patient interactions; biomedical etiologies of mental symptoms; research from successful collaborative models such as geriatrics; and health services research. The journal publishes original research, review articles, innovative educational programs and techniques, and illustrative case reports.
Audience	Providers and researchers in primary care.
Special Themes	Biopsychosocial aspects of primary care such as psychosocial modifiers of illness, physician–patient interactions, geriatrics, health services.
Where Indexed/ Abstracted	Abstracts on Criminology and Penology; Adolescent Mental Health Abstracts; Annals of Behavioral Medicine; Biosciences Information Service of Biological Abstracts; Cambridge Scientific Abstracts; Clinical Medicine; Current Contents: Social and Behavioral Sciences; Current Science; Data TRAQ International, Inc.; Digest of Neurology and Psychiatry; Educational Administration Abstracts/EAA; Human Resources Abstracts/HRA; Excerpta Medica; Index Medicus; Innovations and Research; International Review of Psychiatry; Medical Socioeconomic Research Sources; Mental Health Abstracts Mental Health Book Review Index; Modern Medicine; Psychological Abstracts; Sage Public Administration Abstracts/SPAA; Sage Urban Studies Abstracts/SUSA; Selected List of Tables of Contents of Psychiatric Periodicals and Social Sciences Citation Index; Social Work Abstracts; Violence and Abuse/VAA.
Year Established	1970.
Circulation	Not available.
Frequency	4 issues per year.
Months Issued	April, July, October, January.
No. of Articles	7–10 per issue.

SUBMISSIONS

Address	Thomas S. Oxman, MD, Department of Psychiatry, Dartmouth Hitchcock Medical Center, 1 Medical Center Drive, Lebanon, NH 03756.
Number of Copies	5.
Disk Submission	No.

FORMAT OF MANUSCRIPT

Cover Sheet	Separate sheet, which does not go out for review. Full title, author names, degrees, professional titles; designation of one author as corresponding author with full address, phone numbers, e-mail address, and fax number; date of submission.
Abstract	Abstract should be a single paragraph, approximately 250 words, structured with headings and the following information: Objective—study questions or primary purpose of the article; Method—subjects, design, measurements, data analysis, or number and method of selecting studies for review article; Results—key findings; Conclusions—implications, future directions.

Key Words	After abstract include about 3–10 index words (from MESH list of Index Medicus) and (Intl. J. Psychiatry in Medicine 899-;26:000-000).
Length	No maximum, but prefer fewer than 30 pages.
Margins	Minimum 1 inch on all sides.
Spacing	Double-spaced.

STYLE

Name of Guide	International Committee of Medical Journal Editors. Uniform requirements for manuscripts submitted to biomedical journals *JAMA* 1993R269:2282–2286, instructions available from editor.
Subheadings	Not specified.
References	References are cited in text in numerical order with bracket (1), and are listed in numerical sequence at the end of the article.
Footnotes	Bottom of page where referenced. Numbered with super Arabic numbers, Brief, average length 3 lines.
Tables or Figures	Tables must be cited in text in numbered sequence starting with Table 1. Each table must have a descriptive title. Tables should be typed on separate pages *and* their approximate placement indicated.
	Figures should be referenced in text and appear in numerical sequence starting with Figure 1. Line art must be original drawings in black ink, and suitable for photographing. Labeling should be 8 point type. Clearly identify all figures. Figures should be drawn on separate pages and their placement noted.

REVIEW PROCESS

Type	Peer review; may suggest reviewers, but use not guaranteed.
Queries	Welcomed by editor.
Acknowledgment	By letter.
Review Time	2–3 months.
Revisions	Within 8 weeks.
Acceptance Rate	50%–60%.
Return of Manuscript	Not specified.
Lag Time to Print	6–12 months.

REPRINT, SUBSCRIPTION, AND CONTACT INFORMATION

Reprint Policy	Author receives 20 free reprints and a copy of the journal. Additional reprints may be ordered.
Book Reviews	Yes, send inquiries or books to editor.
Subscriptions	Baywood Publishing Company, Inc., 26 Austin Avenue, P.O. Box 337, Amityville, NY 11701.
E-Mail Address	Editor: thomas.e.oxman@dartmouth.edu Publisher: baywood@baywood.com
Home Page URL	Editor: http://www.dartmouth.edu/dms/~ijpmox Publisher: http://baywood.com

International Social Work

Editorial Focus	To extend knowledge and promote communication in the fields of social work, social development, social welfare, and human services.
Audience	Social work faculty, practitioners, and students in all areas of the profession and in all parts of the world.
Special Themes	Material that addresses between-country issues.
Where Indexed/ Abstracted	Abstracted in Applied Social Sciences Index & Abstracts; caredata Abstracts; Middle East Abstracts & Index; Psychological Abstracts; PsycINFO; Social Work Abstracts; Sociological Abstracts; Southeast Asia Abstracts & Index. Indexed in caredata CD; caredata Information Bulletin; Current Contents: Social and Behavioral Science; International Bibliography of Periodical Literature (IBZ); Research Alert; Social SciSearch.
Year Established	1957.
Circulation	1,000+.
Frequency	Quarterly.
Months Issued	January, April, July, October.
No. of Articles	7–8.

SUBMISSIONS

Address	*International Social Work*, c/o Faculty of Social Work, Wilfrid Laurier University, Waterloo, Ontario, Canada N2L 3C5.
Number of Copies	3.
Disk Submission	No.

FORMAT OF MANUSCRIPT

Cover Sheet	Separate sheet, which does not go out for review. Full name, degrees, and title, phone and fax numbers, and date of submission.
Abstract	Up to 100 words.
Key Words	Not specified.
Length	12–14 pages. Manuscripts exceeding this length will be returned.
Margins	Minimum 1 inch all sides.
Spacing	Double-spaced.

STYLE

Name of Guide	Outline in inside cover of journal.
Subheadings	Not specified.
References	Author–date citation style; see examples in journal.
Footnotes	Collected on a single page at the end of article.

Tables or Figures	Submit camera-ready. Place each table or figure on a separate page and indicate its location in text. Each table must have a short descriptive heading.

REVIEW PROCESS

Type	Blind peer review by 2 readers selected from a worldwide editorial board, plus the editor.
Queries	Welcomed.
Acknowledgment	By letter on receipt.
Review Time	4–6 months.
Revisions	3 copies of revised article with changes identified.
Acceptance Rate	Approximately 60%.
Return of Manuscript	Not returned.
Lag Time to Print	1 year.

REPRINT, SUBSCRIPTION, AND CONTACT INFORMATION

Reprint Policy	All authors receive copy of the edition containing article and 5 reprints of the article.
Book Reviews	Send to Book Review Editor, Ann Lavan, Department of Social Policy and Social Work, University College, Dublin Belfield, Dublin 4 Ireland.
Subscriptions	Individual, $58.
Affiliation	International Association of Schools of Social Work; International Council on Social Welfare; International Federation of Social Workers.

Jewish Social Work Forum

Editorial Focus	Social work, Jewish communal service.
Audience	Social workers, students, alumni, libraries.
Where Indexed/ Abstracted	Social Work Abstracts; Sociological Abstracts.
Year Established	1962.
Circulation	4,200.
Frequency	Annually.
Months Issued	Summer.
No. of Articles	8 on average.

SUBMISSIONS

Address	Editor, *Jewish Social Work Forum,* Wurzweiler School of Social Work Alumni Association, Yeshiva University, 2495 Amsterdam Avenue, New York, NY 10033.
Number of Copies	3.
Disk Submission	Yes, WordPerfect 5.1.

FORMAT OF MANUSCRIPT

Cover Sheet	Title, author, address, and phone.
Abstract	Yes, 50 words.
Key Words	None.
Length	18 pages.
Margins	1 inch on all sides.
Spacing	Double-spaced.

STYLE

Name of Guide	Guide is available to authors.
Subheadings	Not specified.
References	Follow style in *Publication Manual of the American Psychological Association.*
Footnotes	Yes.
Tables or Figures	Provide camera-ready.

REVIEW PROCESS

Type	Journal is refereed. Authors are anonymous.
Queries	The editor welcomes queries.
Acknowledgment	Yes, on receipt of manuscript.
Review Time	3 months.

Revisions	Author is notified of necessary revisions and asked to resubmit the corrected version.
Acceptance Rate	60%.
Return of Manuscript	Only if changes are suggested. Authors should include a return self-addressed envelope.
Lag Time to Print	6 months.

REPRINT, SUBSCRIPTION, AND CONTACT INFORMATION

Reprint Policy	None.
Book Reviews	Most are solicited. They should be sent to the book review editor.
Subscriptions	*Jewish Social Work Forum,* Wurzweiler School of Social Work Alumni Association, Yeshiva University, 2495 Amsterdam Avenue, New York, NY 10033.
	Cost: $10 per year.
Affiliation	Wurzweiler School of Social Work, Yeshiva University.

Journal of Abnormal Psychology

Previous Title   *Journal of Abnormal and Social Psychology.*

Editorial Focus   The *Journal of Abnormal Psychology* publishes articles on basic research and theory in the broad field of abnormal behavior, its determinants, and its correlates. The following general topics fall within its area of major focus: (a) psychopathology—its etiology, development, symptomatology, and course; (b) normal processes in abnormal individuals; (c) pathological or atypical features of the behavior of normal people; (d) experimental studies, with human or animal subjects, relating to disordered emotional behavior or pathology; (e) sociocultural effects on pathological processes, including the influence of gender and ethnicity; and (f) tests of hypotheses from psychological theories that relate to abnormal behavior. Thus, studies of patient populations, analyses of abnormal behavior and motivation in terms of modern behavior theories, case histories, experiments on the nature of hypnosis and the mechanisms underlying hypnotic phenomena, and theoretical papers of scholarly substance on deviant personality and emotional abnormality would all fall within the boundaries of the journal's interests. Each article should represent an addition to knowledge and understanding of abnormal behavior either in its etiology, description, or change. In order to improve the use of journal resources, it has been agreed by the two editors concerned that the *Journal of Abnormal Psychology* will not consider articles dealing with the diagnosis or treatment of abnormal behavior, and the *Journal of Consulting and Clinical Psychology* will not consider manuscripts dealing with the etiology or descriptive pathology of abnormal behavior. Articles that appear to have a significant contribution to both of these broad areas may be sent to either journal for editorial decision.

Audience   Researchers and practitioners in the discipline, faculty, libraries.

Where Indexed/ Abstracted   Academic Index; Biological Abstracts; Child Development Abstracts; Criminal Justice Abstracts; Current Contents; Index Medicus; Management Contents; PsycINFO; Social Sciences Citation Index; Social Sciences Index.

Year Established   1906.

Circulation   8,800.

Frequency   Quarterly.

Months Issued   February, May, August, November.

No. of Articles   18.

SUBMISSIONS

Address   Milton E. Strauss, Department of Psychology, Case Western Reserve University, 10900 Euclid Avenue, Cleveland, OH 44106-7123.

Number of Copies   5.

Disk Submission   Submit manuscripts on paper; disks may be requested of accepted articles.

FORMAT OF MANUSCRIPT

Cover Sheet	Refer to Instructions to Authors in each issue.
Abstract	Manuscripts must include an abstract containing a maximum of 960 characters and spaces (approximately 120 words), typed on a separate sheet.
Key Words	None.
Length	Not specified.
Margins	See style guide.
Spacing	Double-spaced.

STYLE

Name of Guide	*Publication Manual of the American Psychological Association.*
Subheadings	See style guide.
References	See style guide.
Footnotes	See style guide.
Tables or Figures	See style guide; camera-ready copy required for all art.

REVIEW PROCESS

Type	Masked review optional, by request of author.
Queries	No query letters.
Acknowledgment	Editor acknowledges submission by mail.
Review Time	Usually 60–90 days.
Revisions	Editor will notify author if revision is desired (most manuscripts are initially rejected; most published manuscripts have gone through 1 or 2 revisions).
Acceptance Rate	26%.
Return of Manuscript	Manuscripts are not usually returned.
Lag Time to Print	8 months.

CHARGES TO AUTHOR

Author Alterations	Authors are billed for alterations in proofs.

REPRINT, SUBSCRIPTION, AND CONTACT INFORMATION

Reprint Policy	Authors may purchase reprints of their articles (order form accompanies proofs).
Book Reviews	None.
Subscriptions	Subscriptions Department, American Psychological Association, 750 First Street, NE, Washington, DC 20002-4242.
	Yearly rates for nonmembers are $85 domestic, $100 foreign, $108 air mail; insitutional rates are $169 domestic, $199 foreign, $209 air mail. APA members: $42.
Affiliation	Published by the American Psychological Association.
Home Page URL	http://www.apa.org

Journal of Addictive Diseases

Previous Title	*Advances in Alcohol and Substance Abuse.*
Editorial Focus	Epidemiological and clinical studies pertaining to chemical dependency as well as well-constructed reviews of same.
Audience	All health professionals in the field of chemical dependency.
Special Themes	Special issues are published, based on editorial decision.
Where Indexed/ Abstracted	Over 30 services including Academic Abstracts; Addiction Abstracts; Current Contents; Excerpta Medica; Index Medicus/Medicine; Mental Health Abstracts; NIAAA and Alcohol Studies; Psychological Abstracts; Sage Family Studies; Sage Urban Studies; Social Work Abstracts; Sociological Abstracts; Studies on Women Abstracts.
Year Established	1980.
Circulation	5,000.
Frequency	Quarterly.
Months Issued	March, June, September, December.
No. of Articles	5–7 per issue.

SUBMISSIONS

Address	Barry Stimmer, MD, Editor, Dean, Graduate Medical Education, Mt. Sinai School of Medicine, 1 Gustave Levy Place, New York, NY 10029.
Number of Copies	3.
Disk Submission	Yes.

FORMAT OF MANUSCRIPT

Cover Sheet	Not specified.
Abstract	Yes.
Key Words	Yes.
Length	15–20 pages.
Margins	1 inch on all sides.
Spacing	Double-spaced.

STYLE

Name of Guide	*Index Medicus.*
Subheadings	Not specified.
References	See style guide.
Footnotes	None.
Tables or Figures	Type tables double-spaced. Submit camera-ready art. Place each table or figure on a separate numbered page at end of manuscript.

REVIEW PROCESS

Type	2 reviewers and the editor read all papers.
Queries	To editor.
Acknowledgment	Enclose a regular self-addressed, stamped envelope with submission.
Review Time	3 months.
Revisions	3 copies with cover letter noting changes made.
Acceptance Rate	30%.
Return of Manuscript	Not returned.
Lag Time to Print	6–12 months.

REPRINT, SUBSCRIPTION, AND CONTACT INFORMATION

Reprint Policy	Reprint order forms sent.
Book Reviews	None.
Subscriptions	The Haworth Press, Inc., 10 Alice Street, Binghamton, NY 13904-1580. Individual, $45; institutions, $120; libraries, $275.
Affiliation	The journal is sponsored by the American Society of Addiction Medicine.

Journal of Aging & Social Policy

Editorial Focus	Thought and discussion about the pressing policy issues faced by a rapidly changing and aging society.
Audience	All professionals engaged in policy and program development for the elderly.
Special Themes	Public policy, probing the history of contemporary issues, exploring the evolution of policy, and examining the literature in related policy areas to make a point relevant to the aging society and the systems that deliver programs or services.
Where Indexed/ Abstracted	Academic Abstracts/CD-ROM; ALCONLINE Database; Biology Digest; Brown University Digest of Addiction Theory and Application (DATA Newsletter); Cambridge Scientific Abstracts; Child Development Abstracts & Bibliography; CINAHL (Cumulative Index to Nursing & Allied Health Literature); CNPIEC Reference Guide: Chinese National Directory of Foreign Periodicals; Criminal Justice Abstracts; Current Contents; Educational Administration Abstracts (EAA); ERIC Clearinghouse on Counseling and Student Services (ERIC/CASS); Exceptional Child Education Resources (ECER); Family Life Educator "Abstracts Section"; Family Studies Database (online and CD-ROM); Health Source: Indexing & Abstracting of 160 selected health related journals, updated monthly; Health Source Plus; Index to Periodical Articles Related to Law; Institute for Scientific Information; International Bulletin of Bibliography on Education; INTERNET ACCESS (& additional networks) Bulletin Board for Libraries ("BUBL"), coverage of information resources on INTERNET, JANET, and other networks; Medication Use STudies (MUST) DATABASE; Mental Health Abstracts (online through DIALOG); National Criminal Justice Reference Service; NIAAA Alcohol and Alcohol Problems Science Database (ETOH); Psychological Abstracts (PsycINFO); Referativnyi Zhurnal (Abstracts Journal of the Institute of Scientific Information of the Republic of Russia); Sage Family Studies Abstracts (SFSA); Sage Urban Studies Abstracts (SUSA); Social Planning/Policy & Development Abstracts (SOPODA); Social Sciences Citation Index; Social Work Abstracts; Sociological Abstracts (SA); Special Educational Needs Abstracts; Studies on Women Abstracts; Violence and Abuse Abstracts (VAA).
Year Established	1989.
Circulation	380.
Frequency	Quarterly.
Months Issued	Not specified.
No. of Articles	6–10 per issue.

SUBMISSIONS

Address	Editors Scott A. Bass, Francis G. Caro, and Robert Morris, Gerontology Institute, 100 Morrissey Boulevard, Boston, MA 02125-3393.
Number of Copies	4.
Disk Submission	Authors of accepted manuscripts are asked to submit a disk, preferably in Microsoft Word or WordPerfect.

FORMAT OF MANUSCRIPT

Cover Sheet	Separate sheet, which does not go out for review. Full title, author names, degrees, professional titles; designation of one author as corresponding author with full address, phone numbers, e-mail address, and fax number; date of submission.
Abstract	About 100 words.
Key Words	5 or 6 key words that identify article content.
Length	20 pages, including references and abstract. Lengthier manuscripts may be considered, but only at the discretion of the editor. Sometimes, lengthier manuscripts may be considered if they can be divided into sections for publication in successive issues.
Margins	1 inch on all sides.
Spacing	Double-spaced for all copy, except title page.

STYLE

Name of Guide	*Publication Manual of the American Psychological Association.*
Subheadings	Use as needed to guide reader through the article. No more than 4 levels.
References	Author–date citation style; see style guide.
Footnotes	No footnotes preferred; incorporate into text.
Tables or Figures	Type tables double-spaced. Submit camera-ready art (300 dpi printer or better) for all figures. Place each table or figure on a separate, numbered page at the end of the manuscript.

REVIEW PROCESS

Type	"Double blind" anonymous peer review. 3 reviewers plus editor-in-chief read the manuscript in an anonymous review.
Queries	Authors are encouraged to read the journal to determine if their subject matter would be appropriate.
Acknowledgment	Enclose a regular self-addressed, stamped envelope with submission.
Review Time	3–4 months.
Revisions	See journal.
Acceptance Rate	Not specified.
Return of Manuscript	Only if 9″ x 12″ self-addressed, stamped envelope is enclosed.
Lag Time to Print	6 months–1 year.

REPRINT, SUBSCRIPTION, AND CONTACT INFORMATION

Reprint Policy	All authors receive 2 complimentary copies of the issue in which article appears. Authors receive reprint order forms to purchase additional reprinted copies.
Book Reviews	Send to journal editors.
Subscriptions	The Haworth Press, Inc., 10 Alice Street, Binghamton, NY 13904-1580. Individuals, $40; institutions, $80; libraries, $115.
E-Mail Address	norton@umbsky.cc.umb.edu

Journal of Aging Studies

Editorial Focus   Aim is to feature scholarly manuscripts offering new interpretations and challenging existing theory and empirical work. Manuscripts need not deal with the field of aging in general, but with any defensibly relevant topic pertinent to the aging experience and related to the broad concerns and subject matter of the social and behavioral sciences. The journal highlights innovation and critique—new directions in general—regardless of theoretical or methodological orientation. Theoretical, critical, and empirical submissions are welcome.

Audience   Sociologists, psychologists, social workers, political scientists, anthropologists.

Special Themes   Contact editor for details.

Where Indexed/ Abstracted   Abstracts in Social Gerontology; Current Contents; Sociological Abstracts.

Year Established   1986.

Circulation   Not specified.

Frequency   Quarterly.

Months Issued   March, June, September, December.

No. of Articles   Approximately 6.

SUBMISSIONS

Address   Jaber F. Gubrium, Editor, *Journal of Aging Studies,* Department of Sociology, University of Florida, Gainesville, FL 32611-7330.

Number of Copies   4.

Disk Submission   No.

FORMAT OF MANUSCRIPT

Cover Sheet   Not required.

Abstract   150 words maximum.

Key Words   No.

Length   No specific length.

Margins   1.5 inches on all sides.

Spacing   Double-spaced.

STYLE

Name of Guide   Contact editorial office.

Subheadings   Include as necessary.

References   Consult editorial office for reference style.

Footnotes   Not specified.

Tables or Figures   Not specified.

REVIEW PROCESS

Type	Anonymous review by 2 reviewers.
Queries	Yes.
Acknowledgment	Include self-addressed, stamped envelope or postcard when submitting manuscript.
Review Time	4–6 weeks.
Revisions	Not specified.
Acceptance Rate	Not specified.
Return of Manuscript	Not specified.
Lag Time to Print	Not specified.

REPRINT, SUBSCRIPTION, AND CONTACT INFORMATION

Reprint Policy	10 free reprints.
Book Reviews	None.
Subscriptions	JAI Press, 55 Old Post Road, No. 2, P.O. Box 1678, Greenwich, CT 06836-1678.
	Individuals, $35; institutions, $75.

Journal of Analytic Social Work

Previous Title	*Journal of Independent Social Work.*
Editorial Focus	Devoted to addressing myriad contemporary theoretical and clinical issues that confront the social worker with a psychoanalytic orientation. Articles range from detailed intensive single-case studies to scholarly discussions of theoretical psychoanalysis. Articles include clinically focused research investigations of various aspects of psychoanalytic psychotherapy or psychoanalytic developmental psychology; the application of specialized or innovative psychoanalytic techniques and methods in the treatment of various clinical problems; psychoanalytic approaches to special populations and in work with minorities and the underserved; clinical case studies; and reviews of the literature. Both essay-length and more condensed reviews of important publications in the field are also typically included.
Audience	Social work clinicians, psychoanalysts, social work educators, researchers, libraries, social work programs, and psychoanalytic institutes.
Special Themes	Topics of recent special issues include Narration and Therapeutic Action: The Construction of Meaning in Psychoanalytic Social Work, and Psychoanalytic Approaches to Children and Adolescents.
Where Indexed/ Abstracted	Abstracts in Anthropology; Applied Social Sciences Index & Abstracts; caredata CD: the social and community database; CNPIEC Reference Guide: Chinese National Directory of Foreign Periodicals; Criminal Justice Abstracts; Criminology, Penology and Police Science Abstracts; Digest of Neurology and Psychiatry; Family Studies Database; IBZ International Bibliography of Periodical Literature; Family Violence & Sexual Assault Bulletin; INNOVATIONS AND RESEARCH; International Bulletin of Bibliography on Education; INTERNET ACCESS; Mental Health Abstracts; NIAAA Alcohol and Alcohol Problems Science Database; Periodica Islamica; Referativnyi Zhurnal (Abstracts Journal of the Institute of Scientific Information of the Republic of Russia); Sage Family Studies Abstracts; Social Service Abstracts; Social Work Abstracts; Sociological Abstracts; Studies on Women Abstracts.
Year Established	1993.
Circulation	Not available.
Frequency	Quarterly.
Months Issued	Winter, spring, summer, fall.
No. of Articles	3–6 per issue.

SUBMISSIONS

Address	Jerrold R. Brandell, PhD, Editor-in-Chief, *Journal of Analytic Social Work,* Wayne State University, School of Social Work, Thompson Home, Detroit, MI 48202.
Number of Copies	3.
Disk Submission	Authors of manuscripts accepted for publication are asked to submit a disk.

FORMAT OF MANUSCRIPT

Cover Sheet Separate sheet required, which does not go out for review. Information should include: full title, author name(s), degrees, professional title(s); full address, telephone, and fax number of first author.

Abstract Brief abstract not to exceed 200 words.

Key Words None.

Length Optimal length of manuscripts is 25 double-spaced pages (12 characters per inch); however, longer manuscripts will also be considered.

Margins 1 inch on all sides.

Spacing Double-spaced for all copy, with the exception of the title page.

STYLE

Name of Guide *Publication Manual of the American Psychological Association*; a separate *Information for Authors* brochure is available from the editor upon request.

Subheadings As needed throughout article.

References Author–date citation style; see style guide.

Footnotes Material should be incorporated into text whenever possible.

Tables or Figures Type tables double-spaced. Figures should be camera-ready (300 dpi or better).

REVIEW PROCESS

Type "Double-blind" anonymous peer review.

Queries Queries should be addressed to the editor.

Acknowledgment Editor will send letter of acknowledgment upon receipt of manuscript. Authors are asked to enclose a stamped, self-addressed envelope for this purpose.

Review Time 12–16 weeks.

Revisions 3 copies should be submitted with changes clearly described in an accompanying cover letter.

Acceptance Rate Approximately 35%.

Return of Manuscript Manuscripts are not returned to the author. Authors should retain copies.

Lag Time to Print Approximately 9–12 months.

REPRINT, SUBSCRIPTION, AND CONTACT INFORMATION

Reprint Policy Authors receive complimentary copies of the issue in which their article appears. Reprint forms are also sent to authors at the time of publication.

Book Reviews In general, by invitation; however, individuals wishing to review a particular work may write the associate editor, describe the work briefly, and include a curriculum vitae. Contact Roberta A. Shechter, DSW, 141 East 55th Street, Suite 4G, New York, NY 10022.

Subscriptions The Haworth Press, Inc., 10 Alice Street, Binghamton, NY 13904-1580. 1996–97 one-year prices: individuals, $36; institutions, $48.

Journal of Applied Research in Intellectual Disabilities

Previous Title	*Mental Handicap Research.*
Editorial Focus	*Journal of Applied Research in Intellectual Disabilities* aims to draw together the findings derived from original applied research undertaken in the United Kingdom and overseas by authors from all professional disciplines, and to make these available to an international, multidisciplinary readership. Theoretical papers will also be considered provided the implications for treatment are clear and important. Contributions are welcome from authors throughout the world.
Audience	Psychiatrists, psychologists, educationalists, doctors, researchers, health care workers.
Special Themes	Proceedings of the IASSMD Conference, intellectual disabilities and the criminal justice system, challenging behavior, biobehavioral factors, sexuality.
Where Indexed/ Abstracted	British Education Index; Current Contents: Social and Behavioral Sciences; Mental Health Abstracts; PsycINFO; Research Alert; Social SciSearch; Social Work Abstracts.
Year Established	1988.
Circulation	650.
Frequency	Quarterly.
Months Issued	March, June, September, December.
No. of Articles	6–8 per issue.

SUBMISSIONS

Address	Editor, JARID/BILD Publications, Multilingual Matters, Frankfurt Lodge, Clevedon Hall, Victoria Road, Clevedon, BS21 7HJ, England; phone +44 (0)1275-876519; fax: +44 (0)1275-343096; e-mail: multi@multi.demon.co.uk
Number of Copies	4.
Disk Submission	Only when paper has been accepted for publication.

FORMAT OF MANUSCRIPT

Cover Sheet	Full title, authors' names, address, professional titles, phone and fax numbers.
Abstract	Maximum of 200 words.
Key Words	6 key words.
Length	Approximately 2,500–5,000 words.
Margins	1 inch on all sides.
Spacing	Double-spaced.

STYLE

Name of Guide	*Publication Manual of the American Psychological Association,* but please contact the office for more detailed guidelines.
Subheadings	No more than three levels.
References	See style guide.
Footnotes	No footnotes.
Tables or Figures	Type tables double-spaced; provide camera-ready copy for figures. Place tables and figures on a separate page at the end of the manuscript.

REVIEW PROCESS

Type	"Double blind" anonymous peer review, plus editors.
Queries	Write to editor.
Acknowledgment	Letter is sent on receipt of manuscript.
Review Time	3–4 months.
Revisions	Describe the changes made in a separate letter.
Acceptance Rate	Approximately 25%.
Return of Manuscript	Not returned.
Lag Time to Print	6–12 months.

REPRINT, SUBSCRIPTION, AND CONTACT INFORMATION

Reprint Policy	Authors receive 5 copies free, and can purchase additional copies.
Book Reviews	By invitation only. Send books to be reviewed to: Dr. John Harris, JARID/BILD Publications, Frankfurt Lodge, Clevedon Hall, Victoria Road, Clevedon, BS21 7HJ, England.
Subscriptions	Subscription Department, JARID/BILD Publications, Frankfurt Lodge, Clevedon Hall, Victoria Road, Clevedon, BS21 7HJ, England.
	1996 prices: individuals, $65; libraries, $145.
Affiliation	Published by the British Institute of Learning Disabilities.
E-Mail Address	multi@multi.demon.co.uk

The Journal of Applied Social Sciences

Editorial Focus	Application of the social sciences for human services.
Audience	Social workers and social scientists.
Special Themes	None.
Where Indexed/ Abstracted	Psychological Abstracts; Social Work Abstracts.
Year Established	1977.
Circulation	About 600.
Frequency	Semiannually.
Months Issued	October–November (Fall/Winter) and March–April (Spring/Summer).
No. of Articles	6–8 each issue.

SUBMISSIONS

Address	Editor, *The Journal of Applied Social Sciences,* Case Western Reserve University, Cleveland, OH 44106-7164.
Number of Copies	3 copies; authors' names on cover only.
Disk Submission	WordPerfect.

FORMAT OF MANUSCRIPT

Cover Sheet	Required, with authors' names; see style guide.
Abstract	Required.
Key Words	Required.
Length	No more than 24 pages.
Margins	See style guide.
Spacing	Double-spaced.

STYLE

Name of Guide	*Publication Manual of the American Psychological Association.*
Subheadings	Not specified.
References	Not specified.
Footnotes	Not specified.
Tables or Figures	Not specified.

REVIEW PROCESS

Type	Refereed (blind review by peers).
Queries	Not specified.
Acknowledgment	Not specified.
Review Time	3–4 months.

Revisions	If suggested by referees.
Acceptance Rate	Approximately 40%.
Return of Manuscript	Not specified.
Lag Time to Print	Approximately 1 year.

REPRINT, SUBSCRIPTION, AND CONTACT INFORMATION

Reprint Policy	Available on authors' request.
Book Reviews	Yes.
Subscriptions	Springer Publishing Company, Inc., 536 Broadway, 11th Floor, New York, NY 10012-3955.
Affiliation	Mandel School of Applied Social Sciences, Case Western Reserve University.

Journal of Autism and Developmental Disorders

Previous Title	*Journal of Autism and Childhood Schizophrenia.*
Editorial Focus	Journal is devoted to experimental studies into neurobiological issues, implications for normal development, research on diagnosis, new knowledge, and entire spectrum of interventions.
Audience	Not specified.
Special Themes	Autism and pervasive developmental disorders.
Where Indexed/ Abstracted	Acta Paedopsychiatrica; Applied Social Sciences Index & Abstracts; Beck Medical Information; Biological Abstracts; Chicorel Abstracts to Reading and Learning Disabilities; Chicorel Index to Early Childhood Education; Child and Youth Services; Child Development Abstracts and Bibliography; Current Contents; Current Index to Journals in Education; DSH Abstracts; Exceptional Child Education Resources; Excerpta Medica; Family Resources Database; Health Instrument File; Index Medicus; International Journal of Rehabilitation Research; International Review of Psychiatry; Mental Health Abstracts; Multicultural Education Abstracts; NSAC Newsletter; Psychological Abstracts; Referativnyi Zhurnal; Social Work Abstracts.
Year Established	1971.
Circulation	Approximately 4,000.
Frequency	6 times annually.
Months Issued	February, April, June, August, October, December.
No. of Articles	Approximately 100 per year.

SUBMISSIONS

Address	Eric Schopler, Editor, *Journal of Autism and Developmental Disorders,* 310 Medical School Wing E, CB# 7180 UNC–Chapel Hill, Chapel Hill, NC 27599-7180.
Number of Copies	4.
Disk Submission	Yes, same as finalized version of paper.

FORMAT OF MANUSCRIPT

Cover Sheet	Title, names of authors, affiliation.
Abstract	125 words.
Key Words	None.
Length	Average 4,000 words.
Margins	1.5 inches.
Spacing	Double-spaced.

STYLE

Name of Guide	Based on *Publication Manual of the American Psychological Association.*
Subheadings	See style guide.
References	See style guide.
Footnotes	See style guide.
Tables or Figures	See style guide.

REVIEW PROCESS

Type	Peer review, anonymous.
Queries	Welcome.
Acknowledgment	Self-addressed envelope.
Review Time	Approximately 6 months.
Revisions	Specified by reviewers and editor.
Acceptance Rate	45%.
Return of Manuscript	Include self-addressed envelope.
Lag Time to Print	6 months.

CHARGES TO AUTHOR

Author Alterations	No charge up to galleys, no charge for minor revisions.

REPRINT, SUBSCRIPTION, AND CONTACT INFORMATION

Reprint Policy	Reprints can be purchased.
Book Reviews	Contact book review editor.
Subscriptions	6 issues, $325; individual issues, $59.
Affiliation	University of North Carolina at Chapel Hill.
E-Mail Address	Eric_Schopler@UNC.edu

The Journal of Baccalaureate Social Work

Editorial Focus	Undergraduate social work education and practice.
Audience	Baccalaureate/graduate social work faculty, students and practitioners; libraries; schools of social work; and human services organizations.
Special Themes	Human diversity, innovations in BSW education and practice, values and ethics, social and economic justice.
Where Indexed/ Abstracted	Social Work Abstracts.
Year Established	1995.
Circulation	Approximately 500.
Frequency	Semiannually.
Months Issued	April and October.
No. of Articles	8–10.

SUBMISSIONS

Address	*Journal of Baccalaureate Social Work,* Social Work Program, 211 Old Main, University of Arkansas, Fayetteville, AR 72701.
Number of Copies	3.
Disk Submission	Disk must be submitted on acceptance of manuscript; prefer Microsoft Word for Macintosh, but other formats are acceptable.

FORMAT OF MANUSCRIPT

Cover Sheet	All author-identifying information. Cover sheet is removed before the manuscript is sent out for review.
Abstract	150 words.
Key Words	None.
Length	18–20 pages.
Margins	1 inch on all sides.
Spacing	Double-spaced.

STYLE

Name of Guide	*Publication Manual of the American Psychological Association; NASW Press Guidelines for Describing People.*
Subheadings	Encouraged for clarity and organization.
References	See style guide.
Footnotes	No footnotes preferred, unless very necessary.
Tables or Figures	Prefer camera-ready, but will accept clearly typed and double-spaced.

REVIEW PROCESS

Type	Anonymous peer review by 2 consulting editors. Third review or editor review when reviews are widely divergent.
Queries	Phone calls or, preferably, e-mail.
Acknowledgment	Letter acknowledging receipt sent to first author.
Review Time	3–4 months.
Revisions	Depends on original reviewer recommendations. *Accept, Accept with Minor Revisions:* Revisions made and paper and disk copy of revised manuscript submitted with list of changes made in response to reviewers. *Reject, Revise, Resubmit:* Resubmit for complete new review by new reviewers (this policy is currently being reviewed for possible change to re-review by original reviewers. *Reject, Assign Consultant:* Editorial office assists author in finding a consultant to assist in revisions. Re-review process same as for reject, revise, and resubmit. *Reject:* Not appropriate for *JBSW.*
Acceptance Rate	20%–25%.
Return of Manuscript	Not returned.
Lag Time to Print	6 months.

REPRINT, SUBSCRIPTION, AND CONTACT INFORMATION

Reprint Policy	All authors receive 2 complimentary copies of the issue in which the article appears.
Book Reviews	Send book reviews to Murali Nair, *JBSW* Book Review Editor, Cleveland State University, Department of Social Work, 1983 E. 24th Street, Cleveland, OH 44115.
Subscriptions	Free with all categories of BPD membership. Contact Jerry Finn, BPD Treasurer, Arizona State University West, P.O. Box 37100, Phoenix, AZ 85069-7100.
Affiliation	National Association of Baccalaureate Social Work Program Directors. Also supported by National Phi Alpha Social Work Honor Society and the J. William Fulbright College of Arts and Science, University of Arkansas, Fayetteville.
E-Mail Address	jschrive@comp.uark.edu
Home Page URL	http://www.uark.edu/~social/jbsw/jbsw.html http://www.rit.edu/~694www/jbswad.html

Journal of Black Studies

Editorial Focus	Research, review, and theoretical articles on issues in the African world; a full analytical discussion of issues related to people of African descent; manuscripts on a wide range of social sciences issues are invited.
Audience	Not specified.
Special Themes	Several thematic issues each year.
Where Indexed/ Abstracted	ABC Pol Sci; Abstracts of English Studies; Adolescent Mental Health Abstracts; Automatic Subject Citation Alert; Current Contents; Current Index to Journals in Education (CIJE); Historical Abstracts; Human Resources Abstracts; Index to Periodical Articles By and About Blacks; International Political Science Abstracts; PAIS Bulletin; Political Science Abstract; Sage Urban Studies Abstracts; Social Planning/Policy & Development Abstracts; Social Sciences Citation Index; Social Sciences Index; Social Work Abstracts; Sociological Abstracts; United States Political Science Documents; Urban Affairs Abstracts.
Year Established	Not specified.
Circulation	Approximately 2,200.
Frequency	Six times a year.
Months Issued	Not specified.
No. of Articles	6–8.

SUBMISSIONS

Address	Molefi Kete Asante, Editor (since 1969), Terry Kershaw, Co-editor, Department of African American Studies, Temple University, Philadelphia, PA 19122.
Number of Copies	2.
Disk Submission	Yes.

FORMAT OF MANUSCRIPT

Cover Sheet	Title of manuscript; author's name and affiliation; number of pages; brief bibliographic paragraph describing each author's current affiliation, research interests, and recent publications.
Abstract	Not specified.
Key Words	Not specified.
Length	16–25 pages.
Margins	1.5 inches on all sides.
Spacing	Double-spaced.

STYLE

Name of Guide — *Publication Manual of the American Psychological Association;* style sheets available on request.

Subheadings — Include.

References — See style guide.

Footnotes — Avoid using footnotes.

Tables or Figures — Submit camera-ready.

REVIEW PROCESS

Type — Anonymous review by 2 reviewers minimum, occasionally 3.

Queries — Not specified.

Acknowledgment — Include self-addressed, stamped postcard when submitting manuscript.

Review Time — 2–3 months.

Revisions — Not specified.

Acceptance Rate — 20%–25%.

Return of Manuscript — Include self-addressed, stamped envelope when submitting manuscript.

Lag Time to Print — 12–18 months.

REPRINT, SUBSCRIPTION, AND CONTACT INFORMATION

Reprint Policy — Not specified.

Book Reviews — Review essays and bibliographic articles and compilations are sought; contact editor. Send books for review and annotation to: Molefi Kete Asante, Editor, Department of African American Studies, Temple University, Philadelphia, PA 19122.

Subscriptions — Sage Publications, 2111 W. Hillcrest Drive, Newbury Park, CA 91320.

Individuals, $42; institutions, $112.

Journal of Chemical Dependency Treatment

Editorial Focus   Not specified.

Audience   Not specified.

Where Indexed/ Abstracted   Academic Abstracts/CD-ROM; ALCONLINE Database; Brown University Digest of Addiction Theory and Application (DATA Newsletter); Cambridge Scientific Abstracts; CNPIEC Reference Guide: Chinese National Directory of Foreign Periodicals; Criminal Justice Abstracts; Family Studies Database (online and CD-ROM); Health Source; Health Source Plus; Index to Periodical Articles Related to Law; INTERNET ACCESS (& additional networks) Bulletin Board for Libraries ("BUBL"), coverage of information resources on INTERNET, JANET, and other networks; Medication Use STudies (MUST) DATABASE; Mental Health Abstracts (online through DIALOG); NIAAA Alcohol and Alcohol Problems Science Database (ETOH); Referativnyi Zhurnal (Abstracts Journal of the Institute of Scientific Information of the Republic of Russia); Social Work Abstracts; Special Educational Needs Abstracts; Violence and Abuse Abstracts: A Review of Current Literature on Interpersonal Violence (VAA).

Year Established   1987.

Circulation   444.

Frequency   Semiannually.

Months Issued   Not specified.

No. of Articles   6–10 per issue.

SUBMISSIONS

Address   The journal does not accept unsolicited manuscripts; guest-edited only.

Number of Copies   4.

Disk Submission   Authors of accepted manuscripts are asked to submit a disk, preferably in Microsoft Word or WordPerfect.

FORMAT OF MANUSCRIPT

Cover Sheet   Separate sheet, which does not go out for review. Full title, author names, degrees, professional titles; designation of one author as corresponding author with full address, phone numbers, e-mail address, and fax number; date of submission.

Abstract   About 100 words.

Key Words   Not specified.

Length   10–20 pages, including references and abstract. Lengthier manuscripts may be considered, but only at the discretion of the editor. Sometimes, lengthier manuscripts may be considered if they can be divided into sections for publication in successive issues.

Margins   1 inch on all sides.

Spacing   Double-spaced for all copy, except title page.

STYLE

Name of Guide	Not specified.
Subheadings	Use as needed to guide reader through the article. No more than four levels.
References	Author–date citation style; see style guide.
Footnotes	No footnotes preferred; incorporate into text.
Tables or Figures	Type tables double-spaced. Submit camera-ready art (300 dpi printer or better) for all figures. Place each table or figure on a separate, numbered page at the end of the manuscript.

REVIEW PROCESS

Type	"Double blind" anonymous peer review. 3 reviewers plus editor-in-chief read the manuscript in an anonymous review.
Queries	Authors are encouraged to read the journal to determine if their subject matter would be appropriate.
Acknowledgment	Enclose a regular self-addressed, stamped envelope with submission.
Review Time	3–4 months.
Revisions	See journal.
Acceptance Rate	Not specified.
Return of Manuscript	Only if 9″ x 12″ self-addressed, stamped envelope is enclosed.
Lag Time to Print	6 months–1 year.

REPRINT, SUBSCRIPTION, AND CONTACT INFORMATION

Reprint Policy	All authors receive 2 complimentary copies of the issue in which article appears. Authors receive reprint order forms to purchase additional reprinted copies.
Book Reviews	Not specified.
Subscriptions	The Haworth Press, Inc., 10 Alice Street, Binghamton, NY 13904-1580. Individuals, $36; institutions, $90; libraries, $125.

Journal of Child and Adolescent Group Therapy

Editorial Focus Application of theoretical concepts in child and adolescent group therapy; reports on clinical methods and results; innovation on group methods and treatment; manuscripts on techniques, theoretical concepts and research information; brief observation and book review, comments to the editor.

Audience Not specified.

Special Themes Special issues considered by invitation or need and interest.

Where Indexed/ Abstracted Not specified.

Year Established 1990.

Circulation Not specified.

Frequency Quarterly.

Months Issued March, June, September, December.

No. of Articles 3–6.

SUBMISSIONS

Address *Journal of Child and Adolescent Group Therapy,* Edward S. Soo, Editor, P.O. Box 427, Tenafly, NJ 07670.

Number of Copies 3, plus original.

Disk Submission No.

FORMAT OF MANUSCRIPT

Cover Sheet Title page: title of manuscript; author's name (with degree); author's affiliation; suggested running head; complete mailing address and phone number of the one author designated to review proofs. Affiliation: department; institution (usually university or company); city and state (or nation) typed as a numbered footnote to the author's name. Running head: Fewer than 80 characters (including spaces), comprising the title or an abbreviated version thereof.

Abstract 100–150 words maximum.

Key Words 3–5 key words listed directly below the abstract.

Length Approximately 20 pages.

Margins Wide.

Spacing Double-spaced.

STYLE

Name of Guide *Publication Manual of the American Psychological Association*; "Instructions to Contributors" available from editor.

Subheadings Use as needed.

References	See style guide.
Footnotes	Avoid using footnotes. When use is absolutely necessary, number footnotes consecutively, using Arabic numerals, and type at the bottom of the same page as the callout. Place a line above the footnote, so that it is set off from the text. Use the appropriate superscript numeral for citation in text.
Tables or Figures	Number illustrations (photographs, drawings, diagrams, and charts) consecutively, using Arabic numerals. Type legends for illustrations on a separate sheet. Photographs should be large, glossy prints, showing high contrast. Prepare drawings using black India ink. Either the original drawings or good-quality photographic prints are acceptable. Identify figures on the back with author's name and number of the illustration. Number tables and refer to each by number in text. Type each table on a separate sheet. Center the title above the table, and type explanatory footnotes (indicated by superscript letters) below the table.

REVIEW PROCESS

Type	Anonymous review by 2 reviewers minimum.
Queries	Editor welcomes and accepts queries.
Acknowledgment	Editor sends postcard on manuscript receipt.
Review Time	Within weeks.
Revisions	Criticisms and comments.
Acceptance Rate	Not specified.
Return of Manuscript	Include self-addressed, stamped envelope when submitting manuscript.
Lag Time to Print	About 4 months.

CHARGES TO AUTHOR

Author Alterations	Authors will be charged for alterations if the cost of typesetting is increased by more than 10%.

REPRINT, SUBSCRIPTION, AND CONTACT INFORMATION

Reprint Policy	Order forms with the current price schedule are sent with proofs.
Book Reviews	Send reviews to: B. W. MacLennan, PhD, 6307 Crathie Lane, Bethesda, MD 20816.
Subscriptions	Human Sciences Press, 233 Spring Street, New York, NY 10013-1578.
	$42/individual (within U.S.), $145 institution (within U.S.), $49/individual (outside of U.S.), $170 institution (outside of U.S.).
E-Mail Address	plenum@panix.com
Home Page URL	http://www.plenum.com (via gopher)

Journal of Child & Adolescent Substance Abuse

Previous Title	*Journal of Adolescent Chemical Dependency.*
Editorial Focus	The practice and treatment orientation of child and adolescent substance abuse.
Audience	All professionals who work with children and adolescents on a daily basis, chemical dependency clinicians, and prevention/treatment specialists.
Special Themes	Surveys of clinical strategies, treatment modalities, and specific applications.
Where Indexed/ Abstracted	Academic Abstracts/CD-ROM; ALCONLINE Database; Biology Digest; Brown University Digest of Addiction Theory and Application (DATA Newsletter); Cambridge Scientific Abstracts; Child Development Abstracts & Bibliography; CINAHL (Cumulative Index to Nursing & Allied Health Literature); CNPIEC Reference Guide: Chinese National Directory of Foreign Periodicals; Criminal Justice Abstracts; Current Contents; Educational Administration Abstracts (EAA); ERIC Clearinghouse on Counseling and Student Services (ERIC/CASS); Exceptional Child Education Resources (ECER); Family Life Educator "Abstracts Section"; Family Studies Database; Health Source; Health Source Plus; Index to Periodical Articles Related to Law; Institute for Scientific Information; International Bulletin of Bibliography on Education; INTERNET ACCESS (& additional networks) Bulletin Board for Libraries ("BUBL"), coverage of information resources on INTERNET, JANET, and other networks; Medication Use STudies (MUST) DATABASE; Mental Health Abstracts; National Criminal Justice Reference Service; NIAAA Alcohol and Alcohol Problems Science Database (ETOH); Psychological Abstracts (PsycINFO); Referativnyi Zhurnal (Abstracts Journal of the Institute of Scientific Information of the Republic of Russia); Sage Family Studies Abstracts (SFSA); Sage Urban Studies Abstracts (SUSA); Social Planning Policy & Development Abstracts (SOPODA); Social Sciences Citation Index; Social Work Abstracts; Sociological Abstracts (SA); Special Educational Needs Abstracts; Studies on Women Abstracts; Violence and Abuse Abstracts: A Review of Current Literature on Interpersonal Violence (VAA).
Year Established	1990.
Circulation	287.
Frequency	Quarterly.
Months Issued	Not specified.
No. of Articles	6–10 per issue.

SUBMISSIONS

Address	Frank De Piano and Vincent B. Van Hasselt, Center for Psychological Studies, Nova, Southeastern University, 3301 College Avenue, Ft. Lauderdale, FL 33314.
Number of Copies	4.
Disk Submission	Authors of accepted manuscripts are asked to submit a disk, preferably in Microsoft Word or WordPerfect.

FORMAT OF MANUSCRIPT

Cover Sheet	Separate sheet, which does not go out for review. Full title, author names, degrees, professional titles; designation of one author as corresponding author with full address, phone numbers, e-mail address, and fax number; date of submission.
Abstract	About 100 words.
Key Words	5 or 6 key words that identify article content.
Length	20–25 pages, including references and abstract. Lengthier manuscripts may be considered, but only at the discretion of the editor. Sometimes, lengthier manuscripts may be considered if they can be divided up into sections for publication in successive issues.
Margins	1 inch on all sides.
Spacing	Double-spaced for all copy, except title page.

STYLE

Name of Guide	*Publication Manual of the American Psychological Association.*
Subheadings	Use as needed to guide reader through the article. No more than 4 levels.
References	Author–date citation style; see style guide.
Footnotes	No footnotes preferred; incorporate into text.
Tables or Figures	Type tables double-spaced. Submit camera-ready art (300 dpi printer or better) for all figures. Place each table or figure on a separate, numbered page at the end of the manuscript.

REVIEW PROCESS

Type	"Double blind" anonymous peer review. 3 reviewers plus editor-in-chief read the manuscript in an anonymous review.
Queries	Authors are encouraged to read the journal to determine if their subject matter would be appropriate.
Acknowledgment	Enclose a regular self-addressed, stamped envelope with submission.
Review Time	3–4 months.
Revisions	See journal.
Acceptance Rate	Not specified.
Return of Manuscript	Only if 9″ x 12″ self-addressed, stamped envelope is enclosed.
Lag Time to Print	6 months–1 year.

REPRINT, SUBSCRIPTION, AND CONTACT INFORMATION

Reprint Policy	All authors receive 2 complimentary copies of the issue in which article appears. Authors receive reprint order forms to purchase additional reprinted copies.
Book Reviews	Send to journal co-editors.
Subscriptions	The Haworth Press, Inc., 10 Alice Street, Binghamton, NY 13904-1580. Individuals, $36; institutions, $75; libraries, $105.

Journal of Child Psychology and Psychiatry & Allied Disciplines

Editorial Focus	The enhancement of theory, research, and clinical practice in child and adolescent psychology and psychiatry.
Audience	Child psychologists, child psychiatrists, psychotherapists, social workers, pediatricians, and other professionals working in related fields.
Special Themes	None.
Where Indexed/ Abstracted	Applied Social Sciences Index & Abstracts; Automatic Subject Citation Alert; Biosis Data; BRS Data; Chi Abstracts; Current Contents: Social and Behavioral Sciences; ERIC/CIJE; Excerpta Medica; Index Medicus; MEDLINE; PASCAL-CNRS Data; PsycINFO; Psychological Abstracts; Psycscan DP; Social Sciences Citation Index; Social Work Abstracts.
Year Established	1960.
Circulation	5,000.
Frequency	8 times per year.
Months Issued	January, February, March, May, July, September, October, November.
No. of Articles	5–15.

SUBMISSIONS

Address	Journal Secretary, ACPP, St. Saviour's House, 39-41 Union Street, London SE1 SD, England.
Number of Copies	4.
Disk Submission	Disk requested for final accepted manuscript.

FORMAT OF MANUSCRIPT

Cover Sheet	Title, authors' names and affiliations, address of corresponding author.
Abstract	Maximum 300 words.
Key Words	Yes, 4–6 key words.
Length	No limit, but Research Notes would not be expected to exceed 3,000 words.
Margins	Minimum 1 inch on all sides.
Spacing	Double-spaced.

STYLE

Name of Guide	See Notes for Contributors. The journal follows the style of the *Publication Manual of the American Psychological Association*.
Subheadings	Not specified.
References	Not specified.
Footnotes	Not specified.
Tables or Figures	Should be clearly drawn on separate page, with legends for figures and headings for tables on separate sheets, clearly labeled.

REVIEW PROCESS

Type　Anonymous peer review by at least 2 referees. Processing editor reads manuscript. "Blind" review available if requested by author.

Queries　Authors should read the Notes for Contributors carefully to determine if their subject matter is appropriate, but if still in doubt, editors will advise.

Acknowledgment　By letter to corresponding author.

Review Time　4–5 months.

Revisions　Three copies of revisions are required, accompanied by letter from author identifying how he or she has addressed the comments of the referees and editor. Revisions are not always re-reviewed by referees; this depends on the nature and extent of revisions requested. Revisions are always read by editors.

Acceptance Rate　20%–25%.

Return of Manuscript　Rejected manuscripts not returned unless specifically requested by author at time of submission.

Lag Time to Print　6–10 months.

CHARGES TO AUTHOR

Author Alterations　No charges unless alterations are extensive.

REPRINT, SUBSCRIPTION, AND CONTACT INFORMATION

Reprint Policy　First author receives 50 free reprints automatically, and an order form is sent with proofs, on which extra reprints (at author's expense) can be ordered.

Book Reviews　By invitation only. Published in all issues except No.1 (Annual Research Review). Books for review should be sent to: The Book Review Editors (Professor Lionel Hersov), *Journal of Child Psychology & Psychiatry*, ACPP, St. Saviour's House, 39-41 Union Street, London SE1 1SD, England.

Subscriptions　Cambridge University Press, Journals Division, The Edinburgh Building, Shaftesbury Road, Cambridge CB2 2RU, England; phone: +44(0)1223 312393; fax +44 (0)1223 315052.; e-mail: information@cup.cam.ac.uk; journals_subscriptions@cup.cam.ac.uk

For subscribers based in United States, Canada, and Mexico: Cambridge University Press, 40 West 20th Street, New York, NY 10001-4211; phone: +1-914-937-9600, x154; fax: +1-914-937-4712. Orders may be phoned direct (toll-free) at 800-431-1580.

CUP has offices in Australia and New Zealand, Japan, and India.

Affiliation　The *Journal of Child Psychology & Psychiatry* is the official organ of the Association for Child Psychology & Psychiatry, which is affiliated with the International Association for Child & Adolescent Psychiatry & Allied Professions.

E-Mail Address　sgjt400@sghms.ac.uk

Home Page URL　Cambridge: http://www.cup.cam.ack.uk/; New York: http://www.cup.org/ gopher://gopher.cup.cam.ac.uk

Journal of Child Sexual Abuse

Editorial Focus	Research, treatment, prevention programs; legal and criminal justice issues concerning child, adolescent, and adult victims, survivors, and perpetrators of child sexual abuse.
Audience	Interdisciplinary professionals involved in any aspect of working with child sexual abuse issues, victims, or offenders.
Special Themes	Varies.
Where Indexed/ Abstracted	Social work, psychological, sociology, family studies, nursing, legal, and other abstracting sources.
Year Established	1990.
Circulation	1,800.
Frequency	Quarterly.
Months Issued	Generally, March, June, September, and December.
No. of Articles	6–9.

SUBMISSIONS

Address	*Journal of Child Sexual Abuse,* c/o FVSAI, 1121 E SE Loop 323, Suite 130, Tyler, TX 75701.
Number of Copies	5 (1 original with identifying names, etc., and 4 copies without this information).
Disk Submission	Requested on acceptance.

FORMAT OF MANUSCRIPT

Cover Sheet	Title; authors; brief biography of authors including degrees, positions, affiliations, and 1-sentence background; address for reprint requests.
Abstract	Required, 100 words.
Key Words	Optional, 5–10 key words.
Length	20–30 pages including references, abstract, and tables.
Margins	1 inch on all sides.
Spacing	Double-spaced.

STYLE

Name of Guide	*Publication Manual of the American Psychological Association*; instructions for authors available from Family Violence & Sexual Assault Institute.
Subheadings	See style guide.
References	See style guide.
Footnotes	Not suggested unless absolutely needed; see style guide.
Tables or Figures	See style guide. All figures must be camera-ready; the journal can prepare them, but for a fee.

REVIEW PROCESS

Type	Anonymous review by editorial board or ad hoc reviewers.
Queries	Editor welcomes query letters or phone calls.
Acknowledgment	On receipt of manuscript, letter and copyright form sent for all authors to sign in original; must include letter-size self-addressed, stamped envelope and also an envelope for return of the manuscript with feedback.
Review Time	3–5 months.
Revisions	Feedback is given to authors for making revisions, and the number of copies to be sent back is provided. *JCSA* encourages revisions and resubmissions, with a cover letter by the author explaining what has been done to address the concerns.
Acceptance Rate	20% on initial submission, 60% on resubmission (sometimes 2–3 revisions are needed before publishing).
Return of Manuscript	Returned with comments and a letter; self-addressed, stamped envelope needed.
Lag Time to Print	8–11 months.

REPRINT, SUBSCRIPTION, AND CONTACT INFORMATION

Reprint Policy	10 reprints are free, and author can purchase more while issue is in press; publisher sends a form to authors at that time.
Book Reviews	None at present. The Family Violence & Sexual Assault Institute does accept books and book reviews for publication in *Family Violence & Sexual Assault Bulletin.*
Subscriptions	Order through The Haworth Press, Inc., 10 Alice Street, Binghamton, NY 13904-1580.
	Individuals, $34; agencies/institutions, $48; libraries, $85. Individuals and institutions can get discounts of 10% for 1-year subscription, 20% for 2-year subscription, and 30% for 3-year subscription.
Affiliation	Family Violence & Sexual Assault Institute.
E-Mail Address	FVSAI@e-tex.com

Journal of College Student Psychotherapy

Editorial Focus	Not specified.
Audience	Not specified.
Where Indexed/ Abstracted	Applied Social Sciences Index & Abstracts; CNPIEC Reference Guide: Chinese National Directory of Foreign Periodicals; Contents Pages in Education; Educational Administration Abstracts (EAA); Family Studies Database (online and CD–ROM); Higher Education Abstracts; International Bulletin of Bibliography on Education; INTERNET ACCESS (& additional networks) Bulletin Board for Libraries ("BUBL"), coverage of information resources on INTERNET, JANET, and other networks; Mental Health Abstracts (on line through DIALOG); Psychological Abstracts (PsycINFO); Social Planning/Policy & Development Abstracts (SOPODA); Social Work Abstracts; Sociological Abstracts (SA); Special Educational Needs Abstracts.
Year Established	1986.
Circulation	342.
Frequency	Quarterly.
Months Issued	Not specified.
No. of Articles	6–10 per issue.

SUBMISSIONS

Address	Editor, Leighton C. Whitaker, PhD, 220 Turner Road, Wallingford, PA 19086.
Number of Copies	4.
Disk Submission	Authors of accepted manuscripts are asked to submit a disk, preferably in Microsoft Word or WordPerfect.

FORMAT OF MANUSCRIPT

Cover Sheet	Separate sheet, which does not go out for review. Full title, author names, degrees, professional titles; designation of one author as corresponding author with full address, phone numbers, e-mail address, and fax number; date of submission.
Abstract	About 100 words.
Key Words	5 or 6 words that identify article content.
Length	5–20 pages, including references and abstract. Lengthier manuscripts may be considered, but only at the discretion of the editor. Sometimes, lengthier manuscripts may be considered if they can be divided up into sections for publication in successive issues.
Margins	1 inch on all sides.
Spacing	Double-spaced for all copy, except title page.

STYLE

Name of Guide	*Publication Manual of the American Psychological Association.*
Subheadings	Use as needed to guide reader through the article. No more than 4 levels.
References	Author–date citation style; see style guide.
Footnotes	No footnotes preferred; incorporate into text.
Tables or Figures	Type tables double-spaced. Submit camera-ready art (300 dpi printer or better) for all figures. Place each table or figure on a separate, numbered page at the end of the manuscript.

REVIEW PROCESS

Type	"Double blind" anonymous peer review. 3 reviewers plus editor-in-chief read the manuscript in an anonymous review.
Queries	Authors are encouraged to read the journal to determine if their subject matter would be appropriate.
Acknowledgment	Enclose a regular self-addressed, stamped envelope with submission.
Review Time	3–4 months.
Revisions	See journal.
Acceptance Rate	Not specified.
Return of Manuscript	Only if 9″ x 12″ self-addressed, stamped envelope is enclosed.
Lag Time to Print	6 months–1 year.

REPRINT, SUBSCRIPTION, AND CONTACT INFORMATION

Reprint Policy	All authors receive 2 complimentary copies of the issue in which article appears. Authors receive reprint order forms to purchase additional reprinted copies.
Book Reviews	Send to journal editor.
Subscriptions	The Haworth Press, Inc., 10 Alice Street, Binghamton, NY 13904-1580. Individuals, $40; institutions, $75; libraries, $225.

Journal of Community Practice

Editorial Focus	To provide a forum for development of research, theory, practice, and curriculum strategies for the full range of work with community groups, grassroots organizing, and interorganizational and interagency planning, collaboration, and coalition building.
Audience	Public administrations, managers.
Special Themes	Social work, city and regional planning, social and economic development, community organizing, social planning and policy analysis, urban and rural sociology, public administration, and nonprofit management.
Where Indexed/ Abstracted	Alternative Press Index; Applied Social Sciences Index & Abstracts (Online: ASSI via Data-Star) (CD-ROM: ASSIA Plus); caredata CD: the social and commune care database; CINAHL (Cumulative Index to Nursing & Allied Health Literature); CNPIEC Reference Guide: Chinese National Directory of Foreign Periodicals; CPcurrents; Economic Literature Index; Family Studies Database (online and CD-ROM); Family Violence & Sexual Assault Bulletin; Guide to Social Science & Religion in Periodical Literature; Human Resources Abstracts (HRA); IBZ International Bibliography of Periodical Literature; Index to Periodical Articles Related to Law; International Political Science Abstracts; INTERNET ACCESS (& additional networks) Bulletin Board for Libraries ("BUBL"), coverage of information resources on INTERNET, JANET, and other networks; National Library Database on Homelessness; Operations Research/Management Science; Public Affairs Information Bulletin (PAIS); Rural Development Abstracts; Sage Family Studies Abstracts (SFSA); Social Work Abstracts; Sociological Abstracts (SA); Transportation Research Abstracts; Urban Affairs Abstracts.
Year Established	1994.
Circulation	569.
Frequency	Quarterly.
Months Issued	Not specified.
No. of Articles	6–10 per issue.

SUBMISSIONS

Address	Editor, Dr. Marie Weil, Professor, School of Social Work, CB#3550, University of North Carolina, Chapel Hill, Chapel Hill, NC 27599-3550.
Number of Copies	4.
Disk Submission	Authors of accepted manuscripts are asked to submit a disk, preferably in Microsoft Word or WordPerfect.

FORMAT OF MANUSCRIPT

Cover Sheet	Separate sheet, which does not go out for review. Full title, author names, degrees, professional titles; designation of one author as corresponding author with full address, phone numbers, e-mail address, and fax number; date of submission.

Abstract	About 100 words.
Key Words	5 or 6 key words that identify article content.
Length	15–18 pages, including references and abstract. Lengthier manuscripts may be considered, but only at the discretion of the editor. Sometimes, lengthier manuscripts may be considered if they can be divided up into sections for publication in successive issues.
Margins	1 inch on all sides.
Spacing	Double-spaced for all copy, except title page.

STYLE

Name of Guide	*Publication Manual of the American Psychological Association.*
Subheadings	Use as needed to guide reader through the article. No more than 4 levels.
References	Author–date citation style; see style guide.
Footnotes	No footnotes preferred; incorporate into text.
Tables or Figures	Type tables double-spaced. Submit camera-ready art (300 dpi printer or better) for all figures. Place each table or figure on a separate, numbered page at the end of the manuscript.

REVIEW PROCESS

Type	"Double blind" anonymous peer review. 3 reviewers plus editor-in-chief read the manuscript in an anonymous review.
Queries	Authors are encouraged to read the journal to determine if their subject matter would be appropriate.
Acknowledgment	Enclose a regular self-addressed, stamped envelope with submission.
Review Time	3–4 months.
Revisions	See journal.
Acceptance Rate	Not specified.
Return of Manuscript	Only if 9″ x 12″ self-addressed, stamped envelope is enclosed.
Lag Time to Print	6 months–1 year.

REPRINT, SUBSCRIPTION, AND CONTACT INFORMATION

Reprint Policy	All authors receive 2 complimentary copies of the issue in which article appears. Authors receive reprint order forms to purchase additional reprinted copies.
Book Reviews	Send to journal editor.
Subscriptions	The Haworth Press, Inc., 10 Alice Street, Binghamton, NY 13904-1580.
	Individuals, $36; institutions, $48; libraries, $75. ACOSA members receive reduced rates.
Affiliation	Association for Community Organization and Social Administration (ACOSA).
E-Mail Address	jcomm@email.unc.edu

Journal of Consulting and Clinical Psychology

Previous Title	*Journal of Consulting Psychology.*
Editorial Focus	The *Journal of Consulting and Clinical Psychology* publishes original contributions on the following topics: (a) the development, validity, and use of techniques of diagnosis and treatment in disordered behavior; (b) studies of populations of clinical interest, such as hospitals, prison, rehabilitation, geriatric, and similar samples; (c) cross-cultural and demographic studies of interest for the behavior disorders; (d) studies of personality and of its assessment and development where these have a clear bearing on problems of clinical dysfunction; (e) studies of gender, ethnicity, or sexual orientation that have a clear bearing on diagnosis, assessment, and treatment; or (f) case studies pertinent to the preceding topics. The *Journal of Consulting and Clinical Psychology* considers manuscripts dealing with the diagnosis or treatment of abnormal behavior but does not consider manuscripts dealing with the etiology or descriptive pathology of abnormal behavior, which are more appropriate to the *Journal of Abnormal Psychology.* Articles that appear to have a significant contribution to both of these broad areas may be sent to either journal for editorial decision. Papers of a theoretical nature will occasionally be considered within the space limitations of the journal.
Audience	Researchers in the discipline, faculty, libraries.
Where Indexed/ Abstracted	Applied Social Sciences Index & Abstracts; Current Contents; PsycINFO.
Year Established	1937.
Circulation	11,700.
Frequency	Bimonthly.
Months Issued	February, April, June, August, October, December.
No. of Articles	22.

SUBMISSIONS

Address	Philip C. Kendall, *Journal of Consulting and Clinical Psychology,* Department of Psychology, Weiss Hall, Temple University, Philadelphia, PA 19122.
Number of Copies	4.
Disk Submission	Submit manuscripts on paper; disks may be requested of accepted articles.

FORMAT OF MANUSCRIPT

Cover Sheet	Refer to Instructions to Authors in each issue.
Abstract	Manuscripts of regular articles must include an abstract containing a maximum of 960 characters and spaces (approximately 120 words); manuscripts of Brief Reports must include an abstract of 75–100 words.
Key Words	None.
Length	Not specified.

Margins	See style guide.
Spacing	Double-spaced.

STYLE

Name of Guide	*Publication Manual of the American Psychological Association.*
Subheadings	See style guide.
References	See style guide.
Footnotes	See style guide.
Tables or Figures	See style guide; camera-ready copy required for all art.

REVIEW PROCESS

Type	Masked review optional.
Queries	No query letters.
Acknowledgment	Editor acknowledges submission by mail.
Review Time	Usually 60–90 days.
Revisions	Editor will notify author if revision is desired (most manuscripts are initially rejected; most published manuscripts have gone through one or two revisions).
Acceptance Rate	29%.
Return of Manuscript	Manuscripts are not usually returned.
Lag Time to Print	9 months.

CHARGES TO AUTHOR

Author Alterations	Authors are billed for alterations in proofs.

REPRINT, SUBSCRIPTION, AND CONTACT INFORMATION

Reprint Policy	Authors may purchase reprints of their articles (order form accompanies proofs).
Book Reviews	None.
Subscriptions	Subscriptions Department, American Psychological Association, 750 First Street, NE, Washington, DC 20002-4242.
	Yearly rates for nonmembers are $154 domestic, $174 foreign, $187 air mail; institutional rates are $299 domestic, $342 foreign, $354 air mail. APA members: $77.
Affiliation	Published by the American Psychological Association.
Home Page URL	http://www.apa.org

Journal of Continuing Social Work Education

Editorial Focus	Articles on continuing education, staff development, research and evaluation of programs; "Regional Report," "News and Views," book reviews.
Audience	Social work faculty, practitioners, librarians, and research institutions.
Where Indexed/ Abstracted	Social Work Abstracts.
Year Established	1981.
Circulation	300.
Frequency	Semiannually.
Months Issued	Not specified.
No. of Articles	4–8.

SUBMISSIONS

Address	Seymour J. Rosenthal, Editor, or Betty F. Hampton, Assistant to the Editor, *Journal of Continuing Social Work Education*, Temple University, Center for Social Policy and Community Development, 1601 N. Broad Street, Room 100, Philadelphia, PA 19122-6099.
Number of Copies	4.
Disk Submission	If disk is submitted, documents should be in ASCII files.

FORMAT OF MANUSCRIPT

Cover Sheet	Title, authors, affiliations, mailing address, phone number.
Abstract	75–100 words.
Key Words	None.
Length	6–15 pages.
Margins	1 inch on all sides.
Spacing	Double-spaced.

STYLE

Name of Guide	*Chicago Manual of Style.*
Subheadings	No policy.
References	See style guide.
Footnotes	Submit as endnotes.
Tables or Figures	Submit on separate sheets.

REVIEW PROCESS

Type	Anonymous review by 3 reviewers.
Queries	Communicate with editor.

Acknowledgment	Letter sent on manuscript receipt.
Review Time	6–9 months.
Revisions	Revisions requested by reviewers are outlined in letter to authors.
Acceptance Rate	50%.
Return of Manuscript	Not returned.
Lag Time to Print	12–18 months.

REPRINT, SUBSCRIPTION, AND CONTACT INFORMATION

Reprint Policy	Reprints may be ordered at $1 per copy.
Book Reviews	Send unsolicited reviews to Betty F. Hampton, Assistant to the Editor, *Journal of Continuing Social Work Education,* Temple University, Center for Social Policy and Community Development, 1601 N. Broad Street, Room 100, Philadelphia, PA 19122-6099.
Subscriptions	Betty F. Hampton, Assistant to the Editor.
Affiliation	Center for Social Policy and Community Development, School of Social Administration.
E-Mail Address	srosenth@vm.temple.edu

Journal of Counseling Psychology

Editorial Focus	The *Journal of Counseling Psychology* publishes articles on counseling of interest to psychologists and counselors in schools, colleges, universities, private and public counseling agencies, and business, religious, and military settings. The journal gives particular attention to articles reporting the results of empirical studies about counseling processes and interventions, theoretical articles about counseling, and studies dealing with the evaluation of applications of counseling and counseling programs. The journal also considers studies on the selection and training of counselors, the development of counseling materials and methods, and applications of counseling to specific populations and problem areas. Also published occasionally are topical reviews of research and other systematic surveys, as well as research methodology studies directly related to counseling.
Audience	Researchers in the discipline, faculty, libraries.
Where Indexed/ Abstracted	Biological Abstracts; Child Development Abstracts; Current Contents; Current Index to Journals in Education; Ergonomics Abstracts; Index Medicus; Management Contents; PsycINFO; Social Sciences Citation Index; Social Sciences Index.
Year Established	1954.
Circulation	9,900.
Frequency	Quarterly.
Months Issued	January, April, July, October.
No. of Articles	16.

SUBMISSIONS

Address	Clara E. Hill, Department of Psychology, University of Maryland, College Park, MD 20742-4411.
Number of Copies	5.
Disk Submission	Submit manuscripts on paper; disks may be requested of accepted articles.

FORMAT OF MANUSCRIPT

Cover Sheet	Refer to Instructions to Authors in each issue.
Abstract	Manuscripts must include an abstract containing a maximum of 960 characters and spaces (approximately 120 words), typed on a separate sheet of paper.
Key Words	None.
Length	Not specified.
Margins	See style guide.
Spacing	Double-spaced.

STYLE

Name of Guide	*Publication Manual of the American Psychological Association.*
Subheadings	See style guide.
References	See style guide.
Footnotes	See style guide.
Tables or Figures	See style guide; camera-ready copy required for all art.

REVIEW PROCESS

Type	Masked review.
Queries	No query letters.
Acknowledgment	Editor acknowledges submission by mail.
Review Time	Usually 60–90 days.
Revisions	Editor will notify author if revision is desired (most manuscripts are initially rejected; most published manuscripts have gone through 1 or 2 revisions).
Acceptance Rate	20%.
Return of Manuscript	Manuscripts are not usually returned.
Lag Time to Print	6 months.

CHARGES TO AUTHOR

Author Alterations	Authors are billed for alterations in proofs.

REPRINT, SUBSCRIPTION, AND CONTACT INFORMATION

Reprint Policy	Authors may purchase reprints of their articles (order form accompanies proofs).
Book Reviews	None.
Subscriptions	Subscriptions Department, American Psychological Association, 750 First Street, NE, Washington, DC 20002-4242.
	Yearly rates for nonmembers are $73 domestic, $88 foreign, $96 airmail. APA members: $37.
Affiliation	Published by the American Psychological Association.
Home Page URL	http://www.apa.org

Journal of Divorce & Remarriage

Editorial Focus	Clinical studies and research in family therapy, family mediation, family studies, and family law.
Audience	Professionals working with family dissolution.
Special Themes	Understanding of the divorce process, thereby to improve therapeutic, legal, and community services to those who are divorcing and their families.
Where Indexed/ Abstracted	Abstracts of Research in Pastoral Care & Counseling; Applied Social Applied Social Sciences Index & Abstracts; CNPIEC Reference Guide: Chinese National Directory of Foreign Periodicals; Current Contents; Expanded Academic Index; Family Life Educator "Abstracts Section"; Family Studies Database (online and CD-ROM); Guide to Social Science & Religion in Periodical Literature; Index to Periodical Articles Related to Law; Institute for Scientific Information; INTERNET ACCESS (& additional networks) Bulletin Board for Resources Libraries ("BUBL"), coverage of information resources on INTERNET, JANET, and other networks; MasterFILE; Mental Health Abstracts; Periodical Abstracts Research II; Periodical Abstracts Select; Psychological Abstracts (PsycINFO); Published International Literature on Traumatic Stress (The PILOTS Database); Sage Family Studies Abstracts (SFSA); Social Planning/Policy & Development Abstracts (SOPODA); Social Sciences Citation Index; Social Work Abstracts; Sociological Abstracts (SA); Studies on Women Abstracts; Violence and Abuse Abstracts: A Review of Current Literature on Interpersonal Violence (VAA).
Year Established	1977.
Circulation	487.
Frequency	Quarterly.
Months Issued	Not specified.
No. of Articles	6–10 per issue.

SUBMISSIONS

Address	Craig A. Everett, PhD, Editor, Arizona Institute of Family Therapy, 1050 East River Road, Suite 202, Tucson, AZ 85719.
Number of Copies	4.
Disk Submission	Authors of accepted manuscripts are asked to submit a disk, preferably in Microsoft Word or WordPerfect.

FORMAT OF MANUSCRIPT

Cover Sheet	Separate sheet, which does not go out for review. Full title, author names, degrees, professional titles; designation of one author as corresponding author with full address, phone numbers, e-mail address, and fax number; date of submission.

Abstract	About 100 words.
Key Words	5 or 6 words that identify article content.
Length	20 pages, including references and abstract. Lengthier manuscripts may be considered, but only at the discretion of the editor. Sometimes, lengthier manuscripts may be considered if they can be divided up into sections for publication in successive issues.
Margins	1 inch on all sides.
Spacing	Double-spaced for all copy, except title page.

STYLE

Name of Guide	*Publication Manual of the American Psychological Association.*
Subheadings	Use as needed to guide reader through the article. No more than 4 levels.
References	Author–date citation style; see style guide.
Footnotes	No footnotes preferred; incorporate into text.
Tables or Figures	Type tables double-spaced. Submit camera-ready art (300 dpi printer or better) for all figures. Place each table or figure on a separate, numbered page at the end of the manuscript.

REVIEW PROCESS

Type	"Double blind" anonymous peer review. 3 reviewers plus editor-in-chief read the manuscript in an anonymous review.
Queries	Authors are encouraged to read the journal to determine if their subject matter would be appropriate.
Acknowledgment	Enclose a regular self-addressed, stamped envelope with submission.
Review Time	3–4 months.
Revisions	See journal.
Acceptance Rate	Not specified.
Return of Manuscript	Only if 9″ x 12″ self-addressed, stamped envelope is enclosed.
Lag Time to Print	6 months–1 year.

REPRINT, SUBSCRIPTION, AND CONTACT INFORMATION

Reprint Policy	All authors receive 2 complimentary copies of the issue in which article appears. Authors receive reprint order forms to purchase additional reprinted copies.
Book Reviews	Send to journal editor.
Subscriptions	The Haworth Press, Inc., 10 Alice Street, Binghamton, NY 13904-1580. Individuals, $45; institutions, $180; libraries, $325.

Journal of Drug Issues

Editorial Focus	Empirical research, theoretical analysis, policy analysis, clinical developments, theme issues and book digests.
Audience	All who are interested in drug issues in their varied aspects.
Special Themes	Varied and topical.
Where Indexed/ Abstracted	Abstracts on Criminology and Penology; Addiction Abstracts; Alcohol and Alcohol Problems Science Database; Alcohol, Drugs and Traffic Safety; Applied Social Sciences Index & Abstracts; Behavioral Abstracts; Biological Abstracts; Criminal Justice Abstracts; Criminology Abstracts; Current Contents: Social and Behavioral Sciences; Excerpta Medica; Expanded Academic Index; Family Abstracts; Family Resources Database; International Bibliography of Periodical Literature; International Bibliography of Book Reviews; Pharmaceutical Abstracts; PsycINFO; Psychological Abstracts; Research Alert; Social Planning/Policy & Development Abstracts; Social Sciences Citation Index; Sociological Abstracts.
Year Established	1971.
Circulation	1,100.
Frequency	Quarterly.
Months Issued	Winter, spring, summer, and fall.
No. of Articles	10–14 per issue.

SUBMISSIONS

Address	Editor, *Journal of Drug Issues,* 2340 Kilkenny East, Tallahassee, FL 32308-3109.
Number of Copies	3.
Disk Submission	IBM-formatted disk required in WordPerfect or Microsoft Word.

FORMAT OF MANUSCRIPT

Cover Sheet	Name, address, fax number, and e-mail address of contact author.
Abstract	Required. No more than 100 words.
Key Words	2–3 required.
Length	15–40 pages.
Margins	1 inch on all sides.
Spacing	Double-space, including references.

STYLE

Name of Guide	*Chicago Manual of Style.*
Subheadings	See style guide.
References	See style guide.

Footnotes	See style guide.
Tables or Figures	Must be camera-ready and suitable for page size of 4.5″ x 7.5″.

REVIEW PROCESS

Type	Anonymous.
Queries	Accepted.
Acknowledgment	Provide a self-addressed stamped postcard.
Review Time	6–8 weeks.
Revisions	Author provided with reviewer comments as guide to revision.
Acceptance Rate	Approximately 20%.
Return of Manuscript	Provide self-addressed, stamped envelope.
Lag Time to Print	About 1 year.

CHARGES TO AUTHOR

Author Alterations	$2.50 a line for galley corrections if due to author error.

REPRINT, SUBSCRIPTION, AND CONTACT INFORMATION

Reprint Policy	Reprints may be purchased by author at time of publication.
Book Reviews	Book digests published once a year. Book reviews seldom published.
Subscriptions	$90 per year domestic. Contact Subscription Manager, P.O. Box 4021, Tallahassee, FL 32315.
Affiliation	School of Criminology and Criminal Justice, Florida State University, Tallahassee, FL 32306.
E-Mail Address	eczajkos@garnet.acns.fsu.edu
Home Page URL	http://www.mailer.fsu/"crimdo/jrnl-drg.html

Journal of Elder Abuse & Neglect

Editorial Focus	Study of the causes, treatment, effect, and prevention of the abuse and neglect of older people and disabled adults.
Audience	Practitioners, researchers, academics, administrators, policymakers, and educators in the fields of aging, health, social services, domestic violence, law, criminal justice, law enforcement, and other human services.
Where Indexed/ Abstracted	Ageinfo CD-ROM; AgeLine Database; Behavioral Medicine Abstracts; Brown University Geriatric Research Application Digest "Abstracts Section"; Cambridge Scientific Abstracts; caredata CD: the social and community care database; CNPIEC Reference Guide: Chinese National Director of Foreign Periodicals; Communication Abstracts; Criminal Justice Abstracts; Criminal Justice Periodical Index; Current Contents; Current Literature on Aging; Educational Administration Abstracts (EAA); Family Studies Database (online and CD-ROM); Family Violence & Sexual Assault Bulletin; Human Resources Abstracts (HRA); IBZ International Bibliography of Periodical Literature; Index to Periodical Articles Related to Law; Institute for Scientific Information; INTERNET ACCESS (& additional networks) Bulletin Board for Libraries ("BUBL"), coverage of information resources on INTERNET, JANET, and other networks; New Literature on Old Age; Sage Family Studies Abstracts (SFSA); Sage Urban Studies Abstracts (SUSAP): Social Planning/Policy & Development Abstracts (SOPODA); Social Work Abstracts; Sociological Abstracts(SA); Violence and Abuse Abstracts: A Review of Current Literature on Interpersonal Violence (VAA).
Year Established	1989.
Circulation	800.
Frequency	Quarterly.
Months Issued	Spring, summer, fall, winter.
No. of Articles	5–6.

SUBMISSIONS

Address	Rosalie S. Wolf, *Journal of Elder Abuse & Neglect,* c/o Institute on Aging, Medical Center of Central Massachusetts, 119 Belmont Street, Worcester, MA 01605.
Number of Copies	4.
Disk Submission	Authors of accepted manuscripts are asked to submit a disk, preferably in WordPerfect or ASCII.

FORMAT OF MANUSCRIPT

Cover Sheet	Separate sheet with title and abstract.
Abstract	About 100 words.
Key Words	5–6 key words that identify article content.

Length	20–30 pages, including references and tables; lengthier manuscripts considered at the discretion of the editor.
Margins	1 inch on all sides.
Spacing	Double-spaced for all copy.

STYLE

Name of Guide	*Publication Manual of the American Psychological Association.*
Subheadings	Use as needed to guide reader through the article.
References	Author–date citation style; see style guide.
Footnotes	No footnotes; endnotes can be used.
Tables or Figures	All tables, figures, illustrations, etc., must be "camera-ready"; prepare on separate sheets of paper using black ink and professional drawing instruments.

REVIEW PROCESS

Type	Anonymous peer review. At least 2 reviewers plus 2 editors read the manuscript.
Queries	Query letters are encouraged.
Acknowledgment	On receipt of the manuscript, a letter is sent to the senior author.
Review Time	Approximately 3 months.
Revisions	Submit 4 copies with a separate cover sheet describing the changes made in the manuscript and replying to the reviewers' comments.
Acceptance Rate	16% accepted; 16% accepted subject to revisions; 37% recommended to be rewritten; 30% rejected outright.
Return of Manuscript	Not returned.
Lag Time to Print	Approximately 8 months.

REPRINT, SUBSCRIPTION, AND CONTACT INFORMATION

Reprint Policy	Senior author receives 2 copies of the journal issue and 10 complimentary reprints several weeks after the issue is published. The junior author will receive 2 copies of the journal issue.
Book Reviews	Send books for review to: Editor Rosalie S. Wolf, The Haworth Press, Inc., 10 Alice Street, Binghamton, NY 13904-1580. 1996–97 prices: National Committee for the Prevention of Elder Abuse members, free with membership; individual members, $30; institutional members, $100; individual nonmembers, $40; institutional nonmembers, $90; libraries and subscription agencies, $165.
Affiliation	The *Journal of Elder Abuse & Neglect* is a publication of the National Committee for the Prevention of Elder Abuse.

Journal of Emotional Abuse

Editorial Focus	Research, treatment, prevention programs, theories, legal and criminal justice, and legislation issues concerning psychological maltreatment, trauma, and nonphysical aggression in families, schools, workplaces, and relationships; individual or group harassment and nonphysical assaults (including stalking) that degrade or frighten.
Audience	Interdisciplinary professionals involved in any aspect of working with emotional abuse or psychological maltreatment of victims, or by offenders.
Special Themes	Varies.
Where Indexed/ Abstracted	Social work, psychological, sociology, family studies, nursing, legal, and other abstracting sources.
Year Established	1996.
Circulation	Not available (new journal).
Frequency	Quarterly.
Months Issued	March, June, September, December.
No. of Articles	6–9.

SUBMISSIONS

Address	*Journal of Emotional Abuse,* c/o FVSAI, 1121 E SE Loop 323, Suite 130, Tyler, TX 75701.
Number of Copies	5 (1 original with identifying names, etc., and 4 copies without this information).
Disk Submission	Disk requested on acceptance.

FORMAT OF MANUSCRIPT

Cover Sheet	Title; authors; brief biography of authors including degrees, positions, affiliations, and 1-sentence background; address for reprint requests.
Abstract	Required, 100 words.
Key Words	Optional, 5–10 key words.
Length	20–30 pages including references, abstract, and tables.
Margins	1 inch on all sides.
Spacing	Double-spaced.

STYLE

Name of Guide	*Publication Manual of the American Psychological Association;* instructions for authors available from Family Violence & Sexual Assault Institute.
Subheadings	See style guide.
References	See style guide.
Footnotes	Not suggested unless absolutely needed; see style guide.

Tables or Figures See style guide. All figures must be camera-ready; the journal can prepare them, but for a fee.

REVIEW PROCESS

Type Anonymous review by editorial board or ad hoc reviewers.

Queries Editor welcomes query letters or phone calls.

Acknowledgment On receipt of manuscript, letter and copyright form sent for all authors to sign in original; must include letter-size self-addressed, stamped envelope and an envelope for return of the manuscript with feedback.

Review Time 3–5 months.

Revisions Feedback is given to authors for making revisions, and the number of copies to be sent back is provided; the journal encourages revisions and resubmissions, with a cover letter by the author explaining what has been done to address the concerns.

Acceptance Rate Not available (new journal).

Return of Manuscript Manuscripts are returned with comments and a letter; self-addressed, stamped envelope needed.

Lag Time to Print 8–11 months.

REPRINT, SUBSCRIPTION, AND CONTACT INFORMATION

Reprint Policy 10 reprints are free, and author can purchase more while journal is in press; publisher sends a form to authors at that time.

Book Reviews None at present. The Family Violence & Sexual Assault Institute does accept books and book reviews for publication in its *Family Violence & Sexual Assault Bulletin.*

Subscriptions Order through The Haworth Press, Inc., 10 Alice Street, Binghamton, NY 13904-1580.

Individuals, $34; agencies/institutions, $48; libraries, $85. Individuals and institutions can get discounts of 10% for 1-year subscription, 20% for 2-year subscription, and 30% for 3-year subscription.

Affiliation Family Violence & Sexual Assault Institute.

E-Mail Address FVSAI@e-tex.com

Journal of Family Issues

Editorial Focus	Contemporary social issues and problems related to marriage and family life and to theoretical and professional issues of current interest to those who work with and study families.
Audience	Not specified.
Special Themes	Family studies, family violence, gender studies, psychology, social work, and sociology.
Where Indexed/ Abstracted	AGRICOLA; Applied Social Sciences Index & Abstracts; Automatic Subject Citation Alert; Child Development Abstracts & Bibliography; Current Contents; Family Resources Database; Health Instrument File; Psychological Abstracts; PsycINFO; Risk Abstracts; Sage Family Studies Abstracts; Social Planning/Policy & Development Abstracts; Social Sciences Citation Index; Social Science Index; Social Work Abstracts; Sociological Abstracts; Violence and Abuse Abstracts. Also available on microfilm from UMI, Ann Arbor, Michigan.
Year Established	1979.
Circulation	2,000.
Frequency	Bimonthly.
Months Issued	January, March, May, July, September, November.
No. of Articles	7.

SUBMISSIONS

Address	Constance Shehan, Editor, *Journal of Family Issues,* Department of Sociology, University of Florida, Gainesville, FL 32611-2030.
Number of Copies	4.
Disk Submission	Not specified.

FORMAT OF MANUSCRIPT

Cover Sheet	Title, author, affiliation, full mailing address, and acknowledgments.
Abstract	150 words.
Key Words	None.
Length	No more than 30 pages.
Margins	Wide.
Spacing	Double-spaced.

STYLE

Name of Guide	*Publication Manual of the American Psychological Association.*
Subheadings	Not specified.
References	Separate pages.

Footnotes	Separate pages.
Tables or Figures	Separate pages.

REVIEW PROCESS

Type	Not specified.
Queries	Not specified.
Acknowledgment	Enclose stamped postcard to acknowledge receipt of the manuscript.
Review Time	Not specified.
Revisions	Not specified.
Acceptance Rate	Not specified.
Return of Manuscript	Not specified.
Lag Time to Print	Not specified.

REPRINT, SUBSCRIPTION, AND CONTACT INFORMATION

Reprint Policy	May purchase.
Book Reviews	Not specified.
Subscriptions	Sage Publications, Inc., 2455 Teller Road, Thousand Oaks, CA 91320. 1996–97 one-year prices: individuals, $67; institutions, $221.
E-Mail Address	shehan@soc.ufl.edu
Home Page URL	http://www.sagepub.com

Journal of Family Ministry

Editorial Focus	Research findings, theory development, and practice models for family ministry. The journal seeks contributors from the evangelical and ecumenical Christian community.
Audience	Social workers, pastoral counselors, church educators, church agencies, other professional and lay leaders of congregational and denominational services to children and families.
Special Themes	Prevention and community-based services that strengthen families, community development, advocacy.
Where Indexed/ Abstracted	Abstracts of Research in Pastoral Care and Counseling; Guide to Social Science and Religion in Periodical Literature; Social Work Abstracts.
Year Established	1986.
Circulation	500.
Frequency	Quarterly.
Months Issued	March, June, September, December.
No. of Articles	6–8 per issue.

SUBMISSIONS

Address	Editor, *Journal of Family Ministry*, P.O. Box 7354, Louisville, KY 40207.
Number of Copies	5.
Disk Submission	Authors of accepted manuscripts are asked to submit a disk.

FORMAT OF MANUSCRIPT

Cover Sheet	Separate sheet, which does not go out for review. Full title, author names, degrees, professional titles; designation of one author as corresponding author with full address and phone numbers, date of submission, one-sentence description of each author.
Abstract	100-word abstract.
Key Words	None.
Length	Up to 20 pages, including references and tables.
Margins	1 inch on all sides.
Spacing	Double-spaced for all copy.

STYLE

Name of Guide	*Publication Manual of the American Psychological Association.*
Subheadings	Not specified.
References	See style guide.
Footnotes	Endnotes acceptable.
Tables or Figures	Provide camera-ready.

REVIEW PROCESS

Type	Two reviewers plus the editor read the manuscript in anonymous review.
Queries	Queries may be directed to the editor; guidelines are available in each issue, however.
Acknowledgment	Letter sent on receipt of manuscript.
Review Time	3 months.
Revisions	2 copies plus diskette.
Acceptance Rate	Approximately 50%.
Return of Manuscript	Not returned.
Lag Time to Print	3 months.

REPRINT, SUBSCRIPTION, AND CONTACT INFORMATION

Reprint Policy	Authors receive 5 complimentary copies.
Book Reviews	Send to editor.
Subscriptions	*Journal of Family Ministry*, P. O. Box 7354, Louisville, KY 40207.
Affiliation	Independent.
E-Mail Address	drgarland@aol.com

Journal of Family Psychology

Previous Title Division 43 journal; published by Sage.

Editorial Focus The *Journal of Family Psychology* is devoted to the study of the family system from multiple perspectives and to the application of psychological methods of inquiry to that end. The journal publishes original scholarly articles on such topics as the following: (a) marital and family processes, life stages and transitions, and stress and coping; (b) the development and validation of marital and family assessment measures; (c) the outcome and process of marital and family treatment; (d) the development and evaluation of family-focused prevention programs (e.g., preparation for marriage, divorce, teenage pregnancy, transition to parenthood, parenting, and caring for aging relatives); (e) families in transition (separation, divorce, and single parenting; remarriage and the stepfamily; adoption; and death and bereavement); (f) family violence and abuse; (g) employment and the family (e.g., division of household labor, workplace policies, and child care); (h) the family and larger systems (e.g., schools, social agencies, neighborhoods, and governments); (i) ethnicity, social class, gender, and sexual orientation as it relates to the family; and (j) methodological and statistical advances in the study of marriage and the family. The emphasis is on empirical research including, for example, studies involving behavioral, cognitive, emotional, or biological variables. The *Journal of Family Psychology* will publish occasional theoretical articles, literature reviews and meta-analyses, case studies, and brief reports as long as they further the goal of improving scholarship or practice in the field.

Audience Researchers in the discipline, faculty, libraries.

Where Indexed/ Abstracted Ergonomics Abstracts; PsycINFO.

Year Established 1987.

Circulation 6,700.

Frequency Quarterly.

Months Issued March, June, September, December.

No. of Articles 10–11.

SUBMISSIONS

Address Ronald F. Levant, 1093 Beacon Street, Suite 3C, Brookline, MA 02146.

Number of Copies 4.

Disk Submission Submit manuscripts on paper; disks may be requested of accepted articles.

FORMAT OF MANUSCRIPT

Cover Sheet Refer to Instructions to Authors in each issue.

Abstract Manuscripts must include an abstract containing a maximum of 960 characters and spaces (approximately 120 words), typed on a separate sheet of paper.

Key Words	None.
Length	Not specified.
Margins	See style guide.
Spacing	Double-spaced.

STYLE

Name of Guide	*Publication Manual of the American Psychological Association.*
Subheadings	See style guide.
References	See style guide.
Footnotes	See style guide.
Tables or Figures	See style guide; camera-ready copy required for all art.

REVIEW PROCESS

Type	Masked review.
Queries	No query letters.
Acknowledgment	Editor acknowledges submission by mail.
Review Time	Usually 60–90 days.
Revisions	Editor will notify author if revision is desired (most manuscripts are initially rejected; most published manuscripts have gone through 1 or 2 revisions).
Acceptance Rate	30%.
Return of Manuscript	Manuscripts are not usually returned.
Lag Time to Print	7 months.

CHARGES TO AUTHOR

Author Alterations	Authors are billed for alterations in proofs.

REPRINT, SUBSCRIPTION, AND CONTACT INFORMATION

Reprint Policy	Authors may purchase reprints of their articles (order form accompanies proofs).
Book Reviews	None.
Subscriptions	Subscriptions Department, American Psychological Association, 750 First Street, NE, Washington, DC 20002-4242.
	Nonmember individual rates are $60 domestic, $75 foreign, $83 airmail; institutional rates are $95 domestic, $125 foreign, $135 airmail. APA members: $38.
Affiliation	Published by the American Psychological Association.
Home Page URL	http://www.apa.org

Journal of Family Psychotherapy

Previous Title	*Journal of Psychotherapy and the Family.*
Editorial Focus	The quarterly journal of case studies, treatment reports, and strategies in clinical practice.
Audience	All clinical disciplines.
Where Indexed/ Abstracted	Abstracts of Research in Pastoral Care & Counseling; Biology Digest; Cambridge Scientific Abstracts; Digest of Neurology and Psychiatry; Excerpta Medica/Electronic Publishing Division; Family Violence & Sexual Assault Bulletin; Index to Periodical Articles Related to Law; Innovations and Research; Inventory of Marriage and Family Literature; Mental Health Abstracts; Psychological Abstracts (PsychINFO); Referativnyi Zhurnal (Abstracts Journal of the Institute of Scientific Information of the Republic of Russia); Sage Family Studies Abstracts (SFSA); Social Planning/Policy & Development Abstracts (SOPODA); Social Work Abstracts; Sociological Abstracts (SA); Special Educational Needs Abstracts; Studies on Women Abstracts; Violence and Abuse Abstracts: A Review of Current Literature on Interpersonal Violence (VAA).
Circulation	1,000+.
Year Established	1989.
Frequency	Quarterly.
Months Issued	February, May, August, November.
No. of Articles	4–5 regular, 3 brief, 8 book reviews.

SUBMISSIONS

Address	Terry S. Trepper, PhD, Family Studies Center, Purdue University Calumet, Hammond, IN 46323.
Number of Copies	4.
Disk Submission	For final revision.

FORMAT OF MANUSCRIPT

Cover Sheet	Title, author, affiliation, complete address.
Abstract	Yes, 500 words.
Key Words	None.
Length	25 pages maximum, including references.
Margins	1 inch on all sides.
Spacing	Double-spaced.

STYLE

Name of Guide	*Publication Manual of the American Psychological Association.*
Subheadings	See style guide.

References	See style guide.
Footnotes	See style guide.
Tables or Figures	See style guide.

REVIEW PROCESS

Type	Peer-reviewed.
Queries	Yes.
Acknowledgment	Yes.
Review Time	3 months.
Revisions	Not specified.
Acceptance Rate	Not specified.
Return of Manuscript	No, unless requested, and self-addressed, stamped envelope enclosed.
Lag Time to Print	9 months.

REPRINT, SUBSCRIPTION, AND CONTACT INFORMATION

Reprint Policy	The senior author receives 2 copies of the journal issue and 10 complimentary reprints. The junior author receives 2 copies of the journal issue. An order form is sent to the corresponding author for purchase of additional reprints.
Book Reviews	Contact Joe Wetchler, Book Review Editor, Families Studies Center, Purdue University Calumet, Hammond, IN 46323.
Subscriptions	Contact Joe Wetchler at above address.
E-Mail Address	trepper@nwi.calumet.purdue.edu

Journal of Family Social Work

Editorial Focus	New insights to social work practice with families, evaluation of new methodologies and research.
Audience	Social work practitioners, researchers, faculty, students, libraries, and others in family therapy practice.
Special Themes	Social work practice, research social work with families and children.
Where Indexed/ Abstracted	Not specified.
Year Established	1994.
Circulation	Not specified.
Frequency	Quarterly.
Months Issued	Not specified.
No. of Articles	6–7 per issue.

SUBMISSIONS

Address	Donald R. Bardill, Editor, *Journal of Family Social Work,* School of Social Work, Florida State University, Tallahassee, FL 32306.
Number of Copies	3.
Disk Submission	Authors of accepted manuscripts are asked to submit a disk, preferably in Microsoft Word or WordPerfect.

FORMAT OF MANUSCRIPT

Cover Sheet	Separate sheet, which does not go out for review. Full title, author names, degrees, professional titles; designation of one author as corresponding author with full address, phone numbers, e-mail address, and fax number; date of submission.
Abstract	150-word informative abstract.
Key Words	Up to 5 words or key phrases (2–3 word maximum) describing the article.
Length	14–16 pages including references and tables; manuscripts exceeding 25 pages will be returned.
Margins	1 inch on all sides.
Spacing	Double-spaced for all copy, except title page.

STYLE

Name of Guide	*Publication Manual of the American Psychological Association.*
Subheadings	Use as needed to guide reader through the article. No more than 3 levels.
References	See style guide.
Footnotes	See style guide.

Tables or Figures	Type tables double-spaced. Submit camera-ready art (300 dpi printer or better) for all figures. Place each table or figure on a separate, numbered page at the end of the manuscript.

REVIEW PROCESS

Type	"Double blind" anonymous peer review. 2 reviewers plus the editor-in-chief read the manuscript in an anonymous review.
Queries	Discouraged.
Acknowledgment	By postcard on receipt of manuscript.
Review Time	3–4 months.
Revisions	As outlined by the editor-in-chief.
Acceptance Rate	Approximately 40%.
Return of Manuscript	Not returned.
Lag Time to Print	Approximately 6 months–1 year.

REPRINT, SUBSCRIPTION, AND CONTACT INFORMATION

Reprint Policy	Not specified.
Book Reviews	By invitation only; send books for review to: Donald R. Bardill, Editor, *Journal of Family Social Work,* School of Social Work, Florida State University, Tallahassee, FL 32306.
Subscriptions	*Journal of Family Social Work,* School of Social Work, Florida State University, Tallahassee, FL 32306.

Journal of Feminist Family Therapy

Editorial Focus	Critiques family therapy theory and practice from a feminist perspective.
Audience	Family therapy practitioners.
Special Themes	Incest, eating disorders, and domestic abuse; implications of a feminist approach to training and supervision in family therapy, its organizations, and institutional structure from a feminist perspective.
Where Indexed/ Abstracted	Abstracts of Research in Pastoral Care & Counseling; Alternative Press Index; Applied Social Sciences Index & Abstracts; CNPIEC Reference Guide: Chinese National Directory of Foreign Periodicals; Family Studies Database (online and CD-ROM); Family Violence & Sexual Assault Bulletin; Feminist Periodicals: A Current Listing of Contents; IBZ International Bibliography of Periodical Literature; Index to Periodical Articles Related to Law; INTERNET ACCESS (& additional networks) Bulletin Board for Libraries ("BUBL"), coverage of information resources on INTERNET, JANET, and other networks; Mental Health Abstracts (online through DIALOG); Social Work Abstracts; Studies on Women Abstracts; Violence and Abuse Abstracts: A Review of Current Literature on Interpersonal Violence (VAA).
Year Established	1989.
Circulation	402.
Frequency	Quarterly.
Months Issued	Not specified.
No. of Articles	6–10 per issue.

SUBMISSIONS

Address	Editor, Betty Mac Kune-Karrer, MA, *Journal of Feminist Family Therapy*, Family Systems Program, Institute for Juvenile Research, 907 South Wolcott, Chicago, IL 60612.
Number of Copies	4.
Disk Submission	Authors of accepted manuscripts are asked to submit a disk, preferably in Microsoft Word or WordPerfect.

FORMAT OF MANUSCRIPT

Cover Sheet	Separate sheet, which does not go out for review. Full title, author names, degrees, professional titles; designation of one author as corresponding author with full address, phone numbers, e-mail address, and fax number; date of submission.
Abstract	About 100 words.
Key Words	5 or 6 words that identify article content.

Length	15–25 pages, including references and abstract. Lengthier manuscripts may be considered, but only at the discretion of the editor. Sometimes, lengthier manuscripts may be considered if they can be divided into sections for publication in successive issues.
Margins	1 inch on all sides.
Spacing	Double-spaced for all copy, except title page.

STYLE

Name of Guide	*Publication Manual of the American Psychological Association.*
Subheadings	Use as needed to guide reader through the article. No more than 4 levels.
References	Author–date citation style; see style guide.
Footnotes	No footnotes preferred; incorporate into text.
Tables or Figures	Type tables double-spaced. Submit camera-ready art (300 dpi printer or better) for all figures. Place each table or figure on a separate, numbered page at the end of the manuscript.

REVIEW PROCESS

Type	"Double blind" anonymous peer review. 3 reviewers plus editor-in-chief read the manuscript in an anonymous review.
Queries	Authors are encouraged to read the journal to determine if their subject matter would be appropriate.
Acknowledgment	Enclose a regular self-addressed, stamped envelope with submission.
Review Time	3–4 months.
Revisions	See journal.
Acceptance Rate	Not specified.
Return of Manuscript	Only if 9" x 12" self-addressed, stamped envelope is enclosed.
Lag Time to Print	6 months–1 year.

REPRINT, SUBSCRIPTION, AND CONTACT INFORMATION

Reprint Policy	All authors receive 2 complimentary copies of the issue in which article appears. Authors receive reprint order forms to purchase additional reprinted copies.
Book Reviews	Laura Giat Roberto, PsyD, Book Review Editor, 327 West 21st Street, Suite 205, Norfolk, VA 23517-2130.
Subscriptions	The Haworth Press, Inc., 10 Alice Street, Binghamton, NY 13904-1580. Individuals, $40; institutions, $60; libraries, $175.

Journal of Gay & Lesbian Psychotherapy

Editorial Focus	A practical, multidisciplinary professional forum for the exposition and discussion of issues relating to the use of psychotherapy with gay, lesbian, and bisexual clients.
Audience	Clinical and academic psychiatrists, psychologists, social workers, psychiatric nurses, infectuous disease specialists, religious counselors, and others.
Special Themes	The exchange of practical information about lesbian and gay psychotherapy among various specialty groups in the fields of psychology, psychiatry, and social work, as well as various subspecialties such as drug and alcohol counseling, family and couples' therapy, adolescent treatment, group therapy, and bereavement counseling.
Where Indexed/ Abstracted	ABI/INFORM Global; Abstracts in Anthropology; Abstracts of Research in Pastoral Care & Counseling; Academic Index; Cambridge Scientific Abstracts; CNPIEC Reference Guide: Chinese National Directory of Foreign Periodicals; Digest of Neurology and Psychiatry; Expanded Academic Index; Family Violence & Sexual Assault Bulletin; HOMODOK/ "Relevant" Bibliographic database; Index to Periodical Articles Related to Law; INTERNET ACCESS (& additional networks) Bulletin Board for Libraries ("BUBL"), coverage of information resources on INTERNET, JANET, and other networks; Inventory of Marriage and Family Literature (online and CD-ROM); Leeds Medical Information; Mental Health Abstracts (online through DIALOG); MLA International Bibliography; Periodical Abstracts, Research II; PsychNet; Psychological Abstracts (PsycINFO); Referativnyi Zhurnal (Abstracts Journal of the Institute of Scientific Information of the Republic of Russia); Sage Family Studies Abstracts (SFSA); Social Planning/Policy & Development Abstracts (SOPODA); Social Work Abstracts; Sociological Abstracts (SA); Studies on Women Abstracts; Violence and Abuse Abstracts: A Review of Current Literature on Interpersonal Violence (VAA).
Year Established	1989.
Circulation	1,019.
Frequency	Quarterly.
Months Issued	Not specified.
No. of Articles	6–10 per issue.

SUBMISSIONS

Address	Editor, *Journal of Gay & Lesbian Psychotherapy*, 209 N. 4th Street, Suite D5, Philadelphia, PA 19106.
Number of Copies	4.
Disk Submission	Authors of accepted manuscripts are asked to submit a disk, preferably in Microsoft Word or WordPerfect.

FORMAT OF MANUSCRIPT

Cover Sheet	Separate sheet, which does not go out for review. Full title, author names, degrees, professional titles; designation of one author as corresponding author with full address, phone numbers, e-mail address, and fax number; date of submission.
Abstract	About 100 words.
Key Words	Not specified.
Length	30 pages, including references and abstract. Lengthier manuscripts may be considered, but only at the discretion of the editor. Sometimes, lengthier manuscripts may be considered if they can be divided into sections for publication in successive issues.
Margins	1 inch on all sides.
Spacing	Double-spaced for all copy, except title page.

STYLE

Name of Guide	*Publication Manual of the American Psychological Association.*
Subheadings	Use as needed to guide reader through the article. No more than 4 levels.
References	Author–date citation style; see style guide.
Footnotes	No footnotes preferred; incorporate into text.
Tables or Figures	Type tables double-spaced. Submit camera-ready art (300 dpi printer or better) for all figures. Place each table or figure on a separate, numbered page at the end of the manuscript.

REVIEW PROCESS

Type	"Double blind" anonymous peer review. 3 reviewers plus editor-in-chief read the manuscript in an anonymous review.
Queries	Authors are encouraged to read the journal to determine if their subject matter would be appropriate.
Acknowledgment	Enclose a regular self-addressed, stamped envelope with submission.
Review Time	3–4 months.
Revisions	See journal.
Acceptance Rate	Not specified.
Return of Manuscript	Only if 9″ x 12″ self-addressed, stamped envelope is enclosed.
Lag Time to Print	6 months–1 year.

REPRINT, SUBSCRIPTION, AND CONTACT INFORMATION

Reprint Policy	All authors receive 2 complimentary copies of the issue in which article appears. Authors receive reprint order forms to purchase additional reprinted copies.
Book Reviews	Journal editor.
Subscriptions	The Haworth Press, Inc., 10 Alice Street, Binghamton, NY 13904-1580. Individuals, $28; institutions, $48; libraries, $75.

The Journal of General Psychology

Editorial Focus	Experimental, physiological, and comparative psychology.
Audience	Researchers and professors in the field; libraries.
Special Themes	Human and animal studies; mathematical and theoretical investigations; technical reports.
Where Indexed/ Abstracted	Abstracts for Social Workers; Academic Abstracts; Child Development Abstracts & Bibliographies; Current Contents: Social & Behavioral Sciences; Directory of Title Pages, Indexes, and Contents Pages; Exceptional Child Education Resources; Health and Psychosocial Instrument; Index Medicus; Linguistic and Language Behavior Abstracts; Magazine Article Summaries; Mental Health Abstracts; Psychological Abstracts; PsycINFO; Research Alert; Social Planning /Policy and Development Abstracts; Social Science Source; Social Sciences Citation Index; Social Sciences Index; Sociological Abstracts.
Year Established	1927.
Circulation	1,035.
Frequency	Quarterly.
Months Issued	January, April, July, October.
No. of Articles	6–8 per issue.

SUBMISSIONS

Address	Managing Editor, *The Journal of General Psychology,* 1319 18th Street, NW, Washington, DC 20036-1802.
Number of Copies	4.
Disk Submission	Only after acceptance.

FORMAT OF MANUSCRIPT

Cover Sheet	Not specified.
Abstract	Yes, 100–120 words.
Key Words	Not necessary.
Length	Short reports to articles shorter than monograph length.
Margins	1 inch on all sides.
Spacing	Double-spaced.

STYLE

Name of Guide	*Publication Manual of the American Psychological Association.*
Subheadings	See style guide.
References	See style guide.
Footnotes	See style guide.

Tables or Figures	Tables are set for a charge; figures are scanned in for a charge and should be camera-ready.

REVIEW PROCESS

Type	Peer-reviewed by consulting editors and executive editor, anonymous on request.
Queries	Welcome.
Acknowledgment	By postcard.
Review Time	2 months or less.
Revisions	Re-reviewed; submit with copy of original.
Acceptance Rate	50%.
Return of Manuscript	Yes, no need for self-addressed, stamped envelope.
Lag Time to Print	2–6 months.

CHARGES TO AUTHOR

Processing	Charges for setting tables and scanning figures.

REPRINT, SUBSCRIPTION, AND CONTACT INFORMATION

Reprint Policy	Reprint order form is included with acceptance letter. Authors receive 2 complimentary copies of issue in which article appears.
Book Reviews	Not specified.
Subscriptions	*The Journal of General Psychology,* 1319 18th Street, NW, Washington, DC 20036; phone: 800-365-9753.
	$99.50 per year.
E-Mail Address	gen@heldref.org (for author/editor correspondence after manuscript acceptance)
Home Page URL	http://www.heldref.org/

Journal of Genetic Psychology

Editorial Focus	Research and theory in developmental, clinical, and educational psychology.
Audience	Psychology researchers.
Special Themes	Not specified.
Where Indexed/ Abstracted	Abstracts for Social Workers; Biological Abstracts; BIOSIS; Child Development Abstracts & Bibliography; Current Contents: Social & Behavioral Sciences; Directory of Title Pages, Indexes and Contents Pages; Exceptional Child Education Resources; Health & Psychosocial Instrument; Index Medicus; Linguistic and Language Behavior Abstracts; Mental Health Abstracts; Psychological Abstracts; PsycINFO Database; Research Alert; Social Planning/Policy & Development Abstracts; Social Sciences Citation Index; Social Sciences Index; Sociological Abstracts; Sociology of Education Abstracts; and Special Needs Abstracts.
Year Established	1891/1925.
Circulation	1,044.
Frequency	Quarterly.
Months Issued	March, June, September, December.
No. of Articles	10–12 per issue.

SUBMISSIONS

Address	*Journal of Genetic Psychology*, Heldref Publications, 1319 18th Street, NW, Washington, DC 20036.
Number of Copies	Not specified.
Disk Submission	Disk requested on acceptance; Microsoft Word 5.1.

FORMAT OF MANUSCRIPT

Cover Sheet	See style guide.
Abstract	See style guide.
Key Words	See style guide.
Length	See style guide.
Margins	See style guide.
Spacing	See style guide.

STYLE

Name of Guide	*Publication Manual of the American Psychological Association.*
Subheadings	See style guide.
References	See style guide.
Footnotes	See style guide.
Tables or Figures	See style guide.

REVIEW PROCESS

Type	Executive editor and consulting editors.
Queries	Not specified.
Acknowledgment	Not specified.
Review Time	2–3 months.
Revisions	Not specified.
Acceptance Rate	60% after revision.
Return of Manuscript	Not specified.
Lag Time to Print	10–12 months.

CHARGES TO AUTHOR

Author Alterations	$50 per table, $20 per figure.

REPRINT, SUBSCRIPTION, AND CONTACT INFORMATION

Reprint Policy	Not specified.
Book Reviews	Yes.
Subscriptions	Not specified.

Journal of Geriatric Drug Therapy

Editorial Focus	Important findings and exchange of controversial, innovative, and timely views related to geripharmacotherapy.
Audience	Health care professionals.
Special Themes	Drug therapy issues in the geriatric patient.
Where Indexed/ Abstracted	Abstracts in Social Gerontology: Current Literature on Aging; AgeLine Database; Applied Social Sciences Index & Abstracts; Biosciences Information Service of Biological Abstracts (BIOSIS); Brown University Geriatric Research Application Digest "Abstracts Section"; Brown University Long-Term Care Quality Letter "Abstracts Section"; Cambridge Scientific Abstracts; CNPIEC Reference Guide: Chinese National Directory of Foreign Periodicals; Current Awareness in Biological Sciences (CABS); Excerpta Medica/Secondary Publishing Division; Family Studies Database (on line and CD-ROM); Human Resources Abstracts (HRA); Index to Periodical Articles Related to Law; InPharma Weekly DIGEST & NEWS on: Pharmaceutical Literature, Drug Reactions & LMS; International Pharmaceutical Abstracts; INTERNET ACCESS (& additional networks) Bulletin Board for Libraries ("BUBL"), coverage of information resources on INTERNET, JANET, and other networks; Medication Use STudies (MUST) DATABASE; Psychological Abstracts (PsycINFO); Referativnyi Zhurnal (Abstracts Journal of the Institute of Scientific Information of the Republic of Russia); SilverPlatter Information, Inc. "CD-ROM/online"; Social Planning/Policy & Development Abstracts (SOPODA); Social Work Abstracts; Sociological Abstracts (SA).
Year Established	1986.
Circulation	275.
Frequency	Quarterly.
Months Issued	Not specified.
No. of Articles	6–10 per issue.

SUBMISSIONS

Address	Editor, James W. Cooper, PharmD, Professor, Department of Pharmacy Practice, College of Pharmacy, University of Georgia, Athens, GA 30602.
Number of Copies	4.
Disk Submission	Authors of accepted manuscripts are asked to submit a disk, preferably in Microsoft Word or WordPerfect.

FORMAT OF MANUSCRIPT

Cover Sheet	Separate sheet, which does not go out for review. Full title, author names, degrees, professional titles; designation of one author as corresponding author with full address, phone numbers, e-mail address, and fax number; date of submission.

Abstract	About 100 words.
Key Words	5 or 6 words that identify article content.
Length	2–40 pages, including references and abstract. Lengthier manuscripts may be considered, but only at the discretion of the editor. Sometimes, lengthier manuscripts may be considered if they can be divided into sections for publication in successive issues.
Margins	1 inch on all sides.
Spacing	Double-spaced for all copy, except title page.

STYLE

Name of Guide	*Stylebook/Editorial Manual* of the American Medical Association.
Subheadings	Use as needed to guide reader through the article. No more than 4 levels.
References	Author–date citation style; see style guide.
Footnotes	No footnotes preferred; incorporate into text.
Tables or Figures	Type tables double-spaced. Submit camera-ready art (300 dpi printer or better) for all figures. Place each table or figure on a separate, numbered page at the end of the manuscript.

REVIEW PROCESS

Type	"Double blind" anonymous peer review. 3 reviewers plus editor-in-chief read the manuscript in an anonymous review.
Queries	Authors are encouraged to read the journal to determine if their subject matter would be appropriate.
Acknowledgment	Enclose a regular self-addressed, stamped envelope with submission.
Review Time	3–4 months.
Revisions	See journal.
Acceptance Rate	Not specified.
Return of Manuscript	Only if 9" x 12" self-addressed, stamped envelope is enclosed.
Lag Time to Print	6 months–1 year.

REPRINT, SUBSCRIPTION, AND CONTACT INFORMATION

Reprint Policy	All authors receive 2 complimentary copies of the issue in which article appears. Authors receive reprint order forms to purchase additional reprinted copies.
Book Reviews	Send to journal editor.
Subscriptions	The Haworth Press, Inc., 10 Alice Street, Binghamton, NY 13904-1580. Individuals, $48; institutions, $110; libraries, $225.

Journal of Gerontological Social Work

Editorial Focus	Service organization and practice issues.
Audience	Social work practitioners, educators, and administrators.
Special Themes	Impact of settings on practice; demographic trends, relationship between policy research and practice.
Where Indexed/ Abstracted	Abstracts in Social Gerontology; Academic Abstracts; AgeInfo; AgeLine Database; Alzheimer's Disease Education & Referral Center; Applied Social Sciences Index & Abstracts; Behavioral Medicine Abstracts; Bioscience Information Service of Biological Abstracts; Cumulative Index to Nursing & Allied Health Literature; Human Resources Abstracts; New Literature on Old Age; Psychology Abstracts; Social Planning/Policy & Development Abstracts; Social Work Abstracts; Sociological Abstracts.
Year Established	1979.
Circulation	1,252.
Frequency	Quarterly.
Months Issued	Winter, spring, summer, fall.
No. of Articles	10–12 per issue.

SUBMISSIONS

Address	Editor, *Journal of Gerontological Social Work*, 425 East 25th Street, 9th Floor, New York, NY 10010.
Number of Copies	3 (original plus 2 copies).
Disk Submission	Authors of accepted manuscripts are asked to submit a disk. Please specify software used.

FORMAT OF MANUSCRIPT

Cover Sheet	Include only the article title (this is used for anonymous reviewing). Also enclose a second title page which should include full authorship.
Abstract	Approximately 100 words.
Key Words	3–10 key words below abstract to be used for index purposes.
Length	15–20 typewritten pages (lengthier manuscripts may be considered but only at the discretion of the editor).
Margins	1 inch on all sides.
Spacing	Double-spaced for all copies.

STYLE

Name of Guide	*Journal of Gerontological Social Work—Instructions for Authors.*
Subheadings	None.
References	See style guide.

Footnotes	Discouraged; incorporate into text.
Tables or Figures	All tables, figures, illustrations, and so forth should be "camera-ready." They must be prepared on separate sheets of paper. On the back of these items, write the article title and the journal title lightly in pencil.

REVIEW PROCESS

Type	All manuscripts are reviewed anonymously by 2 reviewers and the editor.
Queries	All queries are welcomed; however, we ask that *Instructions for Authors* brochure be read first.
Acknowledgment	Letters of acknowledgment are sent on receipt of manuscript.
Review Time	3–6 months.
Revisions	Submit 1 copy of the revised manuscript with changes, and attach an outline of all the changes made to the manuscript, in response to the reviewers' comments. The revised manuscript is then reviewed by the editor and a final decision is made.
Acceptance Rate	Approximately 50%.
Return of Manuscript	Manuscripts are returned along with the reviewers' comments.
Lag Time to Print	Approximately 6 months–1 year.

REPRINT, SUBSCRIPTION, AND CONTACT INFORMATION

Reprint Policy	The senior author receives 1 copy of the journal issue and 10 complimentary reprints of his or her article. Junior authors receive 1 copy of the journal issue. An order form for the purchase of additional reprints is sent to all authors.
Book Reviews	By invitation only; send books for review to: Book Review Editor, *Journal of Gerontological Social Work,* 425 East 25th Street, New York, NY 10010.
Subscriptions	1996–97 one-year prices: individuals, $36; institutions, $162; libraries, $225.
Affiliation	*JGSW* is affiliated with the Brookdale Center on Aging of Hunter College.

Journal of Health and Social Policy

Editorial Focus	Promoting a forum for those interested in debating and discussing policy formulation, as well as for those desirous of analyzing and investigating responses to policies already enacted. The editors and editorial board vigorously pursue the development of a body of knowledge on the differential effects of health and social policy issues on various populations and will encourage manuscripts form minority authors.
Audience	Practitioners, researchers, faculty, students, libraries, organizations involved in public health such as nursing, health education, allied health, social work, urban affairs, pharmacy, psychology, sociology, mental health, and medicine who want to address public and social policy issues.
Special Themes	Current issues.
Where Indexed/ Abstracted	Abstracts in Anthropology; Academic Abstracts CD/ROM; Biosciences Information Services of Biological Abstracts; CAB Abstracts; Cambridge Scientific Abstracts; Elsevier/Geo Abstracts; Elsevier Science Inc.; Health Care Lit Info/Heclinet; IBZ International Bibliography of Periodicals; International Political Science Abstracts; Joanne Gold Bubl Info Svce (HELMIS); Mental Health Abstracts/Political Science Abstracts; NIAAA; OT Bibsys; PAIS Bulletin; Pat Peters; PsycINFO; Social Work Abstracts.
Year Established	1988.
Circulation	500.
Frequency	Quarterly.
Months Issued	March, June, September, December.
No. of Articles	6–8.

SUBMISSIONS

Address	Marvin D. Feit, PhD, School of Social Work, The University of Akron, Polsky Building, Akron, OH 44325-8001; Stanley Battle, PhD, MPH, School of Social Work, University of Connecticut, 1798 Asylum Avenue, West Hartford, CT 06117.
Number of Copies	3.
Disk Submission	Authors of accepted manuscripts must provide a disk copy, preferably in Microsoft Word or WordPerfect.

FORMAT OF MANUSCRIPT

Cover Sheet	Staple a cover page to each manuscript indicating only the manuscript title on two of the hard copies. Also enclose a separate cover sheet that includes full title, author names, degrees, professional titles; designation of one author as corresponding author with full address, phone numbers, e-mail address, and fax number; date of submission.
Abstract	100–150 word informative abstract.

Key Words	Up to 5 words or key phrases (2–3 word maximum) describing the article.
Length	15–20 pages, including references and tables.
Margins	1 inch on all sides.
Spacing	Double-spaced for all copy, except title page.

STYLE

Name of Guide	*Publication Manual of the American Psychological Association.*
Subheadings	Use as needed to guide reader through the article. No more than 3 levels.
References	References should be double-spaced and in alphabetical order.
Footnotes	No footnotes preferred; incorporate into text.
Tables or Figures	Must be "camera-ready." Each table, figure, or illustration must be prepared on a separate page.

REVIEW PROCESS

Type	"Double-blind" anonymous peer review. 3 reviewers read each submission in an anonymous review.
Queries	Yes.
Acknowledgment	A letter is sent upon receipt of manuscript.
Review Time	3–4 months.
Revisions	Resubmit 3 hard copies with a separate cover sheet describing the alterations made to the manuscript.
Acceptance Rate	Approximately 35%.
Return of Manuscript	Not returned; author should retain copies.
Lag Time to Print	Approximately 9 months–1 year.

REPRINT, SUBSCRIPTION, AND CONTACT INFORMATION

Reprint Policy	The senior author will receive two copies of the journal issues and 10 complimentary reprints of his or her article. The junior author will receive two copies of the journal issue. An order form for the purchase of additional reprints will also be sent to all authors.
Book Reviews	Send books for review to Book Review Editor: Michael Holosko, School of Social Work, University of Windsor, Windsor, Ontario N9B 3P4, Canada.
Subscriptions	The Haworth Press, Inc., 10 Alice Street, Binghamton, NY 13904-1580.
	1996–97 one-year prices: individuals, $37.80; institutions, $67.50; libraries, $145.00.

Journal of Homosexuality

Editorial Focus	A scholarly research on homosexuality, including practices and gender roles and their cultural, historical, interpersonal, and modern social contexts.
Audience	Allied disciplinary and professional groups represented by anthropology, art, history, the law, literature, philosophy, politics, religion, and sociology, as well as research in the biological sciences, medicine, psychiatry, and psychology.
Where Indexed/ Abstracted	Abstracts in Anthropology; Abstracts of Research in Pastoral Care & Counseling; Academic Abstracts/CD-ROM; Academic Search; Applied Social Sciences Index & Abstracts; Book Review Index; Cambridge Scientific Abstracts; CNPIEC Reference Guide: Chinese National Directory of Foreign Periodicals; Criminal Justice Abstracts; Criminology, Penology and Police Science Abstracts; Current Contents: Medicine/Lite Sciences (CC:CM/CS); Digest of Neurology and Psychiatry; Excerpta Medica/ Secondary Publishing Division; Expanded Academic Index; Family Life Educator "Abstracts Section"; Family Studies Database; Family Violence & Sexual Assault Bulletin; HOMODOK/"Relevant" Bibliographic database; IBZ International Bibliography of Periodical Literature; Index Medicus/ MEDLINE; Index to Periodical Articles Related to Law; INTERNET ACCESS (& additional networks) Bulletin Board for Libraries ("BUBL"), coverage of information resources on INTERNET, JANET, and other networks; Leeds Medical Information; MasterFILE: updated database from EBSCO Publishing; Mental Health Abstracts; MLA International Bibliography; PASCAL International Bibliography T205: Sciences de l'information Documentation; Periodical Abstracts Research; Periodical Abstracts Research II; PsychNet; Public Affairs Information Bulletin (PAIS); Religion Index One: Periodicals; Sage Family Studies Abstracts (SFSA); Social Planning Policy & Development Abstracts (SOPODA); Social Sciences Index; Social Science Source; Social Work Abstracts; Sociological Abstracts (SA); Studies on Women Abstracts; Violence and Abuse Abstracts: A Review of Current Literature on Interpersonal Violence (VAA).
Year Established	1974.
Circulation	899.
Frequency	Quarterly.
Months Issued	Not specified.
No. of Articles	6–10 per issue.

SUBMISSIONS

Address	Editor, John P. DeCecco, *Journal of Homosexuality*, Center for Research and Education in Sexuality, San Francisco State University, San Francisco, CA 94132.
Number of Copies	4.
Disk Submission	Authors of accepted manuscripts are asked to submit a disk, preferably in Microsoft Word or WordPerfect.

FORMAT OF MANUSCRIPT

Cover Sheet	Separate sheet, which does not go out for review. Full title, author names, degrees, professional titles; designation of one author as corresponding author with full address, phone numbers, e-mail address, and fax number; date of submission.
Abstract	About 100 words.
Key Words	Not specified.
Length	25 pages, including references and abstract. Lengthier manuscripts may be considered, but only at the discretion of the editor. Sometimes, lengthier manuscripts may be considered if they can be divided into sections for publication in successive issues.
Margins	1 inch on all sides.
Spacing	Double-spaced for all copy, except title page.

STYLE

Name of Guide	*Publication Manual of the American Psychological Association.*
Subheadings	Use as needed to guide reader through the article. No more than 4 levels.
References	Author–date citation style; see style guide.
Footnotes	No footnotes preferred; incorporate into text.
Tables or Figures	Type tables double-spaced. Submit camera-ready art (300 dpi printer or better) for all figures. Place each table or figure on a separate, numbered page at the end of the manuscript.

REVIEW PROCESS

Type	"Double blind" anonymous peer review. 3 reviewers plus editor-in-chief read the manuscript in an anonymous review.
Queries	Authors are encouraged to read the journal to determine if their subject matter would be appropriate.
Acknowledgment	Enclose a regular self-addressed, stamped envelope with submission.
Review Time	3–4 months.
Revisions	See journal.
Acceptance Rate	Not specified.
Return of Manuscript	Only if 9″ x 12″ self-addressed, stamped envelope is enclosed.
Lag Time to Print	6 months–1 year.

REPRINT, SUBSCRIPTION, AND CONTACT INFORMATION

Reprint Policy	All authors receive 2 complimentary copies of the issue in which article appears. Authors receive reprint order forms to purchase additional reprinted copies.
Book Reviews	Send to journal editor.
Subscriptions	The Haworth Press, Inc., 10 Alice Street, Binghamton, NY 13904-1580. Individuals, $40; institutions, $160; libraries, $225.

Journal of Interpersonal Violence

Editorial Focus	Study and treatment of victims and perpetrators of interpersonal violence.
Audience	Not specified.
Special Themes	Domestic violence, child sexual abuse, rape and sexual assault, physical child abuse, and violent crime focusing on both victims and victimizers.
Where Indexed/ Abstracted	Applied Social Sciences Index & Abstracts; caredata ABSTRACTS and caredata CD; Criminal Justice Abstracts; Criminal Justice Periodical Index; Current Contents: Social & Behavioral Sciences; Family Resources Database; Health Instrument File; Index to Periodical Articles Related to Law; International Nursing Index; NIJ/NCJRS Database; PILOTS Database; Psychological Abstracts; PsycINFO; Research Alert; Risk Abstracts; Social Sciences Citation Index; Social Work Abstracts; Sociological Abstracts; Violence and Abuse Abstracts. Also available on microfilm from UMI, Ann Arbor, Michigan.
Year Established	1986.
Circulation	3,000.
Frequency	Bimonthly.
Months Issued	February, April, June, August, October, December.
No. of Articles	8–10.

SUBMISSIONS

Address	Jon R. Conte, Editor, *Journal of Interpersonal Violence,* School of Social Work, University of Washington, 4101 15th Avenue NE, Mailstop 354900, Seattle, WA 98195.
Number of Copies	3.
Disk Submission	Final revised manuscript, saved on IBM-compatible disk, should be included with final revised hard copy.

FORMAT OF MANUSCRIPT

Cover Sheet	Name, affiliation, mailing address, and phone number.
Abstract	An abstract and biographical statement should be included.
Key Words	None.
Length	No more than 22 pages.
Margins	Not specified.
Spacing	Double-spaced.

STYLE

Name of Guide	*Publication Manual of the American Psychological Association.*
Subheadings	Not specified.

References	Separate pages.
Footnotes	Separate pages.
Tables or Figures	Separate pages.

REVIEW PROCESS

Not specified.

REPRINT, SUBSCRIPTION, AND CONTACT INFORMATION

Reprint Policy	May purchase.
Book Reviews	Not specified.
Subscriptions	Sage Publications, Inc., 2455 Teller Road, Thousand Oaks, CA 91320. 1996–97 one-year prices: individual, $52; institution, $146.
E-Mail Address	jiv@u.washington.edu
Home Page URL	http://www.sagepub.com

Journal of Law and Social Work

Editorial Focus	Articles, commentaries (scholarly editorials), and book reviews dealing with international issues and developments arising from the interplay of social work and the law.
Audience	Social workers (practitioners, researchers, faculty, students) who are interested in law; lawyers who are interested in social justice issues; individuals who have both the MSW and JD/LLB; academic libraries.
Special Themes	Research, public policy, social work curriculum, social justice, and human rights.
Where Indexed/ Abstracted	Criminal Justice Abstracts; Human Resources Abstracts; Sage Family Studies Abstracts; Sage Public Administration Abstracts; Social Work Abstracts.
Year Established	1989.
Circulation	500.
Frequency	Semiannually.
Months Issued	Spring and fall.
No. of Articles	4–6 per issue.

SUBMISSIONS

Address	Jannah Hurn Mather, Editor, *Journal of Law and Social Work*, Faculty of Social Work, Wilfrid Laurier University, Waterloo, Ontario, Canada N2L 3C5.
Number of Copies	3.
Disk Submission	All applicants are requested to submit a disk in WordPerfect 6.1 (IBM-compatible).

FORMAT OF MANUSCRIPT

Cover Sheet	Separate sheet, which does not go out for review. Full title, author names, highest degree awarded, institutional affiliations; designation of one author as corresponding author with full address, phone numbers, e-mail address, and fax number; date of submission.
Abstract	200-word informative abstract.
Key Words	Not required.
Length	Up to 4,500 words.
Margins	1 inch on all sides.
Spacing	Double-spaced, except title page.

STYLE

Name of Guide	*Publication Manual of the American Psychological Association; American Bar Association.*
Subheadings	Use as needed to guide reader through the article. No more than 3 levels.
References	Author–date citation style; see style guides.
Footnotes	No footnotes preferred; incorporate into text.
Tables or Figures	Submit camera-ready art. Place each table or figure on a separate, numbered page at the end of the manuscript.

REVIEW PROCESS

Type	Anonymous peer review. 3 reviewers plus the editor-in-chief read the manuscript.
Queries	Query letters are discouraged; authors are encouraged to read the journal to determine if their subject matter would be appropriate.
Acknowledgment	E-mail and/or letter on receipt of manuscript.
Review Time	3–4 months.
Revisions	Submit 3 copies (blinded) describing the changes made in the manuscript and replying to the reviewer's comments. In general, the editor-in-chief reads revisions.
Acceptance Rate	Approximately 50%.
Return of Manuscript	Not returned; author should retain copies.
Lag Time to Print	Approximately 6 months–1 year.

REPRINT, SUBSCRIPTION, AND CONTACT INFORMATION

Reprint Policy	All authors receive 2 complimentary copies of the issue in which the article appears.
Book Reviews	By invitation or submission; send books for review to: Stephen M. Marson, Book Review Editor, *Journal of Law and Social Work*, Social Work Program, University of North Carolina at Pembroke, One University Drive, Pembroke, NC 28372-1510.
Subscriptions	*Journal of Law and Social Work*, WLU Press, Wilfrid Laurier University, Waterloo, Ontario, Canada N2L 3C5.
	1996–97 one-year prices: individuals, $35; institutions, $75; students, $20. (Inside Canada dues are in Canadian dollars; add 7% GST to payment. Outside of Canada dues are in U.S. dollars.)
Affiliation	Wilfrid Laurier University Faculty of Social Work.
E-Mail Address	jkirkpat@mach2.wlu.ca
Home Page URL	www.nconline.com/marson/lawnsoc.htm

Journal of Lesbian Studies

Editorial Focus	Descriptive, theoretical, empirical, applied, and multicultural perspectives on lesbian studies. Also includes book reviews, poetry, letters to the editor, debates, and commentaries.
Audience	Scholars of lesbian studies across disciplines.
Special Themes	3 issues a year will be thematic; contact the editor for upcoming themes.
Where Indexed/ Abstracted	Not available—journal will not appear in print until 1997.
Year Established	1997.
Circulation	Not available.
Frequency	Quarterly.
Months Issued	Not specified.
No. of Articles	7–10.

SUBMISSIONS

Address	Esther Rothblum, PhD, John Dewey Hall, Department of Psychology, University of Vermont, Burlington, VT 05405.
Number of Copies	3.
Disk Submission	Final manuscript only.

FORMAT OF MANUSCRIPT

Cover Sheet	Title, name (without degrees), 1-paragraph biographical description of author(s), correspondence address of primary author.
Abstract	Half page.
Key Words	None.
Length	Up to 15 pages.
Margins	1 inch on all sides.
Spacing	Double-spaced.

STYLE

Name of Guide	Not specified.
Subheadings	Open, but must be consistent.
References	Open, but must be consistent.
Footnotes	Optional.
Tables or Figures	Must be camera-ready.

REVIEW PROCESS

Type	Peer-reviewed, anonymous.
Queries	Welcomed.

Acknowledgment	By letter.
Review Time	3 months.
Revisions	3 months.
Acceptance Rate	Not available.
Return of Manuscript	Yes.
Lag Time to Print	12–18 months.

REPRINT, SUBSCRIPTION, AND CONTACT INFORMATION

Reprint Policy	10 free reprints for each author and 1 free copy of the journal issue.
Book Reviews	Yes, send to editor.
Subscriptions	Individuals, $25.20; institutions, $43.20; libraries, $75.
E-Mail Address	e_rothbl@dewey.uvm.edu

Journal of Long-Term Care Administration

Editorial Focus	The foremost research, developments, and innovative trends in long-term care.
Audience	Long-term care administrators, CEOs, owners, operators.
Special Themes	Critical management issues such as staff recruitment and retention; marketing and strategic planning; delivery of quality care and ethics; financial considerations; and the future of the industry.
Where Indexed/ Abstracted	Cumulative Index to Nursing & Allied Health Literature; National Library of Medicine MEDLINE; Social Work Abstracts. Also available on microfilm from UMI, Ann Arbor, Michigan.
Year Established	1973.
Circulation	6,700.
Frequency	Quarterly.
Months Issued	June, August, November, February.
No. of Articles	10–12.

SUBMISSIONS

Address	Editor, ACHCA, 325 South Patrick Street, Alexandria, VA 22314.
Number of Copies	3.
Disk Submission	Authors of accepted manuscripts are asked to submit a disk, preferably in Microsoft Word or WordPerfect.

FORMAT OF MANUSCRIPT

Cover Sheet	Separate sheet, which does not go out for review: full title, author names, degrees, titles, affiliations; designation of one corresponding author with full address and phone and fax numbers.
Abstract	Not required.
Key Words	None.
Length	12 pages including tables and references.
Margins	At least one inch.
Spacing	Double-spaced.

STYLE

Name of Guide	*Chicago Manual of Style.*
Subheadings	Not specified.
References	See style guide.
Footnotes	Use textnotes.
Tables or Figures	Should enhance understanding of the manuscript and not summarize or repeat information given in the text.

REVIEW PROCESS

Type	Double blind, 2 or more members of editorial review board.
Queries	Call for information.
Acknowledgment	Letter sent upon receipt; no self-addressed, stamped envelope required.
Review Time	6–8 weeks.
Revisions	Resubmission guidelines same as for submissions.
Acceptance Rate	30%–40%.
Return of Manuscript	Returned with reviewers' comments for revision; final copy is not returned.
Lag Time to Print	6–10 months.

REPRINT, SUBSCRIPTION, AND CONTACT INFORMATION

Reprint Policy	Each author receives one copy and reprint information.
Book Reviews	Invitation only; send books for review to the editor.
Subscriptions	Members, free; U.S. & Canada, $70/year; other countries, $80/year.
Affiliation	*JLTCA* is published by the American College of Health Care Administrators.
E-Mail Address	achca@achca.usa.com
Home Page URL	www.achca.org

Journal of Marriage & the Family

Editorial Focus	Original research and theory concerning families, broadly defined, from all disciplines of the social sciences.
Audience	Family scholars; policy analysts.
Special Themes	None.
Where Indexed/ Abstracted	All major social science abstracting services.
Year Established	1939.
Circulation	8,000.
Frequency	4 issues per year.
Months Issued	February, May, August, November.
No. of Articles	20 per issue.

SUBMISSIONS

Address	R. Milardo, Editor, *Journal of Marriage & the Family*, 30 Merrill Hall, University of Maine, Orono, ME 04469-5749.
Number of Copies	5.
Disk Submission	No.

FORMAT OF MANUSCRIPT

Cover Sheet	See any issue of journal for specific guidelines. Generally, the journal requires format of the *Publication Manual of the American Psychological Association*.
Abstract	See style guide.
Key Words	See style guide.
Length	See style guide.
Margins	See style guide.
Spacing	See style guide.

STYLE

Name of Guide	*Publication Manual of the American Psychological Association.*
Subheadings	See style guide.
References	See style guide.
Footnotes	See style guide.
Tables or Figures	See style guide.

REVIEW PROCESS

Type	Anonymous blind review.
Queries	Yes.
Acknowledgment	Include a self-addressed postcard.
Review Time	8–10 weeks.
Revisions	Typically required, as per instructions from the editor.
Acceptance Rate	17%.
Return of Manuscript	Not returned.
Lag Time to Print	6–12 months.

CHARGES TO AUTHOR

Processing	$15.

REPRINT, SUBSCRIPTION, AND CONTACT INFORMATION

Reprint Policy	Available on order directly from the printer.
Book Reviews	Direct inquiries to Marc Baronowski, Book Review Editor, 30 Merrill Hall, University of Maine, Orono, ME 04469-5749.
Subscriptions	National Council on Family Relations, 3989 Central Avenue, NE, Suite 550, Minneapolis, MN 55421.
E-Mail Address	Milardo@Maine.Maine.Edu

The Journal of Mind and Behavior

Editorial Focus	(1) The mind/body problem in the social sciences, psychiatry and the medical sciences, and the physical sciences; (2) the sociology of experimentation and the scientific method; (3) theories of consciousness.
Audience	Psychiatrists, philosophers, social workers, psychologists.
Special Themes	Disquisitions on the biopsychiatric/medical model and its appropriateness to issues of mental health.
Where Indexed/ Abstracted	Current Contents; Excerpta Medica; International Bibliography of Book Reviews; The Philosopher's Index; Physics Abstracts; Psychological Abstracts; Social Sciences Citation Index; Social Work Abstracts; Sociological Abstracts.
Year Established	1980.
Circulation	1,048.
Frequency	Quarterly.
Months Issued	March, June, September, December.
No. of Articles	Average 5 articles and 3 book reviews.

SUBMISSIONS

Address	Dr. Raymond Russ, Editor, *Journal of Mind and Behavior,* Psychology Department, 5742 Little Hall, Orono, ME 04469-5742.
Number of Copies	4.
Disk Submission	After acceptance.

FORMAT OF MANUSCRIPT

Cover Sheet	See style guide.
Abstract	Yes, 150 words.
Key Words	None.
Length	No length requirements.
Margins	1 inch on all sides.
Spacing	Double-spaced.

STYLE

Name of Guide	*Publication Manual of the American Psychological Association.*
Subheadings	Usually three levels.
References	See style guide.
Footnotes	Not encouraged.
Tables or Figures	Camera-ready copy required.

REVIEW PROCESS

Type	Peer review; blind if specified; see authors' instructions.
Queries	Discouraged.
Acknowledgment	On receipt of manuscript.
Review Time	3–4 months.
Revisions	Generally, the original reviewers and editor-in-chief assess revised manuscript.
Acceptance Rate	16%.
Return of Manuscript	Usually returned.
Lag Time to Print	Immediate publication policy: lag time 6–8 months.

REPRINT, SUBSCRIPTION, AND CONTACT INFORMATION

Reprint Policy	Authors must pre-order reprints; pay schedule sent to author.
Book Reviews	By invitation as well as unsolicited. Send reviews to: Dr. Steven Connelly, Department of English, Indiana State University, Terre Haute, IN 47809.
Subscriptions	Institute of Mind and Behavior, P.O. Box 522, Village Station, New York City, NY 10014.
Home Page URL	http://kramer.ume.maine.edu/~jmb

Journal of Multicultural Social Work

Editorial Focus   Ethnic issues in the human services.

Audience   Not specified.

Special Themes   State-of-the-art research and theory on social work issues, practice, and problems.

Where Indexed/ Abstracted   Academic Abstracts/CD-ROM; Academic Search; Book Review Index; caredata CD: the social and community care database; Chicano Periodical Index (plus Chicano Database on CD-ROM); CNPIEC Reference Guide: Chinese National Directory of Foreign Periodicals; ERIC Clearinghouse on Rural Education & Small Schools; Family Studies Database (online and CD-ROM); IBZ International Bibliography of Periodical Literature; Index to Periodical Articles Related to Law; International Bulletin of Bibliography on Education; INTERNET ACCESS (& additional networks) Bulletin Board for Libraries ("BUBL"), coverage of information resources on INTERNET, JANET, and other networks; MasterFILE: updated database from EBSCO Publishing; Multicultural Education Abstracts; National Clearinghouse for Bilingual Education; Public Library FULL TEXT; Referativnyi Zhurnal (Abstracts Journal of the Institute of Scientific Information of the Republic of Russia); Sage Public Administration Abstracts (SPAA); Social Planning Policy & Development Abstracts (SOPODA); Social Science Source; Social Work Abstracts; Sociological Abstracts (SA); Studies on Women Abstracts; Violence and Abuse Abstracts: A Review of Current Literature on Interpersonal Violence (VAA); Vocational Search.

Year Established   1991.

Circulation   479.

Frequency   Quarterly.

Months Issued   Not specified.

No. of Articles   6–10 per issue.

SUBMISSIONS

Address   Diane de Anda, PhD, Department of Social Welfare, UCLA, Box 951452, Los Angeles, CA 90095-1452.

Number of Copies   4.

Disk Submission   Authors of accepted manuscripts are asked to submit a disk, preferably in Microsoft Word or WordPerfect.

FORMAT OF MANUSCRIPT

Cover Sheet   Separate sheet, which does not go out for review. Full title, author names, degrees, professional titles; designation of one author as corresponding author with full address, phone numbers, e-mail address, and fax number; date of submission.

Abstract	About 100 words.
Key Words	5 or 6 key words that identify article content.
Length	20–25 pages, including references and abstract. Lengthier manuscripts may be considered, but only at the discretion of the editor. Sometimes, lengthier manuscripts may be considered if they can be divided into sections for publication in successive issues.
Margins	1 inch on all sides.
Spacing	Double-spaced for all copy, except title page.

STYLE

Name of Guide	*Publication Manual of the American Psychological Association.*
Subheadings	Use as needed to guide reader through the article. No more than 4 levels.
References	Author–date citation style; see style guide.
Footnotes	No footnotes preferred; incorporate into text.
Tables or Figures	Type tables double-spaced. Submit camera-ready art (300 dpi printer or better) for all figures. Place each table or figure on a separate, numbered page at the end of the manuscript.

REVIEW PROCESS

Type	"Double blind" anonymous peer review. 3 reviewers plus editor-in-chief read the manuscript in an anonymous review.
Queries	Authors are encouraged to read the journal to determine if their subject matter would be appropriate.
Acknowledgment	Enclose a regular self-addressed, stamped envelope with submission.
Review Time	3–4 months.
Revisions	See journal.
Acceptance Rate	Not specified.
Return of Manuscript	Only if 9″ x 12″ self-addressed, stamped envelope is enclosed.
Lag Time to Print	6 months–1 year.

REPRINT, SUBSCRIPTION, AND CONTACT INFORMATION

Reprint Policy	All authors receive 2 complimentary copies of the issue in which article appears. Authors receive reprint order forms to purchase additional reprinted copies.
Book Reviews	Books for review should be sent to Dr. Charles Guzzetta, Hunter College School of Social Work, 129 East 29th Street, New York, NY 10021.
Subscriptions	The Haworth Press, Inc., 10 Alice Street, Binghamton, NY 13904-1580. Individuals, $32; institutions, $60; libraries, $125.

Journal of Neuro-AIDS

Editorial Focus	A forum devoted to advances in the neurology and neurobiology of human immunodeficiency virus (HIV), AIDS, and related viral infections of the nervous system.
Audience	Not specified.
Special Themes	The neurology and neurobiology of HIV-1 infection and AIDS.
Where Indexed/ Abstracted	Applied Social Sciences Index & Abstracts; CSA Neurosciences Abstracts; Current AIDS Literature (CAB Abstracts); Digest of Neurology and Psychiatry; INTERNET ACCESS (& additional networks) Bulletin Board for Libraries ("BUBL"), coverage of information resources on INTERNET, JANET, and other networks; Medication Use STudies (MUST) Database; Risk Abstracts; Virology and AIDS Abstracts.
Year Established	1996.
Circulation	213.
Frequency	Quarterly.
Months Issued	Not specified.
No. of Articles	6–10 per issue.

SUBMISSIONS

Address	Editor, Richard W. Price, MD, Department of Neurology, Room 4M62, San Francisco General Hospital, 1001 Potrero Avenue, San Francisco, CA 94110-3518.
Number of Copies	4.
Disk Submission	Authors of accepted manuscripts are asked to submit a disk, preferably in Microsoft Word or WordPerfect.

FORMAT OF MANUSCRIPT

Cover Sheet	Separate sheet, which does not go out for review. Full title, author names, degrees, professional titles; designation of one author as corresponding author with full address, phone numbers, e-mail address, and fax number; date of submission.
Abstract	About 100 words.
Key Words	5 or 6 key words that identify article content.
Length	15–20 pages, including references and abstract. Lengthier manuscripts may be considered, but only at the discretion of the editor. Sometimes, lengthier manuscripts may be considered if they can be divided into sections for publication in successive issues.
Margins	1 inch on all sides.
Spacing	Double-spaced for all copy, except title page.

STYLE

Name of Guide	See journal.
Subheadings	Use as needed to guide reader through the article. No more than 4 levels.
References	Author–date citation style; see style guide.
Footnotes	No footnotes preferred; incorporate into text.
Tables or Figures	Type tables double-spaced. Submit camera-ready art (300 dpi printer or better) for all figures. Place each table or figure on a separate, numbered page at the end of the manuscript.

REVIEW PROCESS

Type	"Double blind" anonymous peer review. 3 reviewers plus editor-in-chief read the manuscript in an anonymous review.
Queries	Authors are encouraged to read the journal to determine if their subject matter would be appropriate.
Acknowledgment	Enclose a regular self-addressed, stamped envelope with submission.
Review Time	3–4 months.
Revisions	See journal.
Acceptance Rate	Not specified.
Return of Manuscript	Only if 9″ x 12″ self-addressed, stamped envelope is enclosed.
Lag Time to Print	6 months–1 year.

REPRINT, SUBSCRIPTION, AND CONTACT INFORMATION

Reprint Policy	All authors receive 2 complimentary copies of the issue in which article appears. Authors receive reprint order forms to purchase additional reprinted copies.
Book Reviews	Send to journal editor.
Subscriptions	The Haworth Press, Inc., 10 Alice Street, Binghamton, NY 13904-1580. Individuals, $45; institutions, $60; libraries, $75.

Journal of Neurovascular Disease

Editorial Focus	To provide a broad academic forum for acute and chronic care physicians and rehab specialists involved in treatment of neurovascular patients.
Audience	Neurologists, rehab MDs, neurosurgeons, neuroradiologists.
Special Themes	Contact publisher.
Where Indexed/ Abstracted	Index Medicus pending.
Year Established	1996.
Circulation	Approximately 3,000.
Frequency	Bimonthly.
Months Issued	February, April, June, August, October, December.
No. of Articles	5–8 per issue.

SUBMISSIONS

Address	R. Patrick Gates, Managing Editor, 470 Boston Post Road, Weston, MA 02193.
Number of Copies	3.
Disk Submission	Mandatory; IBM PC/MS-DOS format disk in ASCII text, Microsoft Word 2.0 or greater, DCA, or WordPerfect 5.1 or greater.

FORMAT OF MANUSCRIPT

Cover Sheet	Title; full name(s); highest academic degrees, affiliations, and address of each author; and phone number of author handling correspondence.
Abstract	100–200 words.
Key Words	Yes.
Length	15–20 pages.
Margins	Wide.
Spacing	Double-spaced.

STYLE

Name of Guide	*MLA Handbook.*
Subheadings	Insert where suitable.
References	Contact publisher for style.
Footnotes	None.
Tables or Figures	Submit 3 copies (paper) of each. Acceptable formats: TIFF, EPS, JPE6, BMP, WFM.

REVIEW PROCESS

Type	Anonymous by 3 reviewers.
Queries	Yes, but not necessary.
Acknowledgment	By mail.
Review Time	10–15 weeks.
Revisions	Reviewer comments and suggestions are mailed to authors for approval or action. If author chooses to make or approve or suggest alternative changes, the manuscript is reviewed again for clarity and content by the previous reviewers or by another party.
Acceptance Rate	50%.
Return of Manuscript	Returned if not published.
Lag Time to Print	6–8 months.

REPRINT, SUBSCRIPTION, AND CONTACT INFORMATION

Reprint Policy	Professional reprints available at discount. Contact publisher.
Book Reviews	Query first.
Subscriptions	Publisher, 470 Boston Post Road, Weston, MA 02193.
E-Mail Address	(AOL) DeVitoR@AOL.COM (CompuServe) 76150.1602 (Internet) radjr@ix.netcom.com

Journal of Nonprofit & Public Sector Marketing

Editorial Focus	The development and extension of marketing knowledge in the voluntary and public sectors.
Audience	Academic (75%) and practitioner (25%).
Special Themes	Guest editors periodically develop thematic special issues.
Where Indexed/ Abstracted	ABSCAN, Inc.; CNPIEC Reference Guide: Chinese National Directory of Foreign Periodicals; Communication Abstracts; Digest of Neurology and Psychiatry; Health Care Literature Information Network/HECLINET; Human Resources Abstracts (HRA); IBZ International Bibliography of Periodical Literature; INTERNET ACCESS (& additional networks) Bulletin Board for Libraries ("BUBL"), coverage of information resources on INTERNET.JANET; Journal of Academic Librarianship: Guide to Professional Literature; Journal of Health Care Marketing (abstracts section); Management & Marketing Abstracts; Marketing Executive Report; Mental Health Abstracts (online through DIALOG); Operations Research/Management Science; OT BibSys, American Occupational Therapy Foundation; Political Science Abstracts; Public Affairs Information Bulletin (PAIS); Social Work Abstracts; Sport Database/Discus.
Year Established	1990.
Frequency	Quarterly.
Months Issued	Not specified.
No. of Articles	5–7 per issue.

SUBMISSIONS

Address	Donald R. Self, Editor, *Journal of Nonprofit & Public Sector Marketing*, Department of Marketing, Auburn University at Montgomery, Montgomery, AL 36117.
Number of Copies	4.
Disk Submission	On acceptance.

FORMAT OF MANUSCRIPT

Cover Sheet	Staple a cover page to the manuscript, indicating only the article title (this is used for refereeing). Enclose a regular title page (but do not staple it to the manuscript) that includes the title plus full authorship, an abstract of about 100 words, and an introductory footnote with authors' academic degrees, professional titles, affiliations, mailing addresses, and any desired acknowledgment of research support or other credit.
Abstract	Approximately 100 words.
Key Words	Optional.
Length	10–30 pages, including references and abstract. Longer manuscripts may be considered.

Margins	At least 1 inch on all sides.
Spacing	Double-spaced.

STYLE

Name of Guide	References, citations, and general style of manuscripts for this journal should follow the *Publication Manual of the American Psychological Association*. If an author wishes to submit a paper that has already been prepared in another style, he or she may do so. However, if the paper is accepted, the author is fully responsible for retyping the manuscript in the correct style as indicated above. Neither the editor nor the publisher is responsible for re-preparing manuscript copy to adhere to the journal's style.
Subheadings	No more than 3 levels (see style guide).
References	See style guide.
Footnotes	No footnotes preferred; incorporate into text.
Tables or Figures	Type tables double-spaced per guide; must be camera-ready, original copies. Place each table or figure on a separate, numbered sheet at the end of the manuscript.

REVIEW PROCESS

Type	"Double-blind" anonymous peer review, 1 internal review.
Queries	To editor.
Acknowledgment	Enclose a regular self-addressed, stamped envelope with submission.
Review Time	2–3 months.
Revisions	Submit 4 copies with a separate cover sheet (not identifying the author) describing the changes made in the manuscript and replying to the reviewers' comments. In general, the original reviewers read revisions.
Acceptance Rate	21%–30%.
Return of Manuscript	Not returned; author should retain copies.
Lag Time to Print	Approximately 6 months–1 year.

REPRINT, SUBSCRIPTION, AND CONTACT INFORMATION

Reprint Policy	The first author will receive 1 copy of the journal issue and 10 complimentary reprints of the article. Other authors will receive 1 copy of the issue. These are sent several weeks after the journal issue is published and in circulation.
Book Reviews	Send books for review to: Book Review Editor, *Journal of Nonprofit and Public Sector Marketing*, Department of Marketing, Auburn University at Montgomery, Montgomery AL 36117.
Subscriptions	The Haworth Press, Inc., 10 Alice Street, Binghamton, NY 13904-1580. 1996–97 one-year prices: Individuals, $36; institutions, $54; libraries, $160.
E-Mail Address	Dself@Monk.Aum.Edu

Journal of Nutrition for the Elderly

Editorial Focus	Multidisciplinary, covers all essential aspects of nutrition, such as the clinical correlation between the pathophysiology of diseases and the role of nutrition, the psychosocial aspects of eating, and client education suggestions.
Audience	Health care professionals who work with older adults—physicians, nurses, nutritionists, public health workers.
Special Themes	All nutrition and food-related topics.
Where Indexed/ Abstracted	Abstracts in Anthropology; Abstracts in Social Gerontology: Current Literature on Aging; Academic Abstracts/CD-ROM; AGRICOLA Database; BIOSIS; BIOSIS Previews; Brown University Geriatric Research Application Digest "Abstracts Section"; Cabell's Directory of Publishing Opportunities in Nursing; Cambridge Scientific Abstracts; CINAHL; CNPIEC Reference Guide: Chinese National Directory of Foreign Periodicals; CHID; Communications Abstracts; CPcurrents; Family Studies Database; Food Institute Report "Abstract Section"; FSTA; Food Adlibra; Heath Promotion and Education Database; Health Source: Indexing & Abstracting; Health Source Plus; HRA; International Nursing Index; International Pharmaceutical Abstracts; INTERNET ACCESS (list on request); Medication Use STudies (MUST) Database; Nutrition Abstracts & Review Series A-Human & Experimental; Nutrition Research Newsletter "Abstract Section"; PsycINFO; Referativnyi Zhurnal (Abstract Journal of the Institute of Scientific Information of the Republic of Russia); Social Work Abstracts.
Year Established	1981.
Circulation	1,000.
Frequency	Quarterly.
Months Issued	Spring, summer, fall, winter.
No. of Articles	3–7.

SUBMISSIONS

Address	*Journal of Nutrition for the Elderly*, P.O. Box 630169, Little Neck, NY 11363-0169.
Number of Copies	4.
Disk Submission	Any format.

FORMAT OF MANUSCRIPT

Cover Sheet	Cover page indicating only the article title (used for anonymous refereeing), abstract on separate page, title page: full authorship with academic degrees, footnote with professional titles, affiliations, mailing address for corresponding author, desired acknowledgment, research support or other credit.
Abstract	Approximately 100–200 words.
Key Words	3–10 words for index purposes.

Length	Approximately 10–30 typed, double-spaced pages including references and abstract. Longer manuscripts may be considered at the discretion of the editor or may be divided into parts.
Margins	1 inch on all sides.
Spacing	Double-spaced, including references, except for title page.

STYLE

Name of Guide	*Chicago Manual of Style.*
Subheadings	As needed to guide reader. Prefer most of the following to be noted in subheads: introduction, literature review, research model, conclusions, implications/discussion.
References	See style guide.
Footnotes	Acceptable in tables, figures, and illustrations, but not in text unless absolutely essential for clarification.
Tables or Figures	Must be "camera-ready," double-spaced. Prepare on separate sheets of paper; on reverse side in pencil indicate article name and journal name. In text leave a space and indicate placement. Photographs are acceptable and will become property of publisher.

REVIEW PROCESS

Type	Anonymous; 2 or more reviewers and 1 editor.
Queries	Accepted, particularly for special sections such as Current Practice and Nutrition Management in Long-Term Care.
Acknowledgment	Provide self-addressed, stamped postcard.
Review Time	8 weeks.
Revisions	Author will be invited to revise paper as directed by reviewers' comments and recommendations.
Acceptance Rate	50%–70%. We encourage and guide authors through revision if manuscript has promise; allow 2–3 revisions if necessary and if author is willing to do such in a timely manner.
Return of Manuscript	Only if revision recommended.
Lag Time to Print	4 months–1 year.

REPRINT, SUBSCRIPTION, AND CONTACT INFORMATION

Reprint Policy	Senior author receives 2 copies of the issue and 10 complimentary reprints; junior authors receive 1 copy of the issue. An order form for the purchase of additional reprints is sent to all authors.
Book Reviews	By invitation only.
Subscriptions	*Journal of Nutrition for the Elderly,* The Haworth Press, Inc., 10 Alice Street, Binghamton, NY 13904-1580; phone: 800-342-9678; fax: 607-722-6362.

Journal of Offender Rehabilitation

Previous Title	*Journal of Offender Counseling, Services & Rehabilitation.*
Editorial Focus	A multidisciplinary journal of innovation in research, services, and programs in corrections and criminal justice.
Audience	Not specified.
Where Indexed/ Abstracted	Abstracts of Research in Pastoral Care & Counseling; Cambridge Scientific Abstracts; CNPIEC Reference Guide: Chinese National Directory of Foreign Periodicals; Criminal Justice Periodical Index; Criminal Justice Abstracts; Criminology Penology and Police Science Abstracts; ERIC Clearinghouse on Counseling and Student Services (ERIC/CASS); Family Studies Database (online and CD-ROM); Family Violence & Sexual Assault Bulletin; IBZ International Bibliography of Periodical Literature; Index to Periodical Articles Related to Law; INTERNET ACCESS (& additional networks) Bulletin Board for Libraries ("BUBL"), coverage of information resources on INTERNET, JANET, and other networks; Mental Health Abstracts (online through DIALOG); National Criminal Justice Reference Service; NIAAA Alcohol and Alcohol Problems Science Database (ETOH); PASCAL International Bibliography T205: Sciences de l'information Documentation; Referativnyi Zhurnal (Abstracts Journal of the Institute of Scientific Information of the Republic of Russia); Sage Urban Studies Abstracts (SUSA); Social Planning/Policy & Development Abstracts (SOPODA); Social Work Abstracts; Sociological Abstracts (SA); Special Educational Needs Abstracts; Violence and Abuse Abstracts: A Review of Current Literature on Interpersonal Violence (VAA).
Year Established	1990.
Circulation	415.
Frequency	Quarterly.
Months Issued	Not specified.
No. of Articles	6–10 per issue.

SUBMISSIONS

Address	Nathaniel J. Pallone, PhD, Editor, *Journal of Offender Rehabilitation*, 360 West Court Street, Doylestown, PA 19801.
Number of Copies	4.
Disk Submission	Authors of accepted manuscripts are asked to submit a disk, preferably in Microsoft Word or WordPerfect.

FORMAT OF MANUSCRIPT

Cover Sheet	Separate sheet, which does not go out for review. Full title, author names, degrees, professional titles; designation of one author as corresponding author with full address, phone numbers, e-mail address, and fax number; date of submission.

Abstract	About 100 words.
Key Words	5 or 6 key words that identify article content.
Length	25 pages, including references and abstract. Lengthier manuscripts may be considered, but only at the discretion of the editor. Sometimes, lengthier manuscripts may be considered if they can be divided into sections for publication in successive issues.
Margins	1 inch on all sides.
Spacing	Double-spaced for all copy, except title page.

STYLE

Name of Guide	*Publication Manual of the American Psychological Association.*
Subheadings	Use as needed to guide reader through the article. No more than 4 levels.
References	Author–date citation style; see style guide.
Footnotes	No footnotes preferred; incorporate into text.
Tables or Figures	Type tables double-spaced. Submit camera-ready art (300 dpi printer or better) for all figures. Place each table or figure on a separate, numbered page at the end of the manuscript.

REVIEW PROCESS

Type	"Double blind" anonymous peer review. 3 reviewers plus editor-in-chief read the manuscript in an anonymous review.
Queries	Authors are encouraged to read the journal to determine if their subject matter would be appropriate.
Acknowledgment	Enclose a regular self-addressed, stamped envelope with submission.
Review Time	3–4 months.
Revisions	See journal.
Acceptance Rate	Not specified.
Return of Manuscript	Only if 9″ x 12″ self-addressed, stamped envelope is enclosed.
Lag Time to Print	6 months–1 year.

REPRINT, SUBSCRIPTION, AND CONTACT INFORMATION

Reprint Policy	All authors receive 2 complimentary copies of the issue in which article appears. Authors receive reprint order forms to purchase additional reprinted copies.
Book Reviews	Send to journal editor.
Subscriptions	The Haworth Press, Inc., 10 Alice Street, Binghamton, NY 13904-1580. Individuals, $45; institutions, $125; libraries, $175.
E-Mail Address	NJP2EDIT@aol.com

Journal of Peace Research

Editorial Focus	Causes of violence and conflict resolution, articles directed toward ways and means of peace favored.
Audience	Researchers, faculty, students, libraries, organizations.
Special Themes	Conversion, disarmament, the environment.
Where Indexed/ Abstracted	ABC Pol Sci; Abstracts of Military Bibliography; Academic Abstracts; The Alternative Newsletter; America: History & Life; Book Review Index; British Humanities Index; Bulletin Analytique de Documentation Politique, Economique et Social Contemporaine; Current Contents: Social & Behavioral Sciences; Current Military & Political Literature; EconLit; The Economic Literature Index; Expanded Academic Index; Future Survey; Historical Abstracts; HRI Reporter; Human Resources Abstracts; Index of Economic Articles; Information-Dokumentation; Inforpaz; Info Trac; International bibliography of Periodical Literature (IBZ); International bibliography of the Social Sciences; International Political Science Abstracts; Middle East Abstracts & Index; Monthly bibliography of the UN Library; Peace Research Abstracts Journal; Periodica Islamica; Political Science Abstracts; PAIS—Public Affairs Information Services; Risk Abstracts; Sage Public Administration Abstracts; Sage Urban Studies Abstracts; Science Culture; Social Science Abstracts; Social Sciences Citation Index; Social Sciences Index; Social Science Source; Social Work Abstracts; Sociological Abstracts; Southeast Asia Abstracts & Index; Violence and Abuse Abstracts.
Year Established	1964.
Circulation	Approximately 1,300.
Frequency	Quarterly.
Months Issued	February, May, August, November.
No. of Articles	Up to 8 per issue.

SUBMISSIONS

Address	Editor, *Journal of Peace Research,* Fuglehauggata 11, 0260 Oslo, Norway.
Number of Copies	4.
Disk Submission	Yes, Microsoft Word or WordPerfect 5.1 for DOS.

FORMAT OF MANUSCRIPT

Cover Sheet	None.
Abstract	200–300 words.
Key Words	None.
Length	No ideal length.
Margins	1 inch on all sides.
Spacing	Double-spaced, except title page.

STYLE

Name of Guide	Provided by the editor.
Subheadings	See style guide.
References	See style guide.
Footnotes	Use endnotes only.
Tables or Figures	See style guide.

REVIEW PROCESS

Type	"Single-blind" anonymous peer review, usually 3 reviewers and 1 of the editors-in-chief.
Queries	Query letters are discouraged; authors are encouraged to read the journal to determine if their subject matter is appropriate.
Acknowledgment	Letter.
Review Time	3 months.
Revisions	When needed.
Acceptance Rate	30%.
Return of Manuscript	If author makes request at time of submission.
Lag Time to Print	6 months after acceptance.

REPRINT, SUBSCRIPTION, AND CONTACT INFORMATION

Reprint Policy	25 free reprints and a copy of the issue in which the article appears.
Book Reviews	By PRIO staff; "Focus On" and "Review Essay" by invitation.
Subscriptions	Sage Publications Ltd., 6 Bonhill Street, London EC2A 4PU, England.
Affiliation	International Peace Research Institute, Oslo (PRIO).
E-Mail Address	jpr@prio.no

Journal of Pediatric Psychology

Editorial Focus	The main emphasis of the journal is on original research. Analytical reviews of research, brief scientific reports, scholarly case studies, and comments to the editor will also be considered for publication.
Audience	Psychologists, physicians, nurses, social workers.
Special Themes	The journal publishes articles related to theory, research, and professional practice in pediatric psychology. Pediatric psychology is an interdisciplinary field addressing physical, cognitive, social, and emotional functioning and development as it relates to health and illness issues in children, adolescents, and families.
Where Indexed/ Abstracted	Beck Medical Information; Behavioral Medical Abstracts; Biological Abstracts; Child and Youth Services; Child Development Abstracts and Bibliography; Cumulative Index to Nursing and Allied Health Literature; Current Contents; Exceptional Child Education Resources; Excerpta Medica; Family Resources Database; Health Instrument File; Index Medicus; Mental Health Abstracts; Psychological Abstracts; Referativnyi Zhurnal; Sage Family Studies Abstracts; Science Citation Index; Selected List of Tables of Contents of Psychiatric Periodicals; Social Work Abstracts; Sociological Abstracts; Special Educational Needs Abstracts; The Psychological Reader's Guide; Zeitschrift fur Kinder- und Jugendpsychiatrie.
Year Established	1976.
Circulation	1,500+.
Frequency	Bimonthly.
Months Issued	February, April, June, August, October, December.
No. of Articles	10–12 per issue.

SUBMISSIONS

Address	Annette M. La Greca, Editor, *Journal of Pediatric Psychology,* Department of Psychology, P.O. Box 249229, University of Miami, Coral Gables, FL 33124.
Number of Copies	4.
Disk Submission	Not applicable.

FORMAT OF MANUSCRIPT

Cover Sheet	A separate title page listing the name and academic affiliations of all authors, the full mailing address of corresponding author, and personal acknowledgments; authors are to avoid identifying information in the body of the manuscript.
Abstract	Must be included and contain a maximum of 960 characters and spaces (100–125 words). Abstracts must begin with a verb and be typed on a separate sheet of paper.
Key Words	3–10 key words or phrases should be placed below the abstract.

Length	Original Research Articles should not exceed 25 pages total, including title page, references, tables, etc.; Scholarly Reviews should not exceed 30 pages total; Case Reports & Brief Scientific Reports should not exceed 12 pages total, including a maximum of 2 tables or illustrations; Comments should not exceed 4 pages including references.
Margins	1 inch on all sides.
Spacing	Double-spaced throughout.

STYLE

Name of Guide	*Publication Manual of the American Psychological Association.*
Subheadings	See style guide.
References	See style guide.
Footnotes	See style guide.
Tables or Figures	See style guide. Tables should be double-spaced, numbered, and referred to by number in the text. Each table should be placed on a separate sheet of paper and have a brief descriptive title. Figures or illustrations are to be numbered in one consecutive series of Arabic numerals. For the initial submission, figures may be laser prints or photocopies. On acceptance, one set of glossy prints, showing high contrast, must be provided. Each figure should have an accompanying caption, with all captions typed as one list on a separate sheet of paper.

REVIEW PROCESS

Type	"Double-blind" anonymous peer review. 2 reviewers plus the editor read the manuscript.
Queries	To editorial office.
Acknowledgment	The editor will notify the author in writing on receipt of manuscript.
Review Time	2–3 months.
Revisions	To be decided by the editor. Directions will be given at that time.
Acceptance Rate	15%.
Return of Manuscript	Not returned; author should retain copies.
Lag Time to Print	Approximately 10 months.

REPRINT, SUBSCRIPTION, AND CONTACT INFORMATION

Reprint Policy	Author can purchase reprints through the publisher, Plenum Publishing Corporation.
Book Reviews	Yes.
Subscriptions	Plenum Publishing Corporation, Subscription Department, 233 Spring Street, New York, NY 10013; phone: 212-620-8468; fax: 212-807-1047.
Affiliation	Society of Pediatric Psychology (American Psychological Association, Division 12, Section V).
Home Page URL	http://macserv.psy.miami.edu/SPP/

Journal of Personality and Social Psychology

Previous Title   *Journal of Abnormal and Social Psychology.*

Editorial Focus   The *Journal of Personality and Social Psychology* publishes original papers in all areas of personality and social psychology. It emphasizes empirical reports but may include specialized theoretical, methodological, and review papers. The journal is divided into three independently edited sections:

• **Attitudes and Social Cognition** addresses those domains of social behavior in which cognition plays a major role, including the interface of cognition with overt behavior, affect, and motivation. Among topics covered are the formation, change, and utilization of attitudes, attributions, and stereotypes, person memory, self-regulation, and the origins and consequences of moods and emotions insofar as these interact with cognition. Of interest also is the influence of cognition and its various interfaces on significant social phenomena such as persuasion, communication, prejudice, social development, and cultural trends.

• **Interpersonal Relations and Group Processes** focuses on psychological and structural features of interaction in dyads and groups. Appropriate to this section are papers on the nature and dynamics of interactions and social relationships, including interpersonal attraction, communication, emotion, and relationship development, and on group and organizational processes such as social influence, group decision making and task performance, intergroup relations and aggression, prosocial behavior and other types of social behavior.

• **Personality Processes and Individual Differences** encourages papers on all aspects of personality psychology. This includes personality assessment, measurement, structure, basic processes, and dynamics. All methodological approaches will be considered.

Audience   Researchers in the discipline, faculty, libraries.

Where Indexed/   Criminal Justice Abstracts; Current Contents; PsycINFO; Sage Family Studies

Abstracted   Abstracts; Social Sciences Citation Index.

Year Established   1965.

Circulation   5,600.

Frequency   Monthly.

No. of Articles   15.

SUBMISSIONS

Address   Section Editors:

Attitudes and Social Cognition: Arie W. Kruglanski, Department of Psychology, University of Maryland, College Park, MD 20742.

Interpersonal Relations and Group Processes: Chester A. Insko, Department of Psychology, CB #3270, Davie Hall, University of North Carolina, Chapel Hill, NC 27599-3270.

Personality Processes and Individual Differences: Russell G. Geen, JPSP-PPID, Department of Psychology, University of Missouri, Columbia, MO 65211.

Number of Copies	6.
Disk Submission	Submit manuscripts on paper; disks may be requested of accepted articles.

FORMAT OF MANUSCRIPT

Cover Sheet	Refer to Instructions to Authors in each issue.
Abstract	Manuscripts must include an abstract containing a maximum of 960 characters and spaces (about 120 words), typed on a separate sheet.
Key Words	None.
Length	Not specified.
Margins	See style guide.
Spacing	Double-spaced.

STYLE

Name of Guide	*Publication Manual of the American Psychological Association.*
Subheadings	See style guide.
References	See style guide.
Footnotes	See style guide.
Tables or Figures	See style guide; camera-ready copy required for all art.

REVIEW PROCESS

Type	Masked review only if requested by author.
Queries	No query letters.
Acknowledgment	Editor acknowledges submission by mail.
Review Time	Usually 60–90 days.
Revisions	Most manuscripts are initially rejected; most published manuscripts have gone through one or two revisions.
Acceptance Rate	17%.
Return of Manuscript	Manuscripts are not usually returned.
Lag Time to Print	6 months.

CHARGES TO AUTHOR

Author Alterations	Authors are billed for alterations in proofs.

REPRINT, SUBSCRIPTION, AND CONTACT INFORMATION

Reprint Policy	Authors may purchase reprints of their articles.
Book Reviews	None.
Subscriptions	Subscriptions Department, American Psychological Association, 750 First Street, NE, Washington, DC 20002-4242.
	Yearly nonmember rates are $238 domestic, $323 foreign, $348 air mail. APA members: $130.
Affiliation	Published by the American Psychological Association.
Home Page URL	http://www.apa.org

Journal of Poetry Therapy

Editorial Focus	The purview of this interdisciplinary journal includes the use of poetry, bibliotherapy, narrative, storytelling, metaphor, journal writing, song lyrics, and the related language/creative arts in therapeutic capacities. The journal welcomes a wide variety of scholarly articles including theoretical, historical, practice, and research (qualitative and quantitative) studies. Brief reports and poetry are also invited. Additional features include book reviews and dissertation abstracts.
Audience	Practitioners, researchers, educators, and students in the helping professions; others studying the therapeutic aspects of the language arts.
Special Themes	Family and group treatment, social welfare, gender and cultural issues, interpersonal violence, social justice, health and mental health, narrative approaches to practice, and theory building.
Where Indexed/ Abstracted	CATLINE from the National Library of Medicine; ERIC/Current Index to Journals in Education (CIJE); Human Resource Abstracts; International Bibliography of Periodical Literature; Linguistics and Language Behavior Abstracts (LLBA); Modern Language Association Abstracts (MLA); Periodical Abstracts (TM) Research II from UMI; Sage Family Studies Abstracts; Social Planning/Policy Development Abstracts; Social Work Abstracts; Sociological Abstracts.
Year Established	1987.
Circulation	500.
Frequency	Quarterly.
Months Issued	Fall, winter, spring, summer.
No. of Articles	4–5 articles; 6–8 poems.

SUBMISSIONS

Address	Nicholas Mazza, PhD, Editor, Journal of Poetry Therapy, Florida State University, School of Social Work, Tallahassee, FL 32306-2024.
Number of Copies	3.
Disk Submission	Disk is requested after a manuscript has been accepted.

FORMAT OF MANUSCRIPT

Cover Sheet	Full title, author names, degrees, author affiliation, complete mailing address, phone number, e-mail address, and fax number.
Abstract	Empirical: 100–150 words; practice/theory: 75–100 words.
Key Words	Up to 5 key words.
Length	14–25 pages for full-length manuscript; 4–6 pages for brief report.
Margins	1 inch on all sides.
Spacing	Double-spaced for all copy.

STYLE

Name of Guide	*Publication Manual of the American Psychological Association.*
Subheadings	See style guide.
References	See style guide.
Footnotes	Avoid using footnotes.
Tables or Figures	Submit camera-ready and include figure legends.

REVIEW PROCESS

Type	Anonymous review by 3 editorial board members.
Queries	Queries are discouraged.
Acknowledgment	Acknowledgment note sent on receipt of manuscript.
Review Time	3 months.
Revisions	Major revision: revised manuscript sent out for review. Minor revision: handled between author and editor only.
Acceptance Rate	Articles, 40%; poetry, 5%.
Return of Manuscript	Returned.
Lag Time to Print	3–9 months.

CHARGES TO AUTHOR

Author Alterations	$5 per line.

REPRINT, SUBSCRIPTION, AND CONTACT INFORMATION

Reprint Policy	Author receives 1 complimentary copy of the journal. Reprints available for purchase from the publisher.
Book Reviews	Contact the editor.
Subscriptions	Human Sciences Press, 233 Spring Street, New York, NY 10013-1578; phone: 800-221-9369.
	Individuals: $44 in U.S., $51 outside U.S.; institutions: $195 in U.S., $230 outside U.S. Authors receive a 15% discount on the first year of any new subscription to a Plenum Press journal.
Affiliation	Sponsored by the National Association for Poetry Therapy.
E-Mail Address	(Editor) nfmazza@mailer.fsu.edu
Home Page URL	(Publisher) Via the World Wide Web: gopher://plenum.titlenet.com:6200
	Via gopher: gopher plenum.titlenet.com 6200

The Journal of Police Negotiations, Crisis Management and Suicidology

Previous Title	*The Journal of Crisis Negotiations.*
Editorial Focus	Police hostage and crisis negotiations, crisis management/intervention, and suicide.
Audience	Police negotiators; plus all others interested in these areas specifically related to police and related groups.
Special Themes	Hostage and crisis negotiations, crisis intervention, suicide, and related areas that provide practical information as well as theory. Practical input from field negotiators and from academics are welcome.
Where Indexed/ Abstracted	Not specified.
Year Established	1996.
Circulation	300.
Frequency	Semiannually.
Months Issued	Approximately March and November.
No. of Articles	6–8.

SUBMISSIONS

Address	Dr. James L. Greenstone, Editor-in-Chief, P.O. Box 670292, Dallas, TX 75367-0292.
Number of Copies	3.
Disk Submission	Encouraged. Microsoft Word 6.0.

FORMAT OF MANUSCRIPT

Cover Sheet	Title, authors, affiliation, address, and phone numbers.
Abstract	500 words.
Key Words	Not specified.
Length	10–15 pages.
Margins	Standard.
Spacing	Double-spaced.

STYLE

Name of Guide	*Publication Manual of the American Psychological Association.*
Subheadings	Not specified.
References	See style guide.
Footnotes	Not specified.
Tables or Figures	Not specified.

REVIEW PROCESS

Type	Anonymous peer review.
Queries	Welcome.
Acknowledgment	Please provide self-addressed, stamped postcard.
Review Time	8–10 weeks.
Revisions	Author is responsible in most cases.
Acceptance Rate	60%–70%.
Return of Manuscript	Not returned.
Lag Time to Print	5–6 months.

CHARGES TO AUTHOR

Author Alterations	Varies.
Page Charges	Varies.

REPRINT, SUBSCRIPTION, AND CONTACT INFORMATION

Reprint Policy	2 copies of issue in which article appears. Additional copies of journal available at $12.50.
Book Reviews	Solicited or unsolicited. Send to Editor-in-Chief.
Subscriptions	Contact editor-in-chief.
	Individuals, $25; institutions, $35.

Journal of Policy Analysis and Management

Editorial Focus   The journal strives for quality, relevance, and originality in its feature articles. The editors give priority to manuscripts that relate their conclusions broadly to a number of substantive fields of public policy or that deal with issues of professional practice in policy analysis and public management. Although an interdisciplinary perspective is usually most appropriate, manuscripts that use the tools of a single discipline are welcome if they have substantial relevance and if they are written for a general rather than disciplinary audience. The editors welcome proposals for articles that review the state of knowledge in particular policy areas. For the "Insights" section, the editors seek manuscripts that present novel policy ideas, challenge common wisdom, report surprising research findings, draw lessons from experience, or illustrate the application of an analytical or managerial method. Wit and verve, and occasionally irreverence, are welcome. For "Curriculum and Case Notes," the editors believe the journal should play a role in improving professional education in policy analysis and public management and, therefore, welcome short manuscripts that deal with broad issues of curriculum or specific aspects of pedagogy.

Audience   Academics, government research staff, government practitioners, consultants; all with public policy and management concerns.

Where Indexed/ Abstracted   Not specified.

Year Established   1981.

Circulation   2,800.

Frequency   Quarterly.

Months Issued   December, March, June, September.

No. of Articles   4–6, plus shorter pieces.

SUBMISSIONS

Address   Janet Rothenberg Pack, Editor, *Journal of Policy Analysis and Management,* Public Policy and Management Department, The Wharton School, University of Pennsylvania, 3620 Locust Walk, Philadelphia, PA 19104-6372.

Number of Copies   3.

Disk Submission   No.

FORMAT OF MANUSCRIPT

Cover Sheet   Title and affiliation of authors.

Abstract   125 words.

Key Words   Not specified.

Length   25–40 pages.

Margins   Wide.

Spacing   Double-spaced.

STYLE

Name of Guide — *Chicago Manual of Style.*

Subheadings — Beginning at the left margin, use initial capitalization for major section headings. Subheadings should be paragraphed, underlined, with period at the end. The text should follow without paragraph. Do not use numbers or letters to identify sections.

References — Cite references in the text and footnotes within brackets that contain the author names and the year of publication. Consult the journal's Notes on Style for more details.

Footnotes — Incorporate footnotes into text when possible. If inclusion proves difficult, that is a strong argument for dropping the point. If, exceptionally, the author decides the idea must be included, then it may be carried in a footnote. Number footnotes consecutively and place at end of manuscript.

Tables or Figures — Rough in first submission; camera-ready for accepted manuscripts. Provide only data relevant to the textual argument. Select headings that communicate the argument being made. Avoid designing tables on dimensions that require printing at right angles to the normal reading position. Number and title all tables.

REVIEW PROCESS

Type — Anonymous review by 2 referees.

Queries — Optional.

Acknowledgment — By card or e-mail.

Review Time — 6–9 weeks.

Revisions — Not specified.

Acceptance Rate — 15%.

Return of Manuscript — Not returned.

Lag Time to Print — 5 months.

CHARGES TO AUTHOR

Author Alterations — The publisher reserves the right to charge no less than $1 per affected line for alterations that are not fault of the typesetter.

REPRINT, SUBSCRIPTION, AND CONTACT INFORMATION

Reprint Policy — Contact: Customer Service Department, John Wiley & Sons, 605 Third Avenue, New York, NY 10158; phone: 212-850-8776.

Book Reviews — Send to: Professor Laurence E. Lynn, Jr., Harris Graduate School of Public Policy Studies, University of Chicago, 1155 E. 60th Street, Chicago, IL 60637.

Subscriptions — John Wiley & Sons, Inc., Subscription Department, 605 Third Avenue, New York, NY 10158. APPAM membership includes subscription.

Affiliation — Association of Public Policy Analysis and Management (APPAM).

E-Mail Address — washburw@wharton.upenn.edu

Home Page URL — http://qsilver.queensu.ca/~appamwww

Journal of Prevention & Intervention in the Community

Previous Title	*Prevention in the Human Services* (until 1996).
Editorial Focus	Research and theoretical articles. Each issue is focused on a current topic.
Audience	Scientists and practitioners, faculty, students, libraries, human service and social welfare professionals.
Special Themes	Coronary heart disease, adolescent health, religion and mental health, AIDS prevention, homelessness, education in community psychology, drunk driving prevention.
Where Indexed/ Abstracted	Current Contents; ERIC; Social Science Index; Social Work Abstracts; among others.
Year Established	1984.
Circulation	300+.
Frequency	Semiannually.
Months Issued	Winter and summer.
No. of Articles	8–10 for single issue, 16–20 for double issue.

SUBMISSIONS

Address	Joseph R. Ferrari, PhD, Editor, *Journal of Prevention & Intervention in the Community*, DePaul University, Department of Psychology, 2219 North Kenmore Avenue, Chicago, IL 60614.
Number of Copies	4.
Disk Submission	Required for all articles; preferably WordPerfect.

FORMAT OF MANUSCRIPT

Cover Sheet	Include author's name and title plus running head.
Abstract	100–120 word informative abstract.
Key Words	None.
Length	15–17 pages (including title page, abstract, references, tables, and figures).
Margins	1 inch on all sides.
Spacing	Double-spaced for all copy.

STYLE

Name of Guide	*Publication Manual of the American Psychological Association.*
Subheadings	Use as needed; no more than 3 levels.
References	Author–date citation style; see style guide.
Footnotes	No footnotes preferred; incorporate into text.
Tables or Figures	Type double-spaced; limit camera-ready art; place each table or figure on a separate, numbered page at the end of the manuscript.

REVIEW PROCESS

Type	Reviewed by guest editor who organized the issue and individuals selected by the guest editor, then by editor-in-chief.
Queries	Query letters are discouraged.
Acknowledgment	Guest editor is phoned or written concerning status.
Review Time	As soon as possible.
Revisions	In general, the guest editor and editor-in-chief read revisions.
Acceptance Rate	Because the papers are pulled together by a guest editor, the acceptance rate is high.
Return of Manuscript	Authors keep a copy of final paper.
Lag Time to Print	6 months–1 year.

REPRINT, SUBSCRIPTION, AND CONTACT INFORMATION

Reprint Policy	Guest editor and editor-in-chief decide on distribution.
Book Reviews	None.
Subscriptions	Journal Subscriptions, The Haworth Press, Inc.,10 Alice Street, Binghamton, NY 13904-1580.
E-Mail Address	jferrari@wppost.depaul.edu

Journal of Progressive Human Services

Editorial Focus	To examine political, professional, and personal issues in the human services.
Audience	Not specified.
Special Themes	Developing knowledge about theories, social policies, clinical practice, organizing, administration, research, and history that reflects and responds to progressive concerns.
Where Indexed/ Abstracted	Alternative Press Index; Applied Social Sciences Index & Abstracts; CNPIEC References Guide: Chinese Directory of Foreign Periodicals; Family Studies Database (online and CD-ROM); IBZ International Bibliography of Periodical Literature; Index to Periodical Articles Related to Law; INTERNET ACCESS (& additional networks) Bulletin Board for Libraries ("BUBL"), coverage of information resources on INTERNET, JANET, and other networks; Left Index; National Library Database on Homelessness; Public Affairs Information Bulletin (PAIS); Referativnyi Zhurnal (Abstracts Journal of the Institute of Scientific Information of the Republic of Russia); Social Planning/Policy & Development Abstracts (SOPODA); Social Work Abstracts; Sociological Abstracts (SA); Sociology of Education Abstracts; Special Educational Needs Abstract; Urban Affairs Abstracts; Violence and Abuse Abstracts: A Review of Current Literature on Interpersonal Violence (VAA).
Year Established	1990.
Circulation	650.
Frequency	Semiannually.
Months Issued	Not specified.
No. of Articles	6–10 per issue.

SUBMISSIONS

Address	JPHS Collective, c/o David Prichard, University of New England, School of Social Work, Hills Beach Road, Biddeford, ME 04005.
Number of Copies	4.
Disk Submission	Authors of accepted manuscripts are asked to submit a disk, preferably in Microsoft Word or WordPerfect.

FORMAT OF MANUSCRIPT

Cover Sheet	Separate sheet, which does not go out for review. Full title, author names, degrees, professional titles; designation of one author as corresponding author with full address, phone numbers, e-mail address, and fax number; date of submission.
Abstract	About 100 words.
Key Words	5 or 6 key words that identify article content.

Length	15–25 pages, including references and abstract. Lengthier manuscripts may be considered, but only at the discretion of the editor. Sometimes, lengthier manuscripts may be considered if they can be divided into sections for publication in successive issues.
Margins	1 inch on all sides.
Spacing	Double-spaced for all copy, except title page.

STYLE

Name of Guide	*Publication Manual of the American Psychological Association.*
Subheadings	Use as needed to guide reader through the article. No more than 4 levels.
References	Author–date citation style; see style guide.
Footnotes	No footnotes preferred; incorporate into text.
Tables or Figures	Type tables double-spaced. Submit camera-ready art (300 dpi printer or better) for all figures. Place each table or figure on a separate, numbered page at the end of the manuscript.

REVIEW PROCESS

Type	"Double blind" anonymous peer review. 3 reviewers plus editor-in-chief read the manuscript in an anonymous review.
Queries	Authors are encouraged to read the journal to determine if their subject matter would be appropriate.
Acknowledgment	Enclose a regular self-addressed, stamped envelope with submission.
Review Time	3–4 months.
Revisions	See journal.
Acceptance Rate	Not specified.
Return of Manuscript	Only if 9" x 12" self-addressed, stamped envelope is enclosed.
Lag Time to Print	6 months–1 year.

REPRINT, SUBSCRIPTION, AND CONTACT INFORMATION

Reprint Policy	All authors receive 2 complimentary copies of the issue in which article appears. Authors receive reprint order forms to purchase additional reprinted copies.
Book Reviews	Send to JPHS Collective.
Subscriptions	The Haworth Press, Inc., 10 Alice Street, Binghamton, NY 13904-1580. Individuals, $36; institutions, $48; libraries, $95.

Journal of Psychology & Human Sexuality

Editorial Focus	Human sexuality.
Audience	Psychologists, therapists, social workers.
Special Themes	Clinical, counseling, educational, social, experimental, psych-endocrinological, or psycho-neuroscience research devoted to the study of human sexuality.
Where Indexed/ Abstracted	Biology Digest; Cambridge Scientific Abstracts; CNPIEC Reference Guide: Chinese National Directory of Foreign Periodicals; Digest of Neurology and Psychiatry; Educational Administration Abstracts (EAA); Family Life Educator "Abstracts Section"; Family Studies Database (online and CD-ROM); Family Violence & Sexual Assault Bulletin; Granta Information Services; Higher Education Abstracts; BZ International Bibliography of Periodical Literature; Index to Periodical Articles Related to Law; INTERNET ACCESS (& additional networks) Bulletin Board for Libraries ("BUBL"), coverage of information resources on INTERNET, JANET, and other networks; Mental Health Abstracts (online through DIALOG); Periodica Islamica; Psychological Abstracts (PsycINFO); Referativnyi Zhurnal (Abstracts Journal of the Institute of Scientific Information of the Republic of Russia); Sage Family Studies Abstracts (SFSA); Sage Urban Studies Abstracts (SUSA); Social Planning/Policy & Development Abstracts (SOPODA); Social Work Abstracts; Sociological Abstracts (SA); Studies on Women Abstracts; Violence and Abuse Abstracts: A Review of Current Literature on Interpersonal Violence (VAA).
Year Established	1988.
Circulation	361.
Frequency	Quarterly.
Months Issued	Not specified.
No. of Articles	6–10 per issue.

SUBMISSIONS

Address	Editor, Eli Coleman, PhD, Program in Human Sexuality, 1300 S. 2nd Street, Suite 180, Minneapolis, MN 55454-1015.
Number of Copies	4.
Disk Submission	Authors of accepted manuscripts are asked to submit a disk, preferably in Microsoft Word or WordPerfect.

FORMAT OF MANUSCRIPT

Cover Sheet	Separate sheet, which does not go out for review. Full title, author names, degrees, professional titles; designation of one author as corresponding author with full address, phone numbers, e-mail address, and fax number; date of submission.

Abstract	About 100 words.
Key Words	5 or 6 key words that identify article content.
Length	25 pages, including references and abstract. Lengthier manuscripts may be considered, but only at the discretion of the editor. Sometimes, lengthier manuscripts may be considered if they can be divided into sections for publication in successive issues.
Margins	1 inch on all sides.
Spacing	Double-spaced for all copy, except title page.

STYLE

Name of Guide	*Publication Manual of the American Psychological Association.*
Subheadings	Use as needed to guide reader through the article. No more than 4 levels.
References	Author–date citation style; see style guide.
Footnotes	No footnotes preferred; incorporate into text.
Tables or Figures	Type tables double-spaced. Submit camera-ready art (300 dpi printer or better) for all figures. Place each table or figure on a separate, numbered page at the end of the manuscript.

REVIEW PROCESS

Type	"Double blind" anonymous peer review. 3 reviewers plus editor-in-chief read the manuscript in an anonymous review.
Queries	Authors are encouraged to read the journal to determine if their subject matter would be appropriate.
Acknowledgment	Enclose a regular self-addressed, stamped envelope with submission.
Review Time	3–4 months.
Revisions	See journal.
Acceptance Rate	Not specified.
Return of Manuscript	Only if 9" x 12" self-addressed, stamped envelope is enclosed.
Lag Time to Print	6 months–1 year.

REPRINT, SUBSCRIPTION, AND CONTACT INFORMATION

Reprint Policy	All authors receive 2 complimentary copies of the issue in which article appears. Authors receive reprint order forms to purchase additional reprinted copies.
Book Reviews	Send to journal editor.
Subscriptions	The Haworth Press, Inc., 10 Alice Street, Binghamton, NY 13904-1580. Individuals, $40; institutions, $120; libraries, $225.

Journal of Psychopathology and Behavioral Assessment

Editorial Focus	Research or reviews of all types of psychopathology and assessment of deviant behavior. The focus is on etiology, description, and measurement. Treatment studies are not published. Theoretical papers are considered if they are of a scientific nature.
Audience	Mental health professionals.
Special Themes	Scientific approach to psychopathology.
Where Indexed/ Abstracted	Various abstracts including Psychological Abstracts.
Year Established	1978.
Circulation	No information available.
Frequency	Quarterly.
Months Issued	March, June, September, December.
No. of Articles	8–10 per issue.

SUBMISSIONS

Address	Henry E. Adams, PhD, Editor, *Journal of Psychopathology and Behavioral Assessment,* Department of Psychology, University of Georgia, Athens, GA 30602-3013.
Number of Copies	4.
Disk Submission	No.

FORMAT OF MANUSCRIPT

Cover Sheet	Full title, authors' names, addresses, designation of corresponding author, phone number, fax number, e-mail address.
Abstract	102–150 words.
Key Words	3–5 key terms, typed at the bottom of the abstract page.
Length	15–50 pages.
Margins	See style guide.
Spacing	Double-spaced.

STYLE

Name of Guide	*Publication Manual of the American Psychological Association.*
Subheadings	See style guide.
References	See style guide.
Footnotes	See style guide.
Tables or Figures	See style guide.

REVIEW PROCESS

Type	Peer-reviewed, 3 editorial referees plus editor or associate editor.
Queries	Not encouraged.
Acknowledgment	On receipt of manuscript.
Review Time	6–12 months.
Revisions	Revisions should be returned within 4–6 weeks. If revisions are major, they may be sent for new review. Minor revisions are processed by editor or associate editors.
Acceptance Rate	Approximately 30%.
Return of Manuscript	Not returned.
Lag Time to Print	4–6 months.

REPRINT, SUBSCRIPTION, AND CONTACT INFORMATION

Reprint Policy	Authors can purchase reprints at a reasonable rate.
Book Reviews	Occasionally, at the invitation of the editor or associate editors.
Subscriptions	Plenum Press, Subscription Department, 233 Spring Street, New York, NY 10013-1578.
E-Mail Address	headams@uga.cc.uga.edu

Journal of Psychosocial Oncology

Editorial Focus	The study of the psychological needs of cancer patients and their families.
Audience	Professional social work clinicians, administrators, educators, and researchers committed to the enhancement of psychological services to cancer patients and their families.
Special Themes	Contemporary clinical and research materials as well as exploratory, hypothesis testing, and program evaluation research for health professionals.
Where Indexed/ Abstracted	Abstracts of Research in Pastoral Care & Counseling; Behavioral Medicine Abstracts; Cabell's Directory of Publishing Opportunities in Nursing; CINAHL (Cumulative Index to Nursing & Allied Health Literature); CNPIEC Reference Guide: Chinese National Directory of Foreign Periodicals; Current Awareness in Biological Sciences (C.A.B.S); Current Contents: Clinical Medicine/Life Sciences (CC: CM/LS); Educational Administration Abstracts (EAA); Excerpta Medica/Secondary Publishing Division; Family Studies Database (online and CD-ROM); INTERNET ACCESS (& additional networks) Bulletin Board for Libraries ("BUBL"), coverage of information resources on INTERNET, JANET, and other networks; Leeds Medical Information; Mental Health Abstracts (online through DIALOG); ONS Nursing Scan in Oncology—NAACOG's Women's Health Nursing Scan; Psychological Abstracts (PsycINFO); Referativnyi Zhurnal (Abstracts Journal of the Institute of Scientific Information of the Republic of Russia); Sage Family Studies Abstracts; Sage Urban Studies Abstracts (SUSA); Sapient Health Network; SilverPlatter Information, Inc. "CD-ROM/ online"; Social Planning/Policy & Development Abstracts (SOPODA); Social Work Abstracts; Sociological Abstracts (SA); Special Educational Needs Abstracts; Violence and Abuse Abstracts: A Review of Current Literature on Interpersonal Violence (VAA).
Year Established	1983.
Circulation	1,336.
Frequency	Quarterly.
Months Issued	Not specified.
No. of Articles	6–10 per issue.

SUBMISSIONS

Address	James R. Zabora, MSW, Co-editor, *Journal of Psychosocial Oncology*, Department of Patient and Family Services, The Johns Hopkins Oncology Center, 600 N. Wolfe Street, Baltimore, MD 21218.
Number of Copies	4.
Disk Submission	Authors of accepted manuscripts are asked to submit a disk, preferably in Microsoft Word or WordPerfect.

FORMAT OF MANUSCRIPT

Cover Sheet	Separate sheet, which does not go out for review. Full title, author names, degrees, professional titles; designation of one author as corresponding

author with full address, phone numbers, e-mail address, and fax number; date of submission.

Abstract	About 100 words.
Key Words	Not specified.
Length	20 pages, including references and abstract. Lengthier manuscripts may be considered, but only at the discretion of the editor. Sometimes, lengthier manuscripts may be considered if they can be divided into sections for publication in successive issues.
Margins	1 inch on all sides.
Spacing	Double-spaced for all copy, except title page.

STYLE

Name of Guide	*Publication Manual of the American Psychological Association.*
Subheadings	Use as needed to guide reader through the article. No more than 4 levels.
References	Author–date citation style; see style guide.
Footnotes	No footnotes preferred; incorporate into text.
Tables or Figures	Type tables double-spaced. Submit camera-ready art (300 dpi printer or better) for all figures. Place each table or figure on a separate, numbered page at the end of the manuscript.

REVIEW PROCESS

Type	"Double blind" anonymous peer review. 3 reviewers plus editor-in-chief read the manuscript in an anonymous review.
Queries	Authors are encouraged to read the journal to determine if their subject matter would be appropriate.
Acknowledgment	Enclose a regular self-addressed, stamped envelope with submission.
Review Time	3–4 months.
Revisions	See journal.
Acceptance Rate	Not specified.
Return of Manuscript	Only if 9″ x 12″ self-addressed, stamped envelope is enclosed.
Lag Time to Print	6 months–1 year.

REPRINT, SUBSCRIPTION, AND CONTACT INFORMATION

Reprint Policy	All authors receive 2 complimentary copies of the issue in which article appears. Authors receive reprint order forms to purchase additional reprinted copies.
Book Reviews	Send to co-editor.
Subscriptions	The Haworth Press, Inc., 10 Alice Street, Binghamton, NY 13904-1580. Individuals, $42; institutions, $140; libraries, $275. Members of AOSW: free.
Affiliation	The Association of Oncology Social Workers (AOSW).

Journal of Sex and Marital Therapy

Editorial Focus	Treatment of sexual and marital disorders.
Audience	Physicians, psychologists, social workers.
Special Themes	Not specified.
Where Indexed/ Abstracted	Current Contents, Index Medicus.
Year Established	1974.
Circulation	1,013.
Frequency	Quarterly.
Months Issued	Winter, spring, summer, fall.
No. of Articles	8–10.

SUBMISSIONS

Address	R. T. Segraves, MD, MHMC-Psychiatry, 2500 MetroHealth Drive, Cleveland, OH 44109-1998.
Number of Copies	3.
Disk Submission	DOS-compatible.

FORMAT OF MANUSCRIPT

Cover Sheet	Name, address.
Abstract	Required.
Key Words	Required.
Length	Variable.
Margins	Standard.
Spacing	Double-spaced.

STYLE

Name of Guide	*Publication Manual of the American Psychological Association.*
Subheadings	Not specified.
References	See style guide.
Footnotes	Not specified.
Tables or Figures	Not specified.

REVIEW PROCESS

Type	Blind.
Queries	Not welcome.
Acknowledgment	Yes.
Review Time	3 months.

Revisions	Not specified.
Acceptance Rate	60%.
Return of Manuscript	Rejected manuscripts are returned.
Lag Time to Print	6 months.

REPRINT, SUBSCRIPTION, AND CONTACT INFORMATION

Reprint Policy	Not specified.
Book Reviews	Yes.
Subscriptions	Susan Cakars, Brunner/Mazel, 19 Union Square West, New York, NY 10003.

Journal of Sex Education and Therapy

Editorial Focus The *Journal of Sex Education and Therapy* is an interdisciplinary journal publishing articles of value to educators and clinicians in all aspects of sexuality, including sexual development and functioning in various populations, evaluation and treatment of sexual problems, sexual boundary issues (e.g., decision-making, abuse), and sexual attitudes and values. Types of articles include research reports, literature reviews, scholarly commentary, program and curriculum development and assessment, clinical cases, educational program reports, media reviews (books, audiovisuals, Internet resources), readers' forum, and letters to the editor.

Audience Sex therapists, sex educators, students, libraries, and all who are interested in issues covered by the journal.

Special Themes Issues relevant to sex education and the evaluation and treatment of sexual disorders. Topical issues with invited articles may be published occasionally.

Where Indexed/ Abstracted Pending.

Year Established 1974.

Circulation 2,000.

Frequency Quarterly (beginning June 1997).

Months Issued March, June, September, December.

No. of Articles 8–10 per issue.

SUBMISSIONS

Address S. Michael Plaut, PhD, Editor, Department of Psychiatry, University of Maryland School of Medicine, 645 W. Redwood Street, Baltimore, MD 21201.

Number of Copies 3.

Disk Submission WordPerfect 5.1, only after acceptance of manuscript.

FORMAT OF MANUSCRIPT

Cover Sheet Full title, author names, professional titles, designation of one author as corresponding author with address, phone, fax, e-mail address.

Abstract 100–150 words

Key Words None required.

Length 25 pages maximum for full-length paper.

Margins 1 inch on all sides.

Spacing Double-spaced throughout, including references.

STYLE

Name of Guide	*Publication Manual of the American Psychological Association.*
Subheadings	As needed; see style guide.
References	See style guide.
Footnotes	With rare exceptions limited to author acknowledgments, including funding and permissions. Separate page entitled "Footnotes."
Tables or Figures	See style guide for tables; camera-ready copy for figures.

REVIEW PROCESS

Type	2–3 reviewers, not anonymous. Reviewers receive each others' reviews after the editorial decision has been made.
Queries	Queries to editor by letter, phone, or e-mail are welcomed.
Acknowledgment	By letter.
Review Time	Authors notified after 1–3 months. Reviewers are asked to submit reviews within 3 weeks of receipt.
Revisions	Manuscripts may be sent to the same or different reviewers after revision. 3 copies of revised manuscript required along with cover letter explaining all modifications and/or reasons for not making recommended changes.
Acceptance Rate	Unknown at present, due to change in editor and format.
Return of Manuscript	Not returned.
Lag Time to Print	6–12 months.

CHARGES TO AUTHOR

Author Alterations	Author alterations after receipt of page proofs may be charged unless changes are requested by the editor.

REPRINT, SUBSCRIPTION, AND CONTACT INFORMATION

Reprint Policy	Each author receives a complimentary copy of the issue in which the article appears. The corresponding author receives a reprint order form.
Book Reviews	By invitation only. Books for review should be sent to Paul Ephross, PhD, School of Social Work, University of Maryland, Baltimore, MD 21201. Audiovisual materials, computer software, and information about Internet resources relevant to issues covered by the journal should be sent to Al Cooper, PhD, San Jose Marital and Sexuality Center, 100 N. Winchester Boulevard, Santa Clara, CA 95050-6567.
Subscriptions	American Association of Sex Educators, Counselors, and Therapists, P.O. Box 238, Mt. Vernon, IA 52314.
	$30 per year.
Affiliation	American Association of Sex Educators, Counselors, and Therapists.
E-Mail Address	mplaut@schmed01.ab.umd.edu

Journal of Sexual Aggression

Editorial Focus   The *Journal of Sexual Aggression* is devoted to the theory, research, and dissemination of information regarding all forms of sexual aggression, regardless of the abuser's age, gender, culture, or sexual preference. Papers also accepted on prevention or impact of sexual aggression on victims, other family members, and caregivers; on judicial and social policy responses.

Audience   Professionals and academics dealing with any aspect of sexual aggression and sexual offending.

Where Indexed/ Abstracted   Applied Social Sciences Index & Abstracts; Bibliographie Zeitschriftenliteratur aller Gebieten des Wissens; Bulletin Signalétique; ICAS; Mental Health Abstracts; Sociological Abstracts.

Year Established   1994.

Circulation   Not specified.

Frequency   Biannually.

Months Issued   April, September.

No. of Articles   4–5 per issue.

SUBMISSIONS

Address   *Journal of Sexual Aggression,* c/o Whiting and Birch Ltd, P.O. Box 872, London SE23 3HZ, England.

Number of Copies   3.

Disk Submission   Disk required for final accepted manuscript. Any word processing format is accepted, but authors using Windows should save to DOS. Avoid using Wordstar.

FORMAT OF MANUSCRIPT

Cover Sheet   Author(s) name, professional address, professional details, title of article, number of words, address/phone/fax for correspondence. Professional addresses of second and subsequent authors welcomed for future communications.

Abstract   Less than 200 words, if possible.

Key Words   Maximum 8 key words.

Length   Up to 6,000 words.

Margins   Generous.

Spacing   Double-spaced.

STYLE

Name of Guide	Notes for contributors are published in journal. Use *Publication Manual of the American Psychological Association* for points of detail.
Subheadings	Preferably no more than 3 levels. Level 1: bold, lowercase; level 2: italics, lowercase; level 3, roman, lowercase. Never use all capitals, and do not capitalize initials except for proper names.
References	Harvard.
Footnotes	Endnotes allowed if absolutely unavoidable.
Tables or Figures	If several tables, group at end of article and indicate position in text. If only 1 or 2 simple tables, include in text. Prepare tables with single right tab between each column. Lines of hyphens should not be included between rows; we will insert rules according to house style. However, authors should add clear indications of how they wish each table to appear. For figures involving any graphics, camera-ready copy should be supplied.

REVIEW PROCESS

Type	Double anonymous.
Queries	Queries are welcomed. Editors especially keen to encourage articles from professionals in practice, and will help as possible.
Acknowledgment	Self-addressed postcard or envelope welcomed.
Review Time	3 months.
Revisions	Material may be accepted subject to minor revisions, rejected, or editors may indicate more substantial rewriting required. In latter case, resubmission required.
Acceptance Rate	40%.
Return of Manuscript	Manuscripts not returned unless adequate postage/international postal reply coupons supplied.
Lag Time to Print	Target is 1 year.

CHARGES TO AUTHOR

Author Alterations	Approximately $6 per page for significant changes. However, we do not charge for alterations that relate to genuinely unpredictable changes since submission that require acknowledgment in text.

REPRINT, SUBSCRIPTION, AND CONTACT INFORMATION

Reprint Policy	10 free reprints, more available at cost.
Book Reviews	We publish book reviews, and accept unsolicited reviews. Submit reviews to Book Review Editor, c/o Whiting and Birch Ltd, P.O. Box 872, London SE23 3HZ, England.
Subscriptions	Whiting and Birch Ltd, P.O. Box 872, London SE23 3HZ, England. North American rates: $65, institutions; $35, individuals.

Journal of Social Issues

Editorial Focus	The psychological analysis of social issues.
Audience	Social scientists and others interested in social issues.
Special Themes	PLEASE NOTE: The *Journal of Social Issues (JSI)* only publishes thematic issues. Each set of papers is coordinated by an issue editor. Individual papers are neither reviewed nor published. Issue editors assemble a proposal for each issue. *JSI* is sponsored by the Society for the Psychological Study of Social Issues (SPSSI). As issue editors develop their proposals, they typically announce the topic of the project in the *SPSSI Newsletter*. Interested authors can submit items for consideration to the person(s) coordinating the proposal.
Where Indexed/ Abstracted	Over 25 places; see inside cover of the journal.
Year Established	1944.
Circulation	Approximately 6,000.
Frequency	Quarterly.
Months Issued	Spring, summer, fall, winter.
No. of Articles	10–12 per issue.

SUBMISSIONS

Address	Dr. Phyllis Katz, Institute for Research on Social Problems, 520 Pearl Street, Boulder, CO 80302. NOTE: Single articles are neither reviewed nor published.
Number of Copies	Not specified.
Disk Submission	Yes.

FORMAT OF MANUSCRIPT

Cover Sheet	Yes.
Abstract	Yes.
Key Words	None.
Length	Per issue editors' instructions.
Margins	1 inch on all sides.
Spacing	Double-spaced.

STYLE

Name of Guide	*Publication Manual of the American Psychological Association.*
Subheadings	Yes, see style guide.
References	See style guide.
Footnotes	Avoid using footnotes.
Tables or Figures	Yes, see style guide.

REVIEW PROCESS

Type	Proposals are reviewed by the journal's editorial board; manuscripts are reviewed by area experts.
Queries	Yes.
Acknowledgment	Manuscript sent to issue editor.
Review Time	Approximately 3 months per review cycle.
Revisions	Not specified.
Acceptance Rate	Not specified.
Return of Manuscript	Not specified.
Lag Time to Print	5 months.

REPRINT, SUBSCRIPTION, AND CONTACT INFORMATION

Reprint Policy	Not specified.
Book Reviews	None.
Subscriptions	Included in membership in the Society for the Psychological Study of Social Issues. For information contact: SPSSI Central Office, P.O. Box 1248, Ann Arbor, MI 48106-1248.
Affiliation	Society for the Psychological Study of Social Issues.
E-Mail Address	katzp@rastro.colorado.edu
Home Page URL	http://www.coled.umn.edu/CAREIwww/SPSSI/JSI.html

The Journal of Social Psychology

Editorial Focus	*The Journal of Social Psychology* is devoted to experimental, empirical, and field studies of groups, cultural effects, cross-national problems, language, and ethnicity. Cross-cultural and field research are given a higher priority than laboratory research using college students.
Audience	Libraries, faculty.
Special Themes	None.
Where Indexed/ Abstracted	Abstracts for Social Workers; Academic Abstracts; Applied Social Sciences Index and Abstracts; Child Development Abstracts and Bibliography; Current Index to Journals in Education; Current Contents: Social & Behavioral Science; Directory of Title Pages, Indexes, and Contents Pages; Family Resources Database; Health & Psychosocial Instruments; Human Resources Abstracts; Magazine Article Summaries; Index Medicus; International Political Science Abstracts; Linguistics and Language Behavior Abstracts; Mental Health Abstracts; Psychological Abstracts; PsycINFO Database; Research Alert; Social Planning/Policy & Development; Social Science Source; Social Sciences Citation Index; Social Studies/Social Science Education (ERIC); Sociology of Education Abstracts; Sociological Abstracts.
Year Established	1929.
Circulation	1,884.
Frequency	Bimonthly.
Months Issued	February, April, June, August, October, December.
No. of Articles	Varies, approximately14 per issue.

SUBMISSIONS

Address	Managing Editor, *The Journal of Social Psychology*, 1319 18th Street, NW, Washington, DC 20036-1802.
Number of Copies	2.
Disk Submission	Encouraged for accepted manuscripts.

FORMAT OF MANUSCRIPT

Cover Sheet	Authors' names, title, authors' affiliations.
Abstract	Approximately120 words.
Key Words	Not required.
Length	5–35 pages.
Margins	1.25 inches on all sides.
Spacing	Double-spaced.

STYLE

Name of Guide	*Publication Manual of the American Psychological Association.*
Subheadings	Not specified.
References	See style guide.
Footnotes	Discouraged.
Tables or Figures	Camera-ready figures, tables set in-house.

REVIEW PROCESS

Type	Anonymous.
Queries	Accepted.
Acknowledgment	By postcard from publisher.
Review Time	2–3 months.
Revisions	2 copies.
Acceptance Rate	Approximately 40%.
Return of Manuscript	Returned if revisions requested.
Lag Time to Print	1 year.

CHARGES TO AUTHOR

Page Charges	No page charges, but $50 for each table and $20 for each figure.

REPRINT, SUBSCRIPTION, AND CONTACT INFORMATION

Reprint Policy	Each author receives a reprint form and 2 complimentary copies of issue in which the article appears.
Book Reviews	None.
Subscriptions	Subscription Department, *The Journal of Social Psychology,* 1319 18th Street, NW, Washington, DC 20036-1802.
	$116 per year.
Affiliation	Helen Dwight Reid Educational Foundation.
E-Mail Address	soc@heldref.org
Home Page URL	http://www.heldref.org

Journal of Social Service Research

Editorial Focus	Scholarly papers ranging from the clinical research of social and behavioral scientists to empirical policy studies from the international social service arena. The primary concern of the *JSSR* is to publish papers that make a conceptual contribution to the fields of social work and social welfare and that are characterized by sophisticated and appropriate designs and rigorous data analysis.
Audience	Scholars, especially social and behavioral scientists; applied researchers; policymakers; policy implementers; administrators, and practitioners.
Special Themes	Quality.
Where Indexed/ Abstracted	Abstracts in Social Gerontology: Current Literature on Aging; Applied Social Sciences Index & Abstracts; Behavioral Medicine Abstracts; caredata CD: The Social and Community Care Database; CNPIEC Reference Guide: Chinese National Directory of Foreign Periodicals; Criminal Justice Abstracts; Criminology, Penology and Police Science Abstracts; Current Contents; Family Studies Database; Human Resources Abstracts (HRA); IBZ International Bibliography of Periodical Literature; Index to Periodical Articles Related to Law; INTERNET ACCESS (& additional networks) Bulletin Board for Libraries ("BUBL"), coverage of information resources on INTERNET, JANET, and other networks; Mental Health Abstracts (online through DIALOG); NIAAA Alcohol and Alcohol Problems Science Database; PASCAL International Bibliography T 205: Sciences de l'information Documentation; Psychological Abstracts (PsycINFO); Social Planning/Policy & Development Abstracts (SOPODA); Social Sciences Citation Index; Social Work Abstracts; Sociological Abstracts (SA).
Year Established	1977.
Circulation	450.
Frequency	Quarterly (4 issues per volume).
Months Issued	Academic year. First issue in each volume begins in September or Fall season.
No. of Articles	Average 4.

SUBMISSIONS

Address	David Gillespie, Editor, *Journal of Social Service Research,* Washington University, Box 1196, Social Work, One Brookings Drive, St. Louis, MO 63130.
Number of Copies	4.
Disk Submission	Required.

FORMAT OF MANUSCRIPT

Cover Sheet	Not specified.
Abstract	About 100 words.

Key Words	5 or 6 key words that identify content.
Length	About 20 pages, including references and abstract.
Margins	At least 1 inch on all sides of 8-1/2″ x 11″ white paper.
Spacing	Double-spaced.

STYLE

Name of Guide	*Publication Manual of the American Psychological Association.*
Subheadings	Yes.
References	Double-spaced in alphabetical order.
Footnotes	Footnotes within text discouraged.
Tables or Figures	Tables are printed as is and are not typeset. Must be prepared on separate pages in the hard copy and on the electronic file. Must be "camera-ready."

REVIEW PROCESS

Type	Peer review.
Queries	Sue Imhoff, Administrative Assistant to the Editor (314-935-6693).
Acknowledgment	Only if a stamped, self-addressed envelope is included with submission of the manuscript.
Review Time	Usually about 3 months.
Revisions	Most papers are accepted contingent on changes recommended by reviewers.
Acceptance Rate	65%.
Return of Manuscript	Only if a 9″ x 12″ stamped, self-addressed envelope is included with submission of manuscript.
Lag Time to Print	About 1 year.

REPRINT, SUBSCRIPTION, AND CONTACT INFORMATION

Reprint Policy	The "senior" author receives 2 copies of the journal and 10 complimentary reprints several weeks after the issue is published. The "junior" author receives two copies of the journal issue. An order form is sent to the corresponding author for the purchase of additional reprints. It takes 4–6 weeks to produce the reprints. Please do not query the journal editor about reprints. All reprint questions should be directed to The Haworth Press, Inc., Production Department, 21 East Broad Street, West Hazleton, PA 18201.
Book Reviews	Nancy Morrow-Howell, Book Review Editor, *Journal of Social Service Research,* Washington University, Box 1196, Social Work, One Brookings Drive, St. Louis, MO 63130.
Subscriptions	Subscriptions through any subscription agency subject to publisher's credit check of subscription agency and payment record history of subscription agency.
E-Mail Address	davidg@gwbssw.wustl.edu
Home Page URL	http://www.gwbssw.wustl.edu/~nethelp/journal/jssr.html

Journal of Social Work Education

Previous Title	*Journal of Education for Social Work* (until 1985).
Editorial Focus	Publishes research-based and theoretical material on education in social work and social welfare at the undergraduate, master's, and doctoral level. Covers trends, new developments, and problems relevant to the education and training of professional social workers, and the implications of practice for education. Publishes articles, research notes, opinion pieces ("Point/ Counterpoint"), book reviews, and letters to the editor.
Audience	Social work faculty, field instructors, researchers, administrators, students, librarians.
Special Themes	Technology, interprofessional education, program evaluation.
Where Indexed/ Abstracted	Applied Social Sciences Index & Abstracts; Current Contents; Current Index to Journals in Education; ProQuest; Research into Higher Education; Sociological Abstracts; Social Sciences Citation Index; Social Sciences Index; Social Work Abstracts.
Year Established	1964.
Circulation	3,500.
Frequency	3 times annually.
Months Issued	January, May, October.
No. of Articles	9–10 per issue.

SUBMISSIONS

Address	Nancy E. Barr, Managing Editor, Council on Social Work Education, 1600 Duke Street, Suite 300, Alexandria, VA 22314-3421.
Number of Copies	4.
Disk Submission	Only for accepted manuscripts. Prefer WordPerfect, Microsoft Word, or ASCII for IBM.

FORMAT OF MANUSCRIPT

Cover Sheet	Manuscript title, name of author(s), title and affiliation of author(s).
Abstract	100–150 words.
Key Words	None.
Length	15–25 pages.
Margins	Not specified.
Spacing	Double-spaced.

STYLE

Name of Guide	*Publication Manual of the American Psychological Association.*
Subheadings	See style guide.

References	See style guide.
Footnotes	See style guide.
Tables or Figures	As part of manuscript or camera-ready.

REVIEW PROCESS

Type	Anonymous peer review by 3 evaluators.
Queries	Accepted on status of manuscript in review process.
Acknowledgment	Sent for all submissions.
Review Time	3 months.
Revisions	Accepted for reject/revise ratings.
Acceptance Rate	20%.
Return of Manuscript	Not returned.
Lag Time to Print	6–9 months.

REPRINT, SUBSCRIPTION, AND CONTACT INFORMATION

Reprint Policy	Authors receive 2 free copies; may order additional copies from: Boyd Printing Company, 49 Sheridan Avenue, Albany, NY 12201.
Book Reviews	By invitation only.
Subscriptions	As part of membership. Contact: Member Services, Council on Social Work Education, 1600 Duke Street, Suite 300, Alexandria, VA 22314-3421.
Affiliation	Council on Social Work Education.
E-Mail Address	cswe@access.digex.net

Journal of Sociology and Social Welfare

Editorial Focus	Articles that analyze social welfare institutions, policies, or problems from a social scientific perspective or otherwise attempt to bridge the gap between social science theory and social work practice; also "Research Notes," book reviews, occasional letters, debates.
Audience	Social science and social work faculty and students, libraries, researchers, practitioners.
Special Themes	1–2 annually; calls for papers published in journal and mailed by special editors.
Where Indexed/ Abstracted	Applied Social Sciences Index & Abstracts; Psychological Abstracts; Social Work Abstracts; Sociological Abstracts.
Year Established	1973.
Circulation	625.
Frequency	Quarterly.
Months Issued	March, June, September, December.
No. of Articles	8–12.

SUBMISSIONS

Address	*Journal of Sociology & Social Welfare,* School of Social Work, Western Michigan University, Kalamazoo, MI 49008-5034.
Number of Copies	3.
Disk Submission	Accepted articles may be sent on disk.

FORMAT OF MANUSCRIPT

Cover Sheet	Title, author names, affiliations, mailing address, phone number, e-mail address, any acknowledgments on one copy only; title only on other two copies.
Abstract	100 words.
Key Words	Not required.
Length	15–18 pages of text; tables and references chosen carefully.
Margins	1 inch all sides.
Spacing	Double-spaced.

STYLE

Name of Guide	*Publication Manual of the American Psychological Association.*
Subheadings	As needed.
References	Author–date style; see style guide.
Footnotes	If it doesn't fit gracefully into the text, you can probably do without it.
Tables or Figures	See style guide.

REVIEW PROCESS

Type	Anonymous review by two editorial board members, sometimes additional reviewers in cases of split decision or when special expertise is required. Editor reads all manuscripts.
Queries	Telephone or e-mail queries welcome, though usually of limited use.
Acknowledgment	Managing editor will acknowledge by letter.
Review Time	4 months usually; traffic is slower in summer and at semester end. Authors can phone or e-mail editor for status report: Robert Leighninger, phone: 504-388-5887; e-mail: swleig@lsuvm.sncc.lsu.edu
Revisions	Editor will advise.
Acceptance Rate	25%–30%.
Return of Manuscript	Not returned.
Lag Time to Print	9–12 months.

CHARGES TO AUTHOR

Author Alterations	Only if excessive.

REPRINT, SUBSCRIPTION, AND CONTACT INFORMATION

Reprint Policy	Consult managing editor.
Book Reviews	By invitation; send books for review to: James Midgley, School of Social Welfare, University of California, Berkeley, CA 94720.
Subscriptions	*Journal of Sociology & Social Welfare*, School of Social Work, Western Michigan University, Kalamazoo, MI 49008-5034.
	$32 individuals (within U.S.), $38 individuals (outside U.S.), $69 institutions (within U.S.), $77 institutions (outside U.S.).
E-mail Address	Editor Robert Leighninger: swleig@lsuvm.sncc.lsu.edu
	Managing Editor Gary Mathews: mathews@gw.wmich.edu

Journal of Traumatic Stress

Editorial Focus	Publication of peer-reviewed original papers (reviewed blind to authorship) on biopsychosocial aspects of trauma. Papers focus on theoretical formulations, research, treatment, prevention, education/training, and legal and policy concerns.
Audience	Professionals who study and treat people exposed to highly stressful and traumatic events.
Special Themes	War, disaster, accident, violence or abuse (criminal or familial), terrorism, or life-threatening illness.
Where Indexed/ Abstracted	Current Contents; Health and Safety Science Abstracts; Health Instrument File; Index Medicus; Psychological Abstracts; Research Alert; Social Sciences Citation Index.
Year Established	1988.
Circulation	Approximately 2,500.
Frequency	Quarterly.
Months Issued	January, April, July, October.
No. of Articles	12–14 per issue.

SUBMISSIONS

Address	*Journal of Traumatic Stress,* Dean Kilpatrick, PhD, Editor, Psychiatry/ Medical University of South Carolina, 171 Ashley Avenue, Charleston, SC 29425-0002.
Number of Copies	3 plus an original.
Disk Submission	Authors of accepted manuscripts are asked to submit an IBM-compatible disk, preferably in Microsoft Word or WordPerfect format (Windows version).

FORMAT OF MANUSCRIPT

Cover Sheet	Title page should include the title of the article, author's name (no degrees), author's affiliation, acknowledgments, and suggested running head. The affiliation should comprise the department, institution, city, and state (or nation) and should be typed as a footnote to the author's name. The suggested running head should be less than 80 characters (including spaces) and should comprise the article title or an abbreviated version thereof. Also include the total word count, and complete mailing address and telephone number for the corresponding author during the review process.
Abstract	120-word informative abstract.
Key Words	4–5 key words provided below the abstract should express the precise content of the manuscript for indexing purposes.
Length	Regular Articles usually no longer than 7,500 words (including references and tables); Brief Reports are 2,500 words (including references and tables); and Commentaries are 1,000 words or less and address responses to previously published articles, or essays on a professional or scientific topic of general interest.

Margins	1 inch on all sides.
Spacing	Double-spaced for all copy; use 12-point font.

STYLE

Name of Guide	*Publication Manual of the American Psychological Association.*
Subheadings	Use as needed to guide the reader through the article. Articles following APA format use from 1 to 5 levels of headings.
References	Author–date citation system; listed alphabetically at the end of the paper.
Footnotes	Footnotes are discouraged; incorporate into text.
Tables or Figures	Should be numbered (with Arabic numerals) and referred to by number in the text. Double-space and place each table or figure on a separate page at the end of the manuscript.

REVIEW PROCESS

Type	Blind anonymous peer review. Up to 3 reviewers read the manuscript in an anonymous review and make recommendations, with the editor making the final decision.
Queries	Query letters are discouraged; authors are encouraged to read the journal to determine if their subject matter would be appropriate.
Acknowledgment	An acknowledgment letter with an assigned manuscript number for tracking is sent to the author upon receipt of his or her manuscript.
Review Time	4–5 months.
Revisions	Submit 3 copies plus an original with a separate cover sheet outlining the changes made and how the reviewers' comments were addressed. Turn-around time is about 3 months.
Acceptance Rate	24%.
Return of Manuscript	The original and 3 copies of an unreviewed manuscript are returned to the author with a letter detailing why it was returned. Reviewed manuscripts are not returned.
Lag Time to Print	9 months.

REPRINT, SUBSCRIPTION, AND CONTACT INFORMATION

Reprint Policy	First authors receive 1 complimentary copy of the issue in which the article appears. Authors receive reprint order forms to purchase additional reprinted copies.
Book Reviews	None.
Subscriptions	Plenum Publishing Corporation, Subscription Department, 233 Spring Street, New York, NY 10013 (fax: 212-807-1047). 1996 prices: institutional subscriptions, $215 (outside the United States, $250); individual subscribers certifying that the journal is for their personal use, $46 (outside the United States, $54).
Affiliation	*The Journal of Traumatic Stress* is published for the International Society for Traumatic Stress Studies.

Journal of Studies on Alcohol

Previous Title	*Quarterly Journal of Studies on Alcohol.*
Editorial Focus	Behavioral, biological, social, and medical research.
Audience	Faculty, libraries, practitioners, students, researchers, organizations.
Special Themes	Alcohol and drugs.
Where Indexed/ Abstracted	Approximately 40 abstracting and indexing services.
Year Established	1940.
Circulation	2,500.
Frequency	Bimonthly.
Months Issued	January, March, May, July, September, November.
No. of Articles	10–14.

SUBMISSIONS

Address	Editor, c/o Patricia Castellano, *Journal of Studies on Alcohol,* Center of Alcohol Studies, P.O. Box 969, Piscataway, NJ 08855-0969.
Number of Copies	4.
Disk Submission	3.5" disk with revised or accepted manuscripts; any popular word processing format.

FORMAT OF MANUSCRIPT

Cover Sheet	Title, author names, degrees, affiliations, grant information and number, corresponding author with complete address.
Abstract	250 words, structured: objective, method, results, conclusions.
Key Words	None.
Length	25 pages.
Margins	Not specified.
Spacing	Double-spaced.

STYLE

Name of Guide	*Publication Manual of the American Psychological Association, Chicago Manual of Style, British Museum.*
Subheadings	No more than 3 levels.
References	See our "Information for Contributors."
Footnotes	Prefer no footnotes; place at end of article.
Tables or Figures	Type tables double-spaced. Camera-ready figures. Place each table or figure on a separate, numbered page at end of manuscript.

REVIEW PROCESS

Type	"Single-blind" anonymous peer review; 2 reviewers plus editor and associate editor.
Queries	Welcome.
Acknowledgment	*JSA* sends postcard giving name of associate editor handling review.
Review Time	2–3 months.
Revisions	Submit 4 hard copies and 1 disk along with a letter describing changes made in the manuscript and replying to the reviewers' comments. Revisions reviewed by associate editor and editor and sometimes original referee.
Acceptance Rate	25%–30%.
Return of Manuscript	Not returned.
Lag Time to Print	10–12 months.

CHARGES TO AUTHOR

Author Alterations	Only if excessive.

REPRINT, SUBSCRIPTION, AND CONTACT INFORMATION

Reprint Policy	All authors receive 1 complimentary copy of the issue in which the article appears. Corresponding author receives reprint order form to purchase reprints of article.
Book Reviews	Reviews are by invitation only. Send academic-oriented books for review to Book Review Editor, c/o Patricia Castellano, *Journal of Studies on Alcohol*, Center of Alcohol Studies, P.O. Box 969, Piscataway, NJ 08855-0969.
Subscriptions	Subscription Department, *Journal of Studies on Alcohol*, Center of Alcohol Studies, P.O. Box 969, Piscataway, NJ 08855-0969.

Journal of Teaching in Social Work

Editorial Focus	Innovations in education, training, and educational practice.
Audience	Not specified.
Where Indexed/ Abstracted	Applied Social Sciences Index & Abstracts; Behavioral Medicine Abstracts; caredata CD: the social and community care database; CNPIEC Reference Guide: Chinese National Directory of Foreign Periodicals; Contents Pages in Education; Family Studies Database (online and CD-ROM); Human Resources Abstracts (HRA); IBZ International Bibliography of Periodical Literature; Index to Periodical Articles Related to Law; International Bulletin of Bibliography on Education; INTERNET ACCESS (& additional networks) Bulletin Board for Libraries ("BUBL"), coverage of information resources on INTERNET, JANET, and other networks; Referativnyi Zhurnal (Abstracts Journal of the Institute of Scientific Information of the Republic of Russia); Social Planning/Policy & Development Abstracts (SOPODA); Social Work Abstracts; Sociological Abstracts (SOPODA); Studies on Women Abstracts.
Year Established	1987.
Circulation	186.
Frequency	Semiannually.
Months Issued	Not specified.
No. of Articles	6–10 per issue.

SUBMISSIONS

Address	Request "Instructions for Authors" from the editors: Florence Vigilante, DSW, or Harold Lewis, PhD, Hunter College School of Social Work, 129 East 79th Street, New York, NY 10021.
Number of Copies	4.
Disk Submission	Authors of accepted manuscripts are asked to submit a disk, preferably in Microsoft Word or WordPerfect.

FORMAT OF MANUSCRIPT

Cover Sheet	Separate sheet, which does not go out for review. Full title, author names, degrees, professional titles; designation of one author as corresponding author with full address, phone numbers, e-mail address, and fax number; date of submission.
Abstract	About 100 words.
Key Words	5 or 6 key words that identify article content.
Length	5–20 pages, including references and abstract. Lengthier manuscripts may be considered, but only at the discretion of the editor. Sometimes, lengthier manuscripts may be considered if they can be divided up into sections for publication in successive issues.

| Margins | 1 inch on all sides. |
| Spacing | Double-spaced for all copy, except title page. |

STYLE

Name of Guide	*Publication Manual of the American Psychological Association.*
Subheadings	Use as needed to guide reader through the article. No more than 4 levels.
References	Author–date citation style; see style guide.
Footnotes	No footnotes preferred; incorporate into text.
Tables or Figures	Type tables double-spaced. Submit camera-ready art (300 dpi printer or better) for all figures. Place each table or figure on a separate, numbered page at the end of the manuscript.

REVIEW PROCESS

Type	"Double blind" anonymous peer review. 3 reviewers plus editor-in-chief read the manuscript in an anonymous review.
Queries	Authors are encouraged to read the journal to determine if their subject matter would be appropriate.
Acknowledgment	Enclose a regular self-addressed, stamped envelope with submission.
Review Time	3–4 months.
Revisions	See journal.
Acceptance Rate	Not specified.
Return of Manuscript	Only if 9″ x 12″ self-addressed, stamped envelope is enclosed.
Lag Time to Print	6 months–1 year.

REPRINT, SUBSCRIPTION, AND CONTACT INFORMATION

Reprint Policy	All authors receive 2 complimentary copies of the issue in which article appears. Authors receive reprint order forms to purchase additional reprinted copies.
Book Reviews	Books for review should be sent to Dr. Charles Guzzetta, Hunter College School of Social Work, 129 East 29th Street, New York, NY 10021.
Subscriptions	The Haworth Press, Inc., 10 Alice Street, Binghamton, NY 13904-1580. Individuals, $40; institutions, $75; libraries, $150.

Journal of Visual Impairment & Blindness

Editorial Focus   In the area of peer-reviewed articles and research notes, *JVIB* is interested in all types of systematic research and reporting: quantitative papers that concentrate on numerical data; qualitative papers that interpret, describe, and narrate what has taken place; and single- and multiple-case histories and ethnographies. *JVIB* also publishes opinion pieces, book reviews, news items, a professional calendar, and product reviews.

Audience   Practitioners (primarily non-medical) in the field of blindness and visual impairment (e.g., orientation and mobility instructors, rehabilitation counselors, etc.), teachers, university professors, social scientists, administrators (e.g., principals of public schools, principals of residential schools for the blind, directors of rehabilitation agencies, etc.), consumers, and parents.

Special Themes   This is only a sampling: the Americans with Disabilities Act, specialized services, employment, attitudes toward blindness, orientation and mobility, public policy, literacy, braille literacy, aging, low vision, early intervention, transition, family issues, deaf-blindness, disability studies.

Where Indexed/ Abstracted   Academic Search; Cumulative Index to Nursing & Allied Health Literature; Current Contents: Social and Behavioral Sciences; Current Index to Journals in Education; Education Index; EMBASE; EP Collection; Exceptional Child Education Resources; Homework Helper; Linguistics and Language Behavior Abstracts; Masterfile; OCLC; PsycINFO; PsycLIT; Psychological Abstracts; Social Sciences Citation Index; Social Work Abstracts; Sociological Abstracts; Telebase; UnCover.

Year Established   1907.

Circulation   3,000.

Frequency   Bimonthly.

Months Issued   January, March, May, July, September, November.

No. of Articles   Varies.

SUBMISSIONS

Address   *Journal of Visual Impairment and Blindness,* 11 Penn Plaza, Suite 300, New York, NY 10001.

Number of Copies   Original plus 5 copies.

Disk Submission   Appreciated but not required.

FORMAT OF MANUSCRIPT

Cover Sheet   Authors' names, academic degrees, professional affiliations with addresses, title of manuscript; also, phone number, fax number, and e-mail address for contact author (usually lead author).

Abstract   Approximately 100 words.

Key Words   None.

Length	2,000–5,000 words.
Margins	1 inch on all sides.
Spacing	Double-spaced.

STYLE

Name of Guide	*Publication Manual of the American Psychological Association.*
Subheadings	As needed; up to 3 levels.
References	See style guide.
Footnotes	None; information should be incorporated into text.
Tables or Figures	Should be on separate numbered pages at end of manuscripts; figures and pictures should be submitted as camera-ready art.

REVIEW PROCESS

Type	"Blind," anonymous outside peer review (2–4 reviewers) plus 3 "blind" in-house reviewers (managing editor and two consulting editors, research), and the editor-in-chief (who knows identity of authors).
Queries	E-mail encouraged for initial contact; letters and phone calls accepted.
Acknowledgment	Letter with copyright transfer agreement enclosed.
Review Time	Approximately 3 months.
Revisions	Submit original plus 5 copies with a cover letter detailing the changes made and explaining why any changes were not made.
Acceptance Rate	Approximately 15%.
Return of Manuscript	Only if manuscript is rejected. If peer review determination is to revise the manuscript, even if authors never comply, manuscript is not returned.
Lag Time to Print	6–12 months.

REPRINT, SUBSCRIPTION, AND CONTACT INFORMATION

Reprint Policy	The lead authors receive 2 complimentary copies of the issue; authors can purchase reprints directly from the printer and they can buy a year's subscription to *JVIB* at a discount.
Book Reviews	By invitation only. Send books for review to *Journal of Visual Impairment and Blindness,* 11 Penn Plaza, Suite 300, New York, NY 10001.
Subscriptions	*JVIB*, c/o Boyd Printing Co., Inc., 49 Sheridan Ave., Albany, NY 12210.
Affiliation	AFB Press of the American Foundation for the Blind.
E-Mail Address	dbrookshire@afb.org sshively@afb.org
Home Page URL	http://www.afb.org/afb

Journal of Volunteer Administration

Editorial Focus	Addresses practical concerns in the management of volunteer programs, philosophical issues in volunteerism, and applicable research.
Audience	Volunteer program administrators in a wide variety of settings, agency executives, association officers, educators, researchers, consultants, students—anyone who shares a commitment to the effective utilization of volunteers.
Special Themes	Not planned specifically; some occur spontaneously. The spring issue usually is devoted in its entirety to proceedings at the annual International Conference on Volunteer Administration sponsored by the Association for Volunteer Administration.
Where Indexed/ Abstracted	Hospital Literature Index; Human Resources Abstracts; Philanthropic Studies Index.
Year Established	1982.
Circulation	2,200.
Frequency	Quarterly.
Months Issued	January, April, July, October.
No. of Articles	4–10 per issue.

SUBMISSIONS

Address	Editor-in-Chief, *The Journal of Volunteer Administration,* Association for Volunteer Administration, 10565 Lee Highway, Suite 104, Fairfax, VA 22030-3135.
Number of Copies	4.
Disk Submission	Authors of accepted manuscripts are asked to submit a disk, preferably in WordPerfect or Microsoft Word.

FORMAT OF MANUSCRIPT

Cover Sheet	Separate sheet that does not go out for review. Full title, author names, degrees, professional titles, designation of one author as corresponding author with full address, phone numbers, e-mail address, and fax number; date of submission. Biographical data (on a separate page) not to exceed 100 words per author.
Abstract	150-word informative abstract.
Key Words	Up to 5 words or key phrases (2–3 word maximum) describing the article.
Length	10–20 pages including references and tables.
Margins	1 inch on all sides.
Spacing	Double-spaced for all copy, except title page.

STYLE

Name of Guide	*Publication Manual of the American Psychological Association.*
Subheadings	Use as needed to guide reader through the article. No more than 3 levels.
References	Author–date citation style; see style guide.
Footnotes	No footnotes preferred; incorporate into text. Where unavoidable, endnotes may be used.
Tables or Figures	See style guide. Place each table or figure on a separate, numbered page at the end of the manuscript.

REVIEW PROCESS

Type	"Double blind" anonymous peer review. Editor reviews for appropriate content then anonymous review by a minimum of 2 reviewers.
Queries	Query letters are encouraged.
Acknowledgment	By letter.
Review Time	2–4 months.
Revisions	*Rejected manuscripts:* Suggestions for a rewrite may be made to author. Revised manuscripts are reviewed again as if they were new submissions. *Accepted manuscripts:* Extensive editing is discussed with the author before publication.
Acceptance Rate	40%.
Return of Manuscript	Not returned; author should retain copies.
Lag Time to Print	Approximately 3 months–1 year.

REPRINT, SUBSCRIPTION, AND CONTACT INFORMATION

Reprint Policy	Each published author receives 2 complimentary copies. Copyright is retained by the Association for Volunteer Administration.
Book Reviews	Send unsolicited reviews to Editor-in-Chief, *The Journal of Volunteer Administration*, Association for Volunteer Administration, 10565 Lee Highway, Suite 104, Fairfax, VA 22030-3135.
Subscriptions	*The Journal of Volunteer Administration*, Association for Volunteer Administration, 10565 Lee Highway, Suite 104, Fairfax, VA 22030-3135.
	1996–97 prices: Association for Volunteer Administration members, free with membership; nonmembers, $29 (one year), $78 (3 years). Postage: Canada and Mexico $3/year; outside U.S., Canada, and Mexico $11/year.
Affiliation	*The Journal of Volunteer Administration* is a publication of the Association for Volunteer Administration.
E-Mail Address	AVAjournal@aol.com

Journal of Youth and Adolescence

Editorial Focus	Empirical research on youth and adolescence.
Audience	Mental health disciplines, as well as pediatrics, education, and social sciences.
Where Indexed/ Abstracted	Abstracts on Criminology and Penology; Adolescent Mental Health Abstracts; Applied Social Sciences Index & Abstracts; Beck Medical Information; Behavioral Abstracts; BIHEP; Biological Abstracts; Child and Youth Services; Child Development Abstracts and Bibliography; Criminal Justice Abstracts; Criminology and Penology Abstracts; Current Contents; Excerpta Medica; Family Planning Perspectives; Health Instrument File; Mental Health Abstracts; Police Science Abstracts; Psychoanalytical Quarterly; Psychological Abstracts; Sage Family Studies Abstracts.
Year Established	1971.
Circulation	3,000.
Frequency	Bimonthly.
Months Issued	February, April, June, August, October, December.
No. of Articles	8 per issue.

SUBMISSIONS

Address	Daniel Offer, MD, Editor, Department of Psychiatry & Behavioral Sciences, Northwestern University Medical School, 303 East Ohio Street, Suite 550, Chicago, IL 60611.
Number of Copies	3 (original and 2 copies).
Disk Submission	Authors of accepted manuscripts are asked to submit a labeled disk identifying software and version number, disk format, and file names.

FORMAT OF MANUSCRIPT

Cover Sheet	Full title, author(s) names, degrees, professional titles, designation of one author as corresponding author with complete address, phone numbers, fax number, and date of submission.
Abstract	An abstract is to be provided, preferably no longer than 150 words.
Key Words	Not required.
Length	25–30 pages including references and tables; manuscripts exceeding 35 pages will be returned.
Margins	1 inch on all sides.
Spacing	Double-spaced for all copy.

STYLE

Name of Guide	The journal follows the recommendations of *Style Manual for Biological Journals*, published by the American Institute of Biological Sciences.
Subheadings	Not required.
References	List references alphabetically at end of paper and refer to them in text by name and year in parentheses. Where there are 3 or more authors, only first author's name is given, followed by et al. References should include titles of papers and should follow style used in the journal.
Footnotes	The present professional affiliation of the contributor(s) should be included in a footnote on the first page. The footnote should also include the background of the author(s): their professional training and where their major interest is at present.
Tables or Figures	Tables should be numbered and referred to by number in text. Each table should by typed on a separate sheet of paper. Illustrations (photographs, drawings, charts) are to be numbered in consecutive series of Arabic numerals. The captions for illustrations should be typed on a separate sheet of paper. Identify figures on the back with author's name and number of the illustration.

REVIEW PROCESS

Type	"Double-blind" anonymous peer review; 2 reviewers, plus the editor-in-chief when necessary.
Queries	Yes.
Acknowledgment	Letter sent on receipt of manuscript.
Review Time	6 months.
Revisions	Submit original plus 2 extra copies. Acknowledgment of the reviews, comments with an explanation of changes made to the manuscript. The original reviewers will review revised manuscript.
Acceptance Rate	30%.
Return of Manuscript	Yes.
Lag Time to Print	Approximately 1 year.

REPRINT, SUBSCRIPTION, AND CONTACT INFORMATION

Reprint Policy	Reprints are available to authors, and order forms with the current price schedule are sent with proofs.
Book Reviews	None.
Subscriptions	Subscription Department, Plenum Publishing Corporation, 233 Spring Street, New York, NY 10013.
Affiliation	American Society of Adolescence Psychiatry.

Marriage & Family Review

Editorial Focus	A multidisciplinary approach to marriage and family issues.
Audience	Counselors, psychologists, health professionals, and social workers.
Special Themes	Leisure time activities, traditional and nontraditional family relationships, societal pressures and impacts on families, and cross-cultural studies on the families.
Where Indexed/ Abstracted	Abstracts in Social Gerontology: Current Literature on Aging, National Council on the Aging; Abstracts of Research in Pastoral Care & Counseling; Academic Abstracts/CD-ROM; AGRICOLA Database; Applied Social Sciences Index & Abstracts; Current Contents: Clinical Medicine/Life Sciences (CC:CM/LS); Family Life Educator "Abstracts Section"; Family Violence & Sexual Assault Bulletin; Guide to Social Science & Religion in Periodical Literature; Index to Periodical Articles Related to Law; Inventory of Marriage and Family Literature; PASCAL International Bibliography T205: Sciences de l'information Documentation; Periodical Abstracts, Research; Periodical Abstracts, Research II; Population Index; Psychological Abstracts (PsycINFO); Sage Family Studies Abstracts (SFSA); Social Planning/Policy & Development Abstracts (SOPODA); Social Sciences Index; Social Work Abstracts; Sociological Abstracts (SA); Special Educational Needs Abstracts; Studies on Women Abstracts; Violence and Abuse Abstracts: A Review of Current Literature on Interpersonal Violence (VAA).
Year Established	1978.
Circulation	402.
Frequency	Quarterly.
Months Issued	Not specified.
No. of Articles	6–10 per issue.

SUBMISSIONS

Address	Marvin B. Sussman, PhD, Unidel Professor of Human Behavior, Emeritus, Department of Individual & Family Studies, College of Human Resources, University of Delaware, Newark, DE 19716.
Number of Copies	4.
Disk Submission	Authors of accepted manuscripts are asked to submit a disk, preferably in Microsoft Word or WordPerfect.

FORMAT OF MANUSCRIPT

Cover Sheet	Separate sheet, which does not go out for review. Full title, author names, degrees, professional titles; designation of one author as corresponding author with full address, phone numbers, e-mail address, and fax number; date of submission.
Abstract	About 100 words.

Key Words	Not specified.
Length	20 pages, including references and abstract. Lengthier manuscripts may be considered, but only at the discretion of the editor. Sometimes, lengthier manuscripts may be considered if they can be divided into sections for publication in successive issues.
Margins	1 inch on all sides.
Spacing	Double-spaced for all copy, except title page.

STYLE

Name of Guide	*Publication Manual of the American Psychological Association.*
Subheadings	Use as needed to guide reader through the article. No more than 4 levels.
References	Author–date citation style; see style guide.
Footnotes	No footnotes preferred; incorporate into text.
Tables or Figures	Type tables double-spaced. Submit camera-ready art (300 dpi printer or better) for all figures. Place each table or figure on a separate, numbered page at the end of the manuscript.

REVIEW PROCESS

Type	"Double blind" anonymous peer review. 3 reviewers plus editor-in-chief read the manuscript in an anonymous review.
Queries	Authors are encouraged to read the journal to determine if their subject matter would be appropriate.
Acknowledgment	Enclose a regular self-addressed, stamped envelope with submission.
Review Time	3–4 months.
Revisions	See journal.
Acceptance Rate	Not specified.
Return of Manuscript	Only if 9″ x 12″ self-addressed, stamped envelope is enclosed.
Lag Time to Print	6 months–1 year.

REPRINT, SUBSCRIPTION, AND CONTACT INFORMATION

Reprint Policy	All authors receive 2 complimentary copies of the issue in which article appears. Authors receive reprint order forms to purchase additional reprinted copies.
Book Reviews	Send to journal editor.
Subscriptions	The Haworth Press, Inc., 10 Alice Street, Binghamton, NY 13904-1580. Individuals, $60; institutions, $160; libraries, $200.

Merrill-Palmer Quarterly: Journal of Developmental Psychology

Editorial Focus	Experimental, theoretical, and review papers concerned with issues in human development. Focus is on infant, child, and adolescent development, and contexts of development, such as the family and school.
Audience	Researchers, graduate students, and professionals in psychology, family relations, nursing, pediatrics, sociology, and education.
Special Themes	Annual invitational issue on selected current topics.
Where Indexed/ Abstracted	Child Development Abstracts & Bibliography; Current Contents: Social & Behavioral Sciences; Current Index to Journals in Education; Linguistics & Language Behavior Abstracts; Psychological Abstracts; PsycSCAN; Developmental Psychology; Sage Family Studies Abstracts; Social Work Abstracts; Sociological Abstracts; Sociology of Education Abstracts (British).
Year Established	1954.
Circulation	Approximately 1,300.
Frequency	Quarterly.
Months Issued	January, April, July, October.
No. of Articles	8–12.

SUBMISSIONS

Address	Dr. Carolyn U. Shantz, Editor, *Merrill-Palmer Quarterly*, Department of Psychology, Wayne State University, Detroit, MI 48202.
Number of Copies	4.
Disk Submission	Disks required for accepted manuscripts; Microsoft Word for Windows or WordPerfect preferred.

FORMAT OF MANUSCRIPT

Cover Sheet	Title and authors; address, phone, fax, and e-mail for corresponding author; statement of compliance with APA ethics guidelines in conducting the research reported; optional, recommendations for possible consulting editors to review manuscript.
Abstract	Required; maximum 120 words for empirical study, 100 words for review or theoretical paper.
Key Words	Not required.
Length	Variable; usually 25–30 pages from title page through tables and figures, including references.
Margins	1 inch minimum on all sides.
Spacing	Double-spaced throughout; regular spaced font (compressed/proportional-spaced font not acceptable).

STYLE

Name of Guide	*Publication Manual of the American Psychological Association.*
Subheadings	3 levels (see style guide).
References	See style guide.
Footnotes	No footnotes preferred.
Tables or Figures	Double-spaced throughout; see style guide.

REVIEW PROCESS

Type	Anonymous peer review; on request, author's identity not provided to reviewers.
Queries	Permitted if questions not answered in "Submission of Manuscripts" directions printed on inside back cover of each issue.
Acknowledgment	A letter of receipt sent immediately to author.
Review Time	3 months in most cases.
Revisions	Submit 4 copies with cover letter describing the changes made and not made in response to the reviewers and editor. Policy is 1 reviewer of original manuscript reviews revised version and 1 reviewer who is "new" to the study, plus the editor or associate editor.
Acceptance Rate	Usually 16%–24% of submitted manuscripts (excluding invited manuscripts).
Return of Manuscript	Not returned; author should retain copies.
Lag Time to Print	Usually 6 months–1 year.

CHARGES TO AUTHOR

Author Alterations	If excessive, publisher charges author.

REPRINT, SUBSCRIPTION, AND CONTACT INFORMATION

Reprint Policy	All authors receive 5 complimentary copies of issue in which article appears; additional reprints may be ordered from publisher.
Book Reviews	Invited and spontaneously submitted to Dr. William G. Graziano, Book Review Editor, Department of Psychology, Texas A&M University, College Station, TX 77843-4235.
Subscriptions	Journal Subscriptions Department, Wayne State University Press, 4809 Woodward Avenue, Detroit, MI 48201.
E-Mail Address	(Publisher) gshurn@cms.cc.wayne.edu (Editor) bmaier@gopher.chem.wayne.edu

Migration World

Editorial Focus	National and international coverage of migration and refugee movements and their impact on local communities.
Audience	Students, immigration lawyers, program managers, immigrant and refugee leaders, caseworkers, paralegals, government personnel, state and local government officials, voluntary agency representatives, academicians.
Special Themes	Immigration reform, refugees/resettlement, migration health, agency prospective, legislative development, profiles, film and book reviews.
Where Indexed/ Abstracted	ABC-CLIO: A Matter of Fact; Baywood Abstracts, ERIC CUE; GEO Abstracts; PAIS Bulletin, Public Affairs Information Service; Sociological Abstracts (SA).
Year Established	1973.
Circulation	5,000.
Frequency	5 times per year.
Months Issued	February, April, June, September, November.
No. of Articles	9 per issue.

SUBMISSIONS

Address	Editor, *Migration World*, 209 Flagg Place, Staten Island, NY 10304-1199.
Number of Copies	3.
Disk Submission	Authors of accepted manuscripts are asked to submit a disk, preferably in IBM-compatible or high-density Macintosh format.

FORMAT OF MANUSCRIPT

Cover Sheet	Not specified.
Abstract	None.
Key Words	None.
Length	10 pages, including illustrations and photos.
Margins	Not specified.
Spacing	Double-spaced.

STYLE

Name of Guide	*Writing for Migration World Magazine: Information for Authors* (free).
Subheadings	Not specified.
References	Author–date citation; see style guide.
Footnotes	No footnotes preferred; incorporate into text.
Tables or Figures	Type tables double-spaced. Submit camera-ready art (300 dpi printer or better) for all figures. Place each table or figure on a separate, numbered page at the end of the manuscript.

REVIEW PROCESS

Type	"Double-blind" anonymous peer review. 2 reviewers plus the editor-in-chief read the manuscript in an anonymous review.
Queries	Query letters are welcome. All authors are encouraged to read *Migration World.*
Acknowledgment	Editorial staff sends postcard on receipt of manuscript.
Review Time	1–2 months.
Revisions	Submit 2 copies with separate cover sheet (not identifying the author) describing the changes made in the manuscript and replying to the reviewers' comments. In general, the original reviewers and the editor-in-chief read revisions.
Acceptance Rate	60%.
Return of Manuscript	Not returned.
Lag Time to Print	2 months.

REPRINT, SUBSCRIPTION, AND CONTACT INFORMATION

Reprint Policy	All authors receive 1 complimentary copy of the issue in which the article appears. Authors receive reprint order forms to purchase additional reprinted copies of their articles.
Book Reviews	By invitation.
Subscriptions	*Migration World,* Center for Migration Studies, 209 Flagg Place, Staten Island, NY 10304-1199. One-year prices: individuals, $21; institutions, $39.
E-Mail Address	cmslft@aol.com
Home Page URL	http://www.cmsny.org

The New Social Worker: The Magazine for Social Work Students and Recent Graduates

Editorial Focus	Career guidance, news, and educational articles for social work students and new graduates. Each issue includes educational articles on field placement issues and social work ethics. Includes articles on practice specialties, book reviews, social work role models, job search tips, news from the profession and from schools of social work, and resources for social workers.
Audience	Social work students, recent graduates, faculty, practitioners, libraries, career placement centers.
Special Themes	Social work ethics, social work field placement.
Where Indexed/ Abstracted	Social Work Abstracts; Sociological Abstracts.
Year Established	1994.
Circulation	5,000.
Frequency	Quarterly.
Months Issued	January, April, July, October.
No. of Articles	Approximately 10 per issue.

SUBMISSIONS

Address	Linda Grobman, ACSW, LSW, Editor, *The New Social Worker*, P.O. Box 5390, Harrisburg, PA 17110-0390.
Number of Copies	1.
Disk Submission	Authors may submit manuscripts on 3-1/2″, IBM-compatible disk. Preferred format is Microsoft Word for Windows or ASCII text. Manuscripts may also be submitted electronically by e-mail to the address below.

FORMAT OF MANUSCRIPT

Cover Sheet	Please include a cover sheet with the author's full name, title, degrees, agency or university affiliation, address, phone numbers, e-mail address, and fax number.
Abstract	None.
Key Words	None.
Length	1,500–2,000 words (4–6 double-spaced pages).
Margins	1/2″–1″ on all sides.
Spacing	Double-spaced.

STYLE

Name of Guide	House style. Articles are written in news or feature style. Please see a back issue for examples of our style.
Subheadings	Use as needed.

References	No references preferred. May include "Recommended Readings" at the end of article.
Footnotes	No footnotes.
Tables or Figures	No tables or figures preferred.

REVIEW PROCESS

Type	All articles are reviewed by the editor.
Queries	Query letters are preferred, to determine editor's interest in the article prior to submission. However, manuscripts may be submitted without a prior query.
Acknowledgment	Approximately 1 month, when status of manuscript is determined. Please include self-addressed, stamped envelope or postcard if you would like immediate acknowledgment of receipt of your manuscript.
Review Time	Approximately 1 month.
Revisions	Submit one copy to the editor.
Acceptance Rate	Approximately 50%.
Return of Manuscript	Manuscripts are not returned. Authors should retain copies.
Lag Time to Print	3–6 months.

REPRINT, SUBSCRIPTION, AND CONTACT INFORMATION

Reprint Policy	All authors receive 2 complimentary copies of the issue in which the article appears. Authors may purchase additional reprinted copies.
Book Reviews	By invitation only. Send books for review or your qualifications for reviewing books to the editor.
Subscriptions	White Hat Communications, P.O. Box 5390, Harrisburg, PA 17110-0390. 1997 prices: 1 year (4 issues), $15; 2 years (8 issues), $26; 3 years (12 issues), $36.
Affiliation	*The New Social Worker* is published by White Hat Communications.
E-Mail Address	linda.grobman@paonline.com
Home Page URL	http://www.xmission.com/~gastown/newsocwk/

Nonprofit and Voluntary Sector Quarterly

Previous Title	*Journal of Voluntary Action Research.*
Editorial Focus	Interdisciplinary research and practice on nonprofit organizations, voluntary action, philanthropy, and community action.
Audience	An international audience of scholars and practitioners from social science, humanities, and practice disciplines.
Special Themes	*NVSQ* is a generalist journal, which means that we publish diverse material. We do publish special focus issues on occasion, and suggestions for them are welcome.
Where Indexed/ Abstracted	Philanthropic Studies Abstracts; Society for Scientific Information; various business abstracts.
Year Established	1972.
Circulation	1,000.
Frequency	Quarterly; we sometimes publish extra issues within a volume.
Months Issued	January, April, July, October.
No. of Articles	6–7.

SUBMISSIONS

Address	Carl Milofsky, Editor-in-Chief, Department of Sociology and Anthropology, Bucknell University, Lewisburg, PA 17837.
Number of Copies	4.
Disk Submission	Disk requested for final copy. We use Macintosh equipment but can read IBM-formatted material. Microsoft Word preferred. If not Macintosh, place footnotes, tables, and body of text in separate files on the disk.

FORMAT OF MANUSCRIPT

Cover Sheet	Use a cover sheet; do not include your name in the body of the manuscript.
Abstract	Yes.
Key Words	Not required.
Length	Flexible, but fewer than 40 pages preferred.
Margins	No requirement.
Spacing	Double-spaced.

STYLE

Name of Guide	*Publication Manual of the American Psychological Association.*
Subheadings	Not specified.
References	See style guide.
Footnotes	We try to minimize the use of footnotes, although in some disciplines they are necessary.

Tables or Figures	Titles should be descriptive of table contents; collapse tables if possible; interpret data for a generalist audience.

REVIEW PROCESS

Type	Blind review by 3 reviewers.
Queries	Not specified.
Acknowledgment	Letter sent on receipt of manuscript.
Review Time	3–6 months.
Revisions	Revisions are generally encouraged and published papers often have been revised several times.
Acceptance Rate	25%.
Return of Manuscript	Not returned.
Lag Time to Print	3–6 months.

REPRINT, SUBSCRIPTION, AND CONTACT INFORMATION

Reprint Policy	Authors receive 2 copies of the issue plus tear sheets from the publisher. Extra reprints may be ordered.
Book Reviews	Send books for review to: Peter D. Hall, Program on Nonprofit Organizations, Yale University, 88 Trumbull St., New Haven, CT 06520-8253.
Subscriptions	$60 per year; $85 with ARNOVA membership.
Affiliation	Association for Research on Nonprofit Organizations and Voluntary Action (ARNOVA), c/o Anita H. Plotinsky, Executive Director, ARNOVA, Indiana University Center on Philanthropy, 550 W. North Street, Suite 301, Indianapolis, IN 46202.
E-Mail Address	milofsky@bucknell.edu
Home Page URL	http://www.yale.edu/isps/ponpo/nvsq/

Occupational Therapy in Health Care

Editorial Focus	A journal of contemporary practice.
Audience	Occupational therapists and occupational therapy assistants.
Special Themes	Information sharing in a variety of practice settings.
Where Indexed/ Abstracted	Abstracts in Social Gerontology: Current Literature on Aging; Academic Abstracts/CD-ROM; Biology Digest; Cambridge Scientific Abstracts; CINAHL (Cumulative Index to Nursing & Allied Health Literature); CNPIEC Reference Guide: Chinese National Directory of Foreign Periodicals; Communication Abstracts; Exceptional Child Education Resources (ECER); Excerpta Medica/Secondary Publishing Division; Health Source; Health Source Plus; Human Resources Abstracts (HRA); INTERNET ACCESS (and additional networks) Bulletin Board for Libraries ("BUBL"), coverage of information resources on INTERNET, JANET, and other networks; Occupational Therapy Database (OTDBASE); Occupational Therapy Index; OT BibSys; Social Work Abstracts; Sport Database/Discus; Violence and Abuse Abstracts: A Review of Current Literature on Interpersonal Violence (VAA).
Year Established	1984.
Circulation	431.
Frequency	Quarterly.
Months Issued	Not specified.
No. of Articles	6–10 per issue.

SUBMISSIONS

Address	Susan Heling Kaplan, PhD, OTR, Associate Professor, Department of Occupational Therapy, Florida International University, University Park Campus, Miami, FL 33199.
Number of Copies	4.
Disk Submission	Authors of accepted manuscripts are asked to submit a disk, preferably in Microsoft Word or WordPerfect.

FORMAT OF MANUSCRIPT

Cover Sheet	Separate sheet, which does not go out for review. Full title, author names, degrees, professional titles; designation of one author as corresponding author with full address, phone numbers, e-mail address, and fax number; date of submission.
Abstract	About 100 words.
Key Words	5 or 6 key words that identify article content.

Length	5–25 pages, including references and abstract. Lengthier manuscripts may be considered, but only at the discretion of the editor. Sometimes, lengthier manuscripts may be considered if they can be divided into sections for publication in successive issues.
Margins	1 inch on all sides.
Spacing	Double-spaced for all copy, except title page.

STYLE

Name of Guide	*Publication Manual of the American Psychological Association.*
Subheadings	Use as needed to guide reader through the article. No more than 4 levels.
References	Author–date citation style; see style guide.
Footnotes	No footnotes preferred; incorporate into text.
Tables or Figures	Type tables double-spaced. Submit camera-ready art (300 dpi printer or better) for all figures. Place each table or figure on a separate, numbered page at the end of the manuscript.

REVIEW PROCESS

Type	"Double blind" anonymous peer review. 3 reviewers plus editor-in-chief read the manuscript in an anonymous review.
Queries	Authors are encouraged to read the journal to determine if their subject matter would be appropriate.
Acknowledgment	Enclose a regular self-addressed, stamped envelope with submission.
Review Time	3–4 months.
Revisions	See journal.
Acceptance Rate	Not specified.
Return of Manuscript	Only if 9″ x 12″ self-addressed, stamped envelope is enclosed.
Lag Time to Print	6 months–1 year.

REPRINT, SUBSCRIPTION, AND CONTACT INFORMATION

Reprint Policy	All authors receive 2 complimentary copies of the issue in which article appears. Authors receive reprint order forms to purchase additional reprinted copies.
Book Reviews	Send to journal editor.
Subscriptions	The Haworth Press, Inc., 10 Alice Street, Binghamton, NY 13904-1580. Individuals, $40; institutions, $75; libraries, $125.
E-Mail Address	kaplan@servax.fiu.edu

Occupational Therapy in Mental Health

Editorial Focus	Psychosocial practice and research.
Audience	Not specified.
Where Indexed/ Abstracted	Abstracts in Social Gerontology: Current Literature on Aging, National Council on the Aging; CINAHL (Cumulative Index to Nursing & Allied Health Literature); CNPIEC Reference Guide: Chinese National Directory of Foreign Periodicals; Developmental Medicine & Child Neurology; Exceptional Child Education Resources (ECER); Excerpta Medica/Secondary Publishing Division; Family Studies Database (online and CD–ROM); INTERNET ACCESS (& additional networks) Bulletin Board for Libraries ("BUBL"), coverage of information resources on INTERNET, JANET, and other networks; Mental Health Abstracts (online through DIALOG); Occupational Therapy Database (OTDBASE); Occupational Therapy Index; OT BibSys; PASCAL International Bibliography T2O5: Sciences de l'information Documention; Psychiatric Rehabilitation Journal; Social Work Abstracts; Sport Database/Discus.
Year Established	1980.
Circulation	742.
Frequency	Quarterly.
Months Issued	Not specified.
No. of Articles	6–10 per issue.

SUBMISSIONS

Address	Editor, Marie-Louise Blount, AM, OTR, New York University, Department of Occupational Therapy, Education Building, 35 West 4th Street, 11th Floor, New York, NY 10012.
Number of Copies	4.
Disk Submission	Authors of accepted manuscripts are asked to submit a disk, preferably in Microsoft Word or WordPerfect.

FORMAT OF MANUSCRIPT

Cover Sheet	Separate sheet, which does not go out for review. Full title, author names, degrees, professional titles; designation of one author as corresponding author with full address, phone numbers, e-mail address, and fax number; date of submission.
Abstract	About 100 words.
Key Words	Not specified.
Length	20 pages, including references and abstract. Lengthier manuscripts may be considered, but only at the discretion of the editor. Sometimes, lengthier manuscripts may be considered if they can be divided into sections for publication in successive issues.

Margins	1 inch on all sides.
Spacing	Double-spaced for all copy, except title page.

STYLE

Name of Guide	*Publication Manual of the American Psychological Association.*
Subheadings	Use as needed to guide reader through the article. No more than 4 levels.
References	Author–date citation style; see style guide.
Footnotes	No footnotes preferred; incorporate into text.
Tables or Figures	Type tables double-spaced. Submit camera-ready art (300 dpi printer or better) for all figures. Place each table or figure on a separate, numbered page at the end of the manuscript.

REVIEW PROCESS

Type	"Double blind" anonymous peer review. 3 reviewers, plus editor-in-chief read the manuscript in an anonymous review.
Queries	Authors are encouraged to read the journal to determine if their subject matter would be appropriate.
Acknowledgment	Enclose a regular self-addressed, stamped envelope with submission.
Review Time	3–4 months.
Revisions	See journal.
Acceptance Rate	Not specified.
Return of Manuscript	Only if 9″ x 12″ self-addressed, stamped envelope is enclosed.
Lag Time to Print	6 months–1 year.

REPRINT, SUBSCRIPTION, AND CONTACT INFORMATION

Reprint Policy	All authors receive 2 complimentary copies of the issue in which article appears. Authors receive reprint order forms to purchase additional reprinted copies.
Book Reviews	Send to journal editor.
Subscriptions	The Haworth Press, Inc., 10 Alice Street, Binghamton, NY 13904-1580. Individuals, $40; institutions, $150; libraries, $175.
E-Mail Address	kaplans@servax.fiu.edu

Omega: Journal of Death and Dying

Editorial Focus	Research articles are a top priority. Journal also publishes quality case studies, theoretical, and review contributions. Original contributions on nontrivial topics are welcomed. Readers include sophisticated researchers, educators, and practitioners from a variety of fields; manuscripts should respect the existing knowledge and offer facts, ideas, or experiences that make a difference. The base fact that a manuscript is "about death" does not automatically qualify it for publication in *Omega*. Journal looks for incisive, thoughtful, challenging manuscripts.
Audience	Not specified.
Special Themes	Contact the editor to express interest in a theme.
Where Indexed/ Abstracted	Abstracts for Social Workers; Applied Social Sciences Index & Abstracts; Behavioral Abstracts; Bibliographic Index of Health Education Periodicals; BioScience Information Service of Biological Abstracts; Chicago Psychoanalytic Literature Index; Excerpta Medica; Family Abstracts; Mental Health Digest; PRE-PSYC Database; PREV; Psychological Abstracts; Social Work Abstracts; Sociological Abstracts.
Year Established	1970.
Circulation	Approximately 1,500.
Frequency	8 times per year.
Months Issued	Not specified.
No. of Articles	Approximately 6.

SUBMISSIONS

Address	Robert Kastenbaum, Editor, Department of Communication, P.O. Box 871205, Tempe, AZ 85284.
Number of Copies	3.
Disk Submission	No.

FORMAT OF MANUSCRIPT

Cover Sheet	Name, address (include zip code), phone number, fax number.
Abstract	100–150 words.
Key Words	Not specified.
Length	No maximum or minimum, average length 20 pages.
Margins	Wide.
Spacing	Double-spaced.

STYLE

Name of Guide	*Publication Manual of the American Psychological Association.*
Subheadings	Include.
References	See style guide.
Footnotes	Include only for acknowledgment and for special circumstances. Generally, avoid using footnotes.
Tables or Figures	Quality word processing printout is acceptable. Include each table and figure on a separate page. Avoid abbreviations. Include a legend and heading.

REVIEW PROCESS

Type	Anonymous review by 2 reviewers minimum.
Queries	Not specified.
Acknowledgment	Include self-addressed, stamped envelope or postcard when submitting manuscript.
Review Time	6 weeks.
Revisions	Author receives detailed comments from reviewers and editor. Most of the published articles have been revised.
Acceptance Rate	15% accepted without revisions; 25%–30% accepted after revisions.
Return of Manuscript	Returned only if requested by author.
Lag Time to Print	1 year.

CHARGES TO AUTHOR

Author Alterations	No charge if minor alterations needed.

REPRINT, SUBSCRIPTION, AND CONTACT INFORMATION

Reprint Policy	Authors receive one free copy of the issue and 20 reprints. Ordering information for additional reprints is sent to author.
Book Reviews	Contact editor. Send a vita and indicate areas of interest and expertise.
Subscriptions	Baywood Publishing Company, Inc., 26 Austin Avenue, P.O. Box 337, Amityville, NY 11701.
	Individuals, $45; institutions, $145.

Physical & Occupational Therapy in Geriatrics

Editorial Focus	Current trends in geriatric rehabilitation.
Audience	Not specified.
Where Indexed/ Abstracted	Abstracts in Social Gerontology: Current Literature on Aging, National Council on the Aging; Academic Abstracts/CD-ROM; Brown University Geriatric Research Application Digest "Abstracts Section"; CINAHL (Cumulative Index to Nursing & Allied Health Literature); CNPIEC Reference Guide: Chinese National Directory of Foreign Periodicals; Communication Abstracts; Excerpta Medica/Secondary Publishing Division; Family Studies Database (online and CD-ROM); Health Source; Health Source Plus; Human Resources Abstracts (HRA); INTERNET ACCESS (& additional networks) Bulletin Board for Libraries ("BUBL"), coverage of information resources on INTERNET, JANET, and other networks; Occupational Therapy Database (OTDBASE); Occupational Therapy Index; OT BibSys; Psychological Abstracts (PsycINFO); Public Affairs Information Bulletin (PAIS); Social Work Abstracts; Sport Database/Discus.
Year Established	1980.
Circulation	537.
Frequency	Quarterly.
Months Issued	Not specified.
No. of Articles	6–10 per issue.

SUBMISSIONS

Address	Editor, Ellen D. Taira, OTR/L, P.O. Box 630242, Bronx, NY 10463.
Number of Copies	4.
Disk Submission	Authors of accepted manuscripts are asked to submit a disk, preferably in Microsoft Word or WordPerfect.

FORMAT OF MANUSCRIPT

Cover Sheet	Separate sheet, which does not go out for review. Full title, author names, degrees, professional titles; designation of one author as corresponding author with full address, phone numbers, e-mail address, and fax number; date of submission.
Abstract	About 100 words.
Key Words	5 or 6 key words that identify article content.
Length	20 pages, including references and abstract. Lengthier manuscripts may be considered, but only at the discretion of the editor. Sometimes, lengthier manuscripts may be considered if they can be divided up into sections for publication in successive issues.
Margins	1 inch on all sides.
Spacing	Double-spaced for all copy, except title page.

STYLE

Name of Guide	*Publication Manual of the American Psychological Association.*
Subheadings	Use as needed to guide reader through the article. No more than 4 levels.
References	Author–date citation style; see style guide.
Footnotes	No footnotes preferred; incorporate into text.
Tables or Figures	Type tables double-spaced. Submit camera-ready art (300 dpi printer or better) for all figures. Place each table or figure on a separate, numbered page at the end of the manuscript.

REVIEW PROCESS

Type	"Double blind" anonymous peer review. 3 reviewers plus editor-in-chief read the manuscript in an anonymous review.
Queries	Authors are encouraged to read the journal to determine if their subject matter would be appropriate.
Acknowledgment	Enclose a regular self-addressed, stamped envelope with submission.
Review Time	3–4 months.
Revisions	See journal.
Acceptance Rate	Not specified.
Return of Manuscript	Only if 9″ x 12″ self-addressed, stamped envelope is enclosed.
Lag Time to Print	6 months–1 year.

REPRINT, SUBSCRIPTION, AND CONTACT INFORMATION

Reprint Policy	All authors receive 2 complimentary copies of the issue in which article appears. Authors receive reprint order forms to purchase additional reprinted copies.
Book Reviews	Send to journal editor.
Subscriptions	The Haworth Press, Inc., 10 Alice Street, Binghamton, NY 13904-1580. Individuals, $40; institutions, $140; libraries, $250.

Physical & Occupational Therapy in Pediatrics

Editorial Focus	Not specified.
Audience	Not specified.
Where Indexed/ Abstracted	Academic Abstracts/CD-ROM; Biosciences Information Service of Biological Abstracts (BIOSIS); Child Development Abstracts & Bibliography; CINAHL (Cumulative Index to Nursing & Allied Health Literature); CNPIEC Reference Guide: Chinese National Directory of Foreign Periodicals; Developmental Medicine & Child Neurology; Educational Administration Abstracts (EAA); Exceptional Child Education Resources (ECER); Excerpta Medica/Secondary Publishing Division; Family Studies Database (online and CD-ROM); Health Source; Health Source Plus; INTERNET ACCESS (& additional networks) Bulletin Board for Libraries ("BUBL"), coverage of information resources on INTERNET, JANET, and other networks; Occupational Therapy Database (OTDBASE); Occupational Therapy Index; OT BibSys; Sage Family Studies Abstracts (SFSA); Sage Urban Studies Abstracts (SUSA); Social Work Abstracts; Sport Database/ Discus; Violence and Abuse Abstracts: A Review of Current Literature on Interpersonal Violence (VAA).
Year Established	1980.
Circulation	885.
Frequency	Quarterly.
Months Issued	Not specified.
No. of Articles	6–10 per issue.

SUBMISSIONS

Address	Editors, Irma J. Whilhelm or Jane Coryell, RFD 1, Box 960, Augusta, ME 04330.
Number of Copies	4.
Disk Submission	Authors of accepted manuscripts are asked to submit a disk, preferably in Microsoft Word or WordPerfect.

FORMAT OF MANUSCRIPT

Cover Sheet	Separate sheet, which does not go out for review. Full title, author names, degrees, professional titles; designation of one author as corresponding author with full address, phone numbers, e-mail address, and fax number; date of submission.
Abstract	About 100 words.
Key Words	5 or 6 key words that identify article content.
Length	12–20 pages, including references and abstract. Lengthier manuscripts may be considered, but only at the discretion of the editor. Sometimes, lengthier manuscripts may be considered if they can be divided into sections for publication in successive issues.

Margins	1 inch on all sides.
Spacing	Double-spaced for all copy, except title page.

STYLE

Name of Guide	Medicus style (as outlined in *Stylebook/Editorial Manual* of the American Medical Association).
Subheadings	Use as needed to guide reader through the article. No more than 4 levels.
References	Author–date citation style; see style guide.
Footnotes	No footnotes preferred; incorporate into text.
Tables or Figures	Type tables double-spaced. Submit camera-ready art (300 dpi printer or better) for all figures. Place each table or figure on a separate, numbered page at the end of the manuscript.

REVIEW PROCESS

Type	"Double blind" anonymous peer review. 3 reviewers plus editor-in-chief read the manuscript in an anonymous review.
Queries	Authors are encouraged to read the journal to determine if their subject matter would be appropriate.
Acknowledgment	See instructions in journal.
Review Time	3–4 months.
Revisions	See journal.
Acceptance Rate	Not specified.
Return of Manuscript	Only if 9" x 12" self-addressed, stamped envelope is enclosed.
Lag Time to Print	6 months–1 year.

REPRINT, SUBSCRIPTION, AND CONTACT INFORMATION

Reprint Policy	All authors receive 2 complimentary copies of the issue in which article appears. Authors receive reprint order forms to purchase additional reprinted copies.
Book Reviews	Send to journal co-editors.
Subscriptions	The Haworth Press, Inc., 10 Alice Street, Binghamton, NY 13904-1580. Individuals, $40; institutions, $160; libraries, $250.

Psychiatric Rehabilitation Journal

Previous Title	*Psychosocial Rehabilitation Journal/Innovations and Research.*
Editorial Focus	Serious mental illness.
Audience	Social work, psychology, psychiatry, psychiatric nursing, rehabilitation.
Special Themes	Not specified.
Where Indexed/ Abstracted	Nursing Abstracts; Psychological Abstracts; Sociological Abstracts.
Year Established	1979.
Circulation	4,500.
Frequency	Quarterly.
Months Issued	January, April, July, October.
No. of Articles	10.

SUBMISSIONS

Address	*Psychiatric Rehabilitation Journal,* 930 Commonwealth Avenue, Boston, MA 02215.
Number of Copies	3.
Disk Submission	Only for accepted manuscripts.

FORMAT OF MANUSCRIPT

Cover Sheet	Not specified.
Abstract	100 words.
Key Words	Not specified.
Length	20 pages.
Margins	1 inch on all sides.
Spacing	Double-spaced.

STYLE

Name of Guide	*Publication Manual of the American Psychological Association.*
Subheadings	Not specified.
References	See style guide.
Footnotes	See style guide.
Tables or Figures	See style guide.

REVIEW PROCESS

Type	Blind review.
Queries	No.
Acknowledgment	By letter.

Review Time	3 months.
Revisions	By author.
Acceptance Rate	50%.
Return of Manuscript	Yes.
Lag Time to Print	1 year.

REPRINT, SUBSCRIPTION, AND CONTACT INFORMATION

Reprint Policy	Available for purchase.
Book Reviews	By invitation.
Subscriptions	LeRoy Spaniol, PhD, Executive Publisher, *Psychiatric Rehabilitation Journal*, 930 Commonwealth Avenue, Boston, MA 02215.
Affiliation	International Association of Psychosocial Rehabilitation Services and Boston University.
E-Mail Address	getgen@acs.bu.edu
Home Page URL	http:/web.bu.edu/sarpsych

Psychiatric Services

Previous Title	*Hospital and Community Psychiatry* (until January 1995).
Editorial Focus	All aspects of psychiatric care, treatment, and service delivery. Strong clinical focus; in-depth coverage of economic, forensic, public policy, and administrative issues. Research, program evaluation, theoretical, and review articles and brief reports, plus columns, commentary, letters, and book reviews.
Audience	Mental health professionals in all disciplines.
Special Themes	Patients with severe and chronic mental illness (treatment and service delivery systems); treatment modalities; all types of service delivery systems including managed care; patient advocacy; families of mentally ill patients.
Where Indexed/ Abstracted	Cumulative Index to Nursing & Allied Health Literature; Current Contents: Social & Behavioral Sciences; EMBASE; HealthSTAR; International Nursing Index; MEDLINE; PsycINFO; Social Sciences Citation Index; Social Work Abstracts; and others.
Year Established	1950.
Circulation	20,000.
Frequency	Monthly.
No. of Articles	11–14.

SUBMISSIONS

Address	John A. Talbott, MD, Editor, *Psychiatric Services,* American Psychiatric Association, 1400 K Street, NW, Washington, DC 20005; phone: 202-682-6070.
Number of Copies	6.
Disk Submission	IBM-compatible disk, if manuscript is accepted.

FORMAT OF MANUSCRIPT

Cover Sheet	Besides manuscript title, list full name, degrees, and primary affiliation (including position title) of each author, plus a second affiliation if desired. For the corresponding author, list mailing address, phone and fax numbers, and e-mail address. List word count, excluding references and tables. In an acknowledgment, list all financial support for the work, plus any financial relationships that may pose a conflict of interest. Individuals contributing to the paper's intellectual or technical content may be acknowledged. Because *Psychiatric Services* uses an anonymous review system, include a second cover sheet with manuscript title only.
Abstract	For full-length research reports and literature reviews, a structured abstract of 250 words maximum. For other full-length articles, a nonstructured informative abstract of 150 words maximum. For brief reports, a nonstructured informative abstract of 100 words maximum.
Key Words	Not required.
Length	For full-length articles, generally a maximum of 3,000 words (excluding tables and references). For brief reports, a maximum of 1,200 words plus no more than 10 references and 1 table or figure.

| Margins | 1.5 inches on all sides. |
| Spacing | Double-spaced for all copy (except title page). |

STYLE

Name of Guide	*Psychiatric Services Information for Contributors,* free from the editorial office (phone: 202-682-6070) and published quarterly in the journal.
Subheadings	Maximum of 3 levels. For research reports, use the standard first-level subheadings of Methods, Results, Discussion, and Conclusions.
References	Reference-number system: arrange and number in order of citation in text.
Footnotes	Not used; incorporate relevant material in text.
Tables or Figures	Use tables and figures only for relevant data. Put each on a separate page. For tables, follow formats in recent issues of the journal; provide specific table titles and indicate all units of measure clearly. The journal recreates figures in-house at no charge to the author.

REVIEW PROCESS

Type	Anonymous peer review by at least three independent reviewers. In addition, separate statistical review is often obtained.
Queries	Query letters are discouraged; authors should consult the journal and its *Information for Contributors* to determine if their topics are appropriate.
Acknowledgment	The journal acknowledges receipt of manuscripts by letter.
Review Time	3–4 months, plus additional time if revisions are reviewed.
Revisions	Submit 4 copies, with a letter briefly describing the changes made and how the reviewers' suggestions have been dealt with. For substantial revisions, the paper is generally sent again to the original reviewers.
Acceptance Rate	30%.
Return of Manuscript	Manuscripts are returned.
Lag Time to Print	4–6 months.

REPRINT, SUBSCRIPTION, AND CONTACT INFORMATION

Reprint Policy	Authors receive 5 copies of the issue, plus a price list for reprints.
Book Reviews	Invited reviews only. Send books for review to the book review editor: Jeffrey L. Geller, MD, Department of Psychiatry, University of Massachusetts Medical School, 55 Lake Avenue North, Worcester, MA 01655.
Subscriptions	Circulation Department, American Psychiatric Association, 1400 K Street, NW, Washington, DC 20005; phone: 202-682-6240.
	One-year subscription prices (1996): In the U.S., $45 for individuals, $75 for institutions, $22.50 for students. Outside the U.S., $65 for individuals, $95 for institutions, $37.50 for students.
Affiliation	American Psychiatric Association.
E-Mail Address	psjournal@psych.org
Home Page URL	www.appi.org/psjournal

Psychological Assessment

Previous Title	*Psychological Assessment: A Journal of Consulting and Clinical Psychology.*
Editorial Focus	*Psychological Assessment* publishes mainly empirical articles concerning clinical assessment and evaluation. Papers that fall within the publication domain include investigations related to the development, validation, and evaluation of assessment techniques. Diverse modalities (e.g., cognitive and motoric) and methods of assessment (e.g., inventories, interviews, direct observations, and psychophysiological measures) are within the domain of the journal, especially as they are evaluated in clinical research or practice. Also included are assessment topics that emerge in the context of such issues as cross-cultural studies, ethnicity, minority status, gender, and sexual orientation. Case studies occasionally will be considered if they identify novel assessment techniques that permit evaluation of the nature, course, or treatment of clinical dysfunction. Nonempirical papers, including highly focused reviews and methodological papers, are considered if they facilitate interpretation and evaluation of specific assessment techniques.
Audience	Researchers in the discipline, faculty, libraries.
Where Indexed/ Abstracted	Academic Index; Addiction Abstract; Applied Social Sciences Index & Abstracts; Biological Abstracts; Child Development Abstracts; Current Advances in Ecological & Environmental Sciences; Current Contents; Current Index to Journals in Education; Ergonomics Abstracts; Index Medicus; Management Contents; PsycINFO; Social Sciences Citation Index; Social Sciences Index.
Year Established	1989.
Circulation	6,500.
Frequency	Quarterly.
Months Issued	March, June, September, December.
No. of Articles	16.

SUBMISSIONS

Address	James N. Butcher, Department of Psychology, Elliott Hall, University of Minnesota, 75 East River Road, Minneapolis, MN 55455.
Number of Copies	3.
Disk Submission	Submit manuscripts on paper; disks may be requested of accepted articles.

FORMAT OF MANUSCRIPT

Cover Sheet	Refer to Instructions to Authors in each issue.
Abstract	Manuscripts must include an abstract containing a maximum of 960 characters and spaces (approximately 120 words), typed on a separate sheet of paper.
Key Words	None.

Length	Not specified.
Margins	See style guide.
Spacing	Double-spaced.

STYLE

Name of Guide	*Publication Manual of the American Psychological Association.*
Subheadings	See style guide.
References	See style guide.
Footnotes	See style guide.
Tables or Figures	See style guide; camera-ready copy required for all art.

REVIEW PROCESS

Type	Masked review optional by request of author.
Queries	No query letters.
Acknowledgment	Editor acknowledges submission by mail.
Review Time	Usually 60–90 days.
Revisions	Editor will notify author if revision is desired (most manuscripts are initially rejected; most published manuscripts have gone through 1 or 2 revisions).
Acceptance Rate	10%.
Return of Manuscript	Manuscripts are not usually returned.
Lag Time to Print	7 months.

CHARGES TO AUTHOR

Author Alterations	Authors are billed for alterations in proofs.

REPRINT, SUBSCRIPTION, AND CONTACT INFORMATION

Reprint Policy	Authors may purchase reprints of their articles (order form accompanies proofs).
Book Reviews	None.
Subscriptions	Subscriptions Department, American Psychological Association, 750 First Street, NE, Washington, DC 20002-4242.
	Yearly nonmember individual rates are $78 domestic, $93 foreign, $101 airmail; institutional rates are $156 domestic, $186 foreign, $196 airmail. APA members: $39.
Affiliation	Published by the American Psychological Association.
Home Page URL	http://www.apa.org

Psychology and Aging

Editorial Focus	*Psychology and Aging* publishes original articles on adult development and aging. Such original articles include reports of research that may be applied, biobehavioral, clinical, educational, experimental (laboratory, field, or naturalistic studies), methodological, or psychosocial. Although the emphasis is on original research investigations, occasional theoretical analyses of research issues, practical clinical problems, or policy may appear, as well as critical reviews of a content area in adult development and aging. Clinical case studies that have theoretical significance are also appropriate. Brief reports are acceptable with the author's agreement not to submit a full report to another journal; a 75–100 word abstract plus 410 60-space lines of text and references constitute absolute limitations on space for such brief reports.
Audience	Researchers in the discipline, faculty, libraries.
Where Indexed/ Abstracted	Addiction Abstracts; Applied Social Sciences Index & Abstracts; Ergonomics Abstracts; PsycINFO.
Year Established	1986.
Circulation	3,400.
Frequency	Quarterly.
Months Issued	March, June, September, December.
No. of Articles	16.

SUBMISSIONS

Address	T.A. Salthouse, School of Psychology, Georgia Institute of Technology, Atlanta, GA 30332-0170.
Number of Copies	4.
Disk Submission	Submit manuscripts on paper; disks may be requested of accepted articles.

FORMAT OF MANUSCRIPT

Cover Sheet	Refer to Instructions to Authors in each issue.
Abstract	Manuscripts must include an abstract containing a maximum of 960 characters and spaces (approximately 120 words), typed on a separate sheet of paper.
Key Words	None.
Length	Not specified.
Margins	See style guide.
Spacing	Double-spaced.

STYLE

Name of Guide	*Publication Manual of the American Psychological Association.*
Subheadings	See style guide.

References	See style guide.
Footnotes	See style guide.
Tables or Figures	See style guide; camera-ready copy required for all art.

REVIEW PROCESS

Type	Masked review optional; must be requested by author.
Queries	No query letters.
Acknowledgment	Editor acknowledges submission by mail.
Review Time	Usually 60–90 days.
Revisions	Editor will notify author if revision is desired (most manuscripts are initially rejected; most published manuscripts have gone through 1 or 2 revisions).
Acceptance Rate	34%.
Return of Manuscript	Manuscripts are not usually returned.
Lag Time to Print	10 months.

CHARGES TO AUTHOR

Author Alterations	Authors are billed for alterations in proofs.

REPRINT, SUBSCRIPTION, AND CONTACT INFORMATION

Reprint Policy	Authors may purchase reprints of their articles (order form accompanies proofs).
Book Reviews	None.
Subscriptions	Subscriptions Department, American Psychological Association, 750 First Street, NE, Washington, DC 20002-4242.
	Yearly nonmember rates are $89 domestic, $104 foreign, $112 airmail. APA members: $45.
Affiliation	Published by the American Psychological Association.
Home Page URL	http://www.apa.org

Psychotherapy

Editorial Focus	*Psychotherapy* welcomes theoretical contributions and research studies. The journal endeavors to foster interactions among training, practice, theory, and research since all are essential to psychotherapy. Authors are asked to submit novel ideas, the controversial, the example of practice-relevant issues that would stimulate another theorist, researcher, or practitioner. We include the widest scope of orientations to inform our readers.
Audience	Researchers in the discipline, faculty, libraries.
Where Indexed/ Abstracted	PsycINFO; PsycLIT.
Year Established	Not specified.
Circulation	Approximately 7,000.
Frequency	Quarterly.
Months Issued	Winter, spring, summer, fall.
No. of Articles	Approximately 15–20.

SUBMISSIONS

Address	Wade H. Silverman, *Journal of Psychotherapy* , 2665 South Bayshore Drive, Suite 406, Coconut Grove, FL 33133.
Number of Copies	4.
Disk Submission	Submit manuscripts on paper; disks may be requested of accepted articles.

FORMAT OF MANUSCRIPT

Cover Sheet	Refer to Instructions to Authors in each issue.
Abstract	100–150 words.
Key Words	None.
Length	Approximately 25 pages.
Margins	1.5 inches on all sides.
Spacing	Double-spaced.

STYLE

Name of Guide	*Publication Manual of the American Psychological Association.*
Subheadings	See style guide.
References	See style guide.
Footnotes	See style guide.
Tables or Figures	See style guide; camera-ready copy required for all art.

REVIEW PROCESS

Type	Anonymous review by 2–3 reviewers.
Queries	No query letters.
Acknowledgment	Editor acknowledges submission by mail.
Review Time	Usually 60–90 days.
Revisions	Editor will notify author if revision is desired (most manuscripts are initially rejected; most accepted manuscripts have gone through 1 or 2 revisions).
Acceptance Rate	20%.
Return of Manuscript	Not returned.
Lag Time to Print	1 year.

CHARGES TO AUTHOR

Author Alterations	Authors are billed for alterations in proofs.

REPRINT, SUBSCRIPTION, AND CONTACT INFORMATION

Reprint Policy	Authors may purchase reprints of their articles (order form accompanies proofs).
Book Reviews	None.
Subscriptions	Subscription Manager, *Psychotherapy*, 3900 E. Camelback Road, Suite 200, Phoenix, AZ 85018-2684.
	1 year—individual: $70/U.S., $85/foreign; institution: $90/U.S., $100/foreign; student: $35/U.S., $50/foreign. 2 years—individual: $120/U.S., $130/foreign; institution: $155/U.S., $170/foreign; student $65/U.S., $80/foreign. Previous single issue—$20/U.S., $25/foreign. Special issue—$25/U.S., $30/foreign.
Affiliation	Published by the American Psychological Association.
Home Page URL	http://www.apa.org

Psychotherapy in Private Practice

Editorial Focus	Innovations in clinical methods and assessment, consultation, and practice management.
Audience	Clinicians and academic researchers.
Special Themes	Forensic issues, types of practices, philosophy, transference issues and the effect of therapist gender, autobiographical essays, humorous monologues.
Where Indexed/ Abstracted	Abstracts of Research in Pastoral Care & Counseling; Periodicals; Excerpta Medica/Secondary Publishing Division; Family Studies Database (online and CD-ROM); Human Resources Abstracts (HRA); Index to Periodical Articles Related to Law; INTERNET ACCESS (& additional networks) Bulletin Board for Libraries ("BUBL"), coverage of information resources on INTERNET, JANET, and other networks; Mental Health Abstracts (online through DIALOG); PASCAL International Bibliography T205: Sciences de l'information Documentation; Psychiatric Rehabilitation Journal; Psychological Abstracts (PsycINFO); Social Work Abstracts.
Year Established	1983.
Circulation	241.
Frequency	Quarterly.
Months Issued	Not specified.
No. of Articles	6–10 per issue.

SUBMISSIONS

Address	Editor, Frank De Piano, PhD, Dean, Center for Psychological Studies, Nova Southeastern University, 3301 College Avenue, Ft. Lauderdale, FL 33314.
Number of Copies	4.
Disk Submission	Authors of accepted manuscripts are asked to submit a disk, preferably in Microsoft Word or WordPerfect.

FORMAT OF MANUSCRIPT

Cover Sheet	Separate sheet, which does not go out for review. Full title, author names, degrees, professional titles; designation of one author as corresponding author with full address, phone numbers, e-mail address, and fax number; date of submission.
Abstract	About 100 words.
Key Words	Not specified.
Length	Not specified.
Margins	1 inch on all sides.
Spacing	Double-spaced for all copy, except title page.

STYLE

Name of Guide	*Publication Manual of the American Psychological Association.*
Subheadings	Use as needed to guide reader through the article. No more than 4 levels.
References	Author–date citation style; see style guide.
Footnotes	No footnotes preferred; incorporate into text.
Tables or Figures	Type tables double-spaced. Submit camera-ready art (300 dpi printer or better) for all figures. Place each table or figure on a separate, numbered page at the end of the manuscript.

REVIEW PROCESS

Type	"Double blind" anonymous peer review. 3 reviewers plus editor-in-chief read the manuscript in an anonymous review.
Queries	Authors are encouraged to read the journal to determine if their subject matter would be appropriate.
Acknowledgment	Enclose a regular self-addressed, stamped envelope with submission.
Review Time	3–4 months.
Revisions	See journal.
Acceptance Rate	Not specified.
Return of Manuscript	Only if 9" x 12" self-addressed, stamped envelope is enclosed.
Lag Time to Print	6 months–1 year.

REPRINT, SUBSCRIPTION, AND CONTACT INFORMATION

Reprint Policy	All authors receive 2 complimentary copies of the issue in which article appears. Authors receive reprint order forms to purchase additional reprinted copies.
Book Reviews	Send to journal editor.
Subscriptions	The Haworth Press, Inc., 10 Alice Street, Binghamton, NY 13904-1580. Individuals, $40; institutions, $85; libraries, $175.

The Psychotherapy Patient

Editorial Focus	Attribute-focused practice.
Audience	Not specified.
Where Indexed/ Abstracted	Abstracts of Research in Pastoral Care & Counseling; CNPIEC Reference Guide: Chinese National Directory of Foreign Periodicals; Family Studies Database (online and CD-ROM); INTERNET ACCESS (& additional networks) Bulletin Board for Libraries ("BUBL"), coverage of information resources on INTERNET, JANET, and other networks; Mental Health Abstracts (online through DIALOG); Psychiatric Rehabilitation Journal; Social Work Abstracts; Special Educational Needs Abstracts; Studies on Women Abstracts.
Year Established	1984.
Circulation	164.
Frequency	Quarterly.
Months Issued	Not specified.
No. of Articles	6–10 per issue.

SUBMISSIONS

Address	Editor, E. Mark Stern, PhD, 215 East 11th Street, New York, NY 10003.
Number of Copies	4.
Disk Submission	Authors of accepted manuscripts are asked to submit a disk, preferably in Microsoft Word or WordPerfect.

FORMAT OF MANUSCRIPT

Cover Sheet	Separate sheet, which does not go out for review. Full title, author names, degrees, professional titles; designation of one author as corresponding author with full address, phone numbers, e-mail address, and fax number; date of submission.
Abstract	About 100 words.
Key Words	Not specified.
Length	20 pages, including references and abstract. Lengthier manuscripts may be considered, but only at the discretion of the editor. Sometimes, lengthier manuscripts may be considered if they can be divided into sections for publication in successive issues.
Margins	1 inch on all sides.
Spacing	Double-spaced for all copy, except title page.

STYLE

Name of Guide	*Publication Manual of the American Psychological Association.*
Subheadings	Use as needed to guide reader through the article. No more than 4 levels.

References	Author–date citation style; see style guide.
Footnotes	No footnotes preferred; incorporate into text.
Tables or Figures	Type tables double-spaced. Submit camera-ready art (300 dpi printer or better) for all figures. Place each table or figure on a separate, numbered page at the end of the manuscript.

REVIEW PROCESS

Type	"Double blind" anonymous peer review. 3 reviewers plus editor-in-chief read the manuscript in an anonymous review.
Queries	Authors are encouraged to read the journal to determine if their subject matter would be appropriate.
Acknowledgment	Enclose a stamped, self-addressed envelope.
Review Time	3–4 months.
Revisions	See journal.
Acceptance Rate	Not specified.
Return of Manuscript	Only if 9″ x 12″ self-addressed, stamped envelope is enclosed.
Lag Time to Print	6 months–1 year.

REPRINT, SUBSCRIPTION, AND CONTACT INFORMATION

Reprint Policy	All authors receive 2 complimentary copies of the issue in which article appears. Authors receive reprint order forms to purchase additional reprinted copies.
Book Reviews	Send to journal editor.
Subscriptions	The Haworth Press, Inc., 10 Alice Street, Binghamton, NY 13904-1580. Individuals, $40; institutions, $90; libraries, $135.

The Public Interest

Editorial Focus	Publish essays and book reviews on a wide array of public policy issues.
Audience	Academics and general readers with a serious interest in public policy and politics.
Special Themes	Social policy; welfare, education, immigration, race, public administration.
Where Indexed/ Abstracted	ABC Pol Sci; Academic Abstracts; America: History and Life; Historical Abstracts; PAIS; Reader's Guide; Social Science Index; Social Science Source; Sociological Abstracts.
Year Established	1965.
Circulation	9,000.
Frequency	Quarterly.
Months Issued	January, April, July, and October.
No. of Articles	10–12 per issue.

SUBMISSIONS

Address	1112 16th Street, NW, Suite 530, Washington, DC 20036.
Number of Copies	2.
Disk Submission	Microsoft Word for Macintosh (or something readable by a Mac).

FORMAT OF MANUSCRIPT

Cover Sheet	Letter with general information: affiliation, topic of paper, etc.
Abstract	None.
Key Words	None.
Length	4,000–5,000 words.
Margins	1 inch on all sides.
Spacing	Double-spaced.

STYLE

Name of Guide	*Chicago Manual of Style.*
Subheadings	None.
References	Not specified.
Footnotes	We do not generally print footnotes for purposes of citation. We sometimes print them if they add something to the article that doesn't fit within the text.
Tables or Figures	Depends on the article (though not usually).

REVIEW PROCESS

Type	Reviewed by 5 editors.
Queries	No. We will only look at completed articles.
Acknowledgment	By letter.
Review Time	2–3 weeks (though sometimes longer).
Revisions	Editors make revisions. Author then has a chance to approve them.
Acceptance Rate	Not specified.
Return of Manuscript	Not returned.
Lag Time to Print	2–3 months.

REPRINT, SUBSCRIPTION, AND CONTACT INFORMATION

Reprint Policy	Authors pay for reprints.
Book Reviews	We publish solicited book reviews, not over the transom.
Subscriptions	*The Public Interest*, Department PI, P.O. Box 3000, Denville, NJ 07834; 800-783-4903.
Affiliation	National Affairs, Inc.

Public Welfare

Editorial Focus	*Public Welfare* covers all aspects of the human services and related fields.
Audience	Human service professionals; federal, state, and local administrators and managers; federal and state legislators and other elected officials and their policy staffs; judges and attorneys; directors of private and voluntary social services agencies; leaders of business and consumer groups; and administrators, educators, and students in schools of social work.
Special Themes	Welfare and welfare reform, Medicaid and health care reform, child welfare and adoption, information systems management, employment, legal services, service integration, housing and homelessness.
Where Indexed/ Abstracted	Academic Abstracts; Social Sciences Index and Abstracts; Social Work Abstracts; Sociological Abstracts; and on the World Wide Web at http://www.apwa.org.
Year Established	1943.
Circulation	5,500.
Frequency	Quarterly.
Months Issued	January, April, July, and October.
No. of Articles	3–5 per issue.

SUBMISSIONS

Address	Editor, *Public Welfare*, American Public Welfare Association, 810 First Street, NE, Suite 500, Washington, DC 20002-4267.
Number of Copies	2.
Disk Submission	With manuscripts submitted for review, prospective authors should also submit their articles on disk. Microsoft Word for Windows is preferred, but *Public Welfare* can accept most IBM-compatible software formats. Contact the editor if you have questions.

FORMAT OF MANUSCRIPT

Cover Sheet	Should include for all authors: name, title, academic degrees, professional affiliations, address, phone and fax numbers, and e-mail address. Should also include date of submission and designate one author as the corresponding author.
Abstract	Prospective authors should submit with their manuscripts a descriptive abstract of no more than 300 words.
Key Words	Unnecessary as we let our abstracting services do this.
Length	Target length is 15–20 pages, double-spaced (4,000–5,000 words), including references, tables, and graphs.
Margins	Prefer 1 inch on top and bottom, 1.25 inches left and right.
Spacing	Double-spaced.

STYLE

Name of Guide
APWA Style Guide, available for purchase from APWA Publication Services for $7.00 ($6.00 for APWA members). Refer also to the *Chicago Manual of Style.*

Subheadings
Use as needed to guide the reader through the article. No more than 1 level.

References
Public Welfare prefers a more informal style, with sources fully identified and worked into the text of the article. When more formal references are necessary, *Public Welfare* requires full endnote citations. See the style guides mentioned above or *A Manual for Term Papers, Theses, and Dissertations,* by Kate Turabian. Refer also to current issues of *Public Welfare* for proper endnote style.

Footnotes
Endnotes rather than footnotes, as described above.

Tables or Figures
In general, *Public Welfare* prefers articles that clearly make their point without need of tables or figures. When they are necessary, two rules should apply: They should be simple, direct, and easily understood; and the fewer the better. Camera-ready copy is not necessary as we often redesign tables and figures to be more reader-friendly.

REVIEW PROCESS

Type
Manuscripts submitted for publication are reviewed by APWA publications and policy staff. There is no blind peer review.

Queries
Queries are discouraged. Interested authors should read current issues of the journal, refer to the manuscript policy on page 2 of each issue, or request a copy of *Public Welfare*'s manuscript requirements.

Acknowledgment
Acknowledgment letter is sent on receipt of manuscript.

Review Time
3–6 months.

Revisions
We will ask for revisions if necessary.

Acceptance Rate
We do not track this information. For unsolicited manuscripts, probably less than 15%; for invited manuscripts, better than 80%.

Return of Manuscript
Not returned. Author should retain copies.

Lag Time to Print
3 months–1 year.

REPRINT, SUBSCRIPTION, AND CONTACT INFORMATION

Reprint Policy
Authors receive complimentary copies of the issue in which the article appears. Reprint information available on request.

Book Reviews
By invitation only. Send books for review to the editor.

Subscriptions
APWA Publication Services, 810 First Street, NE, Suite 500, Washington, DC 20002-4267.

1997 Subscription Rates: APWA members, free with membership; nonmembers, $35 to U.S., $45 to other countries.

Affiliation
American Public Welfare Association.

E-Mail Address
publicwelfare@apwa.org

Home Page URL
http://www.apwa.org

Reflections: Narratives of Professional Helping

Editorial Focus	Narrative inquiry of professional practice. Personal accounts that describe and explain the process of helping others and shaping social change over time: convey immediacy, portray practice across diverse populations; demonstrate the concept of failure as well as success; have a literary presence; and offer new practice perspectives.
Audience	Professional helpers such as ethicists, policymakers, community organizers, psychotherapists, case and group workers, family and child practitioners, health and mental health care providers; and educators, researchers, and administrators in the helping and academic professions. Social workers, educators, nurses, psychologists, students, physicians, libraries, and organizations.
Special Themes	Narratives about practice: diversity, the range and variety of strategies and systems within the helping professions; justice, ethics. Narratives about the helping process, research, and teaching. Interviews and autobiographies.
Where Indexed/ Abstracted	Psychological Abstracts/PsycINFO (pending); Social Work Abstracts.
Year Established	1995.
Circulation	500+.
Frequency	Quarterly.
Months Issued	Winter, spring, summer, fall.
No. of Articles	8–12.

SUBMISSIONS

Address	Sonia Leib Abels, Editor, *Reflections*, California State University Long Beach, Long Beach, CA 90840-0902.
Number of Copies	2.
Disk Submission	Authors of accepted manuscripts are asked to submit a disk for Macintosh or IBM-compatible, formatted in Rich Text format.

FORMAT OF MANUSCRIPT

Cover Sheet	Separate sheet that does not go out for review. Full title, author name(s), degrees, professional titles, full address, phone numbers, fax number, e-mail address, and date of submission.
Abstract	Written in the same language as the narrative.
Key Words	Up to 5 words or key phrases (2–3 word maximum) describing the article.
Length	Depends on the temporal sequence of the narrative.
Margins	1 inch on all sides.
Spacing	Double-spaced.

STYLE

Name of Guide	*Publication Manual of the American Psychological Association.*
Subheadings	Use as needed to guide reader through the article.
References	See style guide.
Footnotes	Footnotes are discouraged. Incorporate content into text.
Tables or Figures	Usually unnecessary.

REVIEW PROCESS

Type	Double-blind anonymous peer review. Two reviewers, plus editor and associate editor.
Queries	S. L. Abels, Editor (phone: 310-985-4626; fax: 310-985-5514).
Acknowledgment	Contract for review.
Review Time	3–4 months.
Revisions	Submit 3 copies with separate cover sheet replying to reviewers' comments.
Acceptance Rate	Approximately 12%.
Return of Manuscript	Manuscripts are not returned.
Lag Time to Print	6 months–1 year.

REPRINT, SUBSCRIPTION, AND CONTACT INFORMATION

Reprint Policy	Authors receive 2 complimentary copies of the issue in which the article appears.
Book Reviews	Send to Book Review Editor. Reviewers may submit; review same as article submission.
Subscriptions	*Reflections,* California State University, Long Beach, CA 90840-0902. Yearly rate: individuals, $25; institutions and libraries, $35. Single copy: $10. Outside United States, add $15.
Affiliation	The University Press, California State University Long Beach, Department of Social Work.
E-Mail Address	sabels@csulb.edu
Home Page URL	http://www.csulb.edu/~reflect

Residential Treatment for Children and Youth

Editorial Focus	Residential treatment of children and youths.
Audience	Not specified.
Where Indexed/ Abstracted	Applied Social Sciences Index & Abstracts; Cambridge Scientific Abstracts; Child Development Abstracts & Bibliography; CNPIEC Reference Guide: Chinese National Directory of Foreign Periodicals; Criminal Justice Abstracts; Criminology, Penology and Police Science Abstracts; Exceptional Child Education Resources (ECER); Index to Periodical Articles Related to Law; International Bulletin of Bibliography on Education; INTERNET ACCESS (& additional networks) Bulletin Board for Libraries ("BUBL"), coverage of information resources on INTERNET, JANET, and other networks; Inventory of Marriage and Family Literature (online and CD-ROM); Mental Health Abstracts (online through DIALOG); Psychological Abstracts (PsycINFO); Sage Family Studies Abstracts (SFSA); Social Planning/Policy & Development Abstracts (SOPODA); Social Work Abstracts; Sociological Abstracts (SA); Sociology of Education Abstracts; Special Education Needs Abstracts; Violence and Abuse Abstracts (VAA).
Year Established	1986.
Circulation	750.
Frequency	Quarterly.
Months Issued	Varies.
No. of Articles	6.

SUBMISSIONS

Address	Gordon Northrup, MD, Editor, RR1, Box 561, Lee, MA 01238-9602.
Number of Copies	3.
Disk Submission	Yes.

FORMAT OF MANUSCRIPT

Cover Sheet	Staple a cover page to the manuscript, indicating only the article title (this is used for anonymous refereeing) and the abstract. Second title page (not stapled to the manuscript): title; full authorship; abstract; key words; introductory footnote with authors' academic degrees, professional titles, affiliations, mailing addresses, and any desired acknowledgment of research support or other credit.
Abstract	Approximately 100 words.
Key Words	5–6 key words that identify article content.
Length	20 pages, including abstract and references.
Margins	1 inch on all sides.
Spacing	Double-spaced.

STYLE

Name of Guide	*Publication Manual of the American Psychological Association.*
Subheadings	As necessary.
References	Double-spaced and in alphabetical order; see style guide.
Footnotes	Footnotes are discouraged.
Tables or Figures	Must be camera-ready.

REVIEW PROCESS

Type	Peer reviewed.
Queries	To editor.
Acknowledgment	By letter.
Review Time	Usually 2 months.
Revisions	As required by editor.
Acceptance Rate	Approximately 85%.
Return of Manuscript	Not returned.
Lag Time to Print	Approximately 9 months.

REPRINT, SUBSCRIPTION, AND CONTACT INFORMATION

Reprint Policy	The senior author receives 2 copies of the journal issue and 10 complimentary reprints. The junior author receives 2 copies of the journal issue. An order form is sent to the corresponding author for the purchase of additional reprints.
Book Reviews	Alan Keith-Lucas, PhD, Book Review Editor, 705 Greenwood Avenue, Chapel Hill, NC 27514.
Subscriptions	The Haworth Press, Inc., 10 Alice Street, Binghamton, NY 13904-1580. Individuals, $45; institutions, $120; libraries, $175.
Affiliation	American Association of Residential Treatment for Children (AACRC).

Research in Pharmaceutical Economics

Editorial Focus	To contribute to knowledge in the pharmaceutical and health sciences and to enhance the economic development through research in the same disciplines.
Audience	Not specified.
Special Themes	Research concerning drug use process, rural health pharmacy, and medical practice.
Where Indexed/ Abstracted	Biosciences Information Service of Biological Abstracts (BIOSIS); CNPIEC Reference Guide: Chinese National Directory of Foreign Periodicals; Economic Literature Index (Journal of Economic Literature); Excerpta Medica/Secondary Publishing Division; Index to Periodical Articles Related to Law; InPharma Weekly DIGEST & NEWS on: Pharmaceutical Literature, Drug Reactions & LMS; International Pharmaceutical Abstracts; INTERNET ACCESS (& additional networks) Bulletin Board for Libraries ("BUBL"), coverage of information resources on INTERNET, JANET, and other networks; Medical Benefits; Medication Use STudies (MUST) DATABASE; Pharmacy Business.
Year Established	1989.
Circulation	277.
Frequency	Quarterly.
Months Issued	Not specified.
No. of Articles	6–10 per issue.

SUBMISSIONS

Address	Mickey C. Smith, PhD, Editor, *Journal of Research in Pharmaceutical Economics,* Research Institute of Pharmaceutical Sciences, School of Pharmacy, University of Mississippi, University, MS 38677.
Number of Copies	4.
Disk Submission	Authors of accepted manuscripts are asked to submit a disk, preferably in Microsoft Word or WordPerfect.

FORMAT OF MANUSCRIPT

Cover Sheet	Separate sheet, which does not go out for review. Full title, author names, degrees, professional titles; designation of one author as corresponding author with full address, phone numbers, e-mail address, and fax number; date of submission.
Abstract	About 100 words.
Key Words	5 or 6 key words that identify article content.

Length	20 pages, including references and abstract. Lengthier manuscripts may be considered, but only at the discretion of the editor. Sometimes, lengthier manuscripts may be considered if they can be divided into sections for publication in successive issues.
Margins	1 inch on all sides.
Spacing	Double-spaced for all copy, except title page.

STYLE

Name of Guide	*ASHP Guidelines.*
Subheadings	Use as needed to guide reader through the article. No more than 4 levels.
References	Author–date citation style; see style guide.
Footnotes	No footnotes preferred; incorporate into text.
Tables or Figures	Type tables double-spaced. Submit camera-ready art (300 dpi printer or better) for all figures. Place each table or figure on a separate, numbered page at the end of the manuscript.

REVIEW PROCESS

Type	"Double blind" anonymous peer review. 3 reviewers plus editor-in-chief read the manuscript in an anonymous review.
Queries	Authors are encouraged to read the journal to determine if their subject matter would be appropriate.
Acknowledgment	Enclose a regular self-addressed, stamped envelope with submission.
Review Time	3–4 months.
Revisions	See journal.
Acceptance Rate	Not specified.
Return of Manuscript	Only if 9″ x 12″ self-addressed, stamped envelope is enclosed.
Lag Time to Print	6 months–1 year.

REPRINT, SUBSCRIPTION, AND CONTACT INFORMATION

Reprint Policy	All authors receive 2 complimentary copies of the issue in which article appears. Authors receive reprint order forms to purchase additional reprinted copies.
Book Reviews	Send to journal editor.
Subscriptions	The Haworth Press, Inc., 10 Alice Street, Binghamton, NY 13904-1580. Individuals, $40; institutions, $80; libraries, $160.

Research on Social Work Practice

Editorial Focus	The journal is devoted to the publication of empirical research concerning the methods and outcomes of social work practice with individuals, couples, families, communities, organizations, and society as a whole. We publish quantitatively oriented, empirical outcome studies which use group- or single-system research designs, reports on the development and validation of social work assessment methods, and empirically based reviews of the literature.
Audience	Social work practitioners, students, academics, institutional libraries, and other human service professionals.
Special Themes	Special issues related to selected themes on social work practice are published. Contact the Editor concerning possible topics for future thematic issues.
Where Indexed/ Abstracted	Applied Social Sciences Index & Abstracts; caredata ABSTRACTS; caredata CD; caredata INFORMATION BULLETIN; Current Contents: Social & Behavioral Sciences; Current Index to Journals in Education; Health and Psychosocial Instrument, Human Resources Abstracts; Linguistics and Language Behavior Abstracts; PsychINFO; Psychological Abstracts; Research Alert; Sage Family Studies Abstracts; Social Planning/Policy & Development Abstracts; Social Sciences Citation Index; Social Work Abstracts; Sociological Abstracts; Violence and Abuse Abstracts.
Year Established	1991.
Circulation	About 800.
Frequency	Quarterly.
Months Issued	January, April, July, October.
No. of Articles	8–10 per issue.

SUBMISSIONS

Address	Bruce A. Thyer, Editor, *Research on Social Work Practice*, School of Social Work, University of Georgia, Athens, GA 30602; phone: 706-542-5440; fax: 706-542-3282.
Number of Copies	5.
Disk Submission	Authors of accepted manuscripts are asked to submit their work on disk, formatted in WordPerfect 5.1 for DOS.

FORMAT OF MANUSCRIPT

Cover Sheet	Separate sheet, which does not go out for review. Full title, author names, designation of one author as corresponding author. Please provide full address, phone numbers, e-mail address, and fax number for *all* authors; date of submission.
Abstract	150-word informative abstract.
Key Words	Up to 5 words or key phrases (2–3 word maximum) describing the article.
Length	No page limits.

Margins	1 inch on all sides.
Spacing	Double-spaced for all copy.

STYLE

Name of Guide	*Publication Manual of the American Psychological Association* (strict compliance with current APA manual is requested).
Subheadings	See style guide.
References	See style guide.
Footnotes	No footnotes preferred; incorporate into text.
Tables or Figures	See style guide.

REVIEW PROCESS

Type	"Double blind" anonymous peer review, usually involving at least 3 social workers.
Queries	Query letters are encouraged, particularly prior to submitting possibly inappropriate manuscripts.
Acknowledgment	Authors receive a letter acknowledging submissions within one month. Inappropriate submissions (e.g., survey studies, nonempirical works, correlational investigations, conceptual or methodological articles, case studies without data) are returned within 2 weeks.
Review Time	3 months or less.
Revisions	Revisions of most accepted articles are requested. Revised articles should be resubmitted within 3 months.
Acceptance Rate	40%–50% of articles that undergo blind peer review are eventually accepted for publication.
Return of Manuscript	Inappropriate manuscripts are returned within 2 weeks. Reviewed manuscripts are not returned, except for 1 copy when an invitation to prepare a revision is issued.
Lag Time to Print	Approximately 1 year.

REPRINT, SUBSCRIPTION, AND CONTACT INFORMATION

Reprint Policy	All authors of accepted articles receive 25 copies of their reprinted article, and a copy of the issue in which it appeared, at no cost.
Book Reviews	Book reviews are published. Contact the editor regarding potential books to review.
Subscriptions	Sage Publications, Inc., P.O. Box 5084, Thousand Oaks, CA 91359; phone: 805-499-0721 (order line/credit card charges); fax: 805-499-0871.
	$48 for individual subscriptions, $129 for institutions/libraries.
E-Mail Address	BThyer@uga.cc.uga.edu for general enquiries.

Scandinavian Journal of Social Welfare

Editorial Focus	Social work and social welfare. Original articles; debate articles, empirical reports, review articles, and contributions in theory and methods.
Audience	Not specified.
Special Themes	Not specified.
Where Indexed/ Abstracted	Current Contents: Social & Behavioral Sciences; Research Alert; Social Sciences Citation Index.
Year Established	1992.
Circulation	Approximately 500.
Frequency	Quarterly.
Months Issued	January, April, July, October.
Number of Articles	Varies.

SUBMISSIONS

Address	Sven Hessle, School of Social Work, Stockholm University, S-106 91 Stockholm, Sweden.
Number of Copies	4.
Disk Submission	Provide manuscript on newly formatted 3.5″ floppy disk. Full details of manuscript submission on disk will be sent following notification of acceptance of manuscript.

FORMAT OF MANUSCRIPT

Please request Instructions for Authors from the publisher: Munksgaard, Journals Division, P.O. Box 2148, DK-1016 Copenhagen, Denmark.

STYLE

Please request Instructions for Authors from the publisher: Munksgaard, Journals Division, P.O. Box 2148, DK-1016 Copenhagen, Denmark.

REVIEW PROCESS

Type	The journal is peer-reviewed.

CHARGES TO AUTHOR

Author Alterations	Only if changes are extensive.
Page Charges	None.
Processing	No charge, except for color illustrations which must be paid by the author.

REPRINT, SUBSCRIPTION, AND CONTACT INFORMATION

Reprint Policy	50 offprints supplied free of charge to authors.
Book Reviews	Yes.
Subscriptions	Individuals: Danish Kroner 350 excl. postage; institutions: Danish Kroner 700 excl. postage.
E-Mail Address	Publisher: journals@mail.munksgaard.dk
Home Page URL	www.munksgaard.dk

SCI Psychosocial Process

Editorial Focus	Psychologists and social workers treating people with spinal cord injury.
Audience	Psychologists and social workers.
Where Indexed/ Abstracted	CINAHL; Human Resources Abstracts; SAGE; Social Work Abstracts.
Year Established	1987.
Circulation	1,500.
Frequency	Quarterly.
Months Issued	February, May, August, November.
No. of Articles	3–6.

SUBMISSIONS

Address	E. Jason Mask, ACSW, Editor, *SCI Psychosocial Process,* Social Work Submission Service (122), Hines VA Hospital, Hines, IL 60141.
Number of Copies	3.
Disk Submission	Required.

FORMAT OF MANUSCRIPT

Cover Sheet	Name, affiliation, job description.
Abstract	Yes.
Key Words	None.
Length	1,000–5,000 words.
Margins	1.5 inches on all sides.
Spacing	Double-spaced.

STYLE

Name of Guide	*Publication Manual of the American Psychological Association.*
Subheadings	Yes.
References	Yes.
Footnotes	None.
Tables or Figures	Yes.

REVIEW PROCESS

Type	Refereed.
Queries	Yes.
Acknowledgment	Yes.
Review Time	Varies.
Revisions	Yes.

Acceptance Rate	Not specified.
Return of Manuscript	Not returned.
Lag Time to Print	Varies by schedule, but can be very short.

REPRINT, SUBSCRIPTION, AND CONTACT INFORMATION

Reprint Policy	Yes, at author's expense (no markup).
Book Reviews	Yes.
Subscriptions	Free to association members and interested, qualified parties.

Small Group Research

Previous Title	*Small Group Behavior.*
Editorial Focus	Advancement of research and theory with reference to small groups.
Audience	Everyone interested in theory and research on groups—students, practitioners, researchers in social work, psychology, sociology, communications, business, etc.
Special Themes	Not specified.
Where Indexed/ Abstracted	Automatic Subject Citation Alert; Communication Abstracts; Human Resources Abstracts; Psychological Abstracts; Social Sciences Citation Index; Social Work Abstracts; among others.
Year Established	1960.
Circulation	Approximately 1,000.
Frequency	Quarterly.
Months Issued	February, May, August, November.
No. of Articles	Approximately 30 per volume.

SUBMISSIONS

Address	*Small Group Research,* c/o Charles Garvin, School of Social Work, University of Michigan, Ann Arbor, MI 48109-1285.
Number of Copies	4.
Disk Submission	Disk required for articles accepted for publication.

FORMAT OF MANUSCRIPT

Cover Sheet	Yes, with title, authors, affiliation, addresses, phone number, e-mail address.
Abstract	Yes, approximately 100 words.
Key Words	None.
Length	Maximum 25 pages.
Margins	1 inch on all sides.
Spacing	Double-spaced.

STYLE

Name of Guide	*Publication Manual of the American Psychological Association.*
Subheadings	Yes, determined by author.
References	See style guide.
Footnotes	As few as possible.
Tables or Figures	Camera-ready.

REVIEW PROCESS

Type	Anonymous peer review.
Queries	Query letters accepted.
Acknowledgment	Only if self-addressed, stamped postcard is enclosed.
Review Time	Approximately 3 months.
Revisions	Author may be asked to revise and resubmit.
Acceptance Rate	Approximately 40%.
Return of Manuscript	Not returned.
Lag Time to Print	9 months.

CHARGES TO AUTHOR

Author Alterations	If exceeding a set number.

REPRINT, SUBSCRIPTION, AND CONTACT INFORMATION

Reprint Policy	An established number supplied to author.
Book Reviews	None.
Subscriptions	Sage Publications, 2455 Teller Road, Thousand Oaks, CA 91320.
	Individuals, $64; institutions, $206.
E-Mail Address	charlesg@umich.edu
Home Page URL	www.sagepub.co.uk/journals/journals.html

Smith College Studies in Social Work

Editorial Focus   The focus is on clinical social work theory and practice. Conceptual frameworks of particular interest include psychodynamic/developmental, object relations, self psychology, social constructivism, and systems theory. The journal publishes reports on innovative practice interventions, particularly in relation to oppressed and underserved client populations, as well as on a wide variety of treatment approaches with other clients. In addition, practice-relevant research reports, literature reviews, editorials, book reviews, and abstracts of Smith College School for Social Work master's theses and doctoral dissertations.

Audience   Clinical social work theorists, practitioners, researchers, and educators, as well as researchers and practitioners from other mental health disciplines.

Special Themes   The application of theory to practice; children and families; traumatized clients; in-depth treatment approaches; community-based interventions; treatment with individuals, couples, families, and groups; and case reports focusing on process issues. Special issues recently published include: "AIDS and Clinical Practice," and "The Human and Corporate Faces of Managed Behavioral Health Care." Manuscripts are solicited through advertising flyers at conferences, mailing lists, conference presentations, and recommendations from members of the editorial board.

Where Indexed/ Abstracted   Social Work Abstracts.

Year Established   1930.

Circulation   1,270.

Frequency   3 times annually.

Months Issued   November, March, June.

No. of Articles   4–8.

SUBMISSIONS

Address   Gerald Schamess, Editor, Smith College School for Social Work, Lilly Hall, Northampton, MA 01063.

Number of Copies   3.

Disk Submission   WordPerfect 5.1 preferred. Most other word processing programs can be accommodated.

FORMAT OF MANUSCRIPT

Cover Sheet   Title, authors' names, home and professional addresses, phone numbers, professional titles, affiliations, degrees.

Abstract   100 words.

Key Words   Up to 8 words or key phrases (2–3 word maximum) describing central themes in the manuscript.

Length	15–25 pages.
Margins	Wide.
Spacing	Double-spaced.

STYLE

Name of Guide	*Publication Manual of the American Psychological Association.*
Subheadings	See style guide.
References	See style guide.
Footnotes	See style guide.
Tables or Figures	Typewritten acceptable; camera-ready if possible.

REVIEW PROCESS

Type	Anonymous review by 2 reviewers. When reviewers disagree, a third reviewer is enlisted. Final decision by the editor.
Queries	To the editor by mail or phone only.
Acknowledgment	Letter sent on receipt of manuscript.
Review Time	3–4 months.
Revisions	Authors are encouraged to resubmit revised manuscripts. If revisions are major, manuscript is reviewed again by the original reviewers whenever possible. If minor, revisions are handled by editor. Editor's revisions are sent to authors for approval.
Acceptance Rate	Approximately 20%.
Return of Manuscript	Not returned. Authors should keep a copy.
Lag Time to Print	3–6 months.

CHARGES TO AUTHOR

Author Alterations	Printer's costs.

REPRINT, SUBSCRIPTION, AND CONTACT INFORMATION

Reprint Policy	May be ordered shortly before printing.
Book Reviews	Unsolicited reviews are welcome. Send them to Katherine Basham, PhD, Book Review Editor, Smith College Studies in Social Work, Lilly Hall, Northampton, MA 01063.
Subscriptions	Smith College School for Social Work, Lilly Hall, Northampton, MA 01063.
	1 year, $20; 2 years, $34; 3 years, $45.
Affiliation	Smith College School for Social Work.

Social Development Issues

Editorial Focus	Perspectives on social and economic practices, projects, and programs in economically developing societies.
Audience	Social workers, academics, and policymakers.
Special Themes	Social services in rural communities and societies; innovative social development projects; poverty, gender, and racial issues; health/mental health; income maintenance; human rights; interaction between economic and social programs; sustainability; education; and community organizing.
Where Indexed/ Abstracted	Academic Abstracts; Applied Social Sciences Index & Abstracts; Geo Abstracts; Social Welfare, Social Planning and Social Development; Social Work Abstracts; Sociological Abstracts.
Year Established	1978.
Circulation	450.
Frequency	3 times a year.
Months Issued	March, August, December.
No. of Articles	7–10 per issue.

SUBMISSIONS

Address	Editor, *Social Development Issues,* School of Social Work, Southern Illinois University, Quigley Hall, Carbondale, IL 62901-4329.
Number of Copies	4.
Disk Submission	Authors of accepted manuscripts are asked to submit a disk, preferably in Microsoft Word or WordPerfect.

FORMAT OF MANUSCRIPT

Cover Sheet	Separate sheet, which does not go out for review. Full title, author names, degrees, professional titles; designation of one author as corresponding author with full address, phone numbers, e-mail address, and fax number; date of submission.
Abstract	60 words or less.
Key Words	Not required.
Length	15–18 pages including references and tables.
Margins	1 inch on all sides.
Spacing	Double-spaced for all copy, except title page.

STYLE

Name of Guide	*Publication Manual of the American Psychological Association.*
Subheadings	Use as needed to guide reader through the article. No more than 2 levels.
References	Author–date citation style: see style guide.

Footnotes	No footnotes preferred; incorporate into text.
Tables or Figures	Submit camera-ready art (300 dpi printer or better) for all figures. Place each table or figure on a separate, unnumbered page at the end of the manuscript.

REVIEW PROCESS

Type	3 reviewers read the manuscript in an anonymous review.
Queries	Authors are encouraged to read the journal to determine if their subject matter would be appropriate.
Acknowledgment	Authors receive a letter or e-mail message on receipt of manuscript.
Review Time	3–4 months.
Revisions	Submit a disk and a hard copy with the revisions with a separate cover letter replying to the reviewers' comments.
Acceptance Rate	Approximately 55%.
Return of Manuscript	Not returned; author should retain copies.
Lag Time to Print	Approximately 9 months–1 year.

REPRINT, SUBSCRIPTION, AND CONTACT INFORMATION

Reprint Policy	No reprints.
Book Reviews	Send books for review to the editor.
Subscriptions	*Social Development Issues,* Dr. Peter C. Y. Lee, Secretary-General, IUCISD, San Jose State University, San Jose, CA 95192.
Affiliation	*Social Development Issues* is published by the Inter-University Consortium for International Social Development (IUCISD) in cooperation with the School of Social Work, Southern Illinois University at Carbondale and The University of Iowa School of Social Work.
E-Mail Address	mbta@siucvmb.siu.edu

Social Policy

Editorial Focus	The "magazine about movements." A fresh, bold look blending theory and action in the social sciences and human services.
Audience	Grassroots activists, policymakers, academicians, libraries, community organizations, others interested in human services and social welfare.
Special Themes	Human services, public policy, social justice, civil society.
Where Indexed/ Abstracted	ABC Pol Sci; Alternative Press Index; Current Contents: Behavioral, Social and Educational Sciences; Current Index to Journals in Education; Medical Socioeconomic Research Sources; Social Sciences Citations Index; Social Sciences Index.
Year Established	1970.
Circulation	4,000+.
Frequency	Quarterly.
Months Issued	Spring, summer, fall, winter.
No. of Articles	7–10.

SUBMISSIONS

Address	Editor, *Social Policy*, 25 West 43rd Street, Suite 620, New York, NY 10036-7406.
Number of Copies	2.
Disk Submission	Authors of accepted manuscripts are asked to submit a disk in Microsoft Word or WordPerfect.

FORMAT OF MANUSCRIPT

Cover Sheet	None.
Abstract	None.
Key Words	None.
Length	10–20 pages, although we are flexible about length.
Margins	1 inch on all sides.
Spacing	Double-spaced.

STYLE

Name of Guide	*Chicago Manual of Style* and *Publication Manual of the American Psychological Association*.
Subheadings	At author's discretion.
References	See style guides.
Footnotes	See style guides.
Tables or Figures	Camera-ready art for figures. Place each table or figure on a separate page at end of article.

REVIEW PROCESS

Type	Nonanonymous; editors read submissions.
Queries	Query letters are accepted.
Acknowledgment	Only if self-addressed, stamped envelope or postcard is provided.
Review Time	4–12 weeks.
Revisions	Revisions are expected only on accepted articles.
Acceptance Rate	20%.
Return of Manuscript	Authors should include self-addressed, stamped envelope for return of manuscript.
Lag Time to Print	6–12 months.

REPRINT, SUBSCRIPTION, AND CONTACT INFORMATION

Reprint Policy	All authors receive 3 complimentary copies of the issue in which the article appears. Reprints are not available.
Book Reviews	Unsolicited book reviews are accepted. Send books for review to: Managing Editor, *Social Policy*, 25 West 43rd Street, Suite 620, New York, NY 10036-7406.
Subscriptions	*Social Policy*, 25 West 43rd Street, Suite 620, New York, NY 10036-7406.
	1996–97 one-year prices: individuals, $20; institutions/libraries, $50; students, $12.
E-Mail Address	socpol@igc.apc.org
Home Page URL	http://www.socialpolicy.org

Social Service Review

Editorial Focus	The journal welcomes manuscripts from social workers and members of allied disciplines engaged in research on human behavior, social systems, and the development of improved social services. Priority is given to research-based articles dealing with subjects central to social welfare research, practice, policy, and history.
Audience	Social work researchers, practitioners, faculty, students, and members of allied disciplines.
Where Indexed/ Abstracted	Abstracts for Social Workers; Criminal Justice Periodical Index; Current Contents: Social and Behavioral Sciences; Sage Family Studies Abstracts; Social Sciences Citation Index; Social Sciences Index; Sociological Abstracts.
Year Established	1927.
Circulation	2,500.
Frequency	Quarterly.
Months Issued	March, June, September, December.
No. of Articles	6–8 each issue.

SUBMISSIONS

Address	Editor, *Social Service Review*, 969 E. 60th Street, Chicago, IL 60637.
Number of Copies	4.
Disk Submission	WordPerfect.

FORMAT OF MANUSCRIPT

Cover Sheet	Separate sheet, which does not go out for review: full title, author names, author affiliations, address, phone, e-mail (if available) of contact author.
Abstract	75–100 words.
Key Words	None.
Length	No limit.
Margins	1 inch on all sides.
Spacing	Double-spaced body and endnotes.

STYLE

Name of Guide	*Chicago Manual of Style*.
Subheadings	Use as needed.
References	*Chicago Manual of Style* endnotes. We do not use author–date style. Submissions *will* be accepted in author–date style for review. If the manuscript is accepted, we will ask that the notes be revised.
Footnotes	None.
Tables or Figures	Use judiciously.

REVIEW PROCESS

Type	Peer review.
Queries	Discouraged.
Acknowledgment	Yes, usually within 2 weeks of receipt.
Review Time	4–6 months.
Revisions	Not accepted unless specifically requested by editor.
Acceptance Rate	Approximately 20%.
Return of Manuscript	Yes.
Lag Time to Print	6 months.

REPRINT, SUBSCRIPTION, AND CONTACT INFORMATION

Reprint Policy   Lead author receives 10 free copies or one-year subscription. Reprints available for a fee.

Book Reviews   By invitation only. Send books for review to: Book Review Editor, *Social Service Review*, 969 E. 60th Street, Chicago, IL 60637.

Subscriptions   *Social Service Review*, University of Chicago Press, Journals Division, P.O. Box 37005, Chicago, IL 60637.

One-year subscription rates:

	Domestic	Canadian	Foreign
Institutions	$81.00	$92.67	$87.00
Individuals	$37.00	$45.59	$43.00
UC SSA Alumni	$25.00	$32.75	$31.00
Students	$25.00	$32.75	$31.00

Affiliation   University of Chicago, School of Social Service Administration; University of Chicago Press.

E-Mail Address   be-ray@uchicago.edu

Home Page URL   http://www.chas.uchicago.edu/ssa/ssr.html

Social Thought (Journal of Religion in the Social Services)

Previous Title	*Catholic Charities USA.*
Editorial Focus	Scholarly papers that focus on topics pertaining to institutional and non-institutional religion in relationship to the development and delivery of social services.
Audience	Social work practitioners, students, and educators.
Special Themes	Social work philosophy, ethics, religion, and spirituality.
Where Indexed/ Abstracted	Abstracts of Research in Pastoral Care & Counseling; caredata CD: the social and community care database; CNPIEC Reference Guide: Chinese National Directory of Foreign Periodicals; Guide to Social Science & Religion in Periodical Literature; IBZ International Bibliography of Periodical Literature; INTERNET ACCESS (& additional networks) Bulletin Board for Libraries ("BUBL"), coverage of information resources on INTERNET, JANET, and other networks; Peace Research Abstracts Journal; Sage Race Relations Abstracts; Sage Urban Studies Abstracts (SUSA); Social Work Abstracts; Sociological Abstracts (SA); Theology Digest; Violence and Abuse Abstracts: A Review of Current Literature on Interpersonal Violence (VAA).
Year Established	1995.
Circulation	102.
Frequency	Quarterly.
Months Issued	Not specified.
No. of Articles	6–10 per issue.

SUBMISSIONS

Address	Joseph Shields, PhD, Editor, *Social Thought,* National Catholic School of Social Service, Shahan Hall, The Catholic University of America, Washington, DC 20064.
Number of Copies	4.
Disk Submission	Authors of accepted manuscripts are asked to submit a disk, preferably in Microsoft Word or WordPerfect.

FORMAT OF MANUSCRIPT

Cover Sheet	Separate sheet, which does not go out for review. Full title, author names, degrees, professional titles; designation of one author as corresponding author with full address, phone numbers, e-mail address, and fax number; date of submission.
Abstract	About 100 words.
Key Words	5 or 6 words that identify article content.

Length	20 pages, including references and abstract. Lengthier manuscripts may be considered, but only at the discretion of the editor. Sometimes, lengthier manuscripts may be considered if they can be divided into sections for publication in successive issues.
Margins	1 inch on all sides.
Spacing	Double-spaced for all copy, except title page.

STYLE

Name of Guide	*Publication Manual of the American Psychological Association.*
Subheadings	Use as needed to guide reader through the article. No more than 4 levels.
References	Author–date citation style; see style guide.
Footnotes	No footnotes preferred; incorporate into text.
Tables or Figures	Type tables double-spaced. Submit camera-ready art (300 dpi printer or better) for all figures. Place each table or figure on a separate, numbered page at the end of the manuscript.

REVIEW PROCESS

Type	"Double blind" anonymous peer review. 3 reviewers plus editor-in-chief read the manuscript in an anonymous review.
Queries	Authors are encouraged to read the journal to determine if their subject matter would be appropriate.
Acknowledgment	Enclose a regular self-addressed, stamped envelope with submission.
Review Time	3–4 months.
Revisions	See journal.
Acceptance Rate	Not specified.
Return of Manuscript	Only if 9″ x 12″ self-addressed, stamped envelope is enclosed.
Lag Time to Print	6 months–1 year.

REPRINT, SUBSCRIPTION, AND CONTACT INFORMATION

Reprint Policy	All authors receive 2 complimentary copies of the issue in which article appears. Authors receive reprint order forms to purchase additional reprinted copies.
Book Reviews	Kathleen M. Shevlin, PhD, Book Review Editor, National Catholic School of Social Service, The Catholic University of America, Washington, DC 20064.
Subscriptions	The Haworth Press, Inc., 10 Alice Street, Binghamton, NY 13904-1580.
	Individuals, $36; institutions, $48; libraries, $75.
Affiliation	National Catholic School of Social Service (NCSSS) of The Catholic University of America (CUA).

Social Work

Editorial Focus	New insights into established social work practices, evaluation of new techniques and research, examination of current social problems, critical analyses of problems in the profession.
Audience	Social work practitioners, researchers, faculty, students, libraries, organizations; others in the human services and social welfare.
Special Themes	Multiculturalism, research, public policy, partnerships/collaboration, social justice and human rights, ethics.
Where Indexed/ Abstracted	Abstracts in Anthropology; Abstracts in Social Gerontology; Academic Abstracts; Age Line; Applied Social Sciences Index and Abstracts; caredata; Cumulative Index to Nursing & Allied Health Literature; Current Contents: Social & Behavioral Sciences; ERIC/Counseling and Student Services Clearinghouse; Exceptional Child Resources, Psychological Abstracts/ PsychINFO; PsychLIT; Public Affairs Information Service; Quality Review Bulletin; Sage Family Studies Abstracts; Social Planning/Policy & Development Abstracts; Social Science Index/Social Science Abstracts; Social Work Abstracts; Sociological Abstracts.
Year Established	1956.
Circulation	163,000+.
Frequency	Bimonthly.
Months Issued	January, March, May, July, September, November.
No. of Articles	10–14 per issue.

SUBMISSIONS

Address	Editor, *Social Work,* NASW Press, 750 First Street, NE, Suite 700, Washington, DC 20002-4241.
Number of Copies	5.
Disk Submission	Authors of accepted manuscripts are asked to submit a disk, preferably in Microsoft Word or WordPerfect.

FORMAT OF MANUSCRIPT

Cover Sheet	Separate sheet, which does not go out for review. Full title, author names, degrees, professional titles; designation of one author as corresponding author with full address, phone numbers, e-mail address, and fax number; date of submission.
Abstract	150-word informative abstract.
Key Words	Up to 5 words or key phrases (2–3 word maximum) describing the article.
Length	14–16 pages including references and tables; manuscripts exceeding 25 pages will be returned.
Margins	1 inch on all sides.
Spacing	Double-spaced for all copy, except title page.

STYLE

Name of Guide	*Writing for the NASW Press: Information for Authors* (free) and *Professional Writing for the Human Services* (for purchase from the NASW Press). Contact NASW Press.
Subheadings	Use as needed to guide reader through the article. No more than 3 levels.
References	Author–date citation style; see style guides.
Footnotes	No footnotes preferred; incorporate into text.
Tables or Figures	Type tables double-spaced. Submit camera-ready art (300 dpi printer or better) for all figures. Place each table or figure on a separate, numbered page at the end of the manuscript.

REVIEW PROCESS

Type	"Double blind" anonymous peer review. 3 reviewers, plus the editor-in-chief, all read the manuscript in an anonymous review.
Queries	Query letters are discouraged; authors are encouraged to read the journal and *Writing for the NASW Press* to determine if their subject matter would be appropriate.
Acknowledgment	The NASW Press sends a postcard on receipt of manuscript.
Review Time	3–4 months.
Revisions	Submit 5 copies with a separate cover sheet (not identifying the author) describing the changes made in the manuscript and replying to the reviewers' comments. In general, the original reviewers and the editor-in-chief read revisions.
Acceptance Rate	Approximately 15%.
Return of Manuscript	Not returned; author should retain copies.
Lag Time to Print	Approximately 6 months–1 year.

REPRINT, SUBSCRIPTION, AND CONTACT INFORMATION

Reprint Policy	All authors receive 5 complimentary copies of the issue in which the article appears. Authors receive reprint order forms to purchase additional reprinted copies.
Book Reviews	By invitation only. Send books for review to: Book Review Editor, *Social Work*, NASW Press, 750 First Street, NE, Suite 700, Washington, DC 20002-4241.
Subscriptions	*Social Work*, P.O. Box 431, Annapolis JCT, MD 20701. 1996–97 one-year prices: NASW members, free with membership; individual nonmembers, $71; libraries/institutions, $98.
Affiliation	The NASW Press is a division of the National Association of Social Workers.
E-Mail Address	press@naswdc.org
Home Page URL	http://www.naswpress.org

Social Work and Christianity: An International Journal

Previous Title	*The Paraclete.*
Editorial Focus	Articles dealing with the issues of the integration of Christian faith and professional practice and other professional concerns that have relevance to Christianity.
Audience	Christians in social work and others who want to understand and interact with a Christian perspective on social work: practitioners, administrators, researchers, educators, students, and libraries.
Special Themes	Values and ethics, approaching issues of diversity with competence and integrity, religion and spirituality in social work practice, practice issues, and research on related topics.
Where Indexed/ Abstracted	Christian Periodical Index; Guide to Social Science and Religion in Periodical Literature; Social Work Abstracts.
Year Established	1974.
Circulation	Approximately 1,300.
Frequency	Semiannually.
Months Issued	Spring and fall.
No. of Articles	3–5.

SUBMISSIONS

Address	Dr. David Sherwood, 65 Cassandra Circle, Churchville, NY 14428.
Number of Copies	4.
Disk Submission	Yes, WordPerfect 3.0 for Macintosh.

FORMAT OF MANUSCRIPT

Cover Sheet	Author's name and address, article title, and abstract.
Abstract	150 words or less.
Key Words	Not specified.
Length	10–20 pages.
Margins	Not specified.
Spacing	Double-spaced.

STYLE

Name of Guide	*Publication Manual of the American Psychological Association.*
Subheadings	Not specified.
References	Not specified.
Footnotes	Not specified.
Tables or Figures	Not specified.

REVIEW PROCESS

Type	Anonymous, with 3 reviewers.
Queries	Yes.
Acknowledgment	By mail.
Review Time	6 months.
Revisions	Major revisions undertaken by the author, editorial revisions by the editor, with extensive editorial revisions reviewed and approved by the author.
Acceptance Rate	60%.
Return of Manuscript	Not returned.
Lag Time to Print	4–6 months.

REPRINT, SUBSCRIPTION, AND CONTACT INFORMATION

Reprint Policy	Permission to reprint may be requested for academic and personal use for a small fee.
Book Reviews	Send to Book Review Editor, P.O. Box 7090, St. Davids, PA 19087-7090.
Subscriptions	P.O. Box 7090, St. Davids, PA 19087-7090.
	$25 in the United States, $27 outside the United States.
Affiliation	North American Association of Christians in Social Work.

Social Work and Social Sciences Review

Editorial Focus   To reinforce and expand the links between social work practice and the various disciplines which inform it. The journal aims: (1) to publicize the results of relevant new research from a variety of sources within the social sciences, including social policy, sociology, and psychology as well as social work itself; (2) to serve as a forum for debate at the highest level for those teaching and undertaking research in social work and allied disciplines.

Audience   It is aimed at fully committed professionals whether practicing in the agencies themselves or in teaching or research in universities and colleges.

Where Indexed/ Abstracted   Applied Social Sciences Index & Abstracts; Bibliographie Zeitschriften-literatur aller Gebieten des Wissens; Bulletin Signalétique; Current Contents: Social and Behavioural Sciences; ICAS; PsychINFO; Research Alert; Social SciSearch; Social Work Abstracts; Sociological Abstracts.

Year Established   1990.

Circulation   Not specified.

Frequency   3 times per year.

Months Issued   March, July, November.

No. of Articles   4–5.

SUBMISSIONS

Address   *Social Work and Social Sciences Review*, c/o Whiting and Birch Ltd, P.O. Box 872, London SE23 3HZ, England.

Number of Copies   3.

Disk Submission   Disks required for final accepted manuscripts. Any word processing format accepted, but authors using Windows should save files in DOS. Avoid using Wordstar.

FORMAT OF MANUSCRIPT

Cover Sheet   Author(s) name, professional address, professional details, title of article, number of words, address/phone/fax for correspondence. Professional addresses of second and subsequent authors welcomed for future communications.

Abstract   Less than 150 words.

Key Words   Maximum 8.

Length   3,000–5,000 words.

Margins   Generous.

Spacing   Double-spaced.

STYLE

Name of Guide	Notes for contributors are published in journal. Use *Publication Manual of the American Psychological Association* for points of detail.
Subheadings	Preferably no more than 3 levels. Level 1: bold, lowercase; level 2: italics, lowercase; level 3: roman, lowercase. Never use all capitals, and do not capitalize initials except for proper names.
References	Harvard.
Footnotes	Endnotes allowed if absolutely unavoidable.
Tables or Figures	If several tables, group at end of article and indicate position in text. If only 1 or 2 simple tables, include in text. Prepare tables with single right tab between each column. Lines of hyphens should not be included between rows; we will insert rules according to house style. However, authors should add clear indications of how they wish each table to appear. For figures involving any graphics, camera-ready copy should be supplied.

REVIEW PROCESS

Type	Double anonymous.
Queries	Queries are welcomed. Editors especially keen to encourage articles from professionals in practice, and will help as possible.
Acknowledgment	Self-addressed postcard/envelope welcomed.
Review Time	3 months.
Revisions	Material may be accepted subject to minor revisions, rejected, or editors may indicate more substantial rewriting required. In latter case, resubmission required.
Acceptance Rate	40%.
Return of Manuscript	Manuscripts not returned unless adequate postage/international postal reply coupons supplied.
Lag Time to Print	Target is 1 year.

CHARGES TO AUTHOR

Author Alterations	Approximately $6 per page for significant changes. However, we do not charge for alterations that relate to genuinely unpredictable changes since submission that require acknowledgment in text.

REPRINT, SUBSCRIPTION, AND CONTACT INFORMATION

Reprint Policy	2 free copies of journal, reprints available at cost.
Book Reviews	We publish book reviews, and will accept unsolicited reviews. Submit unsolicited reviews to: Book Review Editor, c/o Whiting and Birch Ltd, P.O. Box 872, London SE23 3HZ, England.
Subscriptions	Whiting and Birch Ltd, P.O. Box 872, London SE23 3HZ, England.
	North American rates: $90 institutions, $45 individuals.

Social Work Education

Editorial Focus	Social work education, training, and development in all settings—from large local authority departments and the probation service to small, specialized voluntary agencies, as well as college-based work and practice learning centers.
Audience	Social work educators, trainers, and managers.
Special Themes	Special issues have covered social policy context of social work education, black practice teachers, law in social work education.
Where Indexed/ Abstracted	Applied Social Sciences Index & Abstracts; Bibliographie Zeitschriften-literatur aller Gebieten des Wissens; Bulletin Signalétique; ICAS; Sociological Abstracts; Social Work Abstracts.
Year Established	1981.
Circulation	Not specified.
Frequency	4 times per year.
Months Issued	March, June, September, December.
No. of Articles	5–8.

SUBMISSIONS

Address	*Social Work Education,* c/o Whiting and Birch Ltd, P.O. Box 872, London SE23 3HZ, England.
Number of Copies	3.
Disk Submission	Disks required for final accepted manuscripts. Any word processing format accepted, but authors using Windows should save files in DOS. Avoid using Wordstar.

FORMAT OF MANUSCRIPT

Cover Sheet	Author(s) name, professional address, professional details, title of article, number of words, address/phone/fax for correspondence. Professional addresses of second and subsequent authors welcomed for future communications.
Abstract	Less than 200 words.
Key Words	Maximum 8.
Length	2,000–6,000 words (shorter pieces can be accommodated in Ideas in Action section).
Margins	Generous.
Spacing	Double-spaced.

STYLE

Name of Guide
Notes for contributors are published in journal. Use *Publication Manual of the American Psychological Association* for points of detail.

Subheadings
Preferably no more than 3 levels. Level 1: bold, lowercase; level 2: italics, lowercase; level 3: roman, lowercase. Never use all capitals, and do not capitalize initials except for proper names.

References
Harvard.

Footnotes
Endnotes allowed if absolutely unavoidable.

Tables or Figures
If several tables, group at end of article and indicate position in text. If only 1 or 2 simple tables, include in text. Prepare tables with single right tab between each column. Lines of hyphens should not be included between rows; we will insert rules according to house style. However, authors should add clear indications of how they wish each table to appear. For figures involving any graphics, camera-ready copy should be supplied.

REVIEW PROCESS

Type
Double anonymous.

Queries
Queries are welcomed. Editors especially keen to encourage articles from professionals in practice and will help as possible.

Acknowledgment
Self-addressed postcard/envelope welcomed.

Review Time
3 months.

Revisions
Material may be accepted subject to minor revisions, rejected, or editors may indicate more substantial rewriting required. In latter case, resubmission required.

Acceptance Rate
40%.

Return of Manuscript
Manuscripts not returned unless adequate postage/international postal reply coupons supplied.

Lag Time to Print
12–18 months.

CHARGES TO AUTHOR

Author Alterations
Approximately $6 per page for significant changes. However, we do not charge for alterations that relate to genuinely unpredictable changes since submission that require acknowledgment in text.

REPRINT, SUBSCRIPTION, AND CONTACT INFORMATION

Reprint Policy
2 free copies of journal, reprints available at cost.

Book Reviews
We publish book reviews and will accept unsolicited reviews. Submit unsolicited reviews to Book Review Editor, c/o Whiting and Birch Ltd, P.O. Box 872, London SE23 3HZ, England.

Subscriptions
Whiting and Birch Ltd, P.O. Box 872, London SE23 3HZ, England. North American rates: $95 institutions, $50 individuals.

Social Work in Education

Editorial Focus	Social work services in education (preschool, elementary, secondary, and postsecondary). Articles on innovations in practice, interdisciplinary efforts, legislation, policy, planning, research, and administration.
Audience	School social workers, students, faculty, health and mental health agencies, educational institutions, the juvenile justice system, libraries, and other organizations.
Special Themes	Multicultural issues, community services, racial and ethnic diversity, youths as resources.
Where Indexed/ Abstracted	caredata; ERIC; Quality Review Bulletin; Social Work Abstracts; Sociological Abstracts.
Year Established	1978.
Circulation	3,500.
Frequency	Quarterly.
Months Issued	January, April, July, October.
No. of Articles	Generally 5.

SUBMISSIONS

Address	*Social Work in Education,* NASW Press, 750 First Street, NE, Suite 700, Washington, DC 20002-4241.
Number of Copies	5.
Disk Submission	Authors of accepted manuscripts are asked to submit a disk, preferably in Microsoft Word or WordPerfect.

FORMAT OF MANUSCRIPT

Cover Sheet	Separate sheet, which does not go out for review. Full title, author names, degrees, professional titles, designation of one author as corresponding author with full address, phone numbers, e-mail address, and fax number; date of submission.
Abstract	150-word informative abstract.
Key Words	Up to 5 words or key phrases (2–3 word maximum) describing the article.
Length	14–16 pages including references and tables; manuscripts exceeding 25 pages will be returned.
Margins	1 inch on all sides.
Spacing	Double-spaced for all copy, except title page.

STYLE

Name of Guide	*Writing for the NASW Press: Information for Authors* (free) and *Professional Writing for the Human Services* (for purchase from the NASW Press). Contact NASW Press.

Subheadings	Use as needed to guide reader through the article. No more than 3 levels.
References	Author–date citation style; see style guides.
Footnotes	No footnotes preferred; incorporate into text.
Tables or Figures	Type tables double-spaced. Submit camera-ready art (300 dpi printer or better) for all figures. Place each table or figure on a separate, numbered page at the end of the manuscript.

REVIEW PROCESS

Type	"Double blind" anonymous peer review. 3 reviewers plus the editor-in-chief read the manuscript in an anonymous review.
Queries	Query letters are discouraged; authors are encouraged to read the journal and *Writing for the NASW Press* to determine if their subject matter would be appropriate.
Acknowledgment	The NASW Press sends a letter on receipt of manuscript.
Review Time	3–4 months.
Revisions	Submit 5 copies with a separate cover sheet (not identifying the author) describing the changes made in the manuscript and replying to the reviewers' comments. In general, the original reviewers and the editor-in-chief read revisions.
Acceptance Rate	Approximately 25%.
Return of Manuscript	Not returned; author should retain copies.
Lag Time to Print	Approximately 6 months–1 year.

REPRINT, SUBSCRIPTION, AND CONTACT INFORMATION

Reprint Policy	All authors receive 5 complimentary copies of the issue in which the article appears. Authors receive reprint order forms to purchase additional reprinted copies.
Book Reviews	By invitation only; send books for review to: Book Review Editor, *Social Work in Education*, NASW Press, 750 First Street, NE, Suite 700, Washington, DC 20002-4241.
Subscriptions	*Social Work in Education*, P.O. Box 431, Annapolis JCT, MD 20701.
	1996–97 one-year prices: NASW members, $39; individual nonmembers, $62; libraries/institutions, $84.
Affiliation	The NASW Press is a division of the National Association of Social Workers.
E-Mail Address	press@naswdc.org
Home Page URL	http://www.naswpress.org

Social Work in Health Care

Editorial Focus	Articles on practice-program innovation clinical research and program evaluation research, policy issues, letters and book reviews.
Audience	Practitioners, faculties, libraries, hospitals, health systems, and international.
Special Themes	Health care social work practice, managed care, behavioral health, special populations, chronic illness, community health, health status, public health research.
Where Indexed/ Abstracted	Abstracts in Social Gerontology; Academic Abstracts; Applied Social Sciences Index & Abstracts; Behavioral Medicine Abstracts; caredata CD: the social and community care database; CINAHL (Cumulative Index to Nursing & Allied Health Literature); CNPIEC Reference Guide: Chinese National Directory of Foreign Periodicals; Communication Abstracts; Current Contents; Excerpta Medica/Secondary Publishing Division; Family Studies Database; Health Source Plus; Hospital Literature Index; Human Resources Abstracts (HRA); IBZ International Bibliography of Periodical Literature; Index Medicus; Index to Periodical Articles Related to Law; Institute for Scientific Information; INTERNET ACCESS (& additional networks) Bulletin Board for Libraries ("BUBL"); Psychological Abstracts (PsycINFO); Referativnyi Zhurnal (Abstracts Journal of the Institute of Scientific Information of the Republic of Russia); Social Sciences Citation Index; Social Work Abstracts; Sociological Abstracts (SA); SOMED (social medicine) Database; Special Educational Needs Abstracts; Studies on Women Abstracts; Violence and Abuse Abstracts: A Review of Current Literature on Interpersonal Violence (VAA).
Year Established	1975.
Circulation	1,007.
Frequency	Four issues per year (occasional double volume years).
Months Issued	February, May, October, December.
No. of Articles	5–6 per issue.

SUBMISSIONS

Address	Gary Rosenberg, PhD, Editor, *Social Work in Health Care,* Mount Sinai Medical Center, Box 1246. New York, NY 10029.
Number of Copies	4.
Disk Submission	Authors of accepted manuscripts are required to submit a disk. We accept any type of computer program as long as it is labeled.

FORMAT OF MANUSCRIPT

Cover Sheet	Staple a cover page to the manuscript, indicating only the article title (this is used for anonymous refereeing) and the abstract. Second "title page": enclose a regular title page but do not staple it to the manuscript. Include the title again plus full authorship.

Abstract	Approximately 100 words.
Key Words	5–6 key words that identify article content.
Length	Maximum of 20 pages, including references and abstracts. Lengthier manuscripts may be considered, but only at the discretion of the editor.
Margins	1 inch on all sides.
Spacing	Double-spaced.

STYLE

Name of Guide	*Publication Manual of the American Psychological Association.*
Subheadings	Use as needed to guide reader through the article.
References	Double-spaced and placed in alphabetical order.
Footnotes	The use of footnotes within the text is discouraged. Words should be underlined only when it is intended that they be typeset in italics.
Tables or Figures	All tables, figures, illustrations, etc. must be camera-ready.

REVIEW PROCESS

Type	Anonymous review; 2 reviewers, plus the editor, associate editor, and managing editor.
Queries	Query letters are welcome.
Acknowledgment	A letter of acknowledgment is sent on receipt, with a manuscript number assigned.
Review Time	3–4 months.
Revisions	Submit 4 copies with a manuscript number. Mark revisions either by using a word processing program that highlights the revisions or by marking revisions in red pencil.
Acceptance Rate	Approximately 30%.
Return of Manuscript	Generally, only rejected manuscripts are returned.
Lag Time to Print	Approximately 6 months–1 year.

REPRINT, SUBSCRIPTION, AND CONTACT INFORMATION

Reprint Policy	All authors of the manuscript receive a complimentary copy of issue in which the article appears.
Book Reviews	By invitation only. Send books for review to Book Review Editor, Toba Schwaber Kerson, DSW, PhD, Graduate School of Social Work and Social Research, Bryn Mawr College, 300 Airdale Road, Bryn Mawr, PA 19021.
Subscriptions	The Haworth Press, Inc., 10 Alice Street, Binghamton, NY 13904-1580.

	1 Vol.	*2 Vols.*	*3 Vols.*
Individuals	$ 32.40	$ 57.60	$ 75.60
Institutions	$ 81.00	$144.00	$189.00
Libraries	$150.00		

E-Mail Address	lawms@cunyvm.cuny.edu

Social Work Research

Previous Title	*Social Work Research & Abstracts* (changed in 1994 when the two journals were separated.)
Editorial Focus	Research on issues of concern to social workers and other professionals in human services. Analytical reviews of research, theoretical articles, practice-based research, evaluation studies, and other research studies that contribute to knowledge about social issues and social problems.
Audience	Researchers, faculty, students, researchers and writers in allied disciplines, libraries, schools, and other organizations.
Special Themes	Welfare reform, HIV/AIDS, racial and ethnic diversity, research methodologies.
Where Indexed/ Abstracted	Abstracts in Anthropology; Abstracts in Social Gerontology; Academic Abstracts; AgeLine; Applied Social Sciences Index & Abstracts; caredata; Cumulative Index to Nursing & Allied Health Literature (CINAHL); Current Contents: Social & Behavioral Sciences; ERIC/Cass; Exceptional Child Education Resources; Psychological Abstracts/PsycINFO/PsycLIT; Public Affairs Information Service Bulletin (PAIS); Sage Family Studies Abstracts; Social Planning/Policy & Development Abstracts (SOPODA); Social Sciences Index/Social Sciences Abstracts; Social Work Abstracts; Sociological Abstracts (SA).
Year Established	1977.
Circulation	3,500.
Frequency	Quarterly.
Months Issued	March, June, September, December.
No. of Articles	Generally 5.

SUBMISSIONS

Address	*Social Work Research,* NASW Press, 750 First Street, NE, Suite 700, Washington, DC 20002-4241.
Number of Copies	5.
Disk Submission	Authors of accepted manuscripts are asked to submit a disk, preferably in Microsoft Word or WordPerfect.

FORMAT OF MANUSCRIPT

Cover Sheet	Separate sheet, which does not go out for review. Full title, author names, degrees, professional titles, designation of one author as corresponding author with full address, phone numbers, e-mail address, and fax number; date of submission.
Abstract	150-word informative abstract.
Key Words	Up to 5 words or key phrases (2–3 word maximum) describing the article.
Length	14–16 pages including references and tables; manuscripts exceeding 25 pages will be returned.

Margins	1 inch on all sides.
Spacing	Double-spaced for all copy, except title page.

STYLE

Name of Guide	*Writing for the NASW Press: Information for Authors* (free) and *Professional Writing for the Human Services* (for purchase from the NASW Press). Contact the NASW Press.
Subheadings	Use as needed to guide reader through the article. No more than three levels.
References	Author–date citation style; see style guides.
Footnotes	No footnotes preferred; incorporate into text.
Tables or Figures	Type tables double-spaced. Submit camera-ready art (300 dpi printer or better) for all figures. Place each table or figure on a separate, numbered page at the end of the manuscript.

REVIEW PROCESS

Type	"Double-blind" anonymous peer review. 3 reviewers, plus the editor-in-chief read the manuscript in an anonymous review.
Queries	Query letters are discouraged; authors are encouraged to read the journal and *Writing for the NASW Press* to determine if their subject matter would be appropriate.
Acknowledgment	The NASW Press sends a letter on receipt of manuscript.
Review Time	3–4 months.
Revisions	Submit 5 copies with a separate cover sheet (not identifying the author) describing the changes made in the manuscript and replying to the reviewers' comments. In general, the original reviewers and the editor-in-chief read revisions.
Acceptance Rate	Approximately 20%.
Return of Manuscript	Not returned; author should retain copies.
Lag Time to Print	Approximately 6 months–1 year.

REPRINT, SUBSCRIPTION, AND CONTACT INFORMATION

Reprint Policy	All authors receive 5 complimentary copies of the issue in which the article appears. Authors receive reprint order forms to purchase additional reprinted copies.
Book Reviews	Generally none.
Subscriptions	*Social Work Research*, P.O. Box 431, Annapolis JCT, MD 20701.
	1996–97 one-year prices: NASW members, $38; individual nonmembers, $60; libraries/institutions, $84.
Affiliation	The NASW Press is a division of the National Association of Social Workers.
E-Mail Address	press@naswdc.org.
Home Page URL	http://www.naswpress.org

Social Work with Groups

Editorial Focus	A journal of community and clinical practice; practice, theory, research, book reviews, video reviews.
Audience	Faculty, students, practitioners, university libraries in social work and related human services disciplines.
Special Themes	Group work with oppressed populations and in diverse settings.
Where Indexed/ Abstracted	Applied Social Sciences Index & Abstracts; caredata CD: the social and community care database; CNPIEC Reference Guide: Chinese National Directory of Foreign Periodicals; Current Contents; Expanded Academic Index; Guide to Social Science & Religion in Periodical Literature; Index to Periodical Articles Related to Law; Institute for Scientific Information; International Bulletin of Bibliography on Education; INTERNET ACCESS (& additional networks) Bulletin Board for Libraries ("BUBL"), coverage of information resources on INTERNET, JANET, and other networks; Inventory of Marriage and Family Literature (online and CD-ROM); Psychological Abstracts (PsycINFO); Social Planning/Policy & Development Abstracts (SOPODA); Social Work Abstracts; Sociological Abstracts (SA); Special Educational Needs Abstracts; Studies on Women Abstracts; Violence and Abuse Abstracts: A Review of Current Literature on Interpersonal Violence (VAA).
Year Established	1978.
Circulation	1,000.
Frequency	Quarterly.
Months Issued	Spring, summer, fall, winter.
No. of Articles	Approximately 6 per issue, plus editorial commentary and book and video reviews.

SUBMISSIONS

Address	Roselle Kurland, Editor, Hunter College School of Social Work, 129 E. 79th Street, New York, NY 10021.
Number of Copies	4.
Disk Submission	To be included with manuscripts that are accepted for publication.

FORMAT OF MANUSCRIPT

Cover Sheet	Title, author, title of author, mailing address, phone numbers, date of submission.
Abstract	150-word informative abstract.
Key Words	Up to 5 words or key phrases (2–3 word maximum) describing the article.
Length	14–16 pages including references and tables. Excessively lengthy manuscripts will be returned.

| Margins | 1 inch on all sides. |
| Spacing | Double-spaced for all copy. |

STYLE

Name of Guide	*Publication Manual of the American Psychological Association; Writing for the NASW Press.*
Subheadings	Use as needed.
References	Author–date citation style, see style guides.
Footnotes	Incorporate into text.
Tables or Figures	Must be camera-ready.

REVIEW PROCESS

Type	Anonymous peer review, plus editors review.
Queries	Interested authors may write for information: Andrew Malekoff, Editor, North Shore Child and Family Guidance Center, 480 Old Westbury Road, Roslyn Heights, NY 11577.
Acknowledgment	Letter sent on receipt of manuscript.
Review Time	4–6 months.
Revisions	4 copies.
Acceptance Rate	Approximately 15%.
Return of Manuscript	Not returned; author should retain copies.
Lag Time to Print	6–12 months.

REPRINT, SUBSCRIPTION, AND CONTACT INFORMATION

Reprint Policy	Authors receive complimentary copies and reprints from the publisher, as well as order forms for additional reprints.
Book Reviews	By invitation only; send books for review to Andrew Malekoff, Editor, *Social Work with Groups,* North Shore Child and Family Guidance Center, 480 Old Westbury Road, Roslyn Heights, NY 11577.
Subscriptions	The Haworth Press, Inc., 10 Alice Street, Binghamton, NY 13904-1580.

Society

Editorial Focus	New ideas and research findings from all the social sciences.
Audience	Social scientists and others with a proven interest in social and political issues.
Special Themes	Professional ethics; race norming; children and their caretakers; risk, safety, and capitalism; marijuana policy and drug mythology; medicide; safety nets and welfare ceilings; private business and public interests; sexual harassment.
Where Indexed/ Abstracted	ABC Pol Sci: A Bibliography of Contents, Political Science and Government; Academic Abstracts; Book Review for Social Science Eastern Periodicals; Center de Documentation Sciences Humaines; Communication Abstracts; Current Contents: Social, Behavioral, and Managerial Sciences; Current Index to Journals in Education; ERIC Clearinghouse on Urban Education; Linguistic Abstracts; Magazine Article Summaries; Medical Socioeconomic Resource Sources; Periodica Islamica; Political Science Abstracts; Public Affairs Information Service Bulletin; Reader's Guide to Periodical Literature; Research Alert; Social Sciences Citation Index; Social Science Sources; Social Work Abstracts; Sociological Abstracts; United States Political Science Documents; Urban Affairs Abstracts.
Year Established	1963.
Circulation	10,000.
Frequency	Bimonthly.
Months Issued	November, January, March, May, Juiy, September.
No. of Articles	Not specified.

SUBMISSIONS

Address	Transaction Publishers, Attn: Dr. Irving Louis Horowitz, Rutgers University, New Brunswick, NJ 08903.
Number of Copies	Not specified.
Disk Submission	Yes, MS-DOS preferred.

FORMAT OF MANUSCRIPT

Not specified.

STYLE

Name of Guide	*Chicago Manual of Style.*
Subheadings	Not specified.
References	Not specified.
Footnotes	Not specified.
Tables or Figures	Camera-ready.

REVIEW PROCESS

Not specified.

CHARGES TO AUTHOR

Author Alterations 10% waiver.

REPRINT, SUBSCRIPTION, AND CONTACT INFORMATION

Reprint Policy By permission.
Book Reviews Yes.
Subscriptions Individuals: $48 for 1 year, $90 for 2 years, $126 for 3 years; institutions: $108 for 1 year, $204 for 2 years, $288 for 3 years; students: $20 per year.
E-Mail Address ihorowitz@transactionpub.com
Home Page URL http://www.transactionpub.com

Special Services in the Schools

Editorial Focus	Delivery of assessment, instruction-related, personnel development, and administrative services in schools and other educational settings.
Audience	Professionals who provide special services.
Special Themes	Special services delivery, policy perspectives on special education issues and trends.
Where Indexed/ Abstracted	Cabell's Directory of Publishing Opportunities in Education; Child Development Abstracts & Bibliography; CNPIEC Reference Guide: Chinese National Directory of Foreign Periodicals; Contents Pages in Education; Education Digest; Educational Administration Abstracts (EAA); ERIC Clearinghouse on Counseling and Student Services (ERIC/CASS); ERIC Clearinghouse on Rural Education & Small Schools; Exceptional Child Education Resources (ECER); Family Studies Database (online and CD-ROM); International Bulletin of Bibliography on Education; INTERNET ACCESS (& additional networks) Bulletin Board for Libraries ("BUBL"), coverage of information resources on INTERNET, JANET, and other networks; Mental Health Abstracts (online through DIALOG); National Clearinghouse for Bilingual Education; OT BibSys; Social Work Abstracts; Sociology of Education Abstracts; Special Educational Needs Abstracts.
Year Established	1984.
Circulation	154.
Frequency	Semiannually.
Months Issued	Not specified.
No. of Articles	6–10 per issue.

SUBMISSIONS

Address	Charles A. Maher, Department of Applied Psychology, Graduate School of Applied & Professional Psychology, Rutgers University, Box 819, Piscataway, NJ 08855-0819.
Number of Copies	4.
Disk Submission	Authors of accepted manuscripts are asked to submit a disk, preferably in Microsoft Word or WordPerfect.

FORMAT OF MANUSCRIPT

Cover Sheet	Separate sheet, which does not go out for review. Full title, author names, degrees, professional titles; designation of one author as corresponding author with full address, phone numbers, e-mail address, and fax number; date of submission.
Abstract	About 100 words.
Key Words	5 or 6 key words that identify article content.

Length	20 pages, including references and abstract. Lengthier manuscripts may be considered, but only at the discretion of the editor. Sometimes, lengthier manuscripts may be considered if they can be divided into sections for publication in successive issues.
Margins	1 inch on all sides.
Spacing	Double-spaced for all copy except title page.

STYLE

Name of Guide	*Publication Manual of the American Psychological Association.*
Subheadings	Use as needed to guide reader through the article. No more than 4 levels.
References	Author–date citation style; see style guide.
Footnotes	No footnotes preferred; incorporate into text.
Tables or Figures	Type tables double-spaced. Submit camera-ready art (300 dpi printer or better) for all figures. Place each table or figure on a separate, numbered page at the end of the manuscript.

REVIEW PROCESS

Type	"Double blind" anonymous peer review. 3 reviewers, plus editor-in-chief, all read the manuscript in an anonymous review.
Queries	Authors are encouraged to read the journal to determine if their subject matter would be appropriate.
Acknowledgment	Enclose a regular self-addressed, stamped envelope with submission.
Review Time	3–4 months.
Revisions	See journal.
Acceptance Rate	Not specified.
Return of Manuscript	Only if 9″ x 12″ self-addressed, stamped envelope is enclosed.
Lag Time to Print	6 months–1 year.

REPRINT, SUBSCRIPTION, AND CONTACT INFORMATION

Reprint Policy	All authors receive 2 complimentary copies of the issue in which article appears. Authors receive reprint order forms to purchase additional reprinted copies.
Book Reviews	Send to journal editor.
Subscriptions	The Haworth Press, Inc., 10 Alice Street, Binghamton, NY 13904-1580. Individuals, $40; institutions, $75; libraries, $135.

Substance Abuse

Editorial Focus	Empirical research papers and reviews in the field of addiction and substance abuse. The journal is primarily a forum for original empirical research but also includes reviews, editorials, letters to the editor, and book reviews.
Audience	Medical educators, clinical researchers, and other health professionals in the field of alcohol and drug abuse.
Special Themes	Clinical and preclinical research, education, health service delivery, and policy in the field of substance abuse.
Where Indexed/ Abstracted	Not specified.
Year Established	1979.
Circulation	Not specified.
Frequency	Quarterly.
Months Issued	Not specified.
No. of Articles	4–5.

SUBMISSIONS

Address	Marc Galanter, MD, Center for Alcohol and Addiction Studies, Box G-BH, Brown University, Providence, RI 02906.
Number of Copies	4.
Disk Submission	Not required.

FORMAT OF MANUSCRIPT

Cover Sheet	Title of article, author's name (with degree), affiliation, suggested running head.
Abstract	Yes, no more than 150 words.
Key Words	4–5 key words.
Length	No more than 40 pages.
Margins	Not specified.
Spacing	Double-spaced.

STYLE

Name of Guide	Not specified.
Subheadings	Not specified.
References	Type double-spaced, numerically in order of text appearance at the end of the paper (after text and before tables and figure caption list).
Footnotes	Should be avoided, if absolutely necessary should be numbered consecutively with Arabic numerals on the page to which they refer. A line should be placed above the footnote to set it off from the text.
Tables or Figures	Camera-ready copy should be submitted for all tables and figures.

REVIEW PROCESS

Type	All papers are peer-reviewed; they are not anonymous.
Queries	Not specified.
Acknowledgment	By postcard.
Review Time	3–4 months.
Revisions	Authors must submit 4 copies of any revisions that are undertaken. Revised manuscripts may be sent out for further review or reviewed by the editor depending on the extent of the revisions.
Acceptance Rate	50%.
Return of Manuscript	Not returned.
Lag Time to Print	6–9 months.

REPRINT, SUBSCRIPTION, AND CONTACT INFORMATION

Reprint Policy	Reprints are made available to the author and the schedule of charges is distributed by the publisher.
Book Reviews	All books and books reviews may be submitted to the same office. Unsolicited reviews are accepted, however, final decisions on publication are made by the book review editor.
Subscriptions	Contact Plenum Press, Journal Subscription Department, Spring Street, New York, NY 10013.
Affiliation	Association for Medical Education and Research in Substance Abuse (AMERSA).
E-Mail Address	Associate editor: paltibp@brownvm.brown.edu

Substance Use and Misuse

Previous Title	*International Journal of the Addictions.*
Editorial Focus	The use and misuse of illegal and legal drugs, medicines, and social substances; eating disorders and gambling.
Audience	Professionals, policymakers, researchers.
Special Themes	Not specified.
Where Indexed/ Abstracted	Adolescent Mental Health Abstracts; Applied Social Sciences Index & Abstracts; Automatic Subject Citation Alert; Bibliographic Index of Health Education Periodicals (BIHEP); BioSciences Information Service of Biological Abstracts (BIOSIS); Classified Abstracts Archives of the Alcohol Literature; Current Awareness in Biological Sciences; Current Contents: Clinical Practice; Current Contents: Social & Behavioral Sciences; Current Sciences; Excerpta Medica; Gower Academic Journals; Index Medicus; Institute of Scientific Information of the USSR Academy of Sciences; International Pharmaceutical Abstracts; ISI/BIOMED; Psychological Abstracts; Reference Update; Science Citation Index; Selected List of Table of Contents of Psychiatric Periodicals; Social Sciences Citation Index; Social Work Abstracts; Sociological Abstracts; State Central Scientific Medical Library/International Book Exchange-USSR.
Year Established	1956.
Circulation	Not specified
Frequency	Monthly, plus 2 special issues.
Months Issued	14 times a year
No. of Articles	5–7.

SUBMISSIONS

Address	Dr. Stanley Einstein, 113/41 East Talpiot, Jerusalem Israel 93801.
Number of Copies	2.
Disk Submission	No.

FORMAT OF MANUSCRIPT

Cover Sheet	Author's academic degrees; present affiliation; auspices under which work being reported was done, if applicable; addresses to which request for reprints should be sent; begin title with a word useful in indexing; include up to 5 key words/concepts.
Abstract	75–100 words; Spanish and French also requested.
Key Words	Up to 5.
Length	10 pages of text on average.
Margins	Not specified.
Spacing	Double-spaced.

STYLE

Name of Guide	Not specified.
Subheadings	Use major and minor headings. Major headings are uppercase.
References	Author and year.
Footnotes	Avoid using footnotes. When used, group them at the end of the manuscript in their numerical order of appearance.
Tables or Figures	Cite all tables and figures in the text. Give tables titles and provide brief legends for figures. In table, give each column a heading. Indicate units of measure in parentheses in the heading for each column. Use metric units of measure. If measurements were made in English units, give metric equivalents. Do not use vertical rules. Do not use horizontal rules other than those in the heading and at the bottom. Submit photographs as glossy prints, untrimmed and unmounted; identify each with pencil lightly on the back and indicate top.

Publisher will not return artwork unless specifically requested, and will dispose of artwork 3 months after publication.

REVIEW PROCESS

Type	Peer, anonymous.
Queries	Not specified.
Acknowledgment	Author is notified by mail on receipt of copies.
Review Time	2–3 months.
Revisions	Editor notifies authors of necessary revision by letter. Revised manuscripts are returned to editor, who checks for compliance.
Acceptance Rate	50%.
Return of Manuscript	Not returned.
Lag Time to Print	1 year.

REPRINT, SUBSCRIPTION, AND CONTACT INFORMATION

Reprint Policy	Contact the publisher.
Book Reviews	Yes.
Subscriptions	Marcel Dekker, Inc., 270 Madison Avenue, New York, NY 10016. $697.50/students; $1,395/institutions. (Additional cost for foreign postage.)
Affiliation	Institute for the Study of Drug Misuse.
E-Mail Address	einstein@netvision.net.il

Student Assistance Journal

Editorial Focus	News, how-tos, and issues relating to child, youth, and adolescent behavioral health.
Audience	Student assistance professionals, school guidance counselors, and others who work with troubled young people.
Special Themes	Prevention in areas of substance use and abuse by young people and significant adults in their lives; violence; teen pregnancy; other behaviors, attitudes, and practices that affect emotional health.
Where Indexed/ Abstracted	Not available.
Year Established	1987.
Circulation	10,000.
Frequency	Bimonthly.
Months Issued	September through May/June.
No. of Articles	6–7.

SUBMISSIONS

Address	*Student Assistance Journal,* 1270 Rankin Drive, Suite F, Troy, MI 48083.
Number of Copies	1.
Disk Submission	No.

FORMAT OF MANUSCRIPT

Cover Sheet	Cover letter preferred. Must include work and home telephone numbers and addresses.
Abstract	None.
Key Words	None.
Length	No longer than 2,000 words.
Margins	1 inch on all sides.
Spacing	Double-spaced.

STYLE

Name of Guide	Not specified.
Subheadings	Accepted.
References	Standard citation style.
Footnotes	References preferred, tangential information to be included in manuscript or in the form of a "sidebar."
Tables or Figures	Welcomed.

REVIEW PROCESS

Type	Reviewed by staff editors and editorial advisory member when applicable.
Queries	Send a 1-page summary of ideas, with sources indicated. Queries can be discussed by phone: 310-538-7733.
Acknowledgment	Not specified.
Review Time	1 month.
Revisions	Edited by staff editor and returned to writer for polishing.
Acceptance Rate	60%.
Return of Manuscript	If requested and if self-addressed, stamped envelope is enclosed.
Lag Time to Print	3–8 months.

REPRINT, SUBSCRIPTION, AND CONTACT INFORMATION

Reprint Policy	The publisher retains the right to authorize reprints if used for educational purposes and no fee is charged to subsequent readers.
Book Reviews	Not specified.
Subscriptions	$34 per year.
Affiliation	Privately owned and operated. Have a cooperative relationship with National Association of Leadership for Student Assistance Programs.
E-Mail Address	sapeap@ix.netcom.com

Suicide and Life-Threatening Behavior

Editorial Focus	*Suicide and Life-Threatening Behavior* is devoted to emergent approaches in theory and practice related to self-destructive, other-destructive, and life-threatening behaviors. It is multidisciplinary and concerned with a variety of topics related to intentional injuries and self-destructive behavior.
Audience	Practitioners, researchers, support groups, survivors, faculty, students, libraries, organizations, crisis-line workers.
Special Themes	Suicide, suicide prevention, death, accidents, subintentioned destruction, violence, standards of care, nomenclature, survivors, methodology, euthanasia, physician-assisted suicide, bereavement.
Where Indexed/ Abstracted	Abstracts on Criminology and Penology; Automatic Subject Citation Alert; Biological Abstracts; Communication Abstracts; Community Mental Health Review; Current Contents: Behavioral, Social and Educational Sciences; Current Index to Journals in Education; Current Science; Excerpta Medica; Human Resources Abstracts; Information Access; Index Medicus; Mental Health Abstracts; the Psychological Reader's Guide; Safety Science Abstracts; Social Science Periodicals Ondisc; Social Sciences Citation Index; Sociological Abstracts.
Year Established	1970.
Circulation	2,000.
Frequency	Quarterly.
Months Issued	Winter, spring, summer, autumn.
No. of Articles	5–6.

SUBMISSIONS

Address	Morton M. Silverman, MD, Editor, *Suicide and Life-Threatening Behavior,* The University of Chicago, 5737 S. University Avenue, Chicago, IL 60637.
Number of Copies	4 (original plus 3 copies).
Disk Submission	Authors are asked to submit a disk, preferably in Microsoft Word or WordPerfect.

FORMAT OF MANUSCRIPT

Cover Sheet	Separate sheet, which does not go out for review. Full title, author names, degrees, professional titles; designation of one author as corresponding author with full address, e-mail address, and fax number.
Abstract	100–125 word informative abstract.
Key Words	Up to 5 words or key phrases (2–3 word maximum) describing the article.
Length	20 pages maximum.
Margins	1 inch on all sides.
Spacing	Double-spaced for all copy, except title page.

STYLE

Name of Guide	*Publication Manual of the American Psychological Association.*
Subheadings	Use as needed to guide reader through the article. No more than 3 levels.
References	See style guide.
Footnotes	No footnotes preferred; incorporate into text.
Tables or Figures	Type tables double-spaced. Submit camera-ready art (300 dpi printer or better) for all figures. Place each table or figure on a separate, numbered page at the end of the manuscript.

REVIEW PROCESS

Type	"Double blind" anonymous peer review by 3–4 reviewers.
Queries	Editor welcomes query letters or phone calls.
Acknowledgment	Editor acknowledges manuscripts on receipt.
Review Time	2–3 months.
Revisions	Each manuscript receives 3 anonymous reviews. Revised manuscript re-read by at least one previous reviewer and one new reviewer. Decision time for revisions is 1–2 months.
Acceptance Rate	Approximately 30%–35%.
Return of Manuscript	Not returned; author should retain copies.
Lag Time to Print	9 months–1 year.

CHARGES TO AUTHOR

Author Alterations	Charged to author receiving galley proofs.

REPRINT, SUBSCRIPTION, AND CONTACT INFORMATION

Reprint Policy	No free reprints. To purchase, contact: Jody Falco, Guilford Publications, 72 Spring Street, New York, NY 10012.
Book Reviews	By invitation only; send books for review to: Cynthia Pfeffer, MD, Book Review Editor, The New York Hospital-Cornell Medical Center, 21 Bloomingdale Road, White Plains, NY 10605.
Subscriptions	The Guilford Press, 72 Spring Street, New York, NY 10012.
	Individuals, $40; institutions, $168; APA members, $36.
Affiliation	American Association of Suicidology.
E-Mail Address	msilverm@uhs.bsd.uchicago.edu
Home Page URL	samples@guilford.com

Violence Against Women

Editorial Focus	Publication of research and information on all aspects of the problem of violence against women.
Audience	Not specified.
Special Themes	Domestic violence, sexual assault, incest, sexual harassment, female infanticide, female circumcision, and female sexual slavery.
Where Indexed/ Abstracted	Applied Social Sciences Index & Abstracts; Criminal Justice Abstracts; Criminal Justice Periodical Index; Index to Periodical Articles Related to Law; Indian Psychological Abstracts and Reviews; Linguistics and Language Behavior Abstracts; Risk Abstracts; Sage Family Studies Abstracts; Social Planning/Policy & Development Abstracts; Sociological Abstracts; Studies on Women Abstracts; Violence and Abuse Abstracts.
Year Established	1994.
Circulation	2,000.
Frequency	Bimonthly.
Months Issued	February, April, June, August, October, December.
No. of Articles	6.

SUBMISSIONS

Address	Claire Renzetti, Editor, *Violence Against Women,* Department of Sociology, St. Joseph's University, Philadelphia, PA 19131.
Number of Copies	3.
Disk Submission	A copy of the final revised manuscript, saved on an IBM-compatible disk, should be included with the final revised hard copy.

FORMAT OF MANUSCRIPT

Cover Sheet	Name and affiliation on separate page.
Abstract	100 words.
Key Words	None.
Length	No more than 25 pages.
Margins	Not specified.
Spacing	Double-spaced.

STYLE

Name of Guide	*Publication Manual of the American Psychological Association.*
Subheadings	Not specified.
References	Separate pages.
Footnotes	Separate pages.
Tables or Figures	Separate pages.

REVIEW PROCESS

Type	Anonymous editorial evaluation.
Queries	Not specified.
Acknowledgment	Not specified.
Review Time	Not specified.
Revisions	Not specified.
Acceptance Rate	Not specified.
Return of Manuscript	Manuscripts are only returned if they are accompanied, on submission, by a stamped, self-addressed envelope.
Lag Time to Print	Not specified.

REPRINT, SUBSCRIPTION, AND CONTACT INFORMATION

Reprint Policy	May purchase.
Book Reviews	Not specified.
Subscriptions	Sage Publications, Inc., 2455 Teller Road, Thousand Oaks, CA 91320.
	1996–97 one-year prices: individual, $48; institutions, $140.
E-Mail Address	crenzeti@sjuphil.sju.edu
Home Page URL	http://www.sagepub.com

Women and Health

Editorial Focus	Women's health, broad public health issues, epidemiology, psychology.
Audience	Public health professionals.
Special Themes	Numerous over the years. Examples: Women and Cancer, Women's Health and Poverty, The Swedish Alternative, Health of Women as They Age.
Where Indexed/ Abstracted	CINAHL; MEDLINE; more than 40 national and international services.
Year Established	1975.
Circulation	800.
Frequency	Quarterly.
Months Issued	Not specified.
No. of Articles	About 6 per issue.

SUBMISSIONS

Address	Jeanne M. Stellman, PhD, Editor, Columbia University School of Public Health, 600 West 168th Street, New York, NY 10032.
Number of Copies	3.
Disk Submission	No.

FORMAT OF MANUSCRIPT

Cover Sheet	1 with identifiers, 1 anonymous.
Abstract	Yes, 250 words.
Key Words	None.
Length	32 pages.
Margins	1.25 inches on all sides.
Spacing	Double-spaced.

STYLE

Name of Guide	*Publication Manual of the American Psychological Association.*
Subheadings	See style guide.
References	See style guide.
Footnotes	Accepted.
Tables or Figures	Tables will be reset; figures should be camera-ready.

REVIEW PROCESS

Type	Anonymous.
Queries	Yes.
Acknowledgment	All submissions acknowledged; please provide self-addressed, stamped envelope.

Review Time	12–15 weeks.
Revisions	Same as original.
Acceptance Rate	35%.
Return of Manuscript	No.
Lag Time to Print	Approximately 15 months.

REPRINT, SUBSCRIPTION, AND CONTACT INFORMATION

Reprint Policy	Not available.
Book Reviews	Yes, mostly solicited. Send reviews to: Charles R. King, MD, Department of OB/GYN, Medical College of Ohio, P.O. Box 10008, Toledo, OH 43699-0008.
Subscriptions	Haworth Medical Press, 10 Alice Street, Binghamton, NY 13904-1580.
E-Mail Address	jms13@columbia.edu

Women & Politics

Editorial Focus	Research manuscripts on women's roles in society and politics as generally defined.
Audience	Academic journal for anyone with an interest in women's roles in society and politics.
Special Themes	Not specified.
Where Indexed/ Abstracted	ABC Pol Sci: A Bibliography of Contents: Political Science & Government; Academic Abstracts/CD-ROM; Academic Index (on-line); America: History and Life; Current Contents: Clinical Medicine/Life Sciences (CC:CM/LS), and Social Sciences Citation Index. Articles also searchable through Social SciSearch, ISI's online database and in ISI's Research Alert current awareness service; Current Legal Sociology; Feminist Periodicals: A Current Listing of Contents; Historical Abstracts; IBZ International Bibliography of Periodical Literature; Index to Periodical Articles Related to Law; International Political Science Abstracts; Periodical Islamica; Periodical Abstracts, Research I (general & basic reference indexing & abstracting database from University Microfilms International); Periodical Abstracts, Research II (broad coverage indexing & abstracting database from University Microfilms International); Political Science Abstracts; Public Affairs Information Bulletin; Social Planning/Policy & Development Abstracts; Social Work Abstracts; Sociological Abstracts; Studies on Women Abstracts; Urban Affairs Abstracts; Women Studies Abstracts; Women's Studies Index.
Year Established	1981.
Circulation	500.
Frequency	Quarterly.
Months Issued	Winter, spring, summer, fall.
No. of Articles	4.

SUBMISSIONS

Address	Janet Clark, Editor, Department of Political Science, State University of West Georgia, Carrollton, GA 30118.
Number of Copies	Not specified.
Disk Submission	Disks are required on acceptance of the manuscript for publication. 3.5″ computer disk formatted on IBM-compatible computer. WordPerfect 5.1 or higher or ASCII. Type is 10–12 point only.

FORMAT OF MANUSCRIPT

Cover Sheet	Not required.
Abstract	No more than 200-word abstract.
Key Words	None.
Length	25–30 pages.

Margins	1 inch on all sides.
Spacing	Double-spaced.

STYLE

Name of Guide	*Style Manual for Political Science.*
Subheadings	Not required; use as necessary.
References	See style guide.
Footnotes	Endnotes only.
Tables or Figures	Type double-spaced. Camera-ready copy required.

REVIEW PROCESS

Type	Blind, anonymous peer review (3 reviewers). Editor makes final decision based on reviews.
Queries	No.
Acknowledgment	By letter on receipt of manuscript.
Review Time	6–8 weeks.
Revisions	Authors receive copies of the 3 reviews along with the final decision. If the decision is to revise and resubmit to the same reviewers, the author is asked to incorporate the suggestions made by the reviewers. After the revision is complete the author may resubmit the manuscript (4 copies), and the new manuscript is sent out to the same 3 reviewers for a new review. If the original decision was to revise and resubmit for a full new review, 3 different reviewers are selected, and the review process begins again.
Acceptance Rate	Not specified.
Return of Manuscript	Not returned.
Lag Time to Print	8 months.

REPRINT, SUBSCRIPTION, AND CONTACT INFORMATION

Reprint Policy	Contact: The Haworth Press, Inc., 10 Alice Street, Binghamton, NY 13904-1580.
Book Reviews	By invitation only.
Subscriptions	The Haworth Press, Inc., 10 Alice Street, Binghamton, NY 13904-1580.
Affiliation	State University of West Georgia.
E-Mail Address	wandp@westga.edu
Home Page URL	http://www.westga.edu/~wandp/w+p.html

Women and Therapy

Editorial Focus	Descriptive, theoretical, clinical, empirical, and multicultural perspectives on women and therapy.
Audience	Feminist therapists, feminist mental health professionals, feminist graduate students.
Special Themes	Aging, social class, lesbians, women with disabilities, women across cultures. Journal devotes 3 issues per year to thematic issues that are invited by the editor—check with the editors for upcoming themes.
Where Indexed/ Abstracted	Abstracts of Research in Pastoral Care & Counseling; Academic Abstracts/ CD-ROM; Academic Index (on-line); Alternative Press Index; CNPIEC Reference Guide: Chinese National Directory of Foreign Periodicals; Current Contents: Clinical Medicine/Life Sciences (CC: CM/LS); Digest of Neurology and Psychiatry; Expanded Academic Index; Family Violence & Sexual Assault Bulletin; Feminist Periodicals: A Current Listing of Contents; Health Source; Health Source Plus; Higher Education Abstracts; Index to Periodical Articles Related to Law; INTERNET ACCESS (& additonal networks) Bulletin Board for Libraries ("BUBL:), coverage of information resources on INTERNET, JANET, and other networks; Inventory of Marriage and Family Literature (online and CD-ROM); Mental Health Abstracts (online through DIALOG); PASCAL International Bibliography T205: Sciences de l'information Documentation; Periodical Abstracts, Research I; Periodical Abstracts, Research II; PILOTS Database; Psychological Abstracts (PsycINFO); Sage Family Studies Abstracts (SFSA); Social Work Abstracts; Studies on Women Abstracts; Violence and Abuse Abstracts (VAA); Women Studies Abstracts; Women's Studies Index.
Year Established	1982.
Circulation	2,000.
Frequency	Quarterly.
Months Issued	Not specified.
No. of Articles	7–10.

SUBMISSIONS

Address	Dr. Marcia Hill, 25 Court Street, Montpelier, VT 05602.
Number of Copies	3.
Disk Submission	Final manuscript version only.

FORMAT OF MANUSCRIPT

Cover Sheet	Title, name (without degrees), one-paragraph biographical description of author(s), address of primary author.
Abstract	Yes.
Key Words	None.

Length	Up to 15 pages.
Margins	1 inch on all sides
Spacing	Double-spaced.

STYLE

Name of Guide	*Publication Manual of the American Psychological Association.*
Subheadings	See style guide.
References	See style guide.
Footnotes	None.
Tables or Figures	See style guide; must be camera-ready.

REVIEW PROCESS

Type	Peer reviewed, anonymous.
Queries	Welcomed.
Acknowledgment	By letter.
Review Time	3 months.
Revisions	3 months.
Acceptance Rate	12% for unsolicited manuscripts.
Return of Manuscript	Yes.
Lag Time to Print	12–18 months.

CHARGES TO AUTHOR

| Author Alterations | Alterations are discouraged. |

REPRINT, SUBSCRIPTION, AND CONTACT INFORMATION

Reprint Policy	Authors receive 10 free reprints and 1 free copy of the journal issue.
Book Reviews	Dr. Ruth Hall, Book Review Editor, Department of Psychology, Trenton State College, Trenton, NJ 08650-4700.
Subscriptions	The Haworth Press, Inc., 10 Alice Street, Binghamton, NY 13904-1580. Individuals, $40; institutions, $120; libraries, $175.
E-Mail Address	(Rothblum) e_rothbl@dewey.uvm.edu (Hill) rsxg34a@prodigy.com

Appendix: Reference Library for Authors

CITATIONS AND REFERENCES

American Psychological Association. (1994). *Publication manual of the American Psychological Association* (4th ed.). Washington, DC: Author.

Beebe, L. (Ed.). (1993). *Professional writing for the human services.* Washington, DC: NASW Press.

Carner, D. L., & Smith, D. H. (1984). *The complete guide to citing governmental documents: A manual for writers and librarians.* Bethesda, MD: Congressional Information Service.

Harvard Law Review Association. (1981). *A uniform system of citation* (14th ed.). Cambridge, MA: Author.

GRAMMAR

Hodges, J. C., & Whitten, M. E. (1984). *Harbrace college handbook* (9th ed.). New York: Harcourt Brac Jovanovich.

INFORMATION

Barker, R. (1995). *The social work dictionary* (3rd ed.). Washington, DC: NASW Press.

Carter, S. P. (1987). *Writing for your peers: The primary journal paper.* New York: Praeger.

Council of Biology Editors. (1988). *Illustrating science: Standards for publication.* Bethesda, MD: Author.

Day, R. A. (1988). *How to write and publish a scientific paper* (3rd ed.). Phoenix: Oryx Press.

Edwards, R. L. (Ed.-in-Chief). (1995). *Encyclopedia of social work* (19th ed.). Washington, DC: NASW Press.

Ginsberg, L. (1995). *Social work almanac* (2nd ed.). Washington, DC: NASW Press.

NASW Press. (1995). *Writing for the NASW Press: Information for authors* (rev. ed.). Washington, DC: Author.

Tufte, E. (1983). *The visual display of quantitative information.* Cheshire, CT: Graphics Press.

Tufte, E. (1990). *Envisioning information.* Cheshire, CT: Graphics Press.

Zinsser, W. (1988). *Writing to learn.* New York: Harper & Row.

Zinsser, W. (1994). *On writing well: An informal guide to writing nonfiction* (5th ed.). New York: Harper & Row.

SPELLING

Merriam Webster's collegiate dictionary (10th ed.). (1993). Springfield, MA: Merriam-Webster.

Random House dictionary of the English language—Unabridged (2nd ed.). (1987). New York: Random House.

STYLE

Strunk, W., Jr., & White, E. B. (1979). *The elements of style* (3rd ed). New York: Macmillan.

University of Chicago Press. (1993). *The Chicago manual of style* (14th ed.). Chicago: Author.

Words into type (3rd ed.). (1974). Englewood Cliffs, NJ: Prentice Hall.

USAGE

Bernstein, T. M. (1965). *The careful writer: A modern guide to English usage.* New York: Atheneum.

Copperud, R. H. (1980). *American usage and style: The consensus.* New York: Van Nostrand Reinhold.

Fowler, H. W. (1987). *A dictionary of modern English usage* (2nd ed., rev. by E. Gowers). New York: Oxford University Press.

AN AUTHOR'S GUIDE TO SOCIAL WORK JOURNALS, 4TH EDITION

Cover design by Anne Masters Design, Inc.

Interior design by Naylor Design, Inc.

Composed by Fran Pflieger, Maben Publications, Inc., in Adobe Garamond and Univers.

Printed by Boyd Printing Company on 60# Windsor.

TO HELP YOU PUBLISH
FROM THE NASW PRESS

An Author's Guide to Social Work Journals, 4th Edition, *by NASW Press.* The NASW Press has increased the number of listings nearly 50% in the 4th Edition. The *Author's Guide* is an essential reference for authors who want to submit articles to U.S. journals. Writers use it to learn how to package their work to meet the requirements of core social work and social welfare journals.

ISBN: 0-87101-271-5. Item #2715. Price $35.95

Social Work Almanac, Second Edition, *by Leon Ginsberg.* The most comprehensive compilation of statistical social welfare data is now 61% larger, with 69% more tables and 73% more figures. Provides clear, succinct information on virtually every human services category. Entries include basic demographics, children, crime and delinquency, education, health, mental health, older adults, social welfare issues, and the social work profession.

ISBN: 0-87101-248-0. Item #2480. Price $34.95

Professional Writing for the Human Services, *Linda Beebe, Editor.* Learn basic writing techniques, how to conduct literature search, how to write qualitative and quantitative research reports, and how to present statistical data graphically. Delve into the mysteries of the peer review process and discover how to package your journal article or book proposal to best advantage. NASW's own style and citation guides plus references for production techniques, ethical issues, copyright concerns, and more make this the most comprehensive writing guide available for the human services. An excellent resource for all forms of professional writing.

ISBN: 0-87101-199-9. Item #1999. Price $31.95

The Social Work Dictionary, 3rd Edition, *by Robert L. Barker.* The new, updated edition surpasses its predecessor with 60 percent more content. It presents a concise, alphabetized listing of 5,000 social work definitions, organizations, concepts, values, and historical events. One of the most valuable tools ever written for the human services professional—from the beginning student to the seasoned expert.

ISBN: 0-87101-253-7. Item #2537. Price $34.95

(Order form on reverse side)

ORDER FORM

Title	Item #	Price	Total
__ Author's Guide to Social Work Journals	Item 2715	$35.95	_____
__ Social Work Almanac, 2nd Edition	Item 22480	$34.95	_____
__ Professional Writing for			
Human Services	Item 1999	$31.95	_____
__ Social Work Dictionary, 3rd Edition	Item 2537	$34.95	_____
		Subtotal	_____
	+ 10% postage and handling		
		Total	_____

❐   I've enclosed my check or money order for $ _____.

❐   Please charge my   ❐ NASW Visa*   ❐ Other Visa   ❐ MasterCard

_____   _____

Credit Card Number   Expiration Date

Signature _____

Use of this card generates funds in support of the social work profession.

Name_____

Address _____

City _____ State/Province _____

Country _____ Zip _____

Phone _____   _____

NASW Member # (if applicable)

(Please make checks payable to NASW Press. Prices are subject to change.)

NASW PRESS

NASW Press
P.O. Box 431
Annapolis JCT, MD 20701
USA

Credit card orders call
1-800-227-3590
(In the Metro Wash., DC, area, call 301-317-8688)
Or fax your order to 301-206-7989
Or e-mail nasw@pmds.com

Visit our Web site at http://www.naswpress.org   AGBI97